Diego Rotman

The Yiddish Stage as a Temporary Home

Diego Rotman

The Yiddish Stage as a Temporary Home

Dzigan and Shumacher's Satirical Theater (1927–1980)

Translated from the Hebrew by Rebecca Wolpe

DE GRUYTER
OLDENBOURG MAGNES

This book was published with the support of the Israel Science Foundation and the Kronhill Pletka Foundation.

This book is a translation from the Hebrew original:
Diego Rotman. Habama kebayit 'ara'i: Hate'aṭron shel Dzigan ṿeShumacher (1927–1980). Jerusalem: Magnes, 2017.

ISBN 978-3-11-111459-0
e-ISBN (PDF) 978-3-11-071769-3
e-ISBN (EPUB) 978-3-11-071777-8

Library of Congress Control Number: 2021930352

Bibliographic information published by the Deutsche Nationalbibliothek
The Deutsche Nationalbibliothek lists this publication in the Deutsche Nationalbibliografie; detailed bibliographic data are available on the Internet at http://dnb.dnb.de.

This volume is text- and page-identical with the hardback published in 2021.
Cover illustration: "Dzigan and Shumacher 2017–2018" by Adi Kaplan and Shahar Carmel, oil pastel on paper, 24cm x 24cm.
Typesetting: Integra Software Services Pvt. Ltd.
Printing and binding: CPI books GmbH, Leck

www.degruyter.com

Acknowledgements

This book, which is an updated translation of the Hebrew book that developed from my PhD dissertation, was a long journey. I owe a deep debt of gratitude to the many people who accompanied me on it.

The dedicated and generous staff of the various archives I consulted helped me access rare materials and firsthand sources that were vital for my research. I am grateful to the staff of the Yehuda Gabbai Theatre Archive in the Beit Ariela Library in Tel Aviv (BAA), who helped me find files, recordings, and photographs in the collections of Shimen Dzigan and Yisroel Shumacher. I would also like to thank the staff at the Israel Goor Theatre Archives and Museum at The Hebrew University of Jerusalem (IGTA) and the Israeli Center for The Documentation of the Performing Arts at Tel Aviv University (ICDPA). Lydia Shumacher-Ophir z"l was extremely generous, speaking to me at length and helping me in any way she could, including loaning me photographs from her private collection, which are reproduced in this book. I also thank the Ophir family, Kareen and Alexander Israel. Assaf Gallay graciously shared with me the detailed investigation he conducted into Dzigan and Shumacher when making a documentary film about the duo for Israeli television. I am likewise grateful to the many actors and directors who agreed to be interviewed and shared their experiences of working with the artistic duo.

I am deeply grateful to my dissertation advisors Prof. Galit Hasan-Rokem and Prof. Yechiel Szeintuch, for the many years of encouragement and support during the writing of my dissertation and for never giving up on me. They were a source of endless inspiration, ideas, and enlightening comments; without them this book would never have been written. I am also indebted to Avraham Novershtern, who read the Hebrew manuscript, offering important feedback that expanded its perspective and honed many details. I thank my many teachers who instilled in me a love of Yiddish language and culture.

During the writing of this book, Da'at Hamakom: Center for the Study of Cultures of Place in the Modern Jewish World became a temporary home for me. Likewise, I am very grateful to Beth Shalom Aleichem for supporting the publication of the Hebrew version of this book. Thanks to Jonathan Nadav and the Magnes Press for their support and to Julia Barcuh and De Gruyter for joining me as a partner in this English adventure.

Barbara Kirshenblatt-Gimblett, Joel Berkowitz, Jeffrey Shandler, Zehavit Stern, and Andrew Ingall supported the initiative of translating this book into English, offering constructive comments on the manuscript at various stages. I am most deeply grateful to Irene Pletka for encouraging me to publish this English version

https://doi.org/10.1515/9783110717693-202

and to the Kronhill Pletka Foundation and the Israel Science Foundation for making it possible.

Rebecca Wolpe, my brilliant translator, has been a patient and sincere companion throughout this journey. Thanks to Sharon Assaf for her meticulous copyediting and her insightful comments on the manuscript. I am very grateful to Vera Salomon for checking, correcting, editing, and commenting on the Yiddish quotations and translations and offering other important insights. I also thank Adi Kaplan and Shahar Carmel for the beautiful oil paintings they produced when I asked them to design a cover for the book. Today I find myself unable to imagine Dzigan and Shumacher without their visual interpretation, as it appears on the cover of this book.

Finally, I extend my deepest thanks to my family. My beloved children, Ashu and Nahuel, who were born and raised while I was researching and writing this book. They would ask me repeatedly about Dzigan and Shumacher, always confusing the two, and laugh with me while I watched footage of them, even if they could not understand the language. Lea Mauas, my life partner, has been by my side continuously, both while writing – commenting and supporting – and in our work together as artists. Indeed, on more than one occasion we have seen ourselves through the lens of Dzigan and Shumacher, a pair of actors responding critically to the complex surrounding reality. Like them, the stage has often been our home.

Last but not least, I lovingly acknowledge my grandfather, Usher Rotman. It was with him that I first discovered a recording of Dzigan, learned about the beauty of the Yiddish language, and encountered the tradition of listening to skits on records, even before I learned Yiddish. Most of all, I thank my parents, Mery Goldwaser z"l and Samuel Rotman z"l, for their love, their humor, and so many things, big and small.

Contents

Acknowledgements —— V

Introduction —— XI

Chapter 1
Modernism, Avant Garde, and Innovation in Yiddish Theater: Dzigan and Shumacher in Łódź (1925–1933) —— 1
The Influence of Modernism on Yiddish Literature and Theater —— **1**
The Beginnings of Jewish Modernism —— **1**
Moyshe Broderzon's Activities in Łódź —— **4**
The Influence of European and Russian Cabaret —— **9**
The Influence of Traditional Jewish Humor —— **12**
The Ararat Theater —— **14**
Dzigan and Shumacher – Brief Biographies —— **15**
The Łódź Acting Studio —— **20**
The Modernist Characteristics of Ararat and Its Innovations —— **22**
Ararat's Revolutionary Discourse —— **24**
Ararat's Dialogue with the Audience —— **33**
Ararat and the National Union of Jewish Actors —— **37**
Between Avant-Garde and Popular: Theatrical Language, Language in the Theater —— **39**

Chapter 2
From a Collective to an Independent Artistic Endeavor: Dzigan and Shumacher in Warsaw (1934–1939) —— 43
Ararat's First Show in Warsaw —— **43**
The Move to the Capital —— **47**
"A Match Made in Heaven" —— **49**
Aynshteyn-Vaynshteyn —— **51**
From Experimental to Satirical Language —— **53**
Dzigan and Shumacher in the Cinema —— **58**
Al khet (1936) —— **59**
Freylekhe kaptsonim (1937) —— **60**
On a heym (1939) —— **62**
Humor and the Satirical Embodiment of Evil —— **63**
The Depiction of Jewish Life in Poland —— **67**
The Question of Emigration —— **70**
Between Private and Public —— **74**

Last Chance — 75
Humor and Guilt — 77
A Discourse of Opposition — 79

Chapter 3
Tribulations of the Last Decade in Eastern Europe: 1939–1949 — 83
In the Soviet Union (1939–1947) — **84**
Theater as a Means of Indoctrination — **88**
The Attitude of the Soviet Press — **90**
Dzigan's Perception of the Theater's Role in the Soviet Period — **93**
The Breakdown of the Theater — **94**
Return to Poland (1947–1949) — **98**
"Abi m'zet zikh!": Between Silence and Speech, Death and Revival — **102**
Deterritorialization — **110**
Changing Names, Changing Appearance: The New Jewish Identity — **113**
Eternal Wandering — **116**
Memory, Monument, and Theater — **117**
The Film *Undzere Kinder* (1949) — **122**
The Screening in Israel: Translation and Ideology — **136**
Departure from Poland — **139**

Chapter 4
"And They Journeyed and They Encamped": Dzigan and Shumacher in Israel (1950–1980) — 145
Visiting Artists — **146**
The Yiddish Satirical Performance in the State of Israel: Between Admiration and Rejection — **155**
The Israeli Audience — **158**
Israel and the Diaspora — **159**
Reception in Israel — **164**
Language and Nationality — **170**
Ramifications of the Israeli Cultural Policy for Yiddish Artistic Activities — **175**
The End of the Partnership and the Establishment of Shimen Dzigan's Satirical Theater (1961–1980) — **180**
Changes and Influences: Dzigan's Theater at the End of the 1960s — **182**
The Discourse of Sadness — **186**
Dzigan in the Press — **190**

Chapter 5
The Text, the Body, and the Stage — 199
Sources of Humor — **199**
The Jewish and Israeli Reality on the Satirical Stage — **201**
Departure and Wandering as a Personal Solution — **203**
Economy and Livelihood — **206**
The New Immigrant vs. Israeli Bureaucracy — **209**
Wars, Neighbors, and the Arab-Israeli Conflict — **212**
Marriage — **214**
Coming Full Circle: The Soviet Union on Stage — **215**
Criticism of Yiddish Theater — **218**
Dzigan's Satire vs. Hebrew Satire — **219**
The Israeli Political Leadership in the Satire of Dzigan and Shumacher — **221**
"Der nayer dibek" (The New Dybbuk, 1957) — **225**
In the Plonsker Rebbe's Yeshiva — **243**
"Goldenyu" (1971) and "Golde baym poypst" (1973) — **247**
The Poetics of the Diasporic Body and the Zionist Appearance — **252**

Conclusion — 257
The Yiddish Stage as a Temporary Home — **257**

Appendix A – Names of Spectacles and Shows — 263

Appendix B – Movies Starring Dzigan and Shumacher — 271

Appendix C – Television Programs in Israel Starring Shimen Dzigan — 273

Appendix D – List of Artists and the Shows in Which They Participated — 275

Bibliography — 281

Index of Names — 313

Introduction

The stage artists Shimen Dzigan (1905–1980) and Yisroel Shumacher (1908–1961) began their careers in the experimental Yiddish theater in Łódź and started to perform as an independent duo in the second half of the 1930s in Warsaw. During their lengthy careers, the two developed a unique stage language that was appreciated by their admiring audiences throughout Europe, Israel, North and South America, and the Soviet Union. They parted ways in 1960. Shumacher appeared in one dramatic play in the Yiddish repertory theater before his death only one year later. By contrast, Dzigan remained active until 1980 – he established a satirical theater in Tel Aviv and continued to follow the path that the duo had embarked upon. He also produced an Israeli television program and staged highly successful performances throughout the Yiddish-speaking diaspora. This book examines in detail, and from various perspectives, the path of this exceptional artistic duo, which reflects a unique, critical narrative in twentieth century Yiddish culture.

Highbrow Yiddish theater began to develop in the second half of the nineteenth century in Eastern Europe, part of a broader process of secular cultural production that primarily affected Yiddish literature and the Yiddish press. This has been described by Benjamin Harshav as "the modern Jewish" revolution,[1] while Jeffrey Shandler has defined it as "eastern European Jewry's abrupt encounter with the opportunities and challenges posed by new social, political, and economic developments . . ."[2]. Yiddish theater developed at first in a largely popular form and, as a result of the significant Jewish emigration from the Russian Empire, expanded rapidly to Western Europe, North, and South America as well as Australia and South Africa. An increasingly sophisticated and modern Yiddish theater emerged during the second decade of the twentieth century and the interwar years, corresponding with new developments on the European stage and connecting new drama and avant-garde theater to various trends in modern Yiddish literature.

Shimen Dzigan and Yisroel Shumacher began their theatrical careers on the modernist experimental Yiddish stage, as part of the "Ararat" theater company (led by the poet Moyshe Broderzon) that was established in Łódź in 1927. This company was organized as a collective rather than as a hierarchical company, and it developed a unique and challenging artistic language in stark contrast to the conservative trend that governed most contemporary commercial Yiddish theater companies in Poland. The two artists moved to Warsaw in 1933, where

1 Harshav, *The Meaning of Yiddish*, chap. 5.
2 Shandler, *Yiddish*, 126.

https://doi.org/10.1515/9783110717693-204

they established a new company, again named "Ararat," and served as both its star performers and directors. A few years later, the troupe became known (and subsequently was officially publicized) as Dzigan and Shumacher's Theater. Their theater was extremely popular among Polish Jewry in the second half of the 1930s thanks to the duo's acting talents, daring political satire against antisemitism, and creative, virtuoso use of the various means available to artists of the Yiddish word: parody, wordplay, jokes, contemporary satire, and so forth. From the outset, Dzigan and Shumacher used the Łódź Yiddish dialect, and they continued to do so throughout their careers, rather than adopting the standardized language accepted in Eastern European Yiddish theater. This decision expressed their refusal to surrender to cultural and ideological pressures. They remained different, rooted in their linguistic independence.

In the wake of the German invasion of Poland, Dzigan and Shumacher (along with many other Jews from German-occupied Poland) fled from Warsaw to Białystok, which, following the Ribbentrop-Molotov agreement, was under Soviet rule. Similarly to some other refugees, Dzigan and Shumacher chose to become Soviet citizens. In 1940, they became the main actors and stage directors of Der byalistoker melukhisher yidisher minyatur-teater (The Białystok National Jewish Miniature Theater). The company performed in many cities throughout the Soviet Union until the German invasion in June 1941. Weeks after the theater group was disbanded, Dzigan and Shumacher tried to join the Anders Army with the aim of leaving the Soviet Union. However, the two artists were arrested for alleged anti-Soviet activity and imprisoned for four years in the Aktyubinsk labor camp in Kazakhstan. They were released in August 1946 and, after a few months, were able to return to Poland, subsequently establishing in Łódź a new satirical theater group that remained active until 1949. The same year, they also starred in the last Yiddish film made in Poland, produced by Shaul Goskind and directed by Natan Gross, *Undzere kinder* (Our Children). The film focused on how Jewish child survivors dealt with the trauma of the Holocaust and the renewal of Jewish life in Poland after the Second World War, as well as the role of art in tackling these challenges.

In 1949, Dzigan and Shumacher left Poland for a tour of performances in Western Europe. In 1950, they staged their first performance in Israel as "guest actors," a status that allowed them to circumvent the government-sponsored ban prohibiting local actors from performing in Yiddish (in force from 1949 to 1950). Following their success, and in order to limit the power of the Yiddish theater in the State of Israel, the Films and Plays Censorship Committee permitted guest actors to appear in Israel for periods of only six weeks. However, due to their status and fame, Dzigan and Shumacher were allowed to continue performing beyond this limited period, on the condition that they included Hebrew sections amounting to one third of every performance. The duo met this demand mainly by incorporating Hebrew songs performed by Israeli singers between their own skits. Dzigan and Shumacher were received in Israel with great enthusiasm, particularly by the community of Yiddish speakers and theater critics. They were also praised by critics in the Hebrew press, although many expressed reservations regarding their decision to continue performing in Yiddish. They continued their artistic path in an environment that, in the 1950s, rejected Yiddish as a legitimate language and culture. Using their exceptional talents, Dzigan and Shumacher were able to translate the Israeli reality into a satirical theatrical language that became a central tool in the critical representation of Israeli society at a time when light entertainment flourished on the Hebrew stage and Hebrew political satire was almost non-existent in the theater scene. Indeed, skits by the two actors (today available as audio recordings), characterized by a rich variety of subject matter, linguistic finesse, talented performances, and sharp satire, are considered part of the classic treasury of modern Yiddish culture. In 1958, Dzigan and Shumacher settled in Israel, but they continued to perform in the diaspora, mainly in South America and the United States.

Despite Dzigan and Shumacher's central place in the history of Yiddish theater and satirical theater in Israel, no comprehensive study has examined their careers, artistic endeavors, or contribution to these fields. The existing monographs, articles, and studies concerning Yiddish theater and its history in the diaspora focus on specific Yiddish theater troupes, as well as Yiddish theater in various cities and countries. Some of these studies discuss the development of the Jewish performative tradition, while others concentrate on the art of satirical and comic theater among Jews in general and Yiddish speakers in particular.[3] My discussion traces the internal cultural sources that Dzigan and Shumacher drew upon, the duo's place in the chain of Jewish performative tradition, the Jewish and linguistic characteristics of their art, and the cultural and social roles of their theater. In so doing, it relates to existing studies of Yiddish theater, as well as those devoted to Jewish humor, Jewish parody, and humor in Yiddish literature. However, considering the modernist language of the Ararat theater, the duo's work must be examined not only in the context of Jewish theater but also in relation to *Kleynkunst* (miniature theater), the European, Russian, and Polish tradition of cabaret,

3 See, for example, Shiper, *Geshikhte fun yidisher teater-kunst*; Erik, *Di komedyes*; Oyslender, *Yidisher teater*; Mestel, *Undzer teater*; Turkow-Grudberg, "Yidish teater in Varshe"; Belkin, *Hapurim-shpil*; Nahshon, "Habima's Production of 'The Dybbuk'"; Steinlauf, "Y. L. Peretz and the Canonization of Yiddish Theater"; Stern, "From Jester to Gesture"; Berkowitz, "Writing the History of Yiddish Theatre"; Veidlinger, *Moscow State Yiddish Theater*.

and humor in Western culture (for example, the genre of comic duos). All these provide important contexts for understanding Dzigan and Shumacher's artistic path, and I will discuss them at length in this book.

Yiddish theater in Israel has received little attention, both in studies of Yiddish culture in Israel and scholarship on Israeli theater.[4] Academic research has so far focused mainly on the Hebrew theater in Israel, largely ignoring artistic expressions in other languages. This trend began to change in the last two decades, thanks to increasing scholarship on minority cultures in Israel.[5]

The duo specialized in Yiddish satirical performances concerning topics from everyday life. In order to analyze their activities both on and off stage it is vital to understand the milieu in which they performed. Therefore, in addition to the various available sources – such as commercial recordings (audio and video), Dzigan's autobiography, and memoirs penned by theatrical figures – I examined archival material pertinent to the surroundings in which the duo's productions were created and performed – Poland until the outbreak of the Second World War, the USSR, Israel, and the diaspora following the Holocaust. The many archival materials I perused include scripts of plays, recordings of performances for the artists' personal use, directors' notebooks, correspondence with the authorities, reviews in a number of languages, printed playbills for the performances, interviews with the artists, and press cuttings written by the artists themselves.

My analysis of the duo's performances is informed by theories of performance and theater studies. Performance is an aesthetic act of communication that employs cultural symbols and offers the audience an opportunity to partake in a shared experience. Furthermore, it enables the mutual and continued processing of experiences and meanings that constitute culture. A performance must therefore be interpreted within the context of its creation, presentation, and reception.[6] The study of the theatrical event as a context-dependent artistic phenomenon

4 See Pilowsky, *Tsvishn yo un neyn*; Rotman, "Language Politics"; Rojanski, *Yiddish in Israel*.

5 Alongside modern studies of Hebrew theater in Israel – such as those by Alexander, *Leitsan heḥatser*; Orian, *Habe'aya ha'adatit*; Tartakovsky, *Habima*; Gilula, *Hate'aṭron hakameri* – there exist many studies concerning Yiddish theater and theater in Israel in languages other than Hebrew, which are now trickling into the academic discourse on Israeli theater. See, for example, Yerushalmi, "Betsila shel Hanna Rovina"; Yerushalmi, "Hisṭoryot shel 'Hadibuḳ'"; Zer-Zion, "Ha'Vilner trupe'; Kaufman-Simhon, "Lemale' ḥalal"; Lewy, *Hayeḳim*. This change is also evident in the certain degree of recognition accorded to these groups by the government, expressed in grants for cultural activities, changes in educational programs, and the discussion of minority culture in the media. One example is the law passed in 1996 establishing national authorities for Yiddish culture and Ladino culture, and its realization in the founding of these institutions a few years later.

6 See Postlewait, "Autobiography and Theatre History"; Zarrilli, "For Whom Is the King a King?"; Bauman, "Performance."

tends to negate the hierarchy between the aesthetics of the performance and the nature of its reception.[7] In addition to the means of expression, acting style, intonation, and so forth, this study also stresses audience responses, the reactions of reviewers, and the artists' image in the public sphere, outside their activities on stage. According to this approach, the artistic endeavor, the public performance, and the personal story are interwoven.

The Structure of the Book

This book is structured chronologically. Each chapter outlines, characterizes, and analyzes the artistic endeavors of Dzigan and Shumacher, or Dzigan alone, during a certain period. An examination of performances or texts is integrated into a discussion of various facets of their artistic activity – the artists' professional and social biographies; the historical, cultural, economic, and political circumstances in which the art was created and performed; ways of realizing the text; and its reception by critics, alongside other aspects. Thus, the discussion touches upon a range of internal and external aspects – relating to both content and form – of Dzigan and Shumacher's artistic path. I also examine references to them in the press and their behavior vis-à-vis the authorities and various institutions, including their activities in prisons and labor camps in the Soviet Union, in cafes, in the Knesset (Israeli Parliament) cafeteria, or in conversations with reporters. These interactions sometimes complemented (and on other occasions contradicted) their performances on stage.

According to Dzigan, theater and humor can exert great political influence. In his autobiography – entitled *Der koyekh fun yidishn humor* (The Power of Jewish Humor, 1974) – he even claimed that his theater contributed to the historic change in the Israeli political leadership that occurred in the 1970s, a change that reached a peak in 1977, when Menachem Begin came to power, ending three decades of Labor Party dominance. This accords with the findings of contemporary scholars, who regard the theater as an arena of conflict and actors as part of the array of political forces active in society.[8]

The detailed examination of the skits and monologues that Dzigan and Shumacher performed – from the days of Ararat to Dzigan's last show in Israel – emphasizes the performative dimension of their art. This is directly connected

7 See Schechner, *Performance Theory*.

8 Regarding the breakdown of the mechanisms of power and how this is revealed by the study of theater see, for example, Schechner, *Performance Theory*; Kirshenblatt-Gimblett and Taylor, "What's Wrong with These Terms?"; Auslander, "Stand-up Comedy."

with the cultural role that their theater played, its reception by critics and audience, and the means the artists employed in light of their artistic milieu and the socio-political context.[9]

The clearest example of such analysis is the section concerning the skit "Der nayer dibek" (The New Dybbuk), performed in 1957. This skit was a parody of the canonical performance of Sh. An-sky's play *The Dybbuk*, set in Eastern Europe, as staged by the Hebrew Habima theater. However, at the same time, it offered a satirical commentary on Israeli politics during the 1950s – the frustrations felt by immigrants, the unquestioned authority of David Ben-Gurion, and more. Dzigan's performance in a parody of the character Leahele (Leyele), as played by Hanna Rovina, and Shumacher's performance in the role of the Hasidic Tzaddik, a satirical version of Ben-Gurion, here serve as the basis for a discussion of nationalism and theater, the status of immigrants, cultural and linguistic battles, and even gender relations.

About the Sources

There is little scholarly literature relating directly to Dzigan and Shumacher. In her popular book, *Vagabond Stars: A World History of Yiddish Theater*, Nahma Sandrow mentions their artistic endeavors, noting their central place in the history of Yiddish theater.[10] Gilles Rozier, who contributed significantly to the study of Moyshe Broderzon's literary works, discusses the Ararat theater, which was founded by Broderzon, from historical and literary perspectives.[11] Although his study is an important source for examining the initial years of the duo's artistic careers, he focuses on texts rather than theatrical performances and does not discuss Dzigan and Shumacher's art specifically.

The only scholarly works devoted to Dzigan and Shumacher in their own right are an article by the historian John Efron,[12] Uri Vedenyapin's BA Thesis written at Harvard University,[13] and a chapter in Rachel Rojanski's recently published book.[14] Vedenyapin focuses on Dzigan, endeavoring to locate his art within the

---

9 This is influenced principally by the cultural studies approach advanced by Janelle Reinelt and Joseph Roach, who refuse to accept the separation between life and art, attempting to connect both to dynamic cultural processes. See Roach, *Cities*; Reinelt and Roach, *Critical Theory*.
10 Sandrow, *Vagabond Stars*.
11 Rozier, *Moyshe Broderzon*.
12 Efron, "From Łódź to Tel Aviv."
13 Vedenyapin, *Doctors Prescribe Laughter*.
14 Rojanski, *Yiddish in Israel*.

tradition of Jewish theater during various periods of his activity.[15] Efron seeks to characterize Dzigan's political satire and the role of the Yiddish language in his art, based on Dzigan's memoirs, commercial recordings of skits, and historical and social studies. He views Dzigan and Shumacher as continuing the tradition of the *badkhn* (jester) and as the heirs of Sholem Aleichem.[16] Likewise, he discusses Dzigan's status in Israel, which is also the main topic of a chapter in Rojanski's book. In addition, I have published a number of studies concerning the duo: one in the collection *'Al na' tegarshuni* (Do Not Chase Me Away), concerning performance and text in Dzigan and Shumacher's theater, another regarding their political satire of Israeli leaders, published in a collection on Jewish humor,[17] an article on performing homeland in the post-Holocaust era,[18] and my PhD dissertation, upon which this book is based.[19]

Various Yiddish actors described Dzigan and Shumacher at length in their memoirs. These texts contributed to creating the modern mythology of Yiddish theater, which Joel Berkowitz refers to when discussing the scholarly works regarded as "classics" in the historiography of the field.[20] Despite the problems that such works entail, we can glean from them much information about the environment in which the two artists were active, in various periods and different places. The depictions in such literature reveal how key figures interpreted the period and can thus help us to understand the cultural, social, and political meaning of Dzigan and Shumacher's stage art.

In his article "Kleynkunst un marionetn-teaters tsvishn beyde velt-milkhomes" (The Miniature Theater and Puppet Theaters between the Two World Wars), Moyshe Nudelman, one of the central authors of skits and monologues for Ararat and Dzigan and Shumacher's theater, surveys the development of Jewish miniature theater in Poland. In addition to painting a fascinating picture of Ararat in Łódź, Nudelman depicts in detail the duo's Warsaw period, examining how the Jewish audience in the city experienced the artists' theater, their influence

---

15 Vedenyapin depicts Dzigan as a stand-up comedian, although neither Dzigan nor his critics (apart from the reviews of his performances in the United States in the 1970s) identified either him or Shumacher with this genre.

16 Efron, "From Łódź to Tel Aviv."

17 Rotman, "Political Satire."

18 Rotman, "Performing Homeland."

19 The article includes earlier versions of sections found in the fifth chapter of this book. See Rotman, "Hadibuķ 'einenu Moshe Sneh"; Rotman, "Performens kebiķoret tarbut." See also: Rotman, *Habama.*

20 Berkowitz, "Writing the History of Yiddish Theatre." Concerning the study of the theater using memoirs, biographies, and similar materials see Postlewait, "Autobiography and Theatre History."

on the local culture, and their public status in Jewish communal life.[21] A further central source for my research is Moyshe Pulaver's book, *Ararat un lodzher tipn* (Ararat and Łódź types).[22] Pulaver, one of the actors and directors in the Ararat troupe, included in his work documents, pictures, personal memories, and press clippings about Ararat. These constitute important sources for its study, although the book presents a very personal interpretation of the troupe by one of Ararat's central figures and its information is not always accurate.

Shimen Dzigan's autobiography, *Der koyekh fun yidishn humor*, describes the society in which he was raised, his personal development, his theatrical path, and the connection between art and the surrounding political reality. It contains a rich variety of anecdotes as well as portraits of his youthful experiences and artistic career from the actor's own historical perspective. This fascinating book was penned with the help of several writers and editors. Yet despite its comprehensive editing, we clearly hear the actor's voice. The book was written in Yiddish and intended for Yiddish speakers in Israel and the diaspora. The readership that Dzigan imagined was without doubt his own generation, those who attended his theatrical performances – his viewers, and his critics.[23] His autobiography, similarly to any other autobiographical work, is not unproblematic with regard to historical facts, circumstances, and events, but there can be no doubt regarding its contribution to studying the art of Dzigan and Shumacher, as well as Dzigan's life and artistic activities. The book reveals how Dzigan sought to immortalize himself and how he chose to tell his personal story, as well as that of Yiddish theater.[24]

In addition to the materials mentioned above, I relied on many primary sources from various archives. These include scripts and playbills of performances by Dzigan and Shumacher, performed both together and individually; audio recordings of the duo's monologues and dialogues recorded in Poland before World War II; audio recordings made in Israel and other countries and distributed first on vinyl, then commercial tapes, and later on CDs (both Dzigan and Shumacher as a duo and Dzigan's theater); home recordings made by the actors for their personal use in shows and rehearsals; films in which they appeared; extracts from news reports broadcast in Israeli cinemas; and two recordings

---

21 Nudelman, "Kleynkunst."

22 Pulaver, *Ararat*.

23 As far as I know, he did not express any desire to translate the book into Hebrew or other languages.

24 Historians of the theater, among them Postlewait, Barton, and others, have discussed the reliability of autobiographies in establishing historical factors. Berkowitz addresses the topic in his critique of the historiography of Yiddish theater.

of adaptations of theater plays by Dzigan produced especially for Israeli television. The two shows were recorded on tape and distributed on DVD. These materials constitute a major resource in examining the performative aspects of Dzigan and Shumacher's art. I also found useful other materials documenting their activities and creative path, such as director's notebooks, diaries, and correspondence with the authorities. In addition, I availed myself of reviews and articles about Dzigan and Shumacher in the Israeli press in Yiddish, Hebrew, and other languages, in the official languages of Poland, the USSR, the United States, Argentina, and other countries; and interviews with actors and texts that they themselves published in the press.[25] I consulted reviews and photographs from the Ararat collection donated by the actor Moyshe Kosman (Kazanover) to the Israeli Center for the Documentation of the Performing Arts at Tel Aviv University, and interviews with stage artists who collaborated with Dzigan and Shumacher (Shmuel Atzmon-Wircer, Anabela [Ya'akov Kelner], Lea Szlanger), and with Lydia Shumacher-Ophir, Yisroel Shumacher's daughter.

The archival sources are largely located in the Shimen Dzigan collection and the Yisroel Shumacher collection at the Yehuda Gabbai Theatre Archive in the Beit Ariela Library in Tel Aviv (BAA), the Israeli Center for the Documentation of the Performing Arts at Tel Aviv University (ICDPA), the Israel Goor Theatre Archives and Museum at The Hebrew University of Jerusalem (IGTA), the collection of the Yidisher Artistn Farayn (1919–1939), and the collection of the Esther-Rachel Kaminska Theater Museum, both at YIVO in New York.

A Note on Transliteration, Names, and Translation

This book relies extensively on sources in Hebrew and Yiddish. The titles of both first and secondary sources in those languages have been transliterated. Names of newspapers follow the English spelling of the newspaper, where this exists (for example *Yedioth Ahronoth*).

YIVO guidelines were used for transliteration of Yiddish. The Hebrew transliteration follows the ALA (American Library Association) system. According to the

25 Many of the reviews and articles are preserved in the Yehuda Gabbai Theatre Archive at the Beit Ariela Library in Tel Aviv. They were collected by the artists, sometimes without noting the place of publication or date. When I approached the materials in the archive, the articles were not organized in any order and therefore I refer the reader to the archive itself. Online access to many primary and secondary sources is provided nowadays by various websites, including those of The Israel Goor Theatre Archives and Museum, the Index to Yiddish Periodicals, and the Historical Jewish Press.

guidelines of the Academy of the Hebrew Language, prepositions and the article are not separated from the noun (*ha*, *ba*, *la*, etc.). In Hebrew transliteration, the letters Aleph and Ayin are marked with the signs ’ and ‘ respectively. Transliterations use only lower case (apart from the first word in a sentence, private names, and names of countries), in accordance with the fact that both Hebrew and Yiddish have no capital letters.

A particular challenge in writing this book was the spelling of personal names. Indeed, the book includes individuals from a range of countries and cultures. Moreover, Hebrew and Yiddish names can be transliterated in a variety of different ways. Thus, where possible, the spelling of individuals’ names follows the spellings in roman characters found in the authors’ own books, articles, or (more recently) websites and social media, or accords with commonly accepted spellings (for example, Sholem Aleichem, Uri Zvi Greenberg). The names of Yiddish actors are written according to the YIVO encyclopedia, files in the YIVO archives, or Zalmen Zylbercweig’s *Leksikon fun yidishn teater.* Names that do not appear in any of these sources have been transliterated following the YIVO guidelines. Likewise, the names of Hebrew and Yiddish actors, politicians, and other figures have been spelled according to commonly accepted spellings or, in the few cases in which this was not possible, transliterated.

However, a division of the names into Hebrew or Yiddish is not possible. Indeed, some actors performed in both languages and writers wrote in both these tongues. So too, Dzigan and Shumacher were discussed extensively in both the Hebrew and Yiddish press. Thus, spellings are consistent with the context. For example, Dzigan’s first name is spelled Shimon (rather than Shimen) in the transliterated titles of Hebrew articles about him.

All translations from Yiddish and Hebrew within the text are mine, unless indicated otherwise. Quotations from Dzigan and Shumacher’s skits appear in the original Yiddish, followed by an English translation. Lengthy and significant quotations from reviews and other documents have also been included in the original Yiddish, although in most cases these are found in the footnotes, so as not to disrupt the flow of the text.

Chapter 1
Modernism, Avant Garde, and Innovation in Yiddish Theater: Dzigan and Shumacher in Łódź (1925–1933)

The Influence of Modernism on Yiddish Literature and Theater

Dzigan and Shumacher, among the most important figures in the history of Yiddish theater, began their artistic careers with the Yiddish *kleynkunst-bine*[1] troupe Ararat. This troupe was founded in Łódź, Poland, in 1927 by the poet Moyshe Broderzon (1890–1956), who also served as its artistic director. It developed from the Lodzher teater studio (Łódź Theater Studio) that Broderzon had founded two years previously. The name Ararat – an acronym for the Artistisher revolutsyonerer teater (Revolutionary Artistic Theater) or, according to others, the Artistisher revyu-teater (Artistic Revue Theater) – alludes to Mount Ararat, which in Jewish tradition symbolizes rebirth following the flood described in the book of Genesis. Influenced by European and Russian literary cabaret as well as the tradition of Yiddish humor, Ararat became one of the central Jewish theater groups active in Poland in the 1920s and 1930s.

The Beginnings of Jewish Modernism

Following World War I, inspired by contemporaneous modernist artistic and literary movements, groups of Jewish writers and artists emerged in Eastern Europe and Soviet Russia. The influence of modernism was evident in the theater, poetry, literature, music, dance, and plastic arts that these Jewish artists produced: they sought to challenge both artistic language and Jewish literature, developing new, even revolutionary, means of expression in Yiddish, Hebrew, or the vernacular spoken in their surroundings.[2] Authors and artists from various fields cooperated in their quest for change and renewal, making a significant contribution to the modernization and invigoration of Jewish art. However, such instances of collaboration were often short-lived.

1 Literally meaning "little art stage." In Yiddish it was also called "sintetish-teater" (synthetic theater) or "Minyatur-teater" (miniature theater).
2 See Harshav, *Manifesṭim*. See also Kronfeld, *Margins of Modernism*; Wolitz, "Between Folk and Freedom"; Novershtern, *Ḳesem hadimdumim*.

https://doi.org/10.1515/9783110717693-001

Many such groups launched independent frameworks in order to disseminate their works: some organized readings and exhibitions or even established journals in which they published literary works, manifests, and reproductions of the works of art created by their members. The typography and design of these journals reflected the artists' innovative perspectives. Indeed, this is evident in the journals and collections published in various centers of Yiddish culture: *Eygns* (Kiev, 1918–1920) edited by Dovid Bergelson; *Yung-Yidish* (*Yung-Idish*; Łódź, 1919–1921) edited by Moyshe Broderzon; *Albatros* (Warsaw, 1922; Berlin, 1923)[3] edited by Uri Zvi Greenberg; *Khalyastre* (Warsaw, 1922; Paris, 1924)[4] edited by Perets Markish; and others. Efforts were also invested in cultivating an artistic and modern Yiddish theater that would offer an alternative to the existing popular commercial theater, which was often referred to using the derogatory term *shund*.[5] The initiatives to establish an artistic theater were influenced by the thought of Y. L Peretz and the playwright and poet A. Vayter (Ayzik-Meir Devenishsky).

In 1908, Perets Hirshbeyn established a Yiddish art theater troupe in Odessa, the first Yiddish theatrical group to adopt the model developed by Konstantin Stanislavski. It later achieved fame as the Hirshbeyn trupe (Hirshbeyn Troupe), staging plays written by Perets Hirshbeyn himself, Sholem Aleichem, and Sholem Asch. This same vision, the creation of a Yiddish art theater, also motivated the foundation of a number of other troupes: the Vilner trupe (Vilna Troupe), founded in Vilna in 1916, which relocated to Warsaw a year later and was the first theater to stage *Der dibek* (The Dybbuk) by Sh. An-sky, directed by Dovid Herman;[6] the Yung-teater (Young Theater), founded by Dovid Herman and Michael Weichert in Warsaw in 1932,[7] following Weichert's return from his theatrical studies under Max Reinhardt in Berlin;[8] and the VYKT theater, Varshever yidisher kunst-teater

3 See Lipsker, "Young Yiddish Poetry."

4 See Ertel, *Khaliastra*; Wolitz, "Di Khalyastre."

5 This Yiddish term draws on a German word describing the stinking refuse generated when removing the skins of slaughtered animals. The Jewish popular commercial theater was referred to disparagingly as *shund* – this word was also used to describe literature that incorporated comparable content and was written on a similar linguistic level – and became the target of piercing and humiliating criticism. The Jewish intelligentsia viewed this as a social "disease" to be cured, an "evil damaging to the viewers and that must be fought." For examples of this critical discourse, see Mayzel, "Mikoyekh." Turkow, "A mageyfe." For a discussion of the concept *shund*, see Shmeruk, "Sifrut ha'shund.'"

6 See Caplan, *Yiddish Empire.*

7 Rubel, "Lahaḳat ha'Yung-teater.'"

8 See Shner, "Varshever yidisher kunst-teater." Many Jews were active in the Deutsches Theater in Berlin while it was under the management of Max Reinhardt, and they sought to create a unique artistic language that would express or reflect their identity. Jewish actors and directors

(The Warsaw Jewish Art Theater), which was established by Zygmunt Turkow and Ida Kaminska in 1924.[9]

In the Soviet Union two troupes greatly influenced the development of artistic Jewish theater: the Hebrew Habima theater, which began its activities in Moscow in 1917 under the management of Nahum Zemach (following failed attempts to establish such a troupe in Białystok),[10] and the Moskver melukhisher yidisher teater (The Moscow State Jewish Theater), which was founded in Moscow in 1920 (also known as GOSET, the acronym of its Russian name), managed by Aleksandr Granovskii and Solomon Mikhoels.[11]

The first Yiddish troupe in Poland to adopt the modernist tradition of the miniature theater was Azazel. Founded in 1926, Azazel represented a milestone in the evolution of the genre.[12] Its members included director Dovid Herman, painter Henryk Berlewi, composer Henekh Kon, actress Tea Arciszewska, and stage designer Władysław Weintraub. Students from Herman's studio acted alongside veteran performers such as Chaim Sandler, Yoysef Strugatsh, Ola Lilit, and Vladek Godik. Strugatsh appeared a number of years later with the Nayer Ararat (New Ararat) troupe in Łódź and directed seven of its shows. Godik served as "master of ceremonies" in Ararat's Warsaw period, and during World War II, he performed with Der byalistoker melukhisher yidisher minyatur-teater (The Białystok National Jewish Miniature Theater), together with Dzigan and Shumacher.[13]

In its first show, Azazel performed the skits "Tsipele" (Little Tsipe), with lyrics by Moyshe Broderzon, music by Israel Glatstein; "Hoyf-kleyzmer" (The Court Klezmer Musician), also by Broderzon, with music composed by Henekh Kon; "A bank in Krashinskes gortn" (A Bench in Krashinsky's Garden) by Der Tunkeler;[14] "Amerikaner feter" (An American Uncle) by Alter Katsizne, an adaptation of

throughout Europe developed a modernist theatrical language directly connected to visual images from Jewish tradition.

9 Among the attempts that preceded these initiatives were "Dos artistishe vinkele" (The Artistic Corner), a theater group founded in Warsaw in 1916 by Zygmunt and Jonas Turkow.

10 See Zer-Zion, "Beyond Habima," 12–16.

11 The theater was initially managed by Granovskii in St. Petersburg. See Veidlinger, *Moscow State Yiddish Theater* and Béatrice Picon-Vallin, *Le théâtre juif soviétique*.

12 Zylbercweig, *Leksikon*, 2: 1500–3; Nudelman, "Kleynkunst"; Bułat, "Kleynkunst." Bułat notes the appearances of Yaakov Shternberg in Bucharest in 1917–1918 as a first example of the genre.

13 The style of the "master of ceremonies," a central role in European cabaret, was characterized by humoristic comments on the political, economic, and social reality.

14 Der Tunkeler (Yoysef Tunkel, 1881–1949) began his career as an illustrator and author of comics. He also wrote satire, poems, and short stories that were published in various newspapers over many decades. See Yechiel Szeintuch's introduction in Tunkeler, *Sefer hahumoresḳot*, 13–68.

Y. L. Peretz's story "Tsvey yingelekh" (Two Young Men); a monologue by Moyshe Nudelman entitled "Beygl," the song "Azazel-shimi" by Broderzon and Kon, as well as adaptations of popular songs. In other shows, they staged texts by Yankev Oberzhanek, Moyshe-Leyb Halpern, Moyshe Nudelman, and Yekhezkl-Moyshe (Y. M.) Nayman; texts by many of these same writers were later staged by Ararat.[15] Azazael closed in 1928 due to economic difficulties.[16]

Moyshe Broderzon's Activities in Łódź

Łódź, the second largest city in Poland and capital of the textile industry, known as "the Manchester of Poland," was also affected by the new modernist trends. In an article published in Israel in 1950, Y. M. Nayman described how the Jews of Łódź perceived themselves:

> It is impossible to understand Dzigan and Shumacher properly without first becoming acquainted with Łódź, my friends, which excelled in its fabrics and in its jokes . . . In Łódź the joke was like oil for the bonfire, a spice of life. All day long, the activities of a Łódź Jew were accompanied by jokes. It is said that when a Łódź Jew snored and talked in his sleep – he let out a joke. When the joke was good – he woke up. When the joke was bad – he went on sleeping.[17]

In the spirit of futurism, Nahum Sokolow portrayed Łódź as

> neither Polish, nor German, nor Russian, nor Jewish, but all of them combined . . . a great fair, an enormous [cotton] factory, from the beginning of its creation, with Ashkenaziness added its Jewishness, busy streets, noisy, complex, sprawling, [with] machines and smoking chimneys, vibrations and work spasms, wonderful development, a haphazard sense of action, the troubles of business and confusions of trade, Jewish fabricants and their assistants, Jewish-Lithuanian commissioners, traders that set out to conquer all the markets of European and Asian Russia, reaching as far as China, merchandise and merchants and money, a stormy center, boiling, the rule of money.[18]

Stimulated by the Industrial Revolution, from 1821 the city of Łódź entered an era of intensive growth and development, which further increased in the period between 1866 and World War I. Its population rose from 32,500 persons at the

---

15 Weichert, "Azazel"; Mayzel, "Ferter."

16 Dzigan claimed that Azazel's new artistic experiment failed due to the involvement of veteran actors who were unable to liberate themselves from the patterns and molds of the old artistic theater. See Dzigan, *Der koyekh*, 57–58.

17 Nayman, "Dzigan ṿeShumacher." Unless otherwise noted, all translations are original.

18 In Gilboa, *David Frishman*, 76–84.

beginning of the nineteenth century to 63,000 in the second half of that century.[19] During the second decade of the twentieth century, the Jewish population of Łódź grew rapidly, as refugees fled Russia in the wake of the revolution and the wave of pogroms that accompanied it. In 1910, the population of the city had passed 400,000, including 160,000 Jews: around forty percent of the entire population. By 1914 there were around 100,000 Jews living in Bałuty (Yid., Balut), a neighborhood of Jewish workers and craftsmen that became a symbol of the city's Jewish proletariat.[20] In the period 1921–1931, during the economic crisis that followed World War I, 200,000 Jews lived in the city, constituting around thirty-two percent of its population.[21]

The stereotype of the Łódź Jew was immortalized in works of Yiddish literature such as *Di brider Ashkenazi* (The Brothers Ashkenazi, 1936) by Israel Joshua Singer; the novel *Balut: Roman fun a forshtot* (Bałut: Novel of a Suburb, 1934) by Yisroel Rabon; *Der letster lodzher roman* (The Last Łódź Novel, 1951) by Zusman *Segalovitsh*; the memoirs of Yekhiel Yeshaye Trunk, *Poyln – zikhroynes un bilder* (Poland – Memories and Pictures, 1944–1953); and on stage – by Ararat and the theater of Dzigan and Shumacher.

The Jews played a central role not only in the development of the city's industry but also in the cultivation of local culture. The Jewish theater and press began to flourish at the end of the nineteenth century and the beginning of the twentieth century. In 1905, Yitskhok Zandberg, formerly an actor in the Kaminsky family troupe in Warsaw, founded A groyser teater (A Big Theater) at 10 Konstantynowska Street in Łódź.[22] This theater, the first permanent Yiddish theater in the city, was active until 1915, staging performances in the tradition of popular Yiddish theater, among them plays by Avrom Goldfaden, Jacob Gordin, and Sholem Asch. While its performances were not particularly developed in artistic terms, it was a well-organized theater.

In 1907, the local Yiddish newspaper *Lodzher nakhrikhten* began to appear, edited by Yeshaye Uger. When the paper closed a year later, Uger began editing the *Lodzher tageblat*, which published works by Sholem Aleichem, Mendele Moykher Sforim, and Y. L. Peretz, alongside other writers, including David Frishman and Mordkhe Spektor. In 1913, Yulius Adler founded the "Skala-teater" (Skala Theater), located at 18 Ceglana Street. In 1915 the *Lodzher tageblat* (now edited by Lazar Kahn) began to publish the works of Y. M. Nayman, under the penname "A foygl" (A Bird), and Yoysef-Shimen (Y. Sh.) Goldshteyn, who used the penname "Der

19 Pus, "Jews in Lódz."
20 See for example Rabon, *Balut*.
21 Puś, "Jews in Lódz."
22 Mukdoni, *In Varshe un in Lodzh*, 2: 272–79.

lustiker pesimist" (The Joyful Pessimist) – both later wrote for Dzigan and Shumacher's satirical theater in Warsaw. After World War I, two additional Yiddish theaters opened their doors in Łódź: Arkadia on Piotrkowska Street and Urania at 34 Ceglana Street. At the end of the 1920s, following the economic crisis, all the permanent Yiddish theaters in Łódź were forced to close.[23]

Poets, writers, and Jewish artists who played a central role in the Yiddish culture that thrived in Łódź, among them Yitzhak Katzenelson, Yisroel Rabon, Yankl Adler (see below), and Moyshe Broderzon. Broderzon, as noted above, opened an acting studio in Łódź in 1925, became the artistic manager of Ararat, and played a significant role in the careers of Dzigan and Shumacher. He was born in Moscow in 1890, but a year later, when the Jews were expelled from that city, his family settled in Łódź. At seventeen, he wrote his first poems in Russian, and in 1908 he began to publish humoristic texts in the *Lodzher tageblat* under the penname "Broder Zinger," a play on words connecting his family name with the popular, *maskilic* (Jewish enlightenment) humoristic theatrical tradition exemplified by the "Broder Zinger" (The Brody Singers).[24] In 1913, he published his first collection of poetry in Yiddish, entitled *Shvartse fliterlekh* (Black Sparks).

Following the Battle of Łódź (1914) that was fought between the Russians and Germans, Broderzon settled in Moscow, where he was exposed to the artistic activities of young artists who wove Jewish tradition and Jewish folklore into their art.[25] He encountered groundbreaking innovations in the field of theater: from the naturalistic theatrical language developed by Konstantin Stanislavski to searches for an experimental theatrical language led by Vsevolod Meyerhold, a key figure in transforming the Moscow artistic theater into a central tool of the Russian Revolution. The poetry of Vladimir Mayakovsky influenced Broderzon significantly: indeed, upon his return to Łódź in 1918, Broderzon's contemporaries nicknamed him "Der yidisher Mayakovsky" (The Jewish Mayakovsky).

Sitting in the Pittoresque Café in Moscow, the meeting place of Russian futurists, Broderzon met many Jewish writers and artists, among them Viktor Khlebnikov and Meyerhold. His artistic activity in Moscow was multifaceted: together with Yoysef Tshaykov, Yisakhar Rybak, and El Lissitzky, he established the Krayzl fun yidish natsyonaler estetik (Circle for Jewish National Aesthetics), which

23 See Bresler, "Epizodn." Concerning the closure of the Yiddish theaters in Łódź, see Zak, "Di krizis-shtimung."

24 See below pp. 11–14. Broderzon continued to use this penname also a few years later. See, for example, Broderzon, "Di farshtendikung"; Broderzon, "Dos gesheftl."

25 Rozier, *Moyshe Broderzon*.

operated within the small publishing house Shamir. The circle staged exhibitions, established a small acting studio, and in 1917 published Broderzon's first prose work, *Sikhes-khulin*: *Eyne fun di geshikhten* (An Everyday Conversation: A Story) with illustrations by Lissitzky.[26] Together with Gershon Broyde, Daniel Tsharni, and Menashe Halperin, in 1918 he published a collection entitled *Zalbefert* (The Four of Them Together) that included works by all four writers.[27]

Upon his return to Łódź in 1918, Broderzon, together with the visual artists Yitskhok Broyner, Yankl Adler, and Marek Szwarc, founded a group of writers and artists named Yung-Yidish (Young Yiddish).[28] The group declared its experimental and modernist spirit in a poem by Broderzon, "Tsu di shtern" (To the Stars), which was published in the first volume of the group's journal *Yung-Yidish* (*Yung-Idish*):

> מיר יונגע, אַ פֿריילעכע צעזונגענע כאַליאַסטרע, / מיר גייען אין אַן אומבאַוווּסטן וועג, / אין טיפֿע, מרה־שחורהדיקע טעג, / אין נעכטן פֿון שרעק -- / Per aspera ad astra!
>
> [We young people, a happy *khalyastre* (singing bunch),[29] / we walk an unknown path, / in days of deep dejection, / in nights of terror / *Per aspera ad astra*![30]]

The influence of the various artistic movements that the four founding members of Yung-Yidish encountered during their wanderings is evident: Broderzon was affected by futurism and Russian modernism; Adler, who in Germany had close ties to the group Die Aktion (The Action), by German expressionism; Szwarc, who had sojourned in Paris and traveled throughout the Russian Empire, contributed

---

26 On *Sikhes-khulin* and on Moyshe Broderzon as a poet, see the monograph by Rozier, ibid.
27 See Estraikh, *In Harness*, 42.
28 Yitskhok (or Vincenti) Broyner (1887–1944) was the son of a wealthy Łódź family that contributed a great deal to the development of the city's textile industry. The meetings of Yung-Yidish took place in his elegant home. Broyner studied art in Warsaw, Kraków, and Berlin, and he published articles on theater and art in *Lodzher tageblat*, *Folksblat*, and *Nayer folksblat*. Yankl Adler (1895–1949) was born in Tuchin, a small town near Łódź. In 1912, he studied printing in Łódź and a year later left to study art in Dusseldorf, where he encountered the activities of a group of local artists, Das Junge Rheinland (Young Rhineland). The influence of German expressionism is evident in the works he published in the six volumes of the group's journal. He achieved great recognition in Germany. In 1943, he settled in London. See Guralnik, Krempel, and Ładnowska, *Yankl Adler*; Malinowski, "Yung Yiddish." Marek Szwarc (1892–1958) was born in Zgierz, studied art in Paris (1910–1914), and published in the journal for Jewish art *Maḥmadim*, together with Nathan Altman, Yoysef Tshaykov, Yitskhok Lichtenstein, and Leo Kenig. In 1919, he converted to Christianity.
29 Broderzon's poem was also the moto of the journal *Khalyastre* (1922), meaning "band" or "group."
30 From the Latin, meaning "through hardship to the stars!"

his impressions from the dialogue on modern Jewish art; and Broyner, who studied in Berlin, his knowledge of expressionist painting.

The members of Yung-Yidish added new, vibrant colors to the industrial city's grey streets. They met in the Astoria Café, a center of cultural life in Łódź, which was also frequented by leading artists, writers, and musicians active in the city at the time. Some of these artists joined the group's activities, among them Ida Broyner, Henoch Barczyński, Pola Lindenfeld, Dina Matus, Y. M. Nayman, and Yitzhak Katzenelson, and some later collaborated with Ararat. Dzigan describes the café as follows:

> די ווענט און די קעלנער וואָס האָבן אַ גאַנצן טאָג געהערט רעדן וועגן וואָל, צוקער, לעדער און דאָס גלײַכן, האָבן איצט געהערט רעדן וועגן סאָנעטן, מעטאַפֿאָרן, עקספּרעסיאָניזם, אימפּרעסיאָניזם, כאָרעאָגראַפֿיע, נאַטוראַליזם אאַז"וו.[31]
>
> [The walls and the waiters, who all day long heard talk about wool, sugar, leather, etc., now listened to conversations about sonnets, metaphors, expressionism, impressionism, choreography, naturalism, and so forth.]

Yung-Yidish was a groundbreaking development in Jewish art in Poland.[32] It was the first group comprised entirely of members of the young generation, and it succeeded in creating an independent artistic life and establishing links with Polish modernist literary groups.[33] However, Yung-Yidish was short-lived: it disintegrated in 1921, when some of its members left Poland, Szwarc converted to Christianity, and Broderzon began to focus his attention on theater.[34]

In 1922, Broderzon, known as "the prince of Polish Manchester,"[35] Broyner, the composer Henekh Kon, and the author Y. M. Nayman established Khad-gadye – the first Yiddish puppet theater in Poland – in the tradition of the Russian cabaret's puppet theater.[36] The texts for the plays were written by Moyshe Broderzon,

---

31 Dzigan, *Der koyekh*, 68.

32 On this, see Malinowski, "Yung Yiddish."

33 Josef Robakowski claims that the central artists in Yung-Yidish influenced the Polish artistic arena in Łódź. See Robakowski, "Łodz Progressive Art Movement."

34 Szwarc left for Paris. Adler, Broyner, Barczyńsk, and Lindenfeld settled in Germany.

35 Dzigan, *Der koyekh*, 72.

36 Kon studied at the Königliche Hochschule für Musik in Berlin. He was one of the most talented Jewish musicians active in the fields of music and theater in Poland during the interwar period. He wrote music for the miniature theater Azazel and later also for Ararat. Concerning Kon see Fater, *Musiḳa yehudit*. Y. M. Nayman (1893–1956) was born in Zhikhlin (Żychlin). At the age of one, his family moved to Łódź. In his youth, Nayman wrote and published satirical poems and caricatures in local and national Yiddish papers. He edited the humorous-satirical column "Der kibitzer" (The Spectator) in *Dos lodzher morgenblat* (1912–1914), which discussed political events affecting the Jews in Tsarist Russia. He wrote many satires for the theater, published texts

Yankev Oberzhanek, and Y. M. Nayman. The first show also included a work by Froym Kaganovski. The puppets were made by Broyner, who also designed and illustrated the posters. The music was composed by Kon, who played in the performances alongside Sheyne-Miriam, Broderzon's wife. The content of the performances was mainly satirical and concerned Polish Jewry and politics.[37] Khad-gadye ceased performing after only one year, in January 1923.[38] A few years later, its artists played a leading role in establishing Ararat.

In 1924, Broderzon wrote the Yiddish opera *Dovid un bassheve* (*David and Bathsheba*), inspired by the book of Samuel, which was staged in 1924 in the Kaminsky Theater in Warsaw, directed by Dovid Herman and with a musical accompaniment composed by Kon. In 1925, Broderzon established in Łódź the Lodzher teater studyo (Łódź Acting Studio).

The Influence of European and Russian Cabaret

The unique artistic language of European cabaret began to develop in the 1880s with the establishment of the cabaret Le Chat Noir (The Black Cat) in Paris (1881–1897). This cabaret inspired dozens of others in cultural centers throughout Europe: Quatre Gats (Four Cats) opened in Barcelona in 1897, becoming a center of Spanish modernism and hosting groundbreaking art exhibitions; Jung Wien (Young Vienna) was founded in Vienna by Karl Kraus in 1901;[39] Zielony Balonik (Green Balloon) was founded in Kraków in 1905 by Jan August Kisielewski, an attempt to provide an alternative to the local establishment culture.[40] By the end of World War I, cabarets had become unofficial meeting places for painters, poets, musicians, and theatrical artists who endeavored, through their cooperation, to renew their art, widen the accepted boundaries of the genre, and change

in *Yung-Yidish*, and was a member of that group. In 1919, he settled in Warsaw, and in 1933, he became literary editor of the newspaper *Haynt*. He immigrated to Israel after World War II.

37 For example, skits depicted meetings between figures from different worlds or implausible encounters, such as Hillel Zeitlin meeting Moyshe Broderzon; Sholem Asch conversing with Der Tunkeler; Motke Ganev speaking with Sholem Asch, etc. The responses to Khad-gadye's first performance were mixed. See Zeitlin, "Dzigan un Shumacher."

38 Concerning Khad-gadye, see Zylbercweig, *Leksikon*, 1: 799; Nudelman, "Kleynkunst," 163–68; Rozier, *Moyshe Broderzon*. In 1940, while in the Łódź ghetto, Yitskhok Broyner once again established a satirical puppet theater named Khad-gadye that mainly staged parodies of ghetto personalities. See Turkow-Grudberg, "Yidish teater in Varshe."

39 Concerning the European cabaret, see Appignanesi, *Cabaret*; Richard, *Cabarets*; Segel, *Turn-of-the-Century Cabaret*.

40 Segel, *Turn-of-the-Century Cabaret*, 225–26.

the place of art among the bourgeois class.[41] At the same time, the chanson, a popular French song that typically expresses social and political criticism of figures from the margins of society, also underwent a revival. The chanson also offered an artistic avenue via which information not reported in the newspapers, which were controlled by wealthy magnates, could be imparted. Cabaret's combination of "high" and "low" culture was not only an expression of the aesthetic quest characteristic of the period but also a means to express social and political criticism that endeavored to break down social barriers and negate class differences.[42]

Le Picador cabaret was established by Julian Tuwim in Warsaw in 1918; the costumes were designed by the Łódź artist Arthur Szyk, who later worked with Broderzon. A year later Tuwin also founded Quid Pro Quo, which became a source of inspiration among Warsaw artistic circles and to which critics in the Yiddish press compared both Azazel and Ararat.[43] The cabaret Letuchaya Mysh (The Bat), which was established by actors from the Moscow Art Theater in 1908 and managed by Nikita Baliev,[44] staged parodies of the Art Theater's productions performed by the same actors, alongside dances, skits, improvisation, and singing that drew on folkloristic motifs from Russian, Georgian, and Ukrainian folk songs.[45]

A further cabaret that influenced Broderzon, his students, and his acting studio, as well as other Polish artists and writers, was Der Blaue Vogel (The Blue Bird), a Berlin-based cabaret established by Russian artists fleeing the Bolshevik revolution. The cabaret was founded in 1920 by the actor and director Jascha Jushny. Its shows combined Russian folk songs, modernist theater that demonstrated the influence of Russian constructivism, and satirical skits, offering an alternative to the more political content of other Berlin cabarets. Der Blaue Vogel also appeared outside Germany, and in 1924 and 1926 performed in Łódź. During the second visit to Łódź, one of its directors gave a workshop at Broderzon's acting studio.

The combination of entertainment – including folk songs, dances, short skits, and humoristic monologues – with marionette theater, shadow theater, and

41 Appignanesi, *Cabaret*, 5.

42 Ibid., 1–2.

43 Likewise, in their satirical theater, Dzigan and Shumacher staged Yiddish translations of some texts by Julian Tuwim, such as the skit "Meshugene Zashke" (Crazy Zashke) in the show *Tate, du lakhst!* (Father, You're Laughing!), which was staged at the Nowości Theater in 1938.

44 Sullivan, "Nikita Baliev's Le théâtre."

45 Meyerhold himself experimented with cabaret. Cabarets opened in Saint Petersburg, such as Бродя́чая соба́ка, (The Stray Dog), which was a home for the city's intelligentsia, acmeists, and futurists who opposed the Russian symbolists. See Segel, *Turn-of-the-Century Cabaret*, 95–104; Appignanesi, *Cabaret*, 256–303.

pantomime, which were considered minor theatrical forms and expressions of popular art, stimulated poets, theater artists, and plastic artists. Indeed, many saw it as the key to a new stage language.[46] Broderzon described "synthetic theater" as

> די צוזאַמענגיסונג פֿון אַלע קונסט־מעגלעכקייטן, די צונויפֿשמעלצונג פֿון לעבעדיקן וואָרט, פֿון לעבעדיקער פֿאַרב, פֿון לעבעדיקן מוזיקאַלישן קלאַנג, פֿון ריטמישער באַוועגונג, וואָס שאַפֿט איין גאַנצקייט אין שעפֿערישן אחד, וועלכער איז אויסער יעדער טעאַטראַלישער קאָנקורענץ, ומכל שכן פֿון קינאָ.[47]
>
> [The combination of all artistic possibilities, the fusion of living words, living colors, living musical sounds, and rhythmic movement, coming together into one creative whole. It has no rival in the theater, and certainly not in the cinema.]

In the playbill for Meshiekh geyt (*Messiah's Coming*) (1928–1929), Broderzon quoted literary critic and scholar Maks Erik:[48]

> זאָל מען נישט קליין מאַכן דעם באַגריף קליינקונסט. קליינקונסט איז אַ ריין טעכנישער אויסדרוק. אין סוף איז נישטאָ קיין קליינע קונסט אָדער גרויסע קונסט. פֿאַראַן אָדער קונסט, אָדער שונד, אָדער גראַפֿאָמאַניע.[49]
>
> [One should not depreciate the concept "miniature theater." Miniature theater is a completely technical term. At the end of the day, there is no small or big art. There is either art, or *shund*, or graphomania.]

The influence of Jewish folklore on Broderzon's works, motivated by the modernist tendency to reflect on the past as a means to build a modern, secular Jewish culture, was evident not only in the modernist and folksy language of his theater and his literary works – for example, the poem "Ikh – A purim-shpiler" (I – A Purim-shpil Actor, 1919)[50] – but also in his use of the penname Broder Zinger when publishing some of his poems and newspaper articles. The Broder Zinger troupe was named after one of the first Broder Zinger: Berl Broder Margolis (1817–1868). They performed in taverns to audiences of workers who came there to drink and hear popular jokes and improvisations. Their acting style, reminiscent of cabaret, combined singing and dancing, skits, and monologues, foregrounding typical figures from the townspeople's folklore (among other characters, the monologues were given by a poor shepherd, a poor wagon-driver, a moneylender, a wandering Jew, a cantor [*ḥazan*] a marriage-broker [*shadkhn*], and a Hebrew teacher, each

46 Segel, *Turn-of-the-Century Cabaret*, 35–66.
47 Broderzon, in the playbill for *Meshiekh geyt* (1928–1929).
48 Pseudonym of Zalmen Merkin (1898–1937).
49 Ibid.
50 Broderzon, "*Purim-shpiler.*" It should be noted that this is not a case of direct influence but of an accepted, imagined tradition influencing the modern historiographic discourse concerning Yiddish theater. On this, see Stern, "From Jester to Gesture."

one of them wearing typical dress).[51] The content was influenced by the spirit of the Galician Haskalah, manifest also in the anti-Hasidic songs performed.

The Broder Zinger have been considered as the first actors in modern Yiddish theater,[52] and their acting style inspired Goldfaden, who was popularly known as the "father of professional Jewish theater" from the moment that he appeared in his plays with Yisroel Grodner and other Broder Zinger in the garden of Shimen Mark in 1876.

The Influence of Traditional Jewish Humor

The popular historiography of Yiddish theater seeks to discern in the same a continuum of cultural and historical development. The Broder Zinger are perceived as the modern reincarnation of the Jewish *badkhn*,[53] the *badkhn* is in turn the reincarnation of the *marshelik* (the sixteenth-century master of wedding ceremonies and creator of folk songs), and the latter is the re-embodiment of the Talmudic jester.[54] According to this approach, it was only natural to associate Dzigan and Shumacher with central figures in the tradition of humoristic Ashkenazi Jewish performances.[55] Indeed, this is evident in critical texts concerning the artists published in newspapers and scholarly works,[56] in the words of the artists themselves, and in the texts they staged. In the monologue "Reb Leyzer badkhn" (Reb Leyzer the *badkhn*),[57] performed by Yisroel Shumacher in the show

---

51 Shtif, *Yidishe literatur*, 195–99; Sadan, *Masot 'al sofrei yidish*.

52 See Zylbercweig, *Leksikon*, 1: 215–26, 508–15; Dzigan, *Der koyekh*, 320. For criticism of the historiographical discourse concerning Yiddish theater, particularly that which views the Purim-shpil as the beginning of Jewish theater, see Stern, "From Jester to Gesture."

53 Sandrow, *Vagabond Stars*.

54 Yekhezkel Lifshitz described the jester as a "merry-maker," a comedian, satirist, troubadour, and also a musician, similar to the English minstrel or French jongleur. See Lifshitz, "Badkhonim un letsim." In the initial period of the religious *badkhn*'s existence, the sixteenth century, the figure's repertoire was of a serious and scholastic nature. This changed in the nineteenth century with the combining of the role of the traditional jester with the figures of the wise scholar, proficient in customs and religious law, the master of ceremonies, and the author of folk songs. Dissatisfaction with the existing reality constituted one of the sources of the *badkhn*'s creativity and humor. He was a folk artist, combining high and low art, rhyming, and desecration of the holy, and tackling social and national issues through satire, parody, irony, and sarcasm.

55 Max Weinreich calls this kind of connection "vertical legitimization." See Weinreich, *Yidisher shprakh*, 1: 214–18, 231–33. See also Shandler, *Yiddishland*, 126–53.

56 See for example Vedenyapin, *Doctors Prescribe Laughter*.

57 The name of the author does not appear on the manuscript. It can be found in BAA, file 149-02.

Yontef in der vokhn (A Festival Mid-Week) in Israel in 1957, the artist criticizes the modernization of the Jewish wedding, the changing values, the great amounts of money spent on Jewish weddings, and the fact that the figure of the *badkhn* has fallen from prominence:

> איר ווייסט נישט ווער איך בין?... כאָטש ס'איז / אין גאַנצן נישט קיין ווונדער – / ווען איך בין געווען אַ באַרימטער בדחן / זענט איר נאָך געווען קינדער./ . . . חתונות זענען געבליבן, / קלעזמאָרים – געבליבן, / נאָר מיך, דעם מאַרשעליק, האָט מען פֿאַרטריבן. / . . . פֿלעגט דאָך דער מאַרשעליק, דער גראַמען־פֿלעכטער / שאַפֿן פֿרייד, רופֿן געלעכטער / בײַם דרשה־געשאַנק, בײַם עסן... / פֿאַר וואָס האָט איר אין דעם, ייִדן, פֿאַרגעסן?[58]
>
> [Don't you know/ who I am? ... But it's no wonder. – / When I was a famous *badkhn* / you were still children. / . . . There are still weddings, / there are still musicians, / only I, the *marshelik*, have been driven out. / . . . The *marshelik*, who made rhymes / spread happiness, who called forth laughter / at the speech in honor of the wedding presents[59] and during the meal... / why have you, Jews, forgotten this?]

Many theater critics employed the words used to designate humoristic Jewish figures, such as *lets* ("jester," which also used to mean "actor"), *lustik-makher*, or *badkhn*, when describing the artistic duo from Łódź. In so doing, they drew a link between them and the tradition of Jewish popular humoristic performances. Indeed, Y. M. Nayman described Dzigan and Shumacher in the following manner:

> They continue the tradition of Jewish theater from the days of the Broder Zinger or the *badkhn* known in the courts of the Hasidic Rebbes – such as Hershele of Ostropol. They are not alone. Alongside the burial society, there existed a professional union of entertainers. "Words of laughter with tears" – in the style of Charlie Chaplin . . . Dzigan and Shumacher presented the audience with a Jewish "Chapliniada." This means imagination, exaggeration, social criticism, unbounded grotesqueness, with a measure of grief and tears.[60]

In an article written on the first anniversary of Shumacher's death, the journalist Mordkhe (Mordechai) Tsanin depicted the activities of Broderzon, as well as Dzigan and Shumacher, as a direct continuation of the tradition of the *badkhn* and Jewish folk humor:

> Through the *badkhn* and the jester, the singer and the folk moralizer, the people was able to vent its criticism of social deficiencies . . . from the Broder Zinger, Hershele of Ostropol, Shmuel Greidinger, the famous examples of the *badkhn*, to the greatest among them, such as Elikum Tsunzer (Elikum the *badkhn*) . . . afterwards, there slowly emerged a theater of satirical humor that was revived by Moyshe Broderzon – a poet who inherited much from

---

58 The text of the monologue as performed in Argentina can be found in BAA, file 149-02.

59 One of the traditional roles of the *badkhn* was to give a humoristic and ethical speech concerning the wedding presents.

60 Nayman, "Dzigan ṿeShumacher."

> the treasures of Jewish humor and satire bequeathed by our fathers, from the jewels of the *badkhonim* and Jewish folk entertainers . . . Dzigan and Shumacher were the continuation of the theater without a stage, the heirs of the Broder Zinger and the *badkhonim*-actors-humorists of the past, using modern tools and means.[61]

So too, Dzigan himself endeavored to emphasize his connection to two worlds, his merger of Jewish and universal identities. He described presenting monologues in Ararat as bridging "between the good-spirited jester Hershele of Ostropol and the modern philosophical and tragi-comic figure of Charlie Chaplin."[62]

Dzigan and Shumacher's discourse regarding the theater indicates that the audience and critics saw, understood, and interpreted their humoristic endeavors as a direct continuation of the Jewish performance tradition, even if this was an imagined tradition.[63] Unsurprisingly, following Dzigan's death, Shmuel Schnitzer lauded him as "the last of the Jewish *badkhonim* (plural of *badkhn*) and the greatest of them all."[64] In so doing, the critic eulogized not only Dzigan but also the entire tradition of Ashkenazi-Jewish humor. Dzigan and Shumacher were neither *badkhonim* nor jesters,[65] yet they were perceived, under the influence of the historiographical discourse concerning Yiddish theater, as embodying the combination of (a still developing) tradition of Jewish humoristic performance and the modernist European and Yiddish theater.

The Ararat Theater

The activities of the Lodzher teater studyo, under the artistic direction of Moyshe Broderzon, which later formed the basis for the establishment of Ararat, did not begin in a vacuum. Its students were members of the city's various dramatic

61 Tsanin, "Hakokhav hanoded." The introduction to the playbill for Dzigan's anniversary show stated (in Yiddish): "Dzigan's silhouette – half Menakhem-Mendl, half Chaplin. A kind of living continuation of Hershele of Ostropol, a folk-jester."
62 Brat, "40 yor."
63 Marvin Carlson examines how the spectator's reaction to a performance can serve as a tool for understanding the meaning of a theatrical event. He claims that every performance is a "memory machine" and that different interpretations of directors and critics, alongside the previous roles of the actors, constitute various reference points in the spectator's consciousness, endowing the performance with meaning and cultural depth. See Carlson, *Haunted Stage*.
64 Schnitzer, "'Aḥaron habadḥanim."
65 See, for example, the words of Avrom Karpinovitsh in the introduction to Dzigan's memoirs: "Dzigan is no jester. His comedy lies not in situations devoid of content or in his strange appearance. His comedy rests on the strong foundations of our language – Yiddish." See Dzigan, *Der koyekh*, 12.

groups, such as the young people's club Tsukunft (Future), which began its activities in 1919;[66] Undzer vinkl (Our Corner);[67] Sholem Aleichem-krayz (Sholem Aleichem Circle), of which Shmulik (Shmuel) Goldshteyn was a member;[68] and the dramatic group that met in the home of the wealthy Salem family,[69] attended also by Dzigan.[70]

Dzigan and Shumacher – Brief Biographies

Shimen Dzigan was born in 1905 in Łódź. He was raised in the crowded and poor Jewish Bałuty neighborhood. His family lived in an apartment building built around an internal courtyard (hoyf). Dzigan described this building, which was inhabited by tailors, shoemakers, weavers, metalworkers, merchants, and other craftsmen, as "a gants Yiddish shtetl" (a Jewish shtetl in its entirety). Moyshe Dzigan, Shimen's father, was a "simple Jew." He served in the Russian army and, following his discharge, managed the accounts of a wood merchant. He married Nekhe, the daughter of a woodcutter from Tomaszów Lubelski, about whom Dzigan provides no further details. After his marriage, Moyshe Dzigan began to engage in trade, opening a shop in the building in which they lived in Bałuty. This enabled the Dzigan family to live reasonably well, in comparison to the courtyard's other inhabitants.[71]

66 These groups also had predecessors: in 1909, the dramatic circle Dramatishe kunst (Dramatic Art) was founded in the club Hazamir. It aimed to develop an artistic Yiddish theater and stage the works of Y. L. Peretz, Sholem Aleichem, and Yitzhak Katzenelson – one of its founders. See Rozier, *Moyshe Broderzon*, 3–13.

67 "Undzer vinkl" performed at first in small towns outside Łódź and later also in the city itself, in the Urania Theater. See Pulaver, *Ararat*, 74–78.

68 Ibid., 72–82.

69 Among the members of the circle were Y. Levkovitz, Shimen Dzigan, and Moyshe Pulaver. The dramatic circles of Pulaver and Dzigan joined forces to stage the show *Der vilner balebesl* (The Young Gentleman of Vilna) by Mark Arnshteyn in a small town near Łódź.

70 Dzigan remained a member of the dramatic circle until joining the Polish army. According to Pulaver, the army was the first acting test that Dzigan faced. See Pulaver, *Ararat*, 68–73. Dzigan does not mention in his memoirs the existence of this dramatic circle, but he connects the period with his attempts to start more serious acting lessons and mentions his escape from the Polish army. See Dzigan, *Der koyekh*, 47–53, 58–61, 76–77.

71 Ibid., 19–21. Descriptions of Dzigan's childhood in the courtyard of his apartment building in Bałuty can be found in Dzigan, *Der koyekh*, 15–26.

Dzigan's first theatrical role was in a children's play staged in a milkman's stable: the operetta *Dovd in der viste* (David in the Desert) by Heshel Epelberg.[72] Dzigan played a sheep, and his only line was composed of the onomatopoeic interjection "Baa!" From this experience, Dzigan learned that he did not want to be merely another "one of the herd" and discovered the power of humor as a way to stand out and be seen:

> היות איך בין אָבער געווען אַ נײַגעריקער און אַן אומרויִקער איז מיר דאָס קריכן אויף אַלע פֿיר און דאָס ליגן פֿאַרדעקט מיט אַ שעפּסענעם פעלץ גיך נימאס געוואָרן און איך האָב אין אַ געוויסן מאָמענט אונטערגעהויבן דעם פעלץ, כּדי צו כאַפּן אַ קוק אויף דעם אַרום. דערזען דעם עולם קינדער וואָס זייערע שײַנענדיקע אויגן קוקן אויף אונדז פֿון 'זאַל', האָב איך, כ'ווייס אַליין נישט פֿאַר וואָס, אַ מעקע געטאָן, גאָר נישט לויטן פּלאַן פֿון דער רעזשי. ס'איז דווקא געווען אַ 'מאָראַלישער מאָמענט' און מײַן פּלוצעמדיקער 'מע' האָט אַרויסגערופֿן בײַ די קליינע צושויער אַ גרויס געלעכטער. אַז איך האָב דערהערט ווי מען לאַכט האָב איך ערשט אויף אַ רעכטן אמת גענומען מעקען און מאַכן העוויות. הכּלל, איך האָב צוגעגנבֿעט די פֿאָרשטעלונג און מײַן דערפֿאָלג איז געווען זייער גרויס.[73]
>
> [Because by nature I was curious and restless, I quickly grew tired of crawling on all fours and lying covered with a sheepskin. At some point, I lifted up the sheepskin to look around. I saw the audience of children in the "hall," watching us with bright eyes. I don't know why, but I bleated, completely ignoring the director's instructions. It was a significant moment, and my sudden bleat evoked great laughter from the children in the audience. When I heard the audience laughing, I immediately began to bleat more and grimace. In short, I stole the show, and I was a very great success.]

Dzigan attended elementary school (*folksshul*) for seven years, learning Polish and German.[74] When the family's financial situation deteriorated, and his father could no longer fund his children's studies, Dzigan was apprenticed to a tailor. In the 1920s, the economic situation in Łódź was exceedingly difficult, yet the cultural life of the city was extremely vibrant. The libraries, cultural circles, and sports clubs all aroused Dzigan's curiosity far more than his apprenticeship. Dzigan, who, as was noted, did not want to be another "one of the herd," dreamed of being a sports star in the local Bar-Kokhba sports club and indeed managed to become one of its most prominent football players [Figure 1].[75]

---

72 Epelberg, *Dovid in der viste*.

73 Dzigan, *Der koyekh*, 24.

74 According to Dzigan's entrance examination for the National Union of Jewish Actors (Yidisher artistn-fareyn), May 12, 1929. YIVO Archive, file 26.551.2.

75 "Lord of the world, I thought, these are the same Jewish young men and women who are afraid of a non-Jew and of a dog . . . in my fantasy I saw each young man as a Bar-Kokhba, as one of the legendary Maccabees. I signed up for the sport union and very quickly became a good sportsman, and afterwards an even better football player." Dzigan, *Der koyekh*, 36.

Figure 1: Shimen Dzigan the sportsman in the Łódź Bar-Kokhba Club (Dzigan, *Der koyekh*, 37).

Dzigan was introduced to the theater by friends of his who were members of the dramatic circle run by the Po'alei Zion Left Party (Workers of Zion), a party with a militant Marxist-Zionist and Yiddishist approach.[76] However, the real turning point occurred when Dzigan met Broderzon at a party celebrating the local Bar Kokhba Club's tenth anniversary. Also in attendance were central figures from Łódź Jewish society and representatives from other towns and cities. Dzigan, one of the club's soccer stars, who was also known for his talent as a mimic, was invited to perform after the speeches. He began by imitating the people who had spoken before him: his mimicry of their movements and voices as he improvised new speeches evoked great laughter from the audience. At the

76 Po'alei Zion Left, a Jewish Socialist Party, was founded in 1920, after it split from the Po'alei Zion Party. The new movement was influenced by the Russian Revolution, abrogated any connection with the Zionist Union (Histadrut hatsionit), and espoused class warfare and "unrestricted" immigration to Mandatory Palestine.

end of his performance, Broderzon approached him; the latter advised Dzigan to study acting and become a professional actor.[77]

It was at this point that Dzigan started to rediscover Yiddish literature in general and Sholem Aleichem in particular. The works of Sholem Aleichem and his humoristic perspective on daily life were central in the development of Dzigan's humor.[78] He began to divide his time between sport, theater, and his work as a tailor, until, when establishing Ararat, he decided to devote himself entirely to theater.[79]

Dzigan's father opposed his son's new path, and consequently Shimen was forced to leave his parents' home at the age of nineteen. He lived with Moyshe and Sheyne-Miriam Broderzon for two years. In this period, he became acquainted with the rich world of Yiddish theater, literature, and culture. He formed close connections with the veteran and young Yiddish writers, artists, and actors from Poland and other countries who visited the couple's home. The Broderzons' home was no less important than the acting studio in the development of Dzigan's career.[80]

Shumacher, who died at a young age, did not leave a biography like that of Dzigan, and therefore we do not possess much information about his childhood, family, or the years before he joined Ararat. Yisroel Shumacher, the only son of Yankev and Peyke Shumacher, was born on May 20, 1908, in Łódź [Figure 2]. He studied in a traditional religious school (*kheyder*) and at elementary school, completing his studies in the Hebrew gymnasium in the city. His main language was Yiddish, but he apparently knew how to speak, read, and write also in Polish, German, and Hebrew. According to the entrance examination of the National Union of Jewish Actors, Shumacher also knew Latin. Unlike Dzigan, Shumacher grew up in a bourgeois home and acquired experience as an amateur actor in a dramatic group at the Hebrew gymnasium in Łódź, where he played various roles from the Polish theater repertoire. In his entrance examination for the National Union of Jewish Actors, he related that after watching performances of Yiddish theater with his family, he imitated the movements of the actors on the stage. Later, he began to create new characters. He claimed that the theater gradually became a "narcotic" to which he was addicted, unable to live without the "drink known as theater." When asked why he wanted to act in the professional theater, he claimed that the Jewish theatrical stage was "his place in life." Shumacher saw himself as "one part in the endeavor to establish the artistic Jewish theater that

77 Dzigan, *Der koyekh*, 55–54.

78 "I began reading Sholem Aleichem's works and suddenly saw the world around me in a new light. I suddenly saw the comic side of everything around me, and thanks to this comedy I became better acquainted with the surrounding reality." Ibid., 48.

79 Ibid., 41–49.

80 Ibid., 77–79.

still needs to be built."[81] Rather than studying theater in Germany, Shumacher decided to try his luck under the guidance of Broderzon, and he joined Ararat two years after the establishment of the acting studio.[82] Shumacher married Celina Stal (1912–1994), whom he met while she was acting in the Polish theater. Stal wrote for the Polish theater [Figure 3]. She also translated Avrom Goldfaden's Hebrew play *Bar-Kokhba* into Polish, and Shumacher directed its production in the folk theater in Łódź in 1933. Stal also performed in one show staged by Ararat. The couple had a daughter, Lydia, who played one of the children in the feature film *Undzere kinder* (1949).

Figure 2: Yisroel Shumacher with his parents Peyke and Yankev Shumacher (Lydia Shumacher-Ophir collection).

81 This biographical information is found in Yisroel Shumacher's entrance examination for the National Union of Jewish Actors, May 5, 1929. YIVO Archive, file 26.551.2.
82 Pulaver, *Ararat*, 88.

Figure 3: Celina Stal-Shumacher (Lydia Shumacher-Ophir collection).

The Łódź Acting Studio

Broderzon's Łódź Acting Studio was inspired by the similar endeavor established by Dovid Herman and Michael Weichert in Warsaw in 1922.[83] It was intended for young professional and amateur actors alike. Broderzon published an announcement about the studio in local papers, calling for candidates to apply.[84] Around a hundred candidates attended the exams, according to the testimony of the actor Moyshe Pulaver, although Dzigan states that there were around eighty candidates, and Gilles Rozier found approximately forty. Of these, twenty young people were accepted.

The Łódź Acting Studio met in the hall of the Union of Small Merchants. Every week there were three days of rehearsals, during which the students performed texts by Y. L. Peretz, Perets Hirshbeyn, Broderzon, and others. On the other days of the week the students received instruction in a variety of topics: Lazer Kahn

83 Weichert, *Zikhroynes*, vol. 1. See also Edwards, *Stanislavsky Heritage*.
84 Pulaver, *Ararat*, 55.

taught history of Yiddish theater, Yoysef Zelkovits and Broderzon gave lessons in Yiddish literature, Irena Prusicka taught dance, Roman Rozental – art, and Y. Yelin – fencing. Likewise, Broderzon gave a comprehensive course about the art of theater. Acting was taught by two directors: Izidor Levy, formerly an actor in Max Reinhardt's theater, and Yoysef Moskovits. The last had a great influence on Dzigan, who defined him as "the best reader of Sholem Aleichem," stating that he taught him "not what to do on the stage, but rather how to do it."[85] The Łódź Acting Studio provided professional education in the art of theater and more generally concerning Yiddish culture. Pulaver's books about Ararat and Dzigan's autobiography indicate that the studio initiated a fundamental change in the approach to the art of Jewish theater in Łódź.

Pulaver and Dzigan describe in their memoirs a number of events that made a significant impression on the students: the shows by Der Blaue Vogel cabaret in Łódź, the innovations by Alexandr Granovskii in GOSET that they read about, which were discussed heatedly in the studio, and the Hebrew performances of *The Dybbuk* by the Moscow-based Habima theater in Łódź in 1926.[86] The effect of *The Dybbuk* is mentioned also in the essay that Dzigan composed for his entrance examination to the National Union of Jewish Actors. In this essay, Dzigan described the stark impression made by the actors' natural speech, noting that he learned not only from the way that they spoke but also from their silences. He regarded their acting style as in complete opposition to that employed in the popular Yiddish theater, which was characterized, he claimed, by exaggerated gestures and cries.[87]

In its first year, the studio's students staged a full-length performance in the hall of the philharmonic orchestra at 20 Dzielna Street. The performance included works by Y. L. Peretz, Beynish Shteyman (adapted by Yoysef Zelkovits), and Broderzon. The studio also staged other shows: on January 25, 1927, in the Odeon Theater, it performed texts by Y. L. Peretz, Avrom Reyzen, Moyshe-Leyb Halpern, and Moyshe Kulbak, integrated with folk songs.[88] On April 20 of the same year, the students performed the show *Sambatyon* at the Hakoyekh Sports Union.[89]

Following the visit of Der Blaue Vogel, Broderzon invited Dr. Neses, a painter and director active in that cabaret, to meet the students at his studio and give

85 Levin, Interview with Shimon Dzigan.

86 Dzigan, *Der koyekh*, 56.

87 See Archive of the Yidisher artistn-fareyn, YIVO, file 26.551.2.

88 Among those who participated in the performance were Dovid Ogieiv, Leah Zilberman, Moyshe Lipman, Moyshe Pulaver, and Alexander Kein.

89 This show included texts by Moyshe Broderzon and Yoysef Zelkovits, directed by Roman Rozental. Among the actors were Shimen Dzigan, Leah Zilberman, Tabet, Moyshe Pulaver, Feldman, Motl Kon, Kazanover (Moyshe Kosman), Yankev Reynglas, and Shtern.

a workshop.[90] Under the guidance of Neses, the students began rehearsals of *Meshiekh ben-Yoysef* by Beynish Shteyman with a particularly modernist mise-en-scène: scenes replete with numerous performers that integrated dance, music, and vibrant colors.[91] Neses' work impressed the students and influenced their concept of theatrical art. For personal reasons, Neses was forced to leave Łódź during rehearsals, and Broderzon chose Pulaver as his replacement. During the rehearsals, a dispute arose among the members of the studio, giving rise to the idea of establishing a new miniature theater.[92]

The Modernist Characteristics of Ararat and Its Innovations

Around half of the shows staged by Ararat in the first two years of its existence were directed collectively, and many others were directed by Pulaver, one together with Dzigan, and one by Wilhelm Falek. Among the main actors appearing in performances by Ararat during this initial period were: Sheyne-Miriam Broderzon, Zisel Girl Gorlitska, Maria Dolska, Shimen Dzigan, Yehudit Berg (Iza Harari), Leah Zilberman, Lena Man, Moyshe Nelken, Moyshe Elboym, Moyshe Pulaver, Mashe Feterman, Motl Kon, Kazanover (Moyshe Kosman), Yankev Reynglas, and Yisroel Shumacher. The sets were designed mainly by Shmuel Blum and Dina Matus, the costumes by Y. Kenig. Yankl Adler, and Yitskhok Broyner, friends of Broderzon from the Yung-Yidish period, also helped to design some of the scenery and programs. Roman Rozental designed the costumes and scenery for Ararat's first show. Y. Yerozolimski was responsible for lighting design and operation. The music was composed by Henekh Kon, Dovid Beygelman, and Henrik Yavlon. Later, Shaul Berezovsky and Herts Rubin also wrote music for Ararat.[93] The troupe staged texts by Yankev Oberzhanek, Moyshe Broderzon, Der Tunkeler, Moyshe Nadir, Moyshe Nudelman, Y. L. Peretz, Moyshe Kulbak, and many others, although the main writer, Broderzon, also served as artistic manager. Iza Harari, Sheyne-Miriam Broderzon, Shimen Dzigan, and Irena Prusicka were responsible for the choreography.[94]

---

90 Dr. Neses is the name given by Pulaver in his book. I have not been able to find his full name.
91 The play was first published in the journal *Eygns* in 1920, and again in Steyman's book *Dramen*. See Steyman, "Meshiekh ben-Yoysef," in *Dramen*, 27–40.
92 Pulaver, *Ararat*, 56–57.
93 A list of the names of the shows can be found in Appendix A; the actors and the performances in which they appeared are listed in Appendix D.
94 In his book *Ararat*, Pulaver describes some of Ararat's actors and central figures: Iza Harari, who later moved to the Yung-teater and changed her name to Yehudit Berg (98–101); Kazanover

On October 25, 1927, Ararat staged its first show, *Glat kosher* (Glatt Kosher) in the Mont Eiffel Hotel in Łódź. It included modernist stage adaptations of texts by classic Yiddish writers, among them "Der vekhter" (The Guard) by Y. L. Peretz and "Pushketants" (Box Dance) by Avrom Goldfaden, alongside works by contemporary writers such as "Di glokn" (The Bells) by H. Leyvik, an adaptation of "Ikh bin a bokher a hultay" (I Am a Reckless Lad) by Moyshe Kulbak, "Dos tepl" (The Pot) by Yankev Oberzhanek, and the skits "Khasene hobn" (Getting Married) by Der Tunkeler, the satire "Opfal" (Rubbish) by Broderzon, a dance entitled "Glat kosher" by Yankev Rozental, and folk songs, including "Shnayderlekh" (Little Tailors), "Dos kozele" (The Little Goat), and "Shadkhonim" (Matchmakers).[95]

The show *Gut-morgn, koze!* (Good Morning, Goat!), which was first staged in November 1927, reflects the trends that characterized Ararat as it continued its journey – fewer texts by classic writers and an increasing number of works by contemporary authors, mainly Broderzon. The performance included "Shoshanes-Yankev" (The Lily of Jacob), an adaptation of a text by Y. L. Peretz;[96] Broderzon's works "Kleyzmorim" (Musicians), "Bloye mil" (Blue Mill), "Hallo! Hallo!" (Hello! Hello!), "Opgeton af terkish" (Deception), and "Yenke Dovid"; folk songs; the skit "Der nudnik" (The Nuisance) by Der Tunkeler; and the monologue "Der Litvisher Magid" (The Lithuanian Preacher) by the satirist Leyb Berman. The show's music was composed by Kon,[97] and it was directed by Pulaver and Dzigan.

From its establishment, Ararat staged productions at a dizzying pace. Indeed, between October 1927 and December 1928, it staged ten shows, and by the time it relocated to Warsaw in 1934, it had staged more than thirty-five further productions,[98] including also special entertainments for children and for festivals, such as *Latkes* (Potato Pancakes), which was staged in December 1928 in honor of the Hanukkah holiday.[99]

(Moyshe Kosman), the first master of ceremonies (103); Moyshe Nelken, who replaced Kazanover in this role (104); the composer Henekh Kon (106); Yoysef Moskovits (112); the composer Dovid Beygelman (115–17); Yankev Oberzhanek (119); among others.

95 The playbill was published in Pulaver's work. See ibid., 26–27.

96 The playbill includes a photograph of the skit and states that "Shoshanes-Yankev" was an adaptation of "In kretshma" (At the Inn) by Y. L. Peretz.

97 Pulaver notes in his book, mistakenly, that this was the theater's second show (see ibid., 29–30), but reviews in the contemporaneous press demonstrate that this was not the case.

98 It is difficult to determine an exact number of shows due to the lack of sources and the fact that the same performance was staged numerous times under different names with only small changes.

99 Rozier discusses some of the contents of the performances staged by Ararat and the texts written by Broderzon for the troupe. See Rozier, *Moyshe Broderzon*. See also Pulaver, *Ararat*.

It is impossible to glean sufficient information or descriptions from the reviews of the shows for a discussion of the theatrical event itself. Rather, these texts mainly shed light on the central characteristics of the innovative artistic language used by Ararat and the great disparities in the various segments' quality, as will be discussed further below.

Ararat's Revolutionary Discourse

> מיר האָבן זיך דעמאָלט אָפּגעגעבן מיט נײַע פֿאָרמען אין טעאַטער. דאָס זענען געווען עקספּערימענטאַלע אַוואַנגאַרדישע באַנײַונגען אונטערן אײַנפֿלוס פֿון נײַע שטראָמען אין יענער צײַט.
>
> [We were then dealing with new forms of theater. These were avant-garde, experimental innovations influenced by the new streams of that period.]
>
> –Shimen Dzigan

The Ararat theater was driven by young energies – most members were in their twenties. The theater used a modernist and revolutionary language, as is reflected in the search for innovation in performative elements (repertoire, music, scenery, costumes, language, and the director's style), and it successfully integrated the European tradition of the miniature theater with that of the Jewish performance.

This combination of the European modernist spirit and Jewish tradition is manifest in the name of the troupe, "Ararat." As the acronym for Artistisher revolutsyonerer teater,[100] it reflects Broderzon's convention-breaking artistic quest. However, as was noted, is also alludes to the legendary landing of Noah's ark on Mount Ararat. The choice of an explicitly biblical reference reflects the attempt to bridge between Jewish and surrounding cultures.[101]

Broderzon's texts, the theater's main voice during its first period (1927–1935),[102] were characterized by brevity, grace, rhythm, humor, and reference to the contemporary social and economic reality. He was considered a wizard of rhyme and reduction. Broderzon spoke about the need to create a stage for poetic language in

---

100 Sometimes the acronym was interpreted as "Artistisher romantisher teater" (Artistic Romantic Theater). Printed playbills contain the following definition: "Yidisher artistisher revyu un kamer-teater" (Jewish Artistic and Chamber Revue Theater).

101 So too, the names of other miniature theaters, Azazel and Sambatyon, drew on Jewish tradition, as Bułat notes. See: Bułat, "Kleynkunst."

102 I have not been able to restore the contents of all the shows staged by Ararat in this period. However, the available information suggests that Broderzon wrote about seventy percent of the texts.

Yiddish, for the Yiddish color and the Yiddish sound.[103] He argued that not only language should serve as an indication of Ararat's Jewish identity, but the form and content should also contribute to this.

Broderzon's poetic style and the theater's outlook are expressed in Ararat's anthem and declaration of intent, the "Ararat-anthem," which was sung at every performance:

פֿאַרגייט אַ וועלט אין שוואַרצן שימער,
צום מבול נעמט אַן עק –
עס לייגן קלאַפּטער יונגע שווימער,
און זוכן ווו אַ ברעג!
דער חלל איז נאָך אַליץ פֿאַרכמאַרעט,
עס איז נאָך ווײַט פֿון רו...
אָן תּיבֿה צו דעם באַרג אַראַראַט
מיר שווימען שווימען צו! [104]

[A world is passing in a black shimmer,
The flood is coming to an end –
Young swimmers swim front crawl,
And search for a shore!
The skies are still clouded,
It is yet far from calm....
Without an ark, to Mount Ararat,
We swim, and we go on swimming!]

The anthem reflects the feelings of a young generation of artists living in a world devastated by World War I and the Russian Revolution. The feeling of apocalypse mingles with that of the search after the flood. Ararat symbolizes both the revolutionary theater of a group of young people and the aim of the struggle – the Ararat of their dreams, a symbol of rebirth. As Rozier notes in his work on Broderzon,[105] Shumacher stated in his entrance examination for the National Union of Jewish Actors, and Dzigan notes in his memoirs:

. . . איך בין מיט אַ יוגנטלעכן רעוואָלוציאָנערן גלויבן געווען איבערצײַגט אַז דאָס נײַע ייִדישע טעאַטער דאַרף אָנהייבן פֿון סאַמע בראשית און בויען אַליץ פֿון דאָס נײַ.[106]

[With my young revolutionary belief, I was persuaded that the new Yiddish theater must begin anew from genesis and rebuild everything afresh.]

103 Krimsky, "Nokh a mol."
104 Dzigan, *Dzigan-albom.*
105 Rozier, *Moyshe Broderzon*, 172–79.
106 Dzigan, *Der koyekh*, 57.

The concept of Ararat is a myth of creation, salvation, and purity that represented the goal of artists dedicated to revolutionary artistic activity, striding forth toward revolution with nothing but their own might, not even financial means. In one of the playbills, Broderzon wrote:

> דער חלום איז אַ קאַמף געווען, אַ ביטערער קאַמף מיט דחקות, מיט נויט, מיט הונגער (נישט דער סאָציאַליסטישער מאַגיסטראַט, נישט די ייִדישע קהילה האָט אונדז געהאָלפֿן).[107]
>
> [The dream was a battle, a bitter battle against poverty, need, hunger (neither the Socialist city council nor the Jewish community helped us).]

By means of the Ararat theater, they approached Mount Ararat, attempting to realize their dream. The actors in the Ararat troupe were pioneers of theatrical art with no firm ground under their feet – the modernist Yiddish theater possessed no foundations or tradition, and there was no establishment system to support its development. The name transformed the theater at once into a real and mythological place. Broderzon, akin to Noah in the Bible, chose to realize a similar yet unique vision: to establish in Poland a Jewish revolutionary artistic autonomy that was itself a wandering territory.

Songs such as the troupe's anthem or Broderzon's "Koro-grando," which was performed in the show *Afn himl a yarid!* (Much Ado about Nothing!) in 1930, characterize the first period of Ararat – a period rich in modernist language, plays on words and images, and allusions to both the traditional Jewish world and Western culture:

> מיר זינגען אַלע פֿאָרטע־פּיאַנאָ,
> ווי אין 'לאַ־סקאַלאַ' דע מילאַנאָ,
> דאָ-רע-מי-פֿאַ-סאָל-לאַ-סי-דאָ!
> שעבעיאָנו, ועקימאָנו, לאַזמאַנאָזע!
>
> [We all sing forte-piano
> Like "La Scala" in Milano,
> Do, re, mi, fa, so, la, si, do!
> Shehekheyonu-vekimonu-lazmanoze (That He has granted us life, and sustained us,[108] to reach this occasion!)]

---

107 Moyshe Broderzon in the playbill for *Hotel terkalya* (Terkalya Hotel) (1928).

108 From the *shehekheyonu* blessing, which is recited on special occasions (holidays, reaching certain life cycle events, etc.). The full blessing is "Blessed are You, Lord our God, King of the Universe, who has granted us life, and sustained us, and enabled us to reach this occasion." Note that the words "enabled us" are omitted here.

The song continues with critical references to the social and economic situation, evoking the traditional chanson of the French political cabaret:

און ווי זשע אַלע מיר זײַנען אין דער ערד דאָ!
מעצאָ־וואָטשע – בוידעם קלאָטשע,
נישטאָ קיין גראָשן, הענג זיך כאָטשע,
קען מען נישט פֿאַרדינען דאָ![109]

[And we are all deep in the earth here!
Mezzo voce – garbage from the attic,
We haven't a penny, it would be better to hang ourselves,
Here it's impossible to make a living!]

Another example of the occupation with social problems in Broderzon's songs can be found in the skit "Koyln-grebers" (Coal Miners):

בײַ אונדז איז תּמיד פֿינצטער,
קיין שטראַל צו אונדז דערגרייכט,
דער שײַן פֿון טאָג דער מינדסטער,
אין פֿינצטערניש פֿאַרבלײַבט.

[For us it is always dark,
No single ray [of light] reaches us,
The tiniest shine of the day,
Remains in darkness.]

A review of the show testifies to the great effect these words had on the audience:

דאַכט זיך, [אַז] די ווערטער קוילערן זיך אין חלל, שמידן צונויף שוואַרצע הענט און הימלישע נשמות, כּדי בײַ אַ געלעגנהייט צו עקספּלאָדירן אַלס אַ רוף צו באַפֿרײַונג.[110]

[The words seemed to roll in space, melting black hands and heavenly souls, in order to explode at the first opportunity as a call for freedom.]

Although Broderzon's poetics ruled in the innovative language of Ararat, texts by humorists and writers such as Yankev Oberzhanek, Der Tunkeler, Moyshe Nadir, adaptations of Moyshe Kulbak, and later also works by Y. Sh. Goldshteyn, Moyshe

---

109 The text is from a later version, dating from after World War II, which was submitted to the Polish censor in 1948. "Koro-Grando" was also staged in performances by Dzigan and Shumacher in Poland and in the Soviet Union. The copy of the song can be found in BAA, file 149-01.
110 The reviewer praised the acting of Brikn, Dzigan, Nelken, Pulaver, Kon, and Reynglas. See M. H., "'Ararat': Tsu der uffirung fun fertn program," without name of newspaper and date, "Ararat" collection at ICDP.

Nudelman, and many others, also made important contributions to Ararat's repertoire.

A central element in molding the artistic language, no less than the word, is the performative text: the style of music, the direction, and the design of the scenery and costumes. If an analysis of all these aspects – the elements that create "the theatrical event" – were possible, together with an examination of the stage itself, the ages and character of the actors, their facial expressions and gestures, hairstyles and makeup, this would enable us to conduct a semiotic analysis of the theatrical event that occurred between the artists and their audience.[111] However, lacking the necessary information to conduct such an analysis, based on the surviving texts, press reviews, recordings, and memories, we can only highlight the central characteristics of the performance and how it was received and remembered. An in-depth analysis of a performative text will be presented in the discussion of the parody *Der nayer dibek*.[112]

The score for the troupe's anthem, as well as the melodies of musical interludes, the songs sung in the skits, and adaptations of folk songs by poets such as Itsik Manger, Broderzon, Yitskhok Perlov, Moyshe Shimel, Zusman Segalovitsh, Yitzhak Katzenelson, and the songs of Mordkhe Gebirtig, were a central and constitutive element in the artistic language of the young theater, as is clear from press reviews and the actors' memoirs. "The Ararat-music," wrote Yoel Mastboym, "doesn't really include the so-called popular 'hits,' like Kon wrote for the productions of Azazel, but here he [Kon] is sometimes deeper, with a folk character, and more interesting as a musician."[113] The words of the reviewer highlight the composer's quest to combine the popular with a more elaborate style.

Kon played a major role in composing music for the Yiddish miniature theater in general and, together with Dovid Beygelman, during Ararat's first period in particular.[114] Kon was an exceptionally talented musician and one of the main composers for the Yiddish theater (Azazel, Khad-gadye, Yung-teater) and cinema (*Der dibek*, directed by Michał Waszyński, 1937), and he was very active in Poland

111 On the definition of "performative text" see, for example, Dwyer and Marinis, "Dramaturgy"; Rouse, "Textuality." On the classic semiotic analysis see Kowzan, *El Signo*; Elam, *Semiotics*.
112 See below pp. 225–243.
113 'אין דער "אַררט"־מוזיק איז אמת נישט פֿאַראַנען דאָס, וואָס מען רופֿט אָן "שלאַגער־נומערן" פֿאַר דער גאַס, ווי קאָן האָט עס געגעבן אין "אַזאַזעל"־פּראָגראַמען, אָבער ער איז דאָ ערטערווײַז טיפֿער, פֿאָלקסטימלעכער און אינטערעסאַנטער אַלס מוזיקער.'

Mastboym, "In Ararat."
114 See Fater, *Musiḳa yehudit*.

until the outbreak of World War II. After the war, he immigrated to the United States, where he continued to write music.[115]

Beygelman, who perished in Auschwitz, was also a major composer and well-known violinist and conductor. He wrote music for theater and miniature theater in addition to composing operettas. Alongside the music of Kon and Beygelman, the scores that Yisroel Sheybits, Herts Rubin, and Shaul Berezovsky composed for the theater also received much critical acclaim[116] and were popular with audiences. Pulaver, for example, mentions many melodies by Beygelman, such as "Yidn-shmidn" (Jewish Smiths), "A moyd a tsimes," (Maiden *Tsimmes*), "Balut-Balet" (Bałuty Ballet), and "Vaser-treger" (Water Carriers), which became popular hits. Indeed, he states that people could be heard singing them at work, in shops, and in the market place.[117]

As was noted, it is difficult to reconstruct the characteristics of the theatrical elements of the various performances and the acting style in the Ararat period. However, photographs taken during the troupe's performances reveal its modernist character, the innovation of the mise-en-scène, and the influence of the European and Russian cabaret [Figure 4].[118] In an attempt to define the complexity it entailed, Broderzon described directing in the Yiddish theater as at once a tragic, dramatic, and comic experience; in other words, theatrical.[119] Broderzon's connection to central Jewish plastic artists active in Łódź at the time manifested in various aspects of the theater. The scenery that Matus and Blum, and sometimes Broyner, designed and created, and the costumes designed and made by Y. Kenig, became additional agents in the performance, as contemporary theater critics also noted. The central innovations were collective scenes inspired by the Berlin cabaret Der Blaue Vogel (such as the adaptation of "Der vekhter" by Y. L. Peretz and "Marsh" by Broderzon), and the acting style, which was influenced by Habima, notably the attempt to avoid the mannerisms, shouting, and exaggeration associated with popular Yiddish theater.

Broderzon aimed to remold all the aspects of the "sensory shapes" experienced by the Jewish audience. Ararat's desire to offer a young, new, and revolutionary

---

115 For more on Kon, see above, note 36.

116 See, for example, Rozenberg, "Dos 5te program."

117 Pulaver, *Ararat*, 115–18. Dzigan highlights that many songs sung on the Jewish street were first performed in shows by Ararat. See Dzigan, *Der koyekh*, 123–33. See also Bashan, "Monolog." Although most of the reviews of Beygelman's music were positive, there was also criticism of the clichéd characteristics noticeable in some of the melodies. See for example Kipnis, "A shpatsir."

118 The photographs that I relate to were mostly published in Pulaver's book (*Ararat*) and in a number of issues of the journal *Literarishe bleter*. See, for example, "Revyu-teater 'Ararat'"; "Lodzher kameral."

119 Broderzon, "Vegn Ararat."

969 ליטעראַרישע בלעטער Nr. 49

דער לאָדזשער רעווי-טעאַטער „אררט"

דאָס לאָדזשער רעווי - טעאַטער „אררט" האָט דאָ נישט לאַנג גע־פּייערט זיין ערשטן יאָר־טאָג.

דאָס טעאַטער געפינט זיך אונ־טער דער פירונג פון משה בראָ־דערזאָן בײַ דער מיטהילף פון א ריי לאָדזשער קינסטלער און מאָלער.

ס'זענען ביזאהער אויפגעפירט געוואָרן א 10 פּראָגראַמען, וואָס האָבן געהאַט גרויס ערפאָלג.

שוין צייט, דער פריילעכער לאָדזשער „אררט" זאָל אראָפּנידערן פון זיין לאָדזשער הויף קיין וואר־שע. —

Figure 4: Photos of Ararat from 1928, “Der lodzher revyu-teater ‘Ararat’” *Literarishe bleter*, December 7,1928, 5: 969.

response in the field of Yiddish theater was evident both in the troupe's artistic language, its repertoire, and in Broderzon's public statements, as reported by Dzigan: "We must ignite the theatrical forest of Poland, burn and chop the rotten trees."[120] This revolutionary rhetoric also echoed in texts that Broderzon wrote for the playbills of Ararat's performances. In the playbill for *Hotel terkalya* (1928), for example, he cast Ararat in a revolutionary role: "It came into the world in a period of Yiddish theater's premature aging and weakness."[121]

So too, in the playbill for *Latkes*, performed on Hanukkah in that same year, Broderzon described the young artists of Ararat as instigating a revolution:

> יאָ, צוריקגערעדט: עס ווילט זיך שרײַען: ראַטעוועט! מאַכט דעזאינפֿעקציעס, רייניקט, שײַערט, עפֿנט פֿענצטער, ברענט, ראָט אויס . . . ראַטעוועט, צוליב דעם אויפֿבוי פֿון אַ ייִדישער טעאַטער־קונסט! גענוג מיט דער פֿאַרברעכערישער טאָלעראַנץ![122]
>
> [Yes, on the other hand, they want to shout out: Help! Disinfect, clean, polish, open the windows, burn, uproot . . . help build a Jewish theatrical art! Enough with the criminal tolerance!]

It appears that Broderzon repeatedly felt the need to define the genre and goal of the theater and to declare his aims and his artistic language, not only in order to disseminate his ideas but also as a response to critiques concerning the experimental language of Ararat. Such criticism appeared, for example, in a review signed R-K in the bimonthly mouthpiece *Nayer freydenker* (New Freethinker), the organ of the Łódź branch of the Communist Freydenker organization:

> 'אַררט' ווערט אַ צווייטע אויפֿלאַגע פֿון 'אַזאַזעל', אָבער אַן ערגערע. נאָך עפּעס: אין 'אַררט' הערשט ממש אַ בויקאָט אויף דער ייִדישער ליטעראַטור.[123]
>
> [Ararat is becoming a second version of Azazel, but an inferior one. And another thing: Ararat is really boycotting Yiddish literature.]

---

120 Bashan, "Monolog." Jacques Rancière claims that theater, more than any other art form, is connected to the romantic idea of aesthetic revolution. This is not because it can change the systems of government and law, but rather due to its ability to affect the human sensory experience. See Rancière, *Emancipated Spectator*.

121 'אין אַ צײַט פֿון פֿריצײַטיקער זקנה און עלטער־שוואַכקייט אינעם ייִדישן טעאַטער־וועזן איז ער אויף דער וועלט געקומען'.

122 Moyshe Broderzon, playbill for *Latkes* (December 6, 1928). Pulaver, who was influenced by Broderzon, also speaks about the joy of the festival, which allows the audience to escape the heavy burdens of everyday life. See Pulaver, *Ararat*, 12.

123 K-R, "Shoshanes."

Broderzon was not the only one to address the revolutionary motivations of the troupe's members. Dzigan wrote:

> ... ביסלעכווײַז, ביסלעכווײַז האָבן מיר גענומען גלויבן אַז אויף אונדז, יונגע טאַלאַנטן, ליגט די גרויסע אויפֿגאַבע צו רעוואָלוציאָנירן דאָס שאַבלאָנע ייִדישע טעאַטער און אָנצוהייבן אַ נײַ קאַפּיטל אין דער געשיכטע פֿון דער ייִדישער טעאַטער־קונסט.[124]
>
> [... slowly, slowly we began to believe that upon our shoulders, the shoulders of the young talents, lay the great task of revolutionizing the clichéd Yiddish theater and beginning a new chapter in the history of Jewish theatrical art.]

The innovative and revolutionary spirit of Ararat made a great impression on theater critics in Łódź. In reviews of the troupe's shows, critics mainly praised the revolutionary language of the young theater, although they also noted that it had not in fact completed the revolution it declared. One of the central voices in the criticism of Ararat in the local press was Yisroel Rozenberg, who signed his reviews with the penname Y. Dankin. Regarding the theater's first performance, he wrote:

> זענען געקומען אַ צענדליק יונגע ייִדן, וועלכע האָבן נישט דערלאָזט, אַז דער יִאוש זאָל זיך אין גאַנצן אײַנפֿרעסן אין זייער אָרגאַניזם, האָבן נישט דערלאָזט, אַז די האָפֿענונג אויף בעסערע צײַטן זאָל אין גאַנצן צערונען ווערן און – האָבן זיך גענומען צו אַ גרויס ווערק.[125]
>
> [Around ten young Jews (actors), who did not want to allow despair to consume them entirely, came. They did not allow the hope of better times to dissolve completely and devoted themselves to a great endeavor.]

In his review of Ararat's third show, *Nisim min hashomayim* (Miracles from Heaven), Rozenberg emphasized again the efforts of this group of young people, who were optimistically tackling the crisis in theatrical art during a time characterized by a "lack of art." The young people are trying to prove, claimed the critic, that with good intentions it is possible to succeed; the performance staged by Ararat singled out the group of creators as innovative, subversive, forceful, modernist, and daring.[126]

Khayim-Leyb Fuks, another central voice in Łódź theater criticism, argued that the actor's acting language echoed the stylized gestures of Habima. He described Dzigan as "one of the best actors to ever deliver monologues in Yiddish theater." The critic also praised the positive development of the role of the master

---

124 Dzigan, *Der koyekh*, 56.
125 Rozenberg, "Di premyere." See also Rozenberg, "Nisim"; Rozenberg, "Ararat"; Rozenberg, "Dos 5te program"; Pulaver, *Ararat*, 22, 39–44.
126 Rozenberg, "Ararat."

of ceremonies, Kazanover, and the good work of Yankev Reynglas, Moyshe Nelken, Sheyne-Miriam Broderzon, and Yisroel Shumacher.[127] He saw Pulaver and Dzigan, "who play first violin in the troupe," as the "embodiment" of Sholem Aleichem's spirit on stage.[128] Likewise, Rozenberg noted that Pulaver and Dzigan were talented actors whose gestures were modernist and precise, and also lauded Nelken and Shumacher.[129] Most of the critics likewise responded positively to the music and scenery.

However, the critics not only voiced praise; they also commented that the theater was "young" and its steps hesitant. Alongside innovative and excellent segments, the theater staged banal pieces, and the disparities between the various actors' abilities were obvious.[130] Such claims also recurred in reviews of many shows staged by Dzigan and Shumacher's theater. However, Rozenberg and Fuks arguably tried to highlight the new path and avoid sharp criticism. Wishing to be partners to the birth of a modern and quality Yiddish theater, they defended Ararat against more conservative critics who rejected the troupe's modernist language. Thus, they highlighted Ararat's central achievements in acting, scenery, and music, its modernist spirit and progress, and the increasing professionalism evident in each new show.

Ararat's Dialogue with the Audience

The experience of the theatergoers, their role and status, were central elements in Ararat's development. Fascinating descriptions of how the audience behaved during performances, the response to the new developments on stage, their involvement and influence over what happens, as well as the culture of *patriotn* (fans) and the theater's community status are found in many memoirs written

---

127 Yosl Mastboym also praised the performances of Dzigan, Leah Zilberman, Kazanover, and Sheyne-Miriam Broderzon in the production *Salem-Aleykum*. See Mastboym, "In Ararat," December 31, 1928 in Pulaver, *Ararat*, 52–54. According to Dzigan, the well-known German theater critic Alfred Kerr wrote that there were three theaters worth seeing in Poland: Teatr Polski starring Sefan Jaracz, the Reduta theater starring Juliusz Osterwa, and Ararat starring Dzigan. See Dzigan, *Der koyekh*, 116. I have not been able to find Kerr's review.

128 Fuks, "Zikhere trit."

129 Rozenberg, "Di premyere."

130 In his criticism of *Glat kosher*, Rozenberg described most parts of the performance as good, pleasant, modern, and without mannerisms. He praised the combination of classic texts with modern works, although he chose not to review each individual skit due to the great disparities in their quality. See ibid.

by actors and theater critics as well as in many reviews published in the press.[131] Here, within the methodological limitations noted, we will consider the role of the audience and its contribution to the character of the theatrical event, first in Ararat and later in the theater of Dzigan and Shumacher.

The name of the first show staged by Ararat, *Glat kosher*, sought to distinguish the theater from popular theater in the public consciousness. Jewish theatergoers were able to identify a show's genre according to its title. Thus, when theatergoers saw the titles *Mayn vaybs man* (My Wife's Husband),[132] *Di kale fun dray khasonim* (A Bride with Three Grooms),[133] *Khontshe in Amerike* (Chontshe in America),[134] Dzigan relates, they knew that these were operettas featuring singing and dancing. When they saw the titles *Khasye di yesoyme* (Chasye the Orphan Girl), *Mirele Efros*, or *Di shvue* (The Oath),[135] and the name of the playwright, Gordin, they understood that these were dramas with a moral lesson. By contrast, titles such as *A harts vos benkt* (A Heart that Longs)[136] or *S'harts fun a mame* (A Mother's Heart) indicated performances influenced by American melodrama. *Uriel Akosta*[137] and *Di royber* (The Robbers)[138] were part of a higher quality repertoire. In this context, Dzigan claims, Ararat's *Glat kosher* seemed like something staged by a "Turkish theater company." Dzigan emphasized with pride the feeling of innovation and novelty that Ararat brought to the Jewish street. The theater's message was clear, Dzigan claims: theatergoers understood this was not only theater; it was "a real revolution."[139]

Glat kosher's premiere did not go smoothly. The audience failed to respond as expected, laughing during the songs rather than when the artists had intended.[140] Impatient theatergoers, argued the theater critic Rozenberg, buy tickets and demand the goods they want.[141] This applied to many of the theatergoers and

131 Concerning the *patriotn* of Yiddish theater in New York, see Nina Warnke, "Patriotn." Regarding the academic approach to the theatrical event and moving beyond the occupation with what happens on stage to deal with the experience of the theatergoer on his way to the performance, on his return home, during the show etc., see for example Bennett, *Theatre Audiences*, 36.
132 An operetta by Heyman Mayzel.
133 An operetta by Ayzik Somberg
134 An operetta by Nekhemiya Rakov.
135 Three plays by Jacob Gordin.
136 A melodrama by Shmuel Urbakh (Ben-Zvi).
137 A play by Karl Gutskov that was translated several times into Yiddish.
138 A play by Friedrich Schiller. Dovid Kesel translated it into Yiddish.
139 Dzigan, *Der koyekh*, 62–64.
140 Ibid., 65.
141 Rozenberg, "Nisim."

critics who attended performances by Ararat. Indeed, many Łódź theatergoers and some critics opposed the troupe's aesthetic experiments and searches.

Dzigan mentioned the love-hate relationship between Łódź theatergoers and Ararat in an interview with Rafael Bashan. Indeed, he described the complex relations between the theater troupe and its audience at the 1930 premiere of *Bronks ekspres* (Bronx Express), a play by Osip Dymov, in a miniature theater version directed by Dovid Herman:

> The premiere took place, and, after the curtain went down, the audience burst onto the stage and started a pogrom! Yes, a pogrom! Very simply, they tore the actors' clothes, broke the scenery to pieces, shattered the projectors. You hear me? They simply tore it to pieces! That was Łódź. That could happen only in Łódź; there we flourished, there they loved us.[142]

Ararat, and subsequently Dzigan and Shumacher's theater, saw the "common people" as a source of inspiration: "The common people [is] a single party and 'The Internationale' is its art," wrote Broderzon in the playbill for one of Ararat's shows.[143] Dzigan confirms this claim in his memoirs, noting the importance that Dzigan and Shumacher's theater attributed to the public, in particular the simple, working class theatergoer. Dzigan relates that he approached his former colleagues at the tailoring workshop in order to hear their opinions regarding Ararat. The workers told him that they had not enjoyed the performance. They argued that Ararat needed to hone the question of its intended audience, connecting the materials presented on stage with the tastes of the average theatergoer. One expert tailor complained that he did not understand the performance's artistic language. He added that the words used to describe it in reviews – such as "experimental," "avant-garde," and "literary" – discourage theatergoers. Presuming that they will not understand the show, they choose not to go, feeling that it is not meant for them. They seek enjoyment:

> אַז אַ ייִד קומט אין טעאַטער אַרײַן וויל ער פֿאַרגעסן די צרות. ער וויל אַ ביסל פֿרייד. זאָל זײַן, ווי איר זאָגט, 'קונץ', אָבער 'קונץ' טאָר נישט זײַן פֿריילעך? בײַ קונץ מוזן די אַקטיאָרן אַרומגיין אויף דער בינע ווי אויף אַ לוויה? פֿאָלג מיך שמאַי, שפּילט ווי מענטשן, רעדט ווי מענטשן, זינגט ווי מענטשן. גיט דעם עולם אַ ביסל פֿרייד.[144]

> [When a Jew goes to the theater, he wants to forget his sorrows. He wants a bit of joy. It should be, as you say, *kunts*,[145] but can't *kunts* be happy? In *kunts* must the actors go around the stage like they are at a funeral? Listen to me, act like people, speak like people, sing like people. Give the audience a bit of happiness.]

---

142 Bashan, "Monolog."
143 Broderzon quoted in Pulaver, *Ararat*, 12.
144 Dzigan, *Der koyekh*, 84–85.
145 A play on the word *kunts*, "magic trick," and *kunst*, "art."

In an in-depth interview conducted by the historian Dov Levin, Dzigan said that he learned more from the tailor's brief criticism than from the many intellectual discussions among the artists of Ararat regarding culture and theater.[146] Dzigan's story and reviews in the press depicting audience reactions indicate that although the members of Ararat did not abandon their artistic quest, they saw the theatergoer as a central element in molding their artistic language.[147] The theatergoer appears in Dzigan's story as an active partner in creating the theatrical experience.[148]

In this sense, Ararat and the theater of Dzigan and Shumacher offer a unique window onto the role of the theatergoers in creating the meaning of a performance. The spectators at these theatrical events were highly active in comparison to their counterparts in the established European bourgeois theater. The Ararat stage was an arena for encounter between opposing and even ambiguous perspectives in the process of forming a new Jewish theater. The audience reactions – both in the theater itself and in meetings with the artists outside it – influenced the performance and the artists, who understood that they needed to fine-tune their message by altering the style and language, without compromising either their artistic style or aesthetic quests.

---

146 Levin, Interview with Shimen Dzigan (1973).

147 Dzigan mentions in his memoirs that Broderzon customarily published his thoughts about theater in Ararat's playbills:

> 'בראָדערזאָנס הקדמות זענען געווען אין אַ יום־טובֿדיקן טאָן, געשריבן, ווי ס'איז געווען אין דער מאָדע אין יענער צײַט, מיט פֿיל פֿרעמדע ווערטער און דערצו אין אַזאַ פֿאַרוויקלטן סטיל און מיט אַזעלכע אַלוזיעס אַז אַפֿילו גענוג אינטעליגענטע מענטשן פֿלעגן טענהן אַז זיי ווייסן נישט און פֿאַרשטייען נישט וועגן וואָס עס האַנדלט זיך.'
>
> [Broderzon's introductions were written in a festive tone, as was fashionable at the time, with many foreign words and in such a complex style and with such allusions that even sufficiently intelligent people would say that they did not know and don't understand what he was talking about]. See Dzigan, *Der koyekh*, 107.

148 It is interesting to compare the recordings of performances from a later period, made by the artists in Israel using home recording equipment, on which one can hear the audience responses (these are obviously lacking in the official recordings made in studios). Another later example of an audience reaction was mentioned by Shmuel Atzmon-Wircer in an interview that I conducted with him. In the skit "Abi m'zet zikh" (The Main Thing: We Meet Again), Dzigan and Shumacher recalled the Jews of Eastern Europe: Poles, Hungarians, Lithuanians. At their first performance in Israel (March 1950), one of the theatergoers shouted in response: "What about the Romanian Jews?" To this Dzigan replied immediately: "We're not talking about professions!" Thus, the audience reacted not only with laughter but also with words, and spontaneous dialogue became part of the theatrical event.

Ararat and the National Union of Jewish Actors

Some theatergoers and critics did not look favorably upon the revolutionary aspects of the troupe's organization – for example, the collective perspective on directing and allocating roles, or the cooperative that ensured equal distribution of income and expenditures among the actors and other members of theater. Likewise, these elements were frowned upon by the National Union of Jewish Actors in Poland (Yidisher artistn-fareyn in Poyln). A letter sent by the union to the Professional Organization of Łódź (Tsentral-rat fun di profesyonele fareynen in Lodzh) on December 26, 1927, only about two months after Ararat's premiere, expressed the concern the theater aroused among members of the union. In its letter, the union responded to the ironic claim, attributed to Broderzon, that "the amateur theater Ararat became a professional theater not in the sense of a professional union but in its professional approach to the art of theater": as a matter of fact, the National Union of Jewish Actors viewed this as conflicting with its interests. Indeed, according to the union, Ararat was causing chaos in the Polish Jewish theatrical world. Volf Geyhoyz, chair of the union of artists in Łódź, delivered the letter to Broderzon, and the latter responded to it on January 17, 1928.[149] In his reply, Broderzon claimed that Ararat did not pose a threat to professional actors in the Yiddish theater, because the path and status of the actor in Ararat differed completely from those of the professional actor. The actor in Ararat worked for a minimum wage in order to advance the idea that the troupe embodied, while a professional actor could not allow himself to do such a thing. The future income of Ararat and any grants it received were intended only to develop the troupe and not for the benefit of the actors. Broderzon explained in his letter that Ararat was not engaged in a battle against the National Union and that the

149 Among other things, Broderzon wrote in his letter:

'דער אַרטיסטן־פֿאַריין שרײַבט, אַז ער וויל נישט אַנאַליזירן די סיבות וועלכע האָבן גורם געווען דאָס באַשאַפֿן פֿון אַזאַ אומנאָרמאַלקייט, ווי ס'איז "אַררט" . . . אינערלעך איז דער 'אַררט' געבויט אויף ריין חבֿרשע, דעמאָקראַטישע יסודות . . . די מעטאָדן פֿון אונדזער אַרבעט –דאָס זענען די מעטאָדן פֿון זוכן און עקספּערימענטירן, צו באַווײַזן דעם ייִדישן טעאַטער דאָס בעסטע און דאָס שענסטע, וואָס איז אויפֿן טעאַטער־קינסטלערישן געביט דערגרייכט געוואָרן.'

[The artists union writes that it will not get into the reasons behind the creation of an abnormality such as Ararat . . . in its internal organization, Ararat is built on the foundations of pure, democratic friendship . . . the methods of our work – these are the methods of searching and experimenting, to show to the Yiddish theater the best and most beautiful achievements in the field of theatrical art]. The letter is in the archive of the Yidisher artistn-fareyn, YIVO, RG26 F253. Concerning Geyhoz, who was also a prompter in the Łódź philharmonic theater, see Turkow, *Farloshene shtern*, 2: 142–47.

theater valued the actors' devotion to the troupe over profit. His actors did not seek acceptance into the professional union because it was too early to tell which of them would dedicate themselves to theatrical art.[150] Broderzon's rhetoric presents Ararat as the realization of an artistic idea that challenged the Yiddish theater establishment, both in its artistic language and the devotion of its actors to this idea. Ararat's independent mode of organization was a result of Broderzon's idea of theater. The characteristics of his discourse, the uncompromising artistic quest, the collective ideal, and the subversive attitude toward mainstream Yiddish theater in Warsaw placed the troupe in a unique position in the field of contemporary Yiddish theater. Although the troupe's image changed after two years, the spirit of opposition and political and cultural awareness molded the political and aesthetic approaches of Dzigan and Shumacher's theater.

The Ararat troupe encountered economic difficulties, leading to a crisis at the beginning of 1929. Several actors declared a strike, asking for minimum wages in return for their work. The strike ended with the troupe's dissolution, or more precisely, it split into two different factions: the departing actors, among them Shumacher and Pulaver, decided to establish a new troupe, which they also named Ararat.[151] Thus, for some time two troupes with the same name were active: the breakaway Ararat and the original Ararat managed by Broderzon.

The newly established troupe embarked on a tour of performances in Vilna under the artistic management of Roman Rozental, who also directed the shows.[152] It staged a performance comprised of Ararat's "classics," renamed "Ansambl fun Lodzher kamer-teater Ararat" (Ensemble of Łódź Chamber Theater Ararat). This was based mainly on texts by Broderzon, without the author's permission. The troupe met with critical acclaim and was received enthusiastically by audiences. However, its success did not last long.

In Łódź, Broderzon's Ararat staged new shows without great success: *Koym mit tsores* (With Great Difficulty, December 1929); *Khay-gelebt!* (What a Wonderful Life!, January 1930); *On a kop* (Headless, February 1930); *Tshakedik un knakedik* (Spectacular and Festive, April 1930), and another three shows, all directed by

150 The National Union was not pleased that Geyhoyz gave the letter to Broderzon. In a letter dated February 2, 1928, to the Łódź organization, the National Union expressed its disappointment at the fact and alluded to the local organization's "respect" for Ararat. The letter then claimed that the background to the answers given by Ararat was fear of the professional organization and Ararat's desire to avoid punishment. The correspondence, which continued in the same discordant tone, can be found in the archive of the Yidisher artistn fareyn, YIVO, RG26 F253.
151 For the names of the shows that the two theaters staged see Appendix A.
152 See Pulaver, *Ararat*, 139–42.

Yoysef Strugatsh.[153] The theater's innovations on stage were unsuccessful, theatergoers stopped attending performances, and the troupe suffered economic failure.[154] The crisis deepened, according to Dzigan, when Dovid Herman was invited to direct Ararat's staging of *Bronks ekspres*. A great amount was spent on scenery and the luxurious hotel at which Herman stayed while he was in Łódź for rehearsals. Eventually, the play was such a disappointment that theatergoers demanded a return to the original Ararat and asked that Herman "be sent back to the Vilner trupe."[155]

Broderzon argued, apparently following the crisis in the troupe, that in the first two years of Ararat's existence the actors were amateurs. Only in 1930 did the troupe become, under his management, a professional theater.[156] Dzigan made a similar claim: in 1930, the doors were opened to talented individuals whose gifts had previously been lost in scenes featuring numerous actors, because "all the Ivans have the same face."[157]

We learn from Dzigan's memoirs about how the theater became institutionalized. Dzigan depicts the disappearance of the "exceptional scenery," the "strange costumes," and a reduction in the amount of "choral chanting." He indicates a change in the experimental and modernist spirit that characterized Ararat in the first years of its existence, noting that the emphasis shifted to the acting, relying on the unique talents of each actor, and the theatrical language became popular and accessible.

Between Avant-Garde and Popular: Theatrical Language, Language in the Theater

Both in Ararat and later in their own theater, Dzigan and Shumacher engaged in an intensive dialogue with theatergoers, and this was manifest both in direct discourse and stylistic choices. In particular, the decision to use the local Łódź Yiddish vernacular on stage reveals the double dialogue in which the troupe

---

153 Broderzon wrote most of the texts: "A briv," "Di koymen-kerers," "Kaptsonim," "Vayse balade," "Rusishe motivn," "S'vet nokh gut zayn!" "A katerinke," and "Oy pinuse." Other texts included "S'gasn meydl" by Yosl Mastboym, a song by Mordkhe Gebirtig, and folk songs. The veteran actors were joined by Yankev Zustanvits, Yankev Mandelblit, Moyshe Potashinski, Malvina Rappel, with Natan Rikhnberg as master of ceremonies.

154 Dzigan, *Der koyekh*, 82.

155 Ibid., 89–90. See the letter by Geyhoyz, March 1, 1929, Archive of the Yidisher artistn fareyn, YIVO, RG26 F253.

156 Broderzon, "Vegn Ararat."

157 Dzigan, *Der koyekh*, 85.

engaged – with its audience on the one hand and with the field of theater on the other. In 1930, Ararat made the revolutionary decision to employ the local Łódź dialect, thus detaching itself from one of the central conventions of Yiddish theater – the use of *teater-loshn̩* (or *voliner shprakh*), the standardized language used on the Yiddish stage.[158] The employment of a uniform dialect and language in Yiddish theater was a longstanding tradition to ensure that the entire Yiddish-speaking diaspora could understand performances originating from different lands.[159] Broderzon made a daring decision to strike out against this uniformity:

> אַז מען פֿרעגט: דיאַלעקט? ענטפֿערן מיר: – פֿאַר וואָס דווקא ליטווישער? פֿאַר וואָס דווקא וואָלינער? און – פֿאַר וואָס נישט פּוילישער, דער פֿונעם עטלעך מיליאָניקן קיבוץ, דער קלינגענדיק־באַרעדעוודיקער, דער כאַראַקטערפֿולער, קוועלנדיק־אָפּפֿרישנדיקער, און, פֿאַר אונדזער באָדן־נאַטירלעכער?[160]
>
> [So, people ask: Dialect? We answer: – Why Lithuanian specifically? Why Volhynian? And – why not the Polish dialect, replete with pleasantly chiming words, full of character. The refreshing dialect, which flows like a spring and is the most natural to the land of our birth?]

Dzigan noted in his interview with Dov Levin that in Ararat's performances the actors not only employed the local Łódź dialect. Rather, they suited the dialect to the area in which the troupe was performing. Indeed, when they performed in Lemberg (Lwów, Lviv) they spoke Galician Yiddish, in Vilna (Vilnius) they spoke Lithuanian Yiddish. Texts by classic Yiddish writers and the songs and poems that they recited and sung were always in the Volhynian dialect.[161]

Ararat's language thus depended on the location. However, this choice did not receive much attention in the contemporary press, beyond comments regarding the "popular" nature of the troupe – a characterization that could relate to both content and language. One of the few articles to discuss the language

158 This is the date given by Dzigan in his memoirs.

159 In the article "Di yidishe bineshprakh," published in the year Ararat was established, concerning the development of the Deutsche Bühnenaussprache and the precedence of the Vohlin dialect in the theater, Noyekh Pryłucki expressed the opposite approach to Broderzon regarding the need for a uniform stage language in Yiddish theater. Indeed, Pryłucki argued that the diversity of the theater troupes and their performances in various lands necessitated a standardized language. See Pryłucki, "Yidishe bineshprakh." Concerning the language used in Yiddish theater, see also Sauber, "Le Théâtre Yiddish." Regarding the Vilner trupe's decision to use a uniform language, see Zer-Zion, *'Habima' beBerlin*, 53. An exceptional case was the Jewish artistic theater of Shlomo Mikhoels in Moscow. See Veidlinger, *Moscow State Yiddish Theater*.

160 Pulaver, *Ararat*, 14–15.

161 Levin, Interview with Shimen Dzigan (1973). See also Dzigan, *Der koyekh*, 87.

question was penned by the writer Zusman Segalovitsh and concerned Ararat's performance in Warsaw:

> נישט אומזיסט קומען אַלע דרײַ [דזשיגאַן, שומאַכער און גאָלדשטיין] פֿון איין שטאָט, פֿון לאָדזש, און אפֿשר זענען זיי פֿון איין געסל. זיי טראָגן אויף זיך דעם ספּעציפֿישן־ייִדישן קנייטש און וועגן זיי קאָן מען דרײַסט זאָגן, אַז קיין גראַפֿן, קיין באַראָנען וועלן זיי נישט קאָנען שפּילן, קיין מאָל נישט. זאָל דזשיגאַן פּרווון זאָגן 'יאַ' אַנשטאָט 'יאָ' וועט מען לאַכן . . . די דרײַ זענען נישט געבוירן געוואָרן צו שפּילן 'אַריסטאָקראַטן'. זיי זענען 'סאַמאָראָדנע' יאַטן מיט אַלע פּיטשעווקעס. זיי זענען צום טעאַטער געקומען פֿון דער ייִדישער געדיכטעניש. זיי האָבן געבראַכט אויף דער סצענע די ייִדישע מימיק, נו... און דעם עכט־ייִדישן וויץ.[162]
>
> [It's no coincidence that all three of them (Dzigan, Shumacher, and Shmulik Goldshteyn) come from one city, from Łódź, and perhaps even from the same street. They bring with them a specific Yiddish diction, and regarding this, we can dare to say that they would never be able to play a character from the nobility, a duke. Dzigan would only try to say "Ya" instead of "Yo," and the audience would begin to laugh . . . the three of them were not born to play "aristocrats." They are "authentic" guys with all the trimmings. They came to the theater right from the heart of Jewish society. They brought to the theater Jewish mimicry and... the real Jewish joke.]

Segalovitsh highlights the link between the dialect used by the artists and their body language on stage: both are connected to the artists' native culture in Łódź. The Łódź artists play, sometimes unwillingly, characters of simple Jews from their city. This linguistic limitation, in Segalovitsh's opinion, is also an advantage: the cultural specificity is expressed in language, accent, and body language. The process that Segalovitsh describes with regard to Ararat's performances in Warsaw is similar to what Gilles Deleuze and Félix Guattari, forty years later, termed the "deterritorialization of language."[163]

In his book, *Hatsad ha'afel bitseḥoḳo shel Shalom Aleichem* (The Dark Side of Sholem Aleichem's Laughter), Dan Miron applies the theory developed by Deleuze and Guattari to Sholem Aleichem's literary works. Miron claims that the marginal attributes, the exclusion, and the deterritorialization make it possible to describe Sholem Aleichem's works as "minor literature," a term coined by Deleuze and Guattari that was later expanded by other scholars. Miron highlights that Sholem Aleichem intentionally wrote in a simple, folksy language, in contrast to the dominant tendency among contemporary Yiddish writers, who sought to initiate a "majorization" of the language. Sholem Aleichem chose "to adopt the minority and marginal linguistic-cultural feeling, to deepen it and to create through it a

162 Segalovitsh, "Di 'samerodne' yatn"

163 Deleuze and Guattari relate to this as to a process in which mistakes crept into the traditional structures of expression, in contrast to re-territorialization – a process of strengthening those same structures. See Deleuze and Guattari, *Kafka*.

strength of expression and a feeling of political-cultural independence, which was achieved by rejecting the culture of the 'majority' and subverting it."[164]

Similarly to Sholem Aleichem, according to Miron's portrayal, it seems that Broderzon and Dzigan and Shumacher also subverted the political conventions of language in Yiddish theater. It is possible to say that they continued the process begun by Sholem Aleichem, even widening its application to encompass a performative aspect – both spoken and body language, as is evident also in reviews of their performances.[165] Dzigan, Shumacher, and Broderzon brought to the theater stage the intensity of the simple, folksy vernacular, emphasizing it in their performances through words and body language. They elevated the Yiddish language to new heights and dimensions. Their decision to use the spoken language returned the theater "to the people." They spoke to the theatergoers in their language without relinquishing their artistic freedom, and they even challenged the ruling linguistic convention in contemporary Yiddish theater: the subversive artistic decision to perform in a language considered "unartistic" was an additional expression of the revolution that these theater artists initiated in relations between the theater and its spectators.

The first use of the local dialect at the beginning of the 1930s, together with the change in content, which began to focus on satirical and current materials, gave the art of Dzigan and Shumacher a political dimension, as is discussed further in the ensuing chapter that focuses on the Warsaw period. The choice of language was not only a poetic or aesthetic choice due to an inability to perform in another language, another Yiddish, as Segalovitsh fondly claimed in his abovementioned review. This was an explicit political-linguistic choice that Broderzon made consciously. It reveals the intensive dialogue between one artistic periphery and the center. Indeed, Ararat, and subsequently the theater of Dzigan and Shumacher, undermined the reigning convention that Yiddish theater required a uniform language.

---

164 Miron, *Hatsad ha'afel*, 78–79.

165 Dzigan and Shumacher are often compared with Sholem Aleichem in discussions of the actors' style. Early critics described Dzigan and Shumacher as the embodiment of Sholem Aleichem. In an article published in *Haaretz* in 1960, a reviewer defined Dzigan as "the exceptional interpreter of Sholem Aleichem," and Emil Feuerstein wrote about Yisroel Shumacher: "We do not hesitate to mention his name in the same breath as that of Sholem Aleichem." See Fuks, "Zikhere trit"; *Idishe tsaytung*, "A bazukh"; *Haaretz*, "Dzigan metakhnen"; Feuerstein, "Ha'oman shehitsḥiḳ"; Tsanin, "Shumacher z"l."

Chapter 2
From a Collective to an Independent Artistic Endeavor: Dzigan and Shumacher in Warsaw (1934–1939)

> דאָ זענען מיר באַרימט, אָבער דרײַסיק קילאָמעטער פֿון לאָדזש ווייסט מען נישט פֿון אונדז, ווײַל די לאָדזשער פּרעסע לייענט מען בלויז אין לאָדזש.
>
> [Here we are famous, but no one knows us thirty kilometers from Łódź, because the Łódź papers are read only in Łódź.]
>
> – Dzigan, *Der koyekh*

From 1930 to 1933, the Ararat theater experienced an artistic and financial crisis. The troupe relied on only one writer, Moyshe Broderzon. Nothing new was added to the repertoire. With no new shows, its budget dwindled into nonexistence. Consequently, the troupe began to search for new audiences outside Łódź for whom they could perform their existing materials. The peak of these tours were the two shows that Ararat staged at the Scala Theater in Warsaw: *Afn himl a yarid* (Much Ado about Nothing!), performed first in Łódź more than fifty times and seen by over 13,000 theatergoers, in April 1931;[1] and *M'lakht fun der velt!* (Laughing at the World!), in September 1932.

Ararat's First Show in Warsaw

Despite the obstacles the National Union of Jewish Actors tried to place in Ararat's path, demanding that all members of the troupe take the union's admission examination before performing in Warsaw,[2] Ararat reaped great success in the capital. People flocked to the theater, and the shows were a great hit. Likewise, for the first time the troupe also received positive reviews in the national press. The journalist and writer Y. M. Nayman, whose intimate acquaintance with the troupe dated back to its earliest days in Łódź, described Ararat as the best Yiddish miniature theater in Poland.[3] Writing in *Literarishe bleter*, the central Yiddish literary journal in interwar Poland, Nakhmen Mayzel argued that Ararat clearly had the

1 *Literarishe bleter*, "Lodzher kameral."

2 Dzigan and Shumacher passed the examination on May 12, 1929. See Archive of the Yidisher artistn-fareyn, YIVO, file 26.551.2

3 Nayman "Ararat."

https://doi.org/10.1515/9783110717693-002

potential to become an excellent revue theater (see Figure 5).[4] Positive reviews of Ararat's two performances in Warsaw were also published by Menakhem Kipnis in *Haynt* and Yoshue Perle in *Der moment*, the two most influential and widely read Yiddish newspapers in Warsaw.[5] However, in addition to these positive reviews, most critics noted that the quality of the texts varied,[6] and Perle advised that experienced directors were needed in order to maximize the troupe's potential.[7]

Among the troupe's actors, Dzigan, Shumacher, and Shmulik Goldshteyn were singled out with excellent reviews.[8] The critics crowned Dzigan as Ararat's greatest star. Nayman praised his linguistic prowess, which manifested in his exceptional use of idioms and absurd curses. According to the critic, his great talent could carry the entire show singlehandedly.[9] Avrom-Yitskhok Grafman wrote in *Der moment*:

> שוין דאָס אַליין, וואָס דער 'אַראַראַט' האָט אַרויסגענומען אַזאַ פֿולבלוטיקן ייִדישן טאַלענט איז אַ גרויס קולטורעל פֿאַרדינסט. דזשיגאַן דערשײַנט כּמעט אין אַלע נומערן, און מען וויל אים זען נאָך מער.[10]
>
> [The mere fact that such a vigorous Jewish talent has come forth from Ararat is a great cultural service. Dzigan appears in almost all segments, and you want to see him more and more.]

Yoshue Perle depicted Dzigan in the following manner:

> איז דזשיגאַן אַ שטיק פֿײַער – דאָס קינסטלערישע בלוט שפּאַרט פֿון אים אַרויס. עס איז אים אומעטום ענג, מען זעט, אַז ער קען געבן נאָך מער, ווי דאָס וואָס ער גיט. עס איז מיר נאָך כּמעט נישט אויסגעקומען צו זען אַ ייִדישן אַקטיאָר מיט אַזאַ פֿליישיקער, פֿאַרכלינעטער ייִדישער שפּראַך, ווי ס'האָט דער דאָזיקער דזשיגאַן.[11]

4 Mayzel, "Ararat in Lodzh."
5 Kipnis, "A shpatsir"; Perle, "Kleynkunst."
6 A critic, who signed his name A-H, wrote that the troupe was "pleasant" and many of its segments were of good quality. He praised the musical and dancing sections as opposed to the skits, which he did not consider interesting, even though they clearly reflected the actors' talents. The critic concluded by arguing that Ararat was in general a high-quality theater, although not all parts of the show maintained the same level. He praised Sheyne-Miriam Broderzon and Dzigan. See A-H, "Ararat in Varshe," no indication of newspaper or date, BAA, file 153-03.
7 Perle, "Kleynkunst."
8 Segalovitsh, "Ararat"; Mayzel, "Ararat in Varshe."
9 Nayman, "Ararat." One of the skits that drew the attention of critics and audiences alike was the monologue "Tsores fun yo-yo" (Sorrows of a Yoyo), by Y. Sh. Goldshteyn. In this skit, Dzigan appeared on the stage dressed as a Polish Hasid, with a beard, wearing a kaftan, red kerchief, and a *shtreimel* (a fur hat typically worn on holidays and Sabbaths), and playing with a yoyo, the Japanese game popular at the time. In the monologue he relates how he has a yoyo attached to his tefillin, that his wife cooks cholent not with potatoes but with a yoyo, and that his daughter gave birth to twins – Yo and Yo. Dzigan, *Der koyekh*, 94.
10 Grafman, "Yidish teater."
11 Perle, "Kleynkunst."

[Dzigan is a flaming torch – artistic blood gushes from him. Any space is too restrictive for him. You see that he can give even more than he is giving. I have almost never encountered a Yiddish actor with a fleshy, sensual Yiddish language as Dzigan's.]

While Yisroel Shumacher had not attracted attention in the troupe's performances in Łódź, in the Polish capital he became increasingly prominent. Nayman claimed that he was a quiet and shy actor who would be noticed by the discerning,[12] while Perle noted that:

. . . אַזאַ יונגער מענטש, ווי שומאַכער, למשל, רעדט מיט אַ זיסער, איידעלער ייִדישער שפּראַך, מען האָט דעם איַינדרוק, אַז ער שפּילט אויף אַ פֿידל אונטער אַ סורדינקע. בכלל איז דער דאָזיקער שומאַכער אַ מענטש מיט אַ סך ייִדישער ווייַכקייט, מיט דער עכטער ייִדישער נישט איבערגעטריבענער תנועה. ער איז, וואָלט איך געזאָגט, קאַמעראַל – אָפּט מאָל שוין צו פֿיל קאַמעראַל. ער ווייסט אַז מיט געשריי שאַפֿט מען נישט קיין קונסט . . . שומאַכער איז אַ מענטש, וואָס איז איבערגעגעבן דעם 'אַררט' מיט לייב און לעבן. ער איז איינער פֿון יענע געציילטע וואָס וועלן פֿאַרנעמען דאָס ערשטע אָרט, אויב ס'וועט אויף אַן אמת געשאַפֿן ווערן גוט ייִדיש טעאַטער.[13]

[. . . a young man such as Shumacher, for example, speaks with a sweet, gentle Yiddish language, one gets the impression that he is playing the fiddle (on mute). In general, Shumacher is a man characterized by Jewish gentleness, who moves in an authentic, unexaggerated, Jewish manner. He is, I would say, musical, sometimes even too much so. He knows that one does not create art by screaming . . . Shumacher is a man devoted to Ararat with body and soul. He is one of those select few who will take the first place, if a good[14] Jewish theater will truly be created.]

While the creative and economic crisis that Ararat suffered in Łódź signaled the decline of the collective, the tour of performances in Warsaw indicated the move from collective to individual, a change that concluded a few years later with the renaming of the troupe. The new identity of the theater was expressed also in the rejection of standard stage Yiddish in favor of the Łódź Yiddish dialect, and in the abandonment of aesthetic and experimental quests in favor of satirical, political, and social ones.[15] This tour of performances heralded the turning point

12 Nayman, "Ararat."

13 Perle, "Kleynkunst."

14 Meaning the artistic repertory theater in Yiddish.

15 Dzigan, *Der koyekh*, 85–87. Pulaver, who at times provides contradictory details and dates, describes this as the dawn of "stardom" in Ararat, blaming Shumacher for disrupting the troupe's harmony. Shumacher, in Pulaver's opinion, was responsible for creating two camps within Ararat, pulling Dzigan into his camp to the extent that "the two became one." See Pulaver, *Ararat*, 90. Pulaver does not conceal his dislike of Shumacher. He describes him as tense, competitive, and cynical. However, it should be noted that his words also reflect a personal slight: the partnership between Dzigan and Shumacher excluded Pulaver, who ceased to be Dzigan's main partner

ליטעראַרישע בלעטער נומ. 6 (405) זייט 95

לאָדזער קאַמעראַל און קליינ-קונסט-טעאַטער „אַררט“

קינסטלערישער אָנפירער — משה בראָדערזאָן

דאָס 24-סטע פּראָגראַם

ש. דזשיגאַן („גאַנדיי“)

„אררט“-קאָלעקטיוו מיט ג. מייזיל

משה בראָדערזאָן

י. שומאַכער

ש. גאָלדשטיין, מרים דאלסקא, מ. פולאָווער

שיינע מרים

ש. דזשיגאַן, ציליַ סטאָל, שיינע מרים, י. שומאַכער, מ. פולאָוועו

מ. פולאָווער, ש. גאָלדשטיין, י. שומאַכער, צילי סטאָל

Figure 5: Photos of Ararat from 1932, “Lodzher kameral-un kleynkunst-teater ‘Ararat’ – Kinstlerisher onfirer – Moyshe Broderzon, dos 24ste program” Literarishe bleter, February 5, 1932, 9: 95.

in the artistic careers of Shimen Dzigan and Yisroel Shumacher: a comic duo was born, with both partners becoming central figures in the miniature theater and in the Jewish political satire performed on the Yiddish stage.

The Move to the Capital

In 1934, recognizing Ararat's success in Warsaw, and understanding that the theater was in the midst of financial and artistic crises and was thus unable to create any new materials, Henry Ryba and Meyer Vinder, the managers of the Warsaw miniature theater troupe Di yidishe bande (The Jewish Gang),[16] decided to exploit this opportunity. They traveled to Łódź and invited a number of Ararat's actors to join their troupe and perform in a major Warsaw theater. Shimen Dzigan, already convinced that, in his words, "Ararat was on the verge of collapse," accepted the offer, as did Moyshe Broderzon, his wife Sheyne-Miriam, and Yisroel Shumacher.[17]

The artists from Ararat appeared in Di yidishe bande alongside actors Rokhl Holzer, Yokheved Zilberg, Zishe Katz, Dovid Lederman, Lili Liliana, Mark Morevski, Lola Folman, Peysakh Kerman, Malvina Rappel, and Ayzik Rotman. The musical manager was Dovid Beygelman. Dzigan and Shumacher appeared together with the Warsaw troupe in the shows *"Tantst yidelekh!" un "Lakht fun der velt!"* ("Dance Jews!" and "Laugh at the World!," October 1933); *Nisht geshtoygn, nisht gefloygn* (Totally Ludicrous, November 1933); and *Himl efn zikh!* (Gates of Heaven, Open Up!, January 1934). This collaboration with members of Ararat brought Di yidishe bande great success, and the Łódź actors were able to demand the inclusion of additional Ararat members. This anticipated the establishment of Ararat in Warsaw under the artistic management of Moyshe Broderzon, with Dzigan and Shumacher, who eventually left Di yidishe bande, serving as its permanent directors.[18]

---

in acting and directing the troupe. Although Pulaver performed with Ararat again in Warsaw in 1934, he no longer played a central role in the troupe.

16 The miniature theater Di yidishe bande was established in 1932 in Kalisz, under the management of Dovid Lederman and Zishe Katz. Its name was inspired by the successful Polish miniature theater Banda. After suffering failure in Kalisz, the troupe moved to Łódź, where it achieved success. Later, during that same year, it settled in Warsaw. In 1939, the troupe set out on a tour of performances in America. See Nudelman, "Kleynkunst," 160–61.

17 Dzigan, *Der koyekh*, 109–44.

18 See Bashan, "Monolog." Newspaper advertisements and Pulaver's book indicate that Broderzon continued to serve as the troupe's artistic manager until 1936, and Vinder and Ryba remained the general managers. See Pulaver, *Geven iz a geto*, 61–62.

In 1934, Ararat staged two shows in the Nowości theater.[19] The first was *A gdule af der bobe* (A Fat Lot of Good That'll Do). Dzigan and Shumacher directed, with texts by Broderzon, Y. Sh. Goldshteyn, Der Tunkeler, H. Leyvik, Moyshe Nadir, and Moyshe Elboym; songs by Mordkhe Gebirtig, Ludvig Shmargad, and a song written by Izidor Hollender and Shumacher set to music by Herts Rubin. The second show, *Zmires mit lokhsn* (Sabbath Hymns with Noodles), included famous skits by the duo such as "Di koymen-kerers" (The Chimneysweeps) by Broderzon (see below) and "Yidn forn handlen" (Jews Go Off to Do Business) by Y. Sh. Goldshteyn.

In the theatrical seasons of 1935–1936, Ararat staged three new shows and one that reused existing materials: *Khsidish, negidish, mamzerish* (Hasidic, Wealthy, and Sly), *A velt mit nisim* (A World with Miracles), *Moyshe-kapoyer* (Moses the Contrary), and *A nakhes tsu kukn* (A Pleasure to Look). In March 1935, the members of Ararat embarked on their first tour outside the borders of Poland, spending twelve weeks in Western Europe. Their last show in Warsaw before leaving for the tour was entitled *Ararat fort avek* (Ararat Is Departing), which included skits by Broderzon, Y. Sh. Goldshteyn, Der Tunkeler, Moyshe Nadir, Ayzik Plotner, and Zenon Fridvald (later Zenon Verden). The brother of the lawyer and cultural activist Yoysef Veytsman spearheaded and financed this tour, which visited Paris, Brussels, and London. He persuaded the troupe of its financial benefits. Dzigan relates that while the shows received positive reviews from key figures in the theatrical world, among them Sergey Volkonsky and Tristan Bernard, and that the Paris premiere in Paris was attended by the likes of Jewish artists Mark Chagall and Nahum Aronson, in financial terms the tour was a failure.[20]

Upon its return to Warsaw, Ararat staged a number of further shows, which will be discussed in more detail below. Reviews of the troupe's performances in the major Warsaw and Łódź papers echoed the comments on Ararat's guest performances in the city two years previously, and Ararat became the central miniature theater in Poland. In reviews of *A gdule af der bobe* (A Fat Lot of Good That'll Do), Segalovitsh admitted that he lost his critical sense and laughed incessantly throughout the entire performance.[21] Mayzel portrayed with great surprise the joyful atmosphere at the premiere, the success of the shows, and the troupe's

19 The administrative manager in this period was Y. Bergman. The scenery was designed by A. Liberman, the costumes by Dina Matus, the lighting by Ber Shvartshteyn, and the choreographer was J. Wycieczka.

20 Dzigan, *Der koyekh*, 114–15. I have not been able to find the reviews.

21 Segalovitsh mentioned in particular the skit "Mekhile betn" (Asking Forgiveness) by Der Tunkeler, performed by Birenboym and Shmulik Goldshteyn, and the sections "Di kukavke" (The Cuckoo) and "Di lustike brigade" (The Cheerful Brigade) by Broderzon. Like many others,

great promise.[22] Most reviewers praised Ararat's artistic power, noting that, in the tradition of the Polish miniature theater, it staged "cultural [shows] concerning current affairs."[23] Although many reviews mentioned that the quality of the texts varied significantly,[24] negative reviews were rare.[25] Ararat achieved exceptional success among Jewish audiences, exceeding by far the popularity of any other miniature theater. Admiration for the two main actors, who were also the directors, continued to increase, and people began to refer to the troupe as "the theater of Dzigan and Shumacher."[26] The mythical, collective, and geographical name "Ararat" was soon replaced by the surnames of the two artists.

"A Match Made in Heaven"

Dzigan and Shumacher's individual comic talents and their exceptional performative abilities were evident in the monologues they performed. However, in addition, their great flair as a comic duo constituted a significant element of their art. Indeed, they performed extensively in this format during Ararat's Warsaw period. Comic duos, which are found in many different cultures, usually include

---

he praised the acting talents of Dzigan, Shumacher, and Shmulik Goldshteyn. See Segalovitsh, "Di 'samerodne' yatn."

22 Mayzel, "Mikoyekh."

23 Grafman, "Zmires mit lokshn." Grafman praised "Kasrilevker hoteln" (Kasrilevke Hotels), based on Sholem Aleichem's story, and the skit "Di koymen-kerers" (also known as "Palestine-Birobidzhan") by Y. Sh. Goldshteyn. Kipnis noted briefly the skits "In vagon" (In the Wagon) by Yankev Oberzhanek, "Di koymen-kerers" (The Chimneysweeps), and "Baym breg-yam" (At the Seashore) by Broderzon. See Kipnis, "A velt."

24 Mayzel attributes this to a lack of good authors and satirists writing for the revue theater. In his opinion, this also explained why the theater of Dzigan and Shumacher did not manage to reach the level that Azazael and Ararat had achieved in their golden days, despite the fact that the duo's performances were interesting. See Mayzel, "Afn varshever yarid."

25 For an example of a negative review see R-n, "Ararat." This was published in *Fraynd*, a newspaper with a Communist bent, managed by Boris Kletzkin. Among the members of the editorial team were Alter Katsizne, Kadia Molodowsky, and Berl Mark.

26 Dzigan relates that as early as 1933 people began to refer to the theater by this name. See Brat, "40 yor." The theater began to operate as "the theater of Dzigan and Shumacher" following a tour of performances in Europe in 1935. See Dzigan, *Der koyekh*, 114–15. Likewise, Moyshe Nudelman testifies that on the Jewish street people began to refer to Ararat by the name of its two main actors already at the beginning of the 1930s. See Nudelman, "Kleynkunst." See also Pulaver, *Geven iz a geto*, 58. However, advertisements in the press used the moniker "Dzigan and Shumacher" as the name of the theater only from 1937 onwards. In his memoirs from the ghetto period, Pulaver depicts Ararat's final performances in 1939, although he is in fact referring to performances by Dzigan and Shumacher's theater. See ibid., 50

two actors of similar gender, age, and ethnic origin, who are distinguished by different qualities or behavior. The most well known examples are Abbott and Costello, Flanagan and Allen, Gallagher and Shean, Tran and Helle, and Laurel and Hardy; indeed, the last of these achieved great fame and influence following the release of their first short film, *Duck Soup* (1927). One member of the duo is typically serious and logical. In the case of Dzigan and Shumacher, this was Shumacher's role. The other is funny, uneducated, rude, or outlandish – this role fell to Dzigan. Jakub Appenszlak wrote that the two complimented one another astoundingly well.[27] Dzigan appeared as the *horepashnik*, the "laborer," the simple man who does not understand complex matters, who is angry, nimble, and quick to respond. He represented the "average Joe" raging against the authorities. Nayman defined Dzigan as a "primitive force, in a good sense, a man of 'the people,' from the Jewish street, saturated with atmosphere and style."[28] By contrast, he depicted Shumacher as skeptical, unhurried, intelligent, and enlightened.

The contrasts between the two were not only an artistic construction. Off stage, their characters and personalities differed significantly. According to their wives, Eva (Feygnblum) Dzigan and Celina (Stal) Shumacher, Dzigan, who married Eva in 1947 and never had children, slept late and would wake up only a few minutes before a meeting. He was disorganized, lacked a sense of direction, and never remembered dates. Shumacher, by contrast, is depicted as a devoted father, who woke early, performed singing exercises, and in the mornings immersed himself in works of *belles lettres*.[29] Nayman described them as like "Issachar and Zebulun."[30] The duo's dialogue was built on oppositions and reflected the traditional Jewish discourse – the mode of thinking, speaking, and writing that derived from the tradition of rabbinical study and influenced the development of Yiddish daily discourse and humor, as well as literature and theater. This discourse is characterized, as Jordan Finkin notes, by a specific vocabulary, as well

27 Appenszlak, "Nadir un Wejn Niszt."

28 Nayman, "Dzigan ṿeShumacher." It is interesting to compare this description to the characters that Dzigan played in Israel many years later, as depicted by Mirit Shem-Or: "'The eternal Jew,' who never has enough money and is always getting into trouble, the disappointed bridegroom, the dishonest plumber, the street philosopher, the happy idiot, the foolish sage; and, in fact, any person that lives, eats, marries, falls in love (after marriage), pays taxes, learns to understand life the hard way, doesn't understand anything, sighs . . . laughs, and mainly makes people laugh." Shem-Or, "Be'idish ze matsḥiḳ."

29 Avrekh, "Hanashim megalot."

30 Nayman, "Dzigan ṿeShumacher."

as grammatical structures and methods of argumentation, such as "answering a question with a question" or a "competitive" argument.[31] The Jewish dialogical discourse involves interruptions, conceptions, and interpretations that reflect philosophical and cultural perceptions.

The contrasts between the duo became a central component in their shows, making their joint skits extremely powerful. Examples include "Palestine-Birobidzhan" and "Politsyantn in Tel-Aviv" (Police officers in Tel Aviv),[32] "Dzigan un Shumacher in 1980" (Dzigan and Shumacher in 1980), "A heylung far di nervn" (A Cure for the Nerves), "A meshugener" (A Crazy Person), and "Aynshteyn-Vaynsten" (Einstein-Weinstein), the last of which is an example of a light, humorous, and non-political skit by the duo and will be examined here to demonstrate their unique dialogue.

Aynshteyn-Vaynshteyn

"Aynshteyn-Vaynshteyn," by Y. Sh. Goldshteyn and Moyshe Nudelman, is considered one of the duo's classic skits. It was performed in many different contexts: in the Soviet Union, in Poland, following the duo's return in 1947, and in Israel in the 1950s. The skit is based on the confusion caused by two similar sounding surnames, Aynshteyn (Einstein) and Vaynshteyn (Weinstein), which belong to two very different people. This leads to a dialogue constructed from mistakes and misunderstandings: the character played by Shumacher is an intellectual: he is enlightened, well versed in politics, and conversant with the cultural and social reality. Dzigan's character, by contrast, is a simple man with no interest in these topics; he interprets life based on his unmediated acquaintance with reality, drawing on his own personal experience.[33]

The simple man's (exaggerated) ignorance – he has never even heard of Albert Einstein – drives his companion crazy. The latter is not only surprised by this lack of education, but also by the fact that his interlocutor cannot distinguish between Einstein the scientist and Vaynshteyn the exporter, either by name or cultural meaning. The humorous process is classic, simple, and lighthearted,

31 Finkin, "Jewish Jokes," 87–88.

32 See below, pp. 72–73.

33 "The artistic means by which Dzigan and Shumacher affect the theater's audience are apparent when both artists step forth together. The contrasts between their acting styles intensifies the power of the scene. This is not a normal stage-dialogue but rather an artistic embodiment of two separate types." *Letste nayes*, "Dzigan–Shumacher in 'Beit-Lid.'"

based on misunderstandings, a short circuit in communication, listening problems, and plays on words. The actors elaborated on the basic dialogue through various references to intellectual topics that drew on the milieu in which they were performing. For example, in the version recorded in Israel, the "enlightened" character asks "the simple man" if he knows the meaning of the terms dictatorship and democracy; this question was not asked in the previous version of the skit. The response draws on experiences from everyday life: "After twenty years of marriage, you think I don't know what a dictatorship is?"[34] The presentation of two different types of knowledge, the scientific-intellectual and the experiential-personal, is typical of the processes used by comic duos, connecting between private family life and the public sphere, between the individual and the general.

The duo's artistic partnership also received a great deal of press attention after World War II. The two were described as a "match made in heaven," "siamese twins,"[35] "a marriage and a perfect match between two artists."[36] In the newspaper *Nay-velt*, an anonymous journalist wrote: "Together they are one, not partners, but rather one whole, they are an ensemble theater. Together they are a troupe."[37] Likewise, Mordkhe Tsanin commented, "They were as one body."[38] The journalist and critic Yankev Botoshansky depicted the duo as "two that became one whole," adding:

> מאַן און ווײַב וואָלטן אויך ניט געקענט ווערן איינס, ווען זיי זײַנען ניט פֿאַרשידן. זיי ווערן אויף אַזוי פֿיל איינס, אַז טראָץ דער פֿאַרשידנקייט פֿילט איר ניט שטענדיק ווו עס ענדיקט זיך איינער און ווו עס הייבט זיך אָן אַ צווייטער. און ווען זיי באַווײַזן זיך באַזונדער, זײַנען זיי יעדער אויף זײַן שטייגער, גלענצנדיקע שוישפּילער . . . אפֿשר טאַקע דערפֿאַר, ווײַל זיי זײַנען טעזע און אַנטיטעזע און זיי ווערן דורך דעם אַ סינטעז.[39]

> [So too, it would not be possible for man and wife to become one, were they not different. They join together to such an extent that, despite the differences, it is difficult to discern where one ends and the other begins. But when they are apart, each one in his own style is a brilliant actor . . . specifically, because they embody thesis and antithesis, they become synthesis.]

34 It is interesting to note that this question was removed from the version submitted to the Polish censor in 1948. See the manuscript of the script, BAA, file 149-01.
35 *Devar hashavua*, "Mitsrakh ḥiyuni."
36 *Folksblat*, "Dzigan un Shumacher."
37 *Nay-velt*, "Dzigan–Shumacher." Dov-Ber Malkin made a similar claim in his article "Tendo," published in Hebrew translation in the playbill for *Nadir un veyn nisht!* (Take This and Don't Cry!) (1955).
38 Tsanin, "Shumacher z"l."
39 Botoshansky, "Tsvishn yo un neyn."

The duo's partnership on stage and their transformation into one whole was also expressed in the name they used to the sign texts they wrote together, "Y. Shudzig," combining both names into one surname: Shu(macher)Dzig(an).[40]

Another fascinating manifestation of the duo's attitude to partnership and family is the plan for the building they intended to construct on Mandelstam Street, in Tel Aviv, on a plot they purchased in 1951 – a plan that was never realized. The architectural plans depict a unit comprising two identical apartments, one next to the other, with a shared room on the roof level that would serve both families and provide a space for meetings and rehearsals. Each apartment was to have its own, separate access to this room which would connect between the private and the common areas. The planned building was a practical expression of the artistic partnership as parallel to their respective marriages; the name they used to sign their co-written texts was a linguistic amalgamation of the two individuals into one artistic entity; and each new show involved "birth pangs."[41] Indeed, Lydia Shumacher-Ophir, Shumacher's daughter, was always seen as the "daughter of Dzigan and Shumacher," testifying to the public perception of the intimate connection between the two artists. The tension between "amalgamation" and "contrast" is central in understanding their complex relationship.

From Experimental to Satirical Language

When the artists moved to Warsaw, Jewish cultural life in that city was in the midst of a deep crisis. In January 1933, Nayman wrote that the cultural life of Polish Jewry was on the verge of complete disintegration; the last rational stronghold battling for its existence was Mayzel's journal, *Literarishe bleter*.[42] Upon Hitler's rise to power in 1933, Poland was flooded by a wave of antisemitic sentiment, which had serious ramifications for the political, cultural, and social reality of Polish Jewry. This was palpable in the Jewish newspapers, which gradually consolidated a common front in response to the menacing develop-

40 Among the skits they wrote together are: "Abi m'zet zikh!" (The Main Thing: We Meet Again!, 1947); "Di noz" (The Nose, 1947); "A nudnik" (A Nuisance, 1956); "Asirei tsien" (Prisoners of Zion, 1958); "A fli tsu der levone" (A Flight to the Moon, 1958), and "Der shtroyener almen" (The Straw Widower, 1959). The two also cosigned works using the name "Y. Gizdush." Dzigan signed the skits that he wrote himself with the penname Sh. Shimsi, while Shumacher used the penname Y. Tsevi.

41 Avrekh, "Hanashim megalot."

42 Cohen, *Sefer, sofer, ve'iton*, 139. Dovid Bergelson, who visited Warsaw on his way back to the Soviet Union, also claimed that were it not for Nakhmen Mayzel, the city would be suffocating. See ibid., 137. Concerning the difficult situation of the Jewish cultural center in Warsaw in the 1930s, see ibid., 129–41.

ments in Germany, publishing on their front pages fervent calls to arouse public awareness.[43] Likewise, it influenced the stage of Dzigan and Shumacher, who had become Ararat's managers. The artists felt that they could not continue as a theater that provided only entertainment, instead deciding that the content of their shows should respond, directly and immediately, to political events. This decision stemmed not only from the political reality itself but was influenced by similar developments among other contemporaneous cabaret troupes in Warsaw.

Dzigan later recalled that during this period Ararat continued to reflect Jewish suffering, the economic and social crisis, and the Jewish reality. Central themes thus included daily life (marriage, family, modernization); economy (the economic situation, poverty, suggestions for change); Jewish society and identity (religion, arranged marriages, political parties, ideologies, the question of emigration); and Jewish/Yiddish theater (all these will be discussed in the final chapter). The Warsaw version of Ararat began to voice strong, frequent, and immediate reactions to the contemporary political reality. Dzigan and Shumacher integrated into their skits and the shows' opening segments responses to the political developments and even referred directly to the concurrent situation in Germany:[44]

> ס'איז נאָך דאָ מענטשן, וואָס גייט זיי נאָך ערגער. כ'מיין אונדזערע שכנים [די דײַטשן], זיי עסן דאָך נישט ראַיעל,
> הער! הער נאָר! פֿלייש מאַכן זיי פֿון פֿיש, פֿיש מאַכט מען פֿון קאַרטאָפֿל, קאַרטאָפֿל פֿון ברעטער – און שפּײַען
> אַ גאַנצן טאָג מיט זעגעכץ, אַז אויף אַ פֿרישטיק עסט מען גומענע אייער.[45]

> [There are people who are worse off than we are. I mean, our neighbors (the Germans). They're not eating well. Listen! Listen up! They're making meat from fish, fish from potatoes, potatoes from boards – and all day long they're spitting out sawdust, and for breakfast they're eating eggs made from rubber.]

The shift to critical political material was not without its challenges, particularly as freedom of speech became increasingly limited. At the beginning of the 1930s, the Jews in independent Poland still enjoyed a certain degree of freedom of speech, but by the second half of the decade nationalist and antisemitic

43 Ibid., 267. Concerning journalists' responses to Hitler's rise to power, the expression of opinions on national issues, and reactions to events that could be detrimental to the common interests of Polish Jewry, see ibid., 67–69; on writers and journalists' responses to developments in Germany in the years 1933–1939, see ibid., 262–76.

44 See Bashan, "Monolog." Sheyne-Miriam, Broderzon's wife, wrote in her memoirs that her husband stopped writing poetry upon Hitler's rise to power: "When Hitler came to power in Germany, his mood changed. He lost his happy, carefree way of playing with words and rhymes." Broderzon, *Mayn leydns-veg.*

45 "Aḥdut," by Y. Sh. Goldshteyn and Moyshe Nudelman, Yad Vashem Archives (YVA), M10 ARI 1162. I am grateful to Gabriel Finder for helping me to locate this manuscript. Dzigan's monologue was performed in the show *Tate, du lakhst!* (1938).

tendencies had triumphed, bringing in their wake strict censorship, mainly vis-à-vis left wing and national minority elements.[46] The artists were forced to find creative solutions to impart their critical and humoristic messages on stage.[47]

Consequently, one tactic that Dzigan and Shumacher began to implement was the use of silence rather than speech. Just before saying something harsh or completing a joke, they would suddenly stop and fall silent. This exposed the censorship and its practical implications. Using (crude) allusions, the audience members filled in the gap and applauded.[48] This silence played a dual role: it collectively and silently completed what was left unsaid and, at the same time, made the censorship palpable and present. Applying John Austin's concept of performativity, Dzigan and Shumacher "did things" with silence.[49] Sometimes the artists even dared, regardless of the censor, to take aim at a target directly:

> דזשיגאַן: און אַלץ צוליבן דריטן רײַך, זייער דריטער רײַך קומט מיר אויך אויס ווי אַ טראַמוויַ, פֿון פֿראָנט אַן אָנפֿירער, הינטער אים שטייען אַ פּאָר מענטשן און די איבעריקע זיצן.[50]
>
> [Dzigan: And everything's because of the Third Reich. I think their Third Reich looks like a tram, at the front there's a driver, behind him are a few people, and the rest are all "sitting."]

The subversive nature of these words is not limited to a metaphor depicting the German people as passive, sitting in a tram driven by the "Führer" (a play on the Yiddish word for driver, *onfirer*, and the German word for leader, *Führer*). Rather, it is also evident in the double meaning of the Yiddish verb *zitsn*, "to sit," which can also mean to serve a prison sentence. In using this word, Dzigan emphasized the enforced German passivity.

Until the signing of the non-aggression pact between Poland and Germany on January 26, 1934, the Polish authorities looked favorably upon Jewish expressions of anti-German sentiment, mainly in the press, and supported the Jewish initiative to boycott German products. However, this policy changed with the conclusion of the pact, and subsequently anti-German statements became subject to censor-

---

46 As early as 1927, a new regulation concerning newspapers increased censorship, transferring "responsibilities for banning newspapers from the judicial authority to the implementational authority and punishing editors for publishing news that could harm the state or slander the regime and its representatives." Cohen, *Sefer, sofer ye'iton*, 64. See also ibid., 67, 432–41.

47 "Every premiere was a political event," stated Dzigan in an interview with Uri Keisari, "replete with many illusions and echoes. We spoke between the lines, because the authorities were watching . . . this was the period in which Nazism was born, and Hitler had already started barking." Keisari, "Dzigan beli 'ipur." See also Levin, Interview with Shimen Dzigan (1973).

48 See for example Kipnis, "Tate, du lakhst?"

49 Austin, *Things with Words*.

50 "Aḥdut" (above, note 46)

ship.[51] This also applied to the theater, as is demonstrated by the remainder of the monologue quoted above, which was performed in 1938. Immediately following the direct criticism of the Germans, the master of ceremonies says to Dzigan:

> דזשיגאַן, איך בעט אײַך, טשעפּעט נישט אונדזערע שכנים, איבעריקנס די צענזור דערלויבט נישט. האַקט אָפּ![52]
>
> [Dzigan, I beg you, don't bother our neighbors. Apart from that, the censor doesn't allow it. Stop it!]

Another way in which Dzigan and Shumacher tackled the obstacle of censorship, winning a few days' grace and a certain degree of freedom of expression, was by raising the price of tickets for the first three shows to five times the regular price. This prevented the censors from attending the performances, and theatergoers who were able to pay these high prices could see the performance before it was subjected to the censor's pen.[53]

Dzigan and Shumacher's theater responded directly to the surrounding reality, and the censor was not able to stop the spread of their critical jokes. For each joke that was outlawed, Dzigan relates in his memoirs, Moyshe Nudelman and Y. Sh. Goldshteyn invented "another ten new jokes every morning," based on the day's news.[54] Nayman described the authorities' inability to silence the artists in an article published a few years later: "Can you submit to the censor the blinking of an eyelid or the twisting of a nose or winking or waggling three fingers or humming a tune? Indeed, all their power lay in improvisation."[55]

The power of the duo's humor, paraphrasing the title of Dzigan's autobiographical work, came to the fore not only in the performance itself but also in the dissemination of their jokes and songs via word of mouth. These jokes reached even wider audiences through the recordings made by the Polish Syrena Rekord Corporation, which also boosted the duo's popularity, although the recorded segments did not include the most critical remarks.[56]

---

51 Cohen, *Sefer, sofer ṿe'iton*, 267.

52 "Aḥdut" (above, note 46).

53 These performances were attended by members of the Polish theater establishment, writers, and politicians. Dzigan believed that the censors indeed purchased tickets and attended in secret. See Levin, Interview with Shimen Dzigan (1973). See also Dzigan, *Der koyekh*, 119–24; Nudelman, "Kleynkunst."

54 Dzigan, *Der koyekh*, 119–29. In addition to Moyshe Nudelman and Y. Sh. Goldshteyn's words in both the theater and the press, Der Tunkeler penned caustic and amusing humoresques regarding events in Germany, which were printed in *Der moment*. See, for example, Tunkeler, "Vos volt Hitler geven"; "Al khet"; "Hitler"; "Vagones"; "Umshedlekher."

55 Nayman, "Dzigan ṿeShumacher."

56 Among the skits that were included in the recordings and which were reissued in Israel by the Israeli record label Hed-Arzi were: "In Shvitsbod" (In the Mikveh); "Yidn flien in der

It is difficult to determine with any accuracy how quickly the jokes spread among the public. However, according to memoirs written by actors and others involved in the theater, they circulated with great speed. Particularly fascinating is the transfer from the institutionalized theatrical medium to oral dissemination and the link between the popularization of Dzigan and Shumacher's art and the folk humor on which it drew.[57] In an article in the Argentinean newspaper *Di prese*, the theatrical artist and musician Yankev Botoshansky discussed this process and the place of Dzigan and Shumacher in the history of the Jewish humoristic performance:

> זיי זײַנען אַ מין זאַמל־סטאַנציע פֿון ייִדישן פֿאָלקלאָר און זייער 'סטאַנציע' קאָנצענטרירט ווי אין אַ ברענגלאָז דער גאַנצער ייִדישער הומאָר בעל־פּה . . . ניט נאָר אַ סטאַנציע זײַנען דזשיגאַן־שומאַכער, נאָר אַ לאַבאָראַטאָריע. זיי קאָכן כעמיש (קינסטלעריש כעמיש) איבער דעם פֿאָלקלאָר און זיי גיבן אים באַנײַטע פֿאָרעם.[58]
>
> [They are a kind of collection station for Jewish folklore, and their "station" distills, as though through a magnifying glass, all the oral Jewish humor . . . however, Dzigan and Shumacher are not merely a station but rather a laboratory. They concoct (chemically-artistically) Jewish folklore and give it new forms.]

Dzigan recalls in his memoirs that he heard about fans who would recite the duo's skits and that impersonations of them were common on the Jewish street prior to the German invasion, and even afterwards, in the ghettos. The repetition of their jokes and impersonations of the characters portrayed by the artists on stage increased during times of crisis. An example of this can be found in George Topas's book, *The Iron Furnace: A Holocaust Survivor's Story*.[59] Topas describes a young man in the camp of Budzyń[60] who imitated Dzigan's role in Broderzon's skit "In Shvitsbod" (In the Mikveh), a recording of which was made in 1935. The prisoner impersonating Dzigan relates that while sitting at the entrance to the mikveh (ritual bath), a German with a dog walked past him, turned to him, and said: "Hey,

stratosfer" (Jews Flying in the Stratosphere)]; "Kasrilevke sreyfes" (Kasrilevke Fires); "Politsyantn in Tel-Aviv" (Police Officers in Tel Aviv); "Palestine-Birobidzhan" and "Krizhove sokhrim" (Merchants in Crisis). Many of these recordings were reissued in 2004 in three compact discs by the Israel Music company under the name "Di fule zamlung fun Dzigan un Shumacher (1935–1958)" (The Complete Collection of Dzigan and Shumacher ([1935–1958]), ICS 5128. The Warsaw based corporation Syrena Rekord was founded in 1904 by Julius Fejgenbaum and was one of the largest music companies in Europe prior to the Nazi invasion of Poland, when it closed its doors. See Tomasz Lerski, *Syrena Rekord*, 70.

57 On the role of recorded Jewish Hebrew theater, see Abeliovich, *Possessed Voices*.

58 Botoshansky, "Tsvishn yo un neyn."

59 Topas, *Iron Furnace*, 142–43.

60 Budzyń was a work and concentration camp in the Lublin district, around five kilometers from the town of Kraśnik.

Jew, you see the dog? He's your brother!" In response, the Jew answered: "If he's been circumcised, then he is indeed my brother, but if not, he's your brother!"[61] The physical sign that defined the ethnic identity of the victim "saved" him from comparison with a dog; through quick-wittedness, the relationship between aggressor and victim was inverted. The Jew now had the upper hand, and the German's words backfired. The discourse broke through the boundaries of the theater, becoming either stronger or weaker, according to the various contexts in which it was performed and the performers themselves. On stage, Dzigan and Shumacher represented Jewish stereotypes. However, thanks to the dissemination of their jokes and manner of speech, anonymous performers could become, for a moment, Dzigan and Shumacher – that is, they again became those who represented them. Thus, the subversive and therapeutic potential of the duo's humor bourgeoned and flourished.

Dzigan and Shumacher in the Cinema

As their popularity grew, it was only natural that Dzigan and Shumacher would become involved in the Yiddish film industry, which had close ties to the theater.[62] According to his autobiography, Dzigan believed that the cinema offered a unique opportunity for artistic development and publicity.[63]

In this period, which the film director Natan Gross defines as "the golden age" of Yiddish cinema in Poland (1936–1939), the duo appeared in three Yiddish-speaking movies: *Al khet* (For the Sins, 1936), directed by Aleksander Marten (Marek Tenenbaum), the first Yiddish film made in Poland (script by Y. M. Nayman, sets and design by Yankl Adler, and music by Henekh Kon);[64] *Freylekhe kaptsonim* (Jolly Paupers, 1937), directed by Leon Jeannot and Zygmunt Turkow, script

61 In the original skit, the German is sitting at the entrance to the mikveh. The first version was recorded by Syrena Rekord Company, Syrena-Electro 5409/24217. The new recording in Israel was made by Hed-Arzi, Hed-Arzi 707/667.

62 From the very first Yiddish movies, which were recordings of theatrical performances made using a stationary camera – similarly to the first films in the history of cinema – Yiddish theater actors became stars in the Yiddish cinema. Likewise, some of the first scripts were adaptations of classic Yiddish plays, such as Jacob Gordin's *Khasye di yesoyme* (Khasye the Orphan Girl), *Mirele Efros*, and *Got, mentsh un tayvl* (God, Man, and Devil), or *Der dibek* by Sh. An-sky. The theater continued to serve as an important source of inspiration for the plots of Yiddish movies until the very last movies made by this industry.

63 Dzigan, *Der koyekh*, 130–31.

64 The first movie in Yiddish, *East Side Sadie*, directed by Sidney Goldin, was not particularly successful. It was filmed in the United States in 1929, two years after the first movie with sound

by Moyshe Broderzon, adapted by Y. M. Nayman, with music by Henekh Kon; and *On a heym* (Without a Home, 1939), directed by Aleksander Marten, the last film made in Poland before World War II. Dzigan and Shumacher also appeared in the film *Undzere kinder* (Our Children, 1949), directed by Natan Gross, which was made in Poland after the war.[65]

Al khet (1936)

The movie *Al khet* is set during World War I, in the area of Galicia under German control. In the midst of reciting the confessional *'Al ḥeṭ* (Yiddish: *Al khet*) prayer on Yom Kippur, a Jewish officer serving in the German army (played by Khevel Bozgan) is informed that he must leave for the front. The officer bids farewell to his beloved, Esther (Rokhl Holzer). She is the daughter of the local rabbi (played by Avrom Morevski), who opposes the relationship between the two. Before leaving, the officer asks two of his good friends, two *batlonim* (a term describing men who spend their time at the synagogue or study house, and which also indicates lazy or idle persons) played by Dzigan and Shumacher, to look after his beloved [See Figure 6]. The officer dies in battle. Esther, who was pregnant with his child, bears him a daughter, whom she abandons before departing for America. The two *batlonim* care for the child and place her in an orphanage. Sixteen years later, following a successful career as an American singer, Esther is a rich woman, yet she is not happy. She returns to her hometown in search of her daughter, and the two *batlonim* join her quest. They discover that the daughter was adopted by a family named Levin and subsequently embark on a journey to visit all families with that name in the town. During the search, Esther falls in love with a music teacher named Levin (Kurt Katch) and suggests that he join her in America. They discover that Rachel – the musician's adopted daughter – is Esther's child. After a number of complications, mother and daughter are reunited.

The film received negative reviews. Der Tunkeler described the production as uniting excellent artists, producers, and technicians with a terrible scriptwriter.[66] In an article published two years later, Nayman explained that he had decided to write a melodrama in order to help create a real infrastructure for Jewish cinema before embarking on "sophisticated experiments." He claimed that Jewish folklore

in the history of cinema, *The Jazz Singer*, was made. See Gross, *Toldot hakolno'a*; Hoberman, *Bridge of Light*.

65 See pp. 122–135.

66 Tunkeler, "Tsvey yidishe filmen."

Figure 6: Dzigan and Shumacher in the film *Al khet* (1936) (Lydia Shumacher-Ophir collection).

and its motifs constituted an essential pillar of Jewish cinema.[67] In his weekly column in the newspaper *Haynt*, Y. Sh. Goldshteyn published a letter responding to negative reviews of the film. Dzigan and Shumacher signed this letter, although in all likelihood it was penned by Goldshteyn. Among other remarks, the letter stated: "From your reviews it is possible to write a script for a new movie entitled 'About the sin that we sinned before you' . . . one critic says that the technical quality of the movie is terrible, that you can't hear a word. Immediately after this, he claims that we tell stupid jokes. If you can't hear a word, how does he know that the jokes are stupid?" Dzigan and Shumacher laughed at themselves and at the reviews, concluding the letter by announcing that they had received a telegram inviting them to Hollywood.[68]

Freylekhe kaptsonim (1937)

The great success of the film *Yidl mitn fidl* (A Jew with a Violin), directed by Joseph Green (1936), encouraged Shaul Goskind's Kinor production company to produce

67 Nayman, "Planvirtshaft."
68 Goldshteyn, "Nokh der premyere."

its own comedy, *Freylekhe kaptsonim* (1937). Goskind, who wanted to make a movie starring Dzigan and Shumacher, asked Moyshe Broderzon to write the text, which was adapted for the big screen by Y. M. Nayman. Henekh Kon composed the music. The cameraman was Adolf Forbert – one of the best in Polish cinema. Leon Jeannot and Zygmunt Turkow directed.[69]

The plot, reminiscent of Sholem Aleichem's play *Der oytser* (The Treasure), is a comedy of errors. Naftoli the watchmaker (Shumacher) and his friend Kopl the tailor (Dzigan) struggle to make a living and dream of improving their situation. While walking on the outskirts of the shtetl, they stumble upon a puddle of oil. Seeing the puddle, they believe they have found an oil field. The two begin to imagine the great profits they will reap and decide to embark on a partnership. The audience, of course, knows that the puddle was made by a worker spilling oil from his can as he walked through the field. Upon their return home, the two reveal their plan to their wives, swearing them to secrecy. Yet, by the following day, the entire shtetl has heard the news, and great plans are being woven to establish an oil industry. The shtetl's richest Jew is willing to enter into partnership with Naftali and Kopl and offers to invest in the development of the field, while a visiting American tourist wants to win the concession to produce oil. Naftali's wife attempts to arrange a match between the American and her daughter Gitl, while her husband plans to strengthen the partnership with Kopl by marrying Gitl to his friend's son. However, Gitl has other plans. She has fallen in love with a wandering theater star visiting the shtetl. She steals the valuable plans for the oil deal and runs away with her beloved. Subsequently, an engineer arrives and measures the field, revealing that the discovery is nonsense: the field contains only rocks. Naftali and Kopl do not despair and instead plan to establish a tombstone factory.

The film offers no innovative contribution in terms of cinematic language or the depiction of the Jewish shtetl. The traditional Jewish world is molded in a stereotypical manner: the men are henpecked by their gossiping wives; the daughter of marriageable age opposes the matches proposed by her parents and runs away with an actor; the groom chosen by the parents is an idiot. The craftsmen depicted in the movie have no real chance of improving their situation. The exploitation of existing (or imagined) resources, be it oil or stone, provides an opportunity to dream about a revolutionary change in the finances of both the individual and the shtetl. Only the daughter manages to sever ties with traditional life: she leaves

---

69 Other actors in the movie included Menashe Openheim, Maks Buzik, Shmulik Goldshteyn, Zygmunt Turkow, Rut Turkow, Zina Lubitz, Lena Levin, and Simkhe Natan.

behind her family and the shtetl in order to be with her beloved, embarking on a new, modern life on the Jewish stage.

On a heym (1939)

On a heym premiered on March 7, 1939, three years after *Al khet*. This melodrama was based to some degree on a play by Jacob Gordin dating from 1907, which was adapted by Alter Katsizne and directed by Aleksander Marten. This film, the last Yiddish film made in Poland before World War II, starred Ida Kaminska, Marten himself, Adam Dom, and Dzigan and Shumacher.

On a heym tells the story of the fisherman Avrom Rivkin (Marten) and his wife, whose oldest son drowns at sea. The tragedy and the possibilities of a new life in America encourage Rivkin to leave the shtetl and search for a livelihood and a better future for his family across the ocean. Consequently, Rivkin leaves his wife, his second son, and his father, and before departing, he asks the characters played by Dzigan and Shumacher to look after his family (similarly to the role they played in *Al khet*). Rivkin finds work washing dishes in a high-class New York restaurant, and there he falls in love with Bessie, who sings Yiddish songs at the restaurant. He debates whether he should bring his family to America. The movie reflects a family crisis resulting from immigration to America and the process of secularization, a classic theme in modern Yiddish literature. Considering that the movie's creators Marten and Katsizne held left-wing political views, it is unsurprising that America is depicted in a negative light.

Bessie helps Rivkin bring his family to the new continent. However, the family reunion is unsuccessful. Rivkin's long work hours and his great love for Bessie drive a wedge between him and his family, and the new arrivals find themselves unable to acclimate to life in America. The different values, "time is money," and the romance with Bessie cause Rivkin's marriage to flounder and he yearns for the shtetl. Meanwhile, Rivkin's second son disappears, and his wife loses her mind. Finally, his son returns, and a ray of hope seems to shine as the family reunites.

The film presented a picture that was detached from the reality of Jewish life. Audiences and critics alike were disappointed by the production, which failed to tackle current issues, such as the increasing antisemitism and the Nazi threat.[70]

Dzigan and Shumacher's acting talents are evident in these films, and they bring to the fore the play on contrasts at the foundation of their partnership. However, the content of the movies was very different from the subject matter the

---

70 Gross, *Toldot haḳolnoʻa*.

duo tackled on stage. Their theater in Warsaw played a central role in confronting the social, economic, and political reality of Polish Jewry via humor and criticism, while the films were purely for entertainment, examining modern Jewish life only superficially and ignoring the pressing and urgent questions of contemporary reality. In terms of the artists' careers, these movies provide rare documentation of their acting before World War II, even if the style and content are very different from their satirical-political language in the theater. At the time, the films contributed to Dzigan and Shumacher's ever-growing popularity, acquainting wider audiences with their art.

Humor and the Satirical Embodiment of Evil

The performance theory advanced by Richard Schechner emphasizes the transformative aspect of drama – its application in the theater to embody, initiate, or confirm change. Schechner discerns three different dimensions of change in the theater: the drama (the story); the actors themselves, who, in embodying their roles, are liable to change temporarily, physically and mentally (what he calls "transportation"); and the audience, in which the change can be either temporary or permanent. One of the central roles of the theater, argues Schechner, with reference to Levi-Strauss, is to frame and control, to transform the raw into the cooked, in order to deal with the most complicated human interactions – violence, danger, sexual taboos.[71] During the Warsaw period, the theater of Dzigan and Shumacher fulfilled these subversive and transformative functions using satire and humor. This was, in Dzigan's eyes, the uniqueness of Jewish humor:

> דאָס געלעכטער, דאָס באַקאַנטע ייִדישע געלעכטער וואָס חוזקט אויס די שׂונאים און דערלאָזט נישט אַז זיי זאָלן באַהערשן די ייִדישע נשמה מיט זייער קראַפֿט און מיט זייער רישעות.[72]
>
> [The laughter, the well-known Jewish laughter, pokes fun at enemies and does not allow them to conquer the Jewish soul with their force and with their wickedness.]

Dzigan viewed laughter as a means of resistance. He returned to this idea in an interview with Dov Levin, when he claimed that both he and Shumacher attributed great importance to the effect created by laughter: it was a means enabling people to cope with the persecutions.[73]

---

71 Schechner, *Performance Theory*, 190–91.

72 Dzigan, *Der koyekh*, 118.

73 Levin, Interview with Shimen Dzigan.

In the mid-1930s, the artists began to laugh at figures who symbolized oppression of the Jews and discrimination against them or even implemented such policies. At the same time, they voiced criticism of assimilated Jews, "who go on all fours in order to be accepted into circles that reject them."[74] Jokes facilitate the criticism of persons in senior roles and authority figures: the joke is a means to oppose this authority and escape from the pressures it exerts on the individual.[75] Dzigan and Shumacher's jokes and political satire had an effect similar to that posited by Freud and Schechner: they generated an arena of dream-like resistance in which it was possible to confront the hostile political, social, and economic present.

One of the most daring ways to criticize the contemporaneous reality was to place the enemy center stage, making direct jokes at his expense and even impersonating him. For example, one of the duo's jokes – in a skit described in memoirs and press reviews; the original script has not survived – poked fun at German Field Marshal Hermann Göring (a leading figure in Hitler's regime who was among those responsible for the persecution of the Jews) and Polish Foreign Minister Józef Beck (who opposed Germany's demands to transfer the city of Gdansk and the Polish corridor to German control). The joke, which describes the two going for a walk together in the forest, was written following Göring's visit to Poland in January 1935. This trip was portrayed to the public as a hunting expedition in the forests of Białowieża, although Göring's real objective was to secure an alliance with Poland against the USSR (he failed to achieve his aim). In the skit performed by Dzigan and Shumacher, as the two are leaving the forest it suddenly becomes dark and a shot is heard. When the lights come back up, a hunter runs onto the stage, shouting to Beck: "Listen! Mr. Minister! Göring's been shot." The confused Beck answers him with a cry: "I was mistaken, I thought he was a wild boar."[76] The joke ridicules Göring twice and Beck once: Göring is shot and compared to a wild boar, while Beck foolishly divulges his guilt.

The enemy's presence was also felt in the monologue "Der nayer lamdn" (The New Scholar), by Pinchas Katz, performed in the show *Afn varshever yarid* (At the

74 Dzigan, *Der koyekh*, 119.

75 In Freud's view farce and jokes, similarly to dreams, are an expression of unconscious desires, a means to raise repressed topics to the surface. In a joke and a farce, images, actions, and associations are thickened and overturned. Freud argued that the joke "enables the psychical reliefs experienced in jokes, as they 'evade restrictions and open sources of pleasure that have become inaccessible.'" See Salisbury, *Samuel Beckett*, 165. For Freud's discussion see Freud, *Jokes*.

76 Dzigan, *Der koyekh*, 122.

Warsaw Fair), which was staged in March 1937 in the Nowości theater. This monologue is a first-person speech by the antisemitic priest and scholar Stanisław Trzeciak, played by Shumacher.[77] Trzeciak, proud of his wisdom, claims that he can use his great knowledge of the Talmud to prove that Jews are cheats, scoundrels, and traitors to the Polish nation.[78] He rapidly blurts out sections of the Talmud, and his erroneous interpretations reveal his ignorance. He ends his show with a song and, before leaving the stage, stops and assumes the classic Napoleonic stance, signifying megalomania. He points to his head and says

> מען דאַרף האָבן אַ ייִדישע קעפּעלע, ווי הייסט עס אין תּלמוד? אַהאַ! תּחת, אַ תּחת דאַרף מען האָבן.[79]

> [One must have a Jewish head. How do they say it in the Talmud? Aha! A *tukhes* (ass). You need a *tukhes* (ass).]

The cynical approach to the priest's learning and the inversion of his knowledge are acts of poetic-humoristic protest against Trzeciak's antisemitic expressions and actions. Mikhail Mikhailovich Bakhtin, highlighting the link between laughter and the artistic and historical consciousness, argues that laughter is in fact the contemplation of the world from a different viewpoint, one that interprets the world only through laughter.[80] In this monologue, reclamation of Jewish knowledge and the clear demonstration of the other's ignorance with regard to Jewish culture humiliate the enemy, if not on the practical plain then at least symbolically. This subversive act aroused strong emotional responses among the Jewish audience.

The duo's most provocative act in portraying the enemy was without doubt the staging of a skit written by Broderzon in which Moyshe Pulaver played Adolf Hitler, as described by Pulaver in his book *Geven iz a geto* (There Was a Ghetto). Hitler, a painter, stands on stage with a bucket in his hand and a ladder on his back – an ironic allusion to his failed attempt to become an artist. Using hand gestures, he demonstrates his intention to paint any area that he can reach. Pulaver related that when he entered the stage "there were raucous whistles from

---

77 Trzeciak was a vitriolic antisemite who penned religious and antisemitic works. In 1936, his well-known book about Jewish conspiracies was published in Polish. See Modras, "The Catholic Church and Antisemitism."

78 Concerning the skit, see Grafman, "Beys der hafsoke"; Mayzel, "Afn varshever yarid"; Kipnis, "Afn varshever yarid." The reconstruction of the monologue herein is based on memoirs and reviews of the show.

79 Dzigan, *Der koyekh*, 121. See also Nudelman, "Kleynkunst."

80 Bakhtin, *Rabelais*, 66, 72–73.

the crowd and wild laughter."[81] Pulaver-Hitler places the ladder to one side, opens his mouth, and barks. The audience reacted with excitement:

> דער שטורעם אין טעאַטער איז געוואָרן מעכטיקער. דער עולם האָט געהאַט אַ גרויסע הנאה פֿון אויספֿײַפֿן, אויסזידלען דעם גרעסטן רשע היטלער, וועמען זיי קאָנען זען פּנים־אל־פּנים, כאָטש דורך דער מאַסקע פֿון אַן אַקטיאָר.[82]
>
> [The frenzy in the theater intensified. The crowd greatly enjoyed mocking and condemning Hitler, the greatest criminal, who they can see face to face, albeit through the mask of an actor.]

This offered the audience a great sense of release, Pulaver recalls. After the performances in Łódź, the troupe staged the show in Warsaw. However, in the capital city Pulaver's Hitler was not a painter but rather the Führer himself. "I went on stage barking like a dog, and I shouted out '*Lebenrsaum*' and barked again."[83]

Depicting Hitler as a dog, devoid of language and humanity, was not only a subversive act but also inverted the classic antisemitic motif comparing the Jew to a dog, a reversal that Dzigan and Shumacher had previously employed in the skit "In shvitsbod."[84] This constituted collective revenge, exacted between the walls of the theater, in a carnival at which everything was possible. The theater of Dzigan and Shumacher created an arena of rhetorical and critical opposition, in which change was possible on stage or in the audience's imagination.

---

81 Pulaver, *Geven iz a geto*, 62. The depiction here is based solely on Pulaver's memoir. This skit was apparently staged in the show *Tate, du lakhst!* in Łódź in 1939. It was also part of the last performance given by Dzigan and Shumacher before the war, *Nadir un veyn nisht!* (Take This and Don't Cry!), staged in Warsaw in April 1939.

82 Ibid., 62.

83 'איך בין אַרויס אויף דער בינע געבילט ווי אַ הונט און געשריִען "לעבנסראַום" און ווידער געבילט'
At the same time, a well-known Polish actor, Ludwik Sempoliński, performed one of his famous parodies of Hitler in the Ali Baba Theater in Warsaw in the show "Panopticum." Alongside Sempoliński as Hitler were Wojciech Ruszkowski as Mussolini and Mieczysław Fogg as Chamberlain. In the parody, Sempoliński sang a new version of the popular song "Je cherche après Titine" by Louis Mauban and Marcel Bertal, the melody for which was composed by Leo Daniderff. This was the song that Charlie Chaplin sang in gibberish in the movie *Modern Times* in 1936. Sempoliński sang an adaptation of the song, "Waşik, ach ten waşik" (Moustache, What a Moustache!), while trying to determine which of the two, Chaplin or Hitler, is funnier and which of them had offered a greater contribution to the world. The Gestapo searched for Sempoliński, without success. Pulaver and Sempoliński preceded Chaplin, who played Hitler two years later in his famous movie *The Great Dictator* (1940).

84 On the antisemitic image of the Jew as a dog, see Stow, *Jewish Dogs*.

The Depiction of Jewish Life in Poland

ס'איז שוין בײַ אונדז געוואָרן, ברוך־השם, אַזאַ מינהג, אַז עס קומט די צײַט, וואָס מען הייבט אָן רעדן פֿון פּאָגראָמען, הייבן ייִדן אָן צו לויפֿן פֿון איין שטאָט אין דער אַנדערער, ווי אין פּסוק שטייט: ויסעו ויחנו, ויחנו ויסעו – איז דער טײַטש: פֿאָר דו צו מיר, וועל איך פֿאָרן צו דיר.

[It has become a custom among us, blessed be His name, that when there is a rumor of a pogrom, Jews run from one city to another, as it says in the verse: *And they journeyed and they encamped and they encamped and they journeyed* – which means: you come to me, and I'll go to you.

– Sholem Aleichem, "Tevye the Dairyman"

Prior to the German invasion, Dzigan and Shumacher had no reason to leave Poland – they were popular, and they enjoyed a good income and a respected social status.[85] However, on stage the duo raised questions about emigration, wandering, and flight. These central topics in the general Jewish discourse became particularly relevant due to the economic crisis, the political situation, intensifying antisemitism, and the physical threats that the Jews in Poland faced.[86]

In the second half of the 1930s, as Dzigan and Shumacher performed before audiences of Jews who found themselves "unable to leave," emigration became a central issue in their theater.[87] Throughout that decade, the duo proposed a range of practical, immediate, or absurd solutions to the problem of Jewish existence in Poland , including "laughing cures" of various kinds,[88] Hasidic dances by Breslov Hasidim in order to dispel despair,[89] immigration to Palestine, to Birobidzhan, or the stratosphere, or even dispensing completely with humanity.

In the monologue "A shmues mitn kind" (Conversation with a Child), by Moyshe Nudelman, a father pushes a baby in a baby-carriage, all the while

85 The two artists decided to flee occupied Poland only after discovering that their names appeared on a Gestapo blacklist. Prior to this, they considered accepting invitations to embark on a tour of performances in Europe and in Mandatory Palestine, which would increase their popularity outside Poland's borders. See Goldshteyn, "Dzigan un Shumacher."

86 Cohen notes that many authors and journalists discussed the question of emigration on both the ideological and practical levels. Cohen also highlights the high percentage of Jews among the emigrants leaving Warsaw in the years 1927–1938: in the years 1931–1935, Jews constituted 92.8 percent of emigrants, while in 1935 they accounted for only fifty-seven percent. See Cohen, *Sefer, sofer ve'iton*, 254–55.

87 Dzigan, *Der koyekh*, 118.

88 In the skits "Undzer opteyk" (Our Pharmacy) and "Politik hintern oyvn" (Politics behind the Oven). See Fertreter, "Nadir un veyn nisht!" The critic, who signed with the penname "A fertreter," which means "a representative," describes these skits, the audience's need to laugh, and how the artists helped the theatergoers face the impossible reality.

89 In the skit "Politik hintern oyvn," ibid.

describing to his child, with humor and pragmatism, the dangers hovering over the Jews in Poland and their difficult situation. He also portrays violent incidents, such as publicly shaving off Jews' beards and antisemitic attacks perpetrated by student members of the ND (National Democracy) Party[90] in the city's streets and squares. The father endeavors to project a feeling of security for the sake of his baby. However, when he finishes speaking, the audience discovers that the carriage is wrapped with barbed wire to protect the baby from ND party members bearing sticks and stones. Using exaggeration and absurdity, the scene emphasizes the disparity between confidence and hope in the father's words on the one hand and feelings of terror that reigned among Jews on the other.[91]

In independent Poland, numerous Jewish parties and movements advocated a range of political and ideological tendencies. The left-wing parties – the Communist Party, the Bund, and Po'alei Zion Left (of which Dzigan and Shumacher were members in their youth) – envisioned a future for the Jews in Poland, with the Polish socialists as their allies, and regarded modern Yiddish culture as the embodiment of the new Jewish national experience. In contrast, the Zionist parties focused on physically and spiritually preparing Jews, mainly the youth, to realize the Zionist dream in Palestine. Although the Orthodox Party, Agudes (Agudat) Israel, opposed secular Zionism, its members did not oppose settlement in Palestine. The tactics adopted by the various parties aroused disagreements within the Jewish public, and the political leaders were unable to bridge the gaps between their parties or suggest practical solutions for the existential problems facing the Jews. The parties were a target for Dzigan and Shumacher's satirical criticism, as we find in the song "Shumacherishe kupletn" (Shumacher's Couplets), of which a handwritten copy from prewar Poland has survived.[92]

Likewise, the skit "Suke-politik" (Sukkah Politics), as depicted in memoirs and the press, targeted the Jewish political parties. Two Jews, political opponents,

90 The Narodowa Demokracja Party (ND) was established in the mid-nineteenth century, during the period of Poland's partition (1795–1918), and it collapsed at the end of the Second Republic (1939). Its original goal was to advance the battle for Polish sovereignty against the Imperialist powers, although it subsequently became a right wing, nationalist, and antisemitic party.

91 The text of the monologue itself has not survived. It is described in memoirs and contemporary reviews. Several years later, in Israel, Shumacher performed a monologue entitled "Oy, dokter nebekh" (Oy, Poor Doctor), written by Yoysef Heyblum, in which he also played the part of a father pushing a child in a carriage. The central themes in the new version were the child's future profession and livelihood and the difficulties that the father, a doctor, encountered in trying to make a living.

92 See below, p. 117.

Figure 7: Dzigan and Shumacher with other unidentified actors in a performance at a Warsaw theater prior to the outbreak of World War II (Lydia Shumacher-Ophir collection).

sit in the sukkah eating a festive meal. As they eat, they discuss the global crisis, the question of a Jewish state, and the possibility of emigration. The sukkah symbolizes the liminal state of the Jews on their journey from slavery in Egypt and freedom in the Promised Land. The discussion in the sukkah is closely linked to both the festival and central themes in the concurrent political climate. The ideological argument exposes the ineffectiveness of the Jewish political parties, and this causes – at least on the symbolic plain – the roof of the sukkah to cave in on the two men, symbolizing the Jewish political parties' collapse.[93]

93 Nudelman, "Kleynkunst." On the crisis in the Jewish political leadership in Poland, see, for example, Melzer, *Ma'avaḳ medini bemalkodet*, 299–303, 352–60. It is interesting to note in this respect a caricature signed with the initials Sh. G., which was published in 1921 in the book *Di royte fon* (The Red Flag), edited by Der Tunkeler. This caricature depicts the leaders of the Jewish political parties sitting in a sukkah, holding the party newspapers, and arguing with one another. A pig wearing a ribbon emblazoned with the words *Konter-revolutsye*, "Counterrevolution," leans on the shaky poles holding up the sukkah, causing it to collapse. See Tunkeler, *Di royte fon*.

The Question of Emigration

ניטאָ קיין היים, ניטאָ קיין הויז, / ניטאָ, ניטאָ, / ניטאָ דערווײַל.

[No home, no house, / nothing, nothing, / nothing in the meantime.]
– From the skit "Marsh" by Moyshe Broderzon

The 1934 program *Zmires mit lokshn* (Sabbath Hymns with Noodles) included a skit that focused on the question of emigration rather than finding solutions for survival or self-defense: "Di koymen-kerers" (The Chimneysweeps), written by Y. Sh. Goldshteyn (signed "Shteyngold"), in which Dzigan and Shumacher play chimneysweeps sitting on a Warsaw roof. One of them (Shumacher) is learning the trade of chimneysweep before leaving for Palestine, while his friend wants to go to Birobidzhan. This skit, which is also known by the name "Palestine-Birobidzhan" (the title it was given on the recording made in Poland),[94] was praised by reviewers, who were impressed by its content, relevance, and the quality of the performance.[95]

The skit poses questions about the possibility of a national and territorial solution, presenting two major ideological streams then popular among Polish Jewry:[96] the Zionists advocated immigration to Palestine, while those faithful to Stalin proposed settlement in Birobidzhan.[97] In 1928, it was decided that part of Birobidzhan would be allocated for pro-Soviet Jewish settlement, and Jewish Communists all around the globe supported this solution to the Jewish national question; some of them even subsequently immigrated to Birobidzhan.[98]

The skit is set in a space between heaven and earth, an appropriate place to contemplate dreams. The dialogue confronts the tension between the hope of finding a better home and the impossibility of leaving Poland. Each charac-

94 A skit with an identical name was written by Moyshe Broderzon and performed by Shimen Dzigan and Sheyne-Miriam in Ararat's show *Tshakedik un knakedik* (Spectacular and Festive) (1930). These skits were recorded in Poland and distributed for the first time on records produced by the Syrena Rekord Company and again in Israel by the Hed-Arzi music label. The skit was around three minutes in length, and thus was recorded on one side of a shellac. The discussion below concerns the full-length version performed on stage.

95 See Grafman, "Zmires mit lokshn." Chimneysweeps are a classic motif in folk literature and in the cinema. For another discussion of this skit, see Vedenyapin, *Doctors Prescribe Laughter*.

96 Concerning discussions of the topic in the contemporaneous Jewish press, see, for example, Neyr, "In gevirbl"; Katsizne, "Milkhike gevisns"; Khrabolovsky, "Palestine, Birobidzhan."

97 Prior to the Birobidzhan program, Jewish agricultural settlements were established in the Ukraine, Crimea, Belorussia, and other places. See Levavi, *Hahityashvut*, 40.

98 See for example Levavi, *Hahityashvut*; Kagedan, *Soviet Zion*; Weinberg, *Stalin's Forgotten Zion*.

ter proposes a different destination, questioning the solution advocated by the other: Zion or the Soviet Zion. The chimneysweep who dreams of Birobidzhan relates that he received a letter from his son, already living in the autonomous Jewish region, according to which Birobidzhan is the land described in Jewish tradition as "a desirable, good, and spacious land." These words, which are part of the grace after meals, relocates the biblical Jewish narrative, situating it in the Soviet Union: if Birobidzhan is indeed the Soviet Zion, it is a desirable, good, and spacious land. The Zionist highlights the ostensible "mistake" in this interpretation. He corrects the error, explaining to his friend and political opponent that these words refer to Mandatory Palestine: a "desirable, good, and spacious land, *shteyt es for bay Erets-Yisroel* (meaning the Land of Israel)." The Communist rejoins with a play on the word *shteyt*, which can signify either "meaning" or "standing": Azoy... bay Erets-Yisroel shteyt der Englender (So... the English are standing in Mandatory Palestine). The Zionist becomes confused and argues that Birobidzhan is inhabited by the Japanese, "there in Manchuria" (an area bordering Birobidzhan), and the play on words continues: "Mayn zhsuria, dayn zshuria (mayn, pronounced "man" in Polish Yiddish: my churia, your churia)." Indeed, one of the reasons that Stalin encouraged Jewish settlement in Birobidzhan was to prevent the settlement of the Japanese in Manchuria.[99]

As the dialogue continues, the argument intensifies. Each character expresses his opinion about the other's destination, claiming that the respective political and economic conditions preclude any possibility of immigration. The skit reflects disappointment at Jewish life in Poland and at the same time voices doubts regarding the two solutions suggested. The skepticism regarding Birobidzhan is evident in the last song, in which the Communist proclaims his naive hope that Stalin himself will come to his grandson's circumcision ceremony in Birobidzhan – cynically disparaging the naïve Jews who believed Stalin's false promises and grasped at the glimmer of hope he offered. Yet, due to the Arab threat, the British rule in Palestine, and the dire economic situation, the Zionist solution too seems doubtful.

However, the skit continues. The conclusion of the dialogue is followed by the screening of a film illustrating the two characters' dreams: their journey and their later employment, one in Tel Aviv and one in Birobidzhan. Based on the reviews of the show in the press, it is difficult to determine whether the audience understood this film as a cinematic expression of the characters' dreams or "a documentation" of their realization.

---

99 See also Vedenyapin, *Doctors Prescribe Laughter*, 28–29.

The skit does not propose a real solution for emigration but rather expresses the Jews' inability to leave their homes and prevent the approaching tragedy. This situation was also depicted in Yiddish literature, for example in the works of Sholem Aleichem. In his story "Di groyse beheyle fun di kleyne mentshelekh" (The Great Panic of the Little People)], the residents of Kasrilevke flee to the town of Kozodoyevke during a pogrom, while the residents of Kozodoyevke escape to Kasrilevke.

Immediately after the skit "Suke-politik," which, as was mentioned above, concerned the failure of the political parties to find a solution for the Jews, Dzigan and Shumacher performed the skit "Yidn flien in der stratosfer" (Jews Flying in the Stratosphere) by Y. Sh. Goldshteyn. In this skit, they appeared as two simple Jews searching for a way to escape the world. Their quest leads them to construct a "Jewish" hot air balloon (with a mezuzah) and take flight in it, consequently becoming true *luftmentshn* (air-people). They declare their intention to travel to the stratosphere, the only place where Jews can find "a little peace."[100]

Thus, the theater of Dzigan and Shumacher expressed the desire to emigrate, a longing shared by many Jews, and also enabled the symbolic enaction of the emigration on stage. In the skit "Politsyantn in Tel-Aviv" (Police Officers in Tel Aviv), by Y. Sh. Goldshteyn, which was performed in 1935 and a recording of which has survived, two Jewish, Yiddish-speaking policemen from Poland wander around the Hebrew city of Tel Aviv. The city is depicted as an exotic place: the skit opens with Oriental music, alluding to the oriental character of Mandatory Palestine. One of the policemen relates how a young man courted his beloved by reciting the Song of Songs in Hebrew. Courting in Hebrew was only possible using the biblical tongue, because the newly revived language lacked words to articulate modern day conceptions of love.[101] The irony concerns not only language but also the return to Jewish sources: in this mythical Zionist reality, a young man is afraid to swim in the sea, fearing that he will encounter the Leviathan.[102] In Dzigan and Shumacher's Tel Aviv, the new Hebrew does not experience the change that Herzl envisioned for those arriving in Altneuland: the transfer from dark cellars to the sun, from the poor shtetl to nature and wealth.[103] Rather, the sabra as portrayed

100 Nudelman, "Kleynkunst." This skit was recorded in Poland and distributed by the Syrena Rekord Company and again in Israel by Hed-Arzi. For a discussion of the image of the *luftmentsh* and the motif of wandering see below, pp....

101 See also the analysis by Vedenyapin, *Doctors Prescribe Laughter*, 30.

102 Mentions of the Leviathan in the Bible include, for example, Isaiah 27:1; Psalm 74:14. It is discussed in Midrash Tanḥuma, parshat Nitsavim, paragraph 4; Tanḥuma, parshat Sheminit, paragraph 7, and other places.

103 On Herzl and the Zionist body, see Gluzman, *Haguf hatsioni*, 21.

by Dzigan and Shumacher is a naïve and romantic coward, and the Zionist dream is a myth.[104] The policemen are frustrated: while walking down Rothschild Boulevard, one of them states that he would like to switch places with Rothschild himself, who is in Paris, while his friend expresses a desire to leave for Germany.

One of the skits that challenged both the Jewish and Polish imagination was "Der letster yid in Poyln" (The Last Jew in Poland), which was performed in 1938 in the show *Tate, du lakhst!* (Father, You're Laughing!). The skit visualizes Warsaw in 1939, after Poland has been made *Judenrein*. Having forcibly expelled the Jews from Poland, the Poles discover that their country can no longer function: trade collapses, the economy and cultural life come to a standstill, the antisemitic students have no one to attack, and Café Ziemiańska (Mała Ziemiańska), a café frequented by Jews, has been replaced by a cemetery. The only hope for the country is the one last Jew still in its borders, a Jew who had not met the deadline for departure. A government delegation is dispatched, begging him to stay. To persuade him, the students organize a meal in his honor and play Yiddish music. The Jew promises to remain on one condition: that they will make him traditional Jewish foods, such as gefilte fish and cholent. The Polish radio rallies in the efforts to find someone able to prepare these dishes. Finally, the government decorates this Jew with the Order of "Polonia Restituta." He takes the medal, places it on his lower back, and, when he turns around, the audience discovers that he is already wearing a golden service cross awarded to him by the Polish government. The spotlight focuses on the medals, and the Poles sing to the Jews the well-known Polish birthday song, *Sto lat*, "Until one hundred and twenty."

The skit shifts between an apocalyptic scene depicting the expulsion of the Jews from Poland and the utopian desire that they should remain – rather than chasing the Jews in order to expel them, the Poles are pursuing them to keep them in the country. However, this is not because they are loved, valued, or because their contribution to the nation is recognized, but rather because the Poles are unable to ensure their own comfortable existence without Jews.[105] The skit was so

---

104 According to tradition, the Leviathan is served as a dish to the righteous in the Garden of Eden. Thus, Dzigan and Shumacher present Israel as a modern Eden. See Vedenyapin, *Doctors Prescribe Laughter*, 30.

105 The skit is apparently inspired by an Austrian avant-garde film *Die Stadt ohne Juden* (A City without Jews, 1924), directed by Hans Karl Breslauer, which itself was based on a book of the same name by Hugo Betauer. The book describes how a fascist party rises to power in Austria. The new chancellor, a declared antisemite, deports all the Jews from Vienna, with dire ramifications for the cultural, culinary, and economic life of the city. The solution is the return of the Jews. At the end of the film, it is revealed that the entire episode in fact took place in the chancellor's nightmare.

caustic that Dzigan and Shumacher were forced to remove it from the show after only five performances in order to avoid arrest.[106]

Between Private and Public

One of the few reported instances in which Dzigan and Shumacher confronted antisemitism outside the theater occurred in 1936. While the two were busy filming the movie *Al khet*, Antonti Słonimski published an antisemitic article in his weekly column for the Polish paper *Wiadomości Literackie*.[107] The filming of the movie took place in a studio located adjacent to the expensive and luxurious IPS café,[108] a meeting place of Warsaw's intelligentsia. Dzigan relates:

> During lunch break, we talked excitedly about Słonimski's article: Moyshe Broderzon, the writer Y. M. Nayman, the artist Yenkele [Yankl] Adler, Shumacher, and I. Both of us were made up for the movie: beard and skull cap, kaftan, in the best of Jewish tradition. Yenkele Adler suddenly said: "I'll give you a bottle of champagne if you'll go, dressed like that, with kaftan, beard, and side curls, to 'IPS' and order something!" Everyone burst out laughing . . . Shumacher looked at me, we got up, and we went out into the street. I went in first. I crossed the threshold – around me, everyone fell silent. The goyim [non-Jews] looked at me with wonder, and the Jewish intellectuals Jews who were sitting in the café bowed their heads in shame. One of the waiters approached me and said, "This is no place for you." I turned to the manager of the café: "Sir, why is the waiter saying that this is no place for me?" The manager was a sharp-witted non-Jew, and he replied, "Because here everything is non-kosher." "No problem," I said, "I'll just have tea." At that moment, Shumacher appeared at the door, an innocent look on his face and a skull cap on his head. "Oy!" the waiter blurted, "It's an invasion!" I took the opportunity provided by the confusion to sit down at a table. With sure steps, Shumacher approached me, greeted me, and sat down. We began speaking loudly in Yiddish, all the while talking with our hands.[109]

This deliberate appearance in a place that did not welcome Jews, while dressed in traditional Jewish garb, constituted an artistic intervention in the "other's" symbolic space, as part of an attempt to challenge the deep-seated prejudice

---

106 The description of the skit herein is based on Dzigan's memoirs, which contain the only surviving portrayal of it. However, due to the great deal of discussion it evoked, this became one of the duo's most frequently mentioned skits. See Dzigan, *Der koyekh*, 121.

107 The article to which Dzigan refers is Słonimski, "Kronika Tygodniowa." Concerning Słonimski, an author and publicist who was active among liberal circles, and regarding *Wiadomości Literackie*, see Opalski, "Polemics on the Jewish Question."

108 An acronym of the Instytut Propagandy Sztuki, the institute for the dissemination of art, in which the café was located.

109 Bashan, "Dzigan." For a Yiddish version of this story, see Dzigan, *Der koyekh*, 133–34.

against Jews. Using their performative presence to underscore the Polish intelligentsia's discriminatory feelings and practices vis-à-vis the Jewish minority, Dzigan and Shumacher sought to provoke a reaction. The artists' bravery in stepping forward to challenge the reality testifies to the subversive nature of their activities: they struggled to achieve freedom of expression and equal rights not only on stage, in their home environment, among a supportive Jewish audience, but also in a contested arena, face to face with non-Jewish Polish citizens and assimilated Jews.

Last Chance

The termination of the non-aggression pact between Poland and Germany in 1939 enabled criticism of the Germans, although strict censorship continued, and the situation of the Jews did not improve. The last shows that Dzigan and Shumacher staged in Poland were replete with acute political satire aimed at the Nazis and Hitler, such as the skit in which Pulaver played Adolf Hitler.[110] On May 30, 1939, they staged the show *Nadir un veyn nisht!* (Take This and Don't Cry!) in the Scala Theater in Warsaw, in which they were joined by Yoysef Kamen, an actor who had previously performed in the Vilner trupe. This was to be their last performance before the outbreak of the war in Poland.[111] The theater critic and publicist Jakub Appenszlak wrote in *Nasz Przegląd*, a Polish-language Zionist, Jewish newspaper, that in this show, "Jewish humor reached a peak" and all the original qualities of Jewish folklore were brought to the fore in the most beautiful manner. According to his report, the shows were full, with no empty seats in the house.[112]

In this program, the duo conveyed a different attitude to emigration: the discussion of this topic no longer concerned the preference for one ideology or another but rather emphasized the despondency felt by Polish Jews with regard to their future as equal citizens in Poland. In one of the skits, Shumacher talks about the difficulties and challenges faced by the Jews and his character announces his intention to leave the country. He then bids farewell to every character he

---

110 Dzigan, *Der koyekh*, 138. Concerning the responses of Jewish journalists and authors to contemporaneous developments, see Cohen, *Sefer, sofer ṿe'iton*, 286–87.

111 In January 1939, Dzigan and Shumacher premiered (alone on the stage) a show entitled *A sho tsum lakhn* (Time to Laugh), which included texts by Moyshe Nudelman and Y. Sh. Goldshteyn. It was staged in the Nowości theater.

112 Appenszlak, "Nadir un Wejn Niszt."

encounters on stage, even the fly he catches in the air. In his parting words to the fly, he declares:

> זײַ געזונט, פֿליג! איך פֿאָר אַוועק און לאָז דיך איבער. גלייב מיר, פֿליג, איך בין דיך מקנא. דו קענסט פֿרײַ פֿליִען וווּהין דו ווילסט און ווען דו ווילסט. דו ווייסט ניט פֿון קיין עמיגראַציע־שוועריקייטן, פֿון קיין פּאַס, פֿון קיין וויזע, פֿון קיין אַפֿידייוויט. גלייב מיר, פֿליג, איך בין שוואַכער פֿון דיר...[113]
>
> [Goodbye, fly! I'm going away and leaving you here. Believe me, fly, I envy you. You can go freely wherever you wish, whenever you wish. You don't know anything about the difficulties of emigration, about passports, about visas, about affidavits. Believe me, fly, I am weaker than you...]

Later in the skit, Kamen appears on stage, stating that he wants to transform himself into a rooster. Subsequently, Reb Shimen (Dzigan) and Reb Yisroel (Shumacher) enter, dressed as bears, wearing realistic costumes.[114] The two explain why they are wearing such costumes: if the Jews in Poland cannot live like people, they must protect themselves by wearing the skins of animals – perhaps this will help them ensure a more secure future, perhaps it is a recipe for survival.[115] The image of the man-bear was a central image in European folklore in the Middle Ages and at carnivals – people wearing bear masks danced while bound in chains. Unlike the image of the bear bound in chains, which signifies man's control of the beast, Dzigan and Shumacher proposed a vision that embodies man's control over his fellow man and the transformation of man into an animal. This represents the ostensible freedom of which Jews, as humans, are deprived, and it eventually creates an image of control, of freedom that has been restricted.

Many of the jokes in the skits from this period depict the Jews' enemies as animals (Hitler, Göring, the antisemitic German walking with a dog). However, this last skit turned the tables. Dzigan and Shumacher presented for the first time a scene of surrender or helplessness in the face of the hostile reality, or, in the best case, they adopted the enemy's discourse (the Jew as an animal) as a last chance for personal survival. In this skit, the Jews try to survive by becoming animals. It reflects – as no other skit by the duo did – the feeling that the forces at work in this period were not satisfied with power over life and death, with the

---

113 Nudelman, "Kleynkunst." The skit has not survived. It is mentioned in memoirs and press reviews.

114 Some versions note that only Dzigan appeared as a bear. It is not clear whether the description refers to the same scene. Appenszlak describes a skit in which Dzigan and Shumacher played two Hasidim in Zakopane who make a living by impersonating white bears and charging tourists to have their photograph taken with them. See Appenszlak, "Nadir un Wejn Niszt."

115 See Nudelman, "Kleynkunst." See also Fertreter, "Nadir un veyn nisht!"

ability to kill, but also sought to control people's very lives, a time that Foucault described as the "biopolitical" age.[116]

The skit unfurls before the eyes of the audience the tragic future: both options, leaving or remaining, are no longer relevant. Even the stratosphere, a utopian destination in one of the duo's earlier skits, is now inaccessible. The hope that there will be a call for the last Jew to remain is also in the realm of the utopian; even its artistic expression is outlawed by the authorities. The change of identity, the transformation into an animal, abandoning the cultural world in favor of wild nature, this is ironically the only human solution remaining to the Jews in Poland in 1939: "No longer either *to make die* or to *make live*, but *to make survive*. The decisive activity of biopower in our time consists in the production not of life or death, but rather of a mutable and virtually infinite survival" (emphasis in original).[117]

Giorgio Agamben discusses the processes in political history that excluded certain entities from the law. He describes these entities as *Homo sacer*, similar to the status that Roman law accorded to the sacred: a certain body, sanctified, is liable to become a victim without any legal implications. The public life of the *Homo sacer* is a biological life without legal rights. This is the new status of the Jews, and Dzigan and Shumacher presented it on stage.

If the process of destruction begins by negating the possibility that man can be a citizen,[118] arguably, the presentation of the Jew as a bear or a rooster, or as someone whose status is lower than that of a fly, is an artistic and satirical depiction of the Jews in Poland that heralded the destruction of the Jews or, more precisely, signaled a process of dehumanization that was already underway. The theater of Dzigan and Shumacher realized the desire to imagine a different social order by creating a parallel artistic reality that interpreted, criticized, or corrected the surrounding reality or, alternatively, ridiculed it. The duo's theatrical activities can be viewed as a suggestion for changing or correcting the political, economic, and social reality and as a struggle against the dehumanization of the individual.

Humor and Guilt

In his discussion of the complex manner in which Jewish journalists and authors responded to the Nuremberg Laws in 1935,[119] Nathan Cohen notes that some Jewish

116 Agamben, *Homo Sacer*, 4.
117 Ibid., 155.
118 Schmitt, *Political Theology*.
119 Cohen, *Sefer, sofer ve'iton*, 268–69.

writers tried to minimize the importance of these laws. Others reacted to Hitler's show of force with irony, while a few emphasized the threat they represented to the Jews of Poland and Germany alike. Cohen also depicts the reactions of Jewish authors and journalists to the events of Kristallnacht (November 9–10, 1938), highlighting that Jewish journalists in Poland criticized the verbal protests with which the world seem satisfied and demanded instead an active response.[120] Yet Zionist journalists were more concerned with developments in Palestine, and Yiddish writers for the most part avoided discussing events in Germany. Uri Zvi Greenberg, in an article published in *Der moment* in May 1939, ridiculed "our clean-shaven writers and politicians (Zionist and socialist) who sit in cafes and in newspaper editorial offices and ignore [the attempts to underscore] the danger as rude and 'ridiculous.'" According to Greenberg, the Jews of Poland had convinced themselves that the Nazi regime would not endure for long. However, he believed that "pacifist chatter and Bundist feuilletons" were no longer sufficient: rather, hatred of the Germans was to be expressed using all possible means.[121]

The theater of Dzigan and Shumacher responded immediately by criticizing the Jewish reality – political, social, and economic. Despite this, Dzigan later wondered:

> ווי אַזוי איז דאָס מעגלעך געווען? זענען מיר געווען בלינד, טויב און טעמפּ צו די דראָענדיקע צייכנס פֿון דער צײַט? איך האָב אויף דעם נישט קיין ענטפֿער.[122]
>
> [How was this possible? Were we blind, deaf, and dumb to the threatening signs of the time? I have no answer to that.]

In his memoirs, Dzigan explained the theater's activities and its focus on humor as life's final gesture in opposition to death, at a time when the verdict was already sealed:

> מיר האָבן מיט אַ שוימיקער, ברויזנדיקער פֿרייד געוואָלט פֿאַרטרײַבן דעם נאָגנדיקן טרויער, די אימה און דעם פּחד וואָס האָבן טיף אין אונדז גענעסטיקט און אונדז געמאַטערט. מיר זענען געווען ווי אַ שיף וואָס זינקט צום אָפּגרונט און וואָס טיפֿער זי זינקט אין די וואַסערן פֿון אומקום, אַלץ העכער און לוסטיקער שפּילט איר אָרקעסטער.[123]
>
> [Using a vigorous, strong gaiety, we wanted to drive away the gnawing sadness, the terror and the fear that had taken root deep inside us and exhausted us. We were like a ship sinking in the depths, and the deeper it sinks in the waters of [destruction], so its orchestra plays louder and more vigorously.]

---

120 Ibid., 275–76.

121 Greenberg, "Amalek"; Greenberg, "Tsu tsar." A Hebrew translation can be found in Cohen, *Sefer, sofer ve'iton*, 278–79.

122 Dzigan, *Der koyekh*, 124.

123 Ibid.

This tragic image, which clearly describes the sinking ship of the duo's theater (and seemingly alludes to the sinking of the Titanic in 1912, during which the ship's orchestra continued to play in an effort to calm the passengers), also rhetorically concluded a process that began with a more optimistic maritime motive in Ararat's anthem – young Jewish artists, without a boat, swimming with all their strength to Mount Ararat in their quest for rebirth. In 1939, after these young people had reached Ararat and been reborn as artists, they continued to perform and make the Jews of Poland laugh, even in their last days, as the art, the mountain, the artists, and their audience began to drown together.

A Discourse of Opposition

In a staged reality in which Göring was a wild boar, the priest Trzeciak was an ignorant fool, Hitler was a dog, an uncircumcised dog was a German antisemite, and the last Jew in Poland was a lifesaver for Polish Jewry, the satire of Dzigan and Shumacher enabled the artists and audience to take collective – ceremonial and symbolic – revenge on the oppressing power. This non-violent vengeance was realized by presenting the opposition "at home" (apart from the incident at the IPS café).

Subordinate groups can take action in various ways and in a range of spheres to express or challenge the relationship between oppressor and oppressed (jokes, gossip, folk tales, incitement, pretense). These can potentially serve the subordinate as tools in their class, ideological, and psychological struggle against the dominant group.[124] "The imaginary lives" of oppressed groups are not an abstract exercise. They negate the existing order, envisaging an alternative order that can act as an ideological basis for rebellion.[125]

The duo's performances contributed to creating a discourse of opposition in the face of the oppressive reality, not only in the theater but also outside it, when people repeated the jokes, songs, and skits that they had heard in the theater. The political satires of Dzigan and Shumacher (and their repetition or recreation by the audience) transformed feelings of helplessness and passivity into poetic or creative rebellion, reinforcing the Jewish self-image, which was attacked and undermined by the Polish antisemitic discourse. On stage, they annulled the existing order and imagined a different one. "Lacking other options, we created

124 Scott, *Domination*, 79.
125 Ibid., 80–81.

illusions and lived with them," claimed Dzigan in his memoirs.[126] The potential for rebellion, for a utopian revolution, remained in the realm of the possible for the creators of the theater and its spectators, in the critical discourse in the press, and among those who duplicated and disseminated the duo's subversive works off stage. Theater does not lead directly to social change, claims John McGrath. It can only increase the social pressure for change and help people to develop revolutionary thinking. More than any other medium, theater can provide a space in which an audience finds its voice and becomes conscious of solidarity.[127]

The targets of Dzigan and Shumacher's criticism – the antisemitic Polish government and the German authorities – saw the duo's theater as a threat. This is apparent not only from comments made by the actors but was also evidenced by the regime's political persecution of them, its censorship of their works, the inclusion of their names in a Gestapo black list, and their arrest in the Soviet Union following a political satire that critiqued antisemitism in prewar Poland.

Dzigan claimed that their theater sought to lift the Jews' spirits, to prevent the Jewish essence from being broken beyond repair, and to battle for the Jews' rights as citizens of the Polish nation at a time when emigration was not possible.[128] According to reviews of the duo's shows, their art achieved these aims.[129] In Warsaw in the mid-1930s, Dzigan and Shumacher played a role that was not only critical but also therapeutic (which again came to the fore in the last years of Dzigan's activity in Israel).[130] The Jewish comedian, according to Dzigan,

---

126 Dzigan, *Der koyekh*, 139.

127 McGrath, "The Cheviot," xxvii.

128 "The great Jewish masses, those who had no opportunity to emigrate to the lands over the sea, lived with that same hope, and the majority of the Jewish intelligentsia fed that hope." Dzigan, *Der koyekh*, 118.

129 See, for example, Grafman's 1937 article: "In the midst of the breaking of the windowpanes, right at the time when they were apparently 'outlawing' ritual slaughter by Jews – I sat, together with another thousand or even 1,500 Jews, at the premiere in the Nowości theater and I laughed. Jokes about your isolation, about your sorrows – and you laugh." Grafman, "Beys der hafsoke." In a review published in the newspaper *Haynt*, the author wrote: "These comedians carried out an 'Anschluss' before the word became popular and political . . . despite all the sorrows, the Jews still laugh." Fertreter, "Nadir un veyn nisht!" So too, Nayman commented: "We laughed, and at the same time the sadness accosted us, because the performance touched upon a sensitive point." Nayman, "Dzigan veShumacher" See also Kipnis, "Tate, du lakhst?"; Appenszlak, "Nadir un Wejn Niszt."

130 The names of Dzigan's later shows also reflect this sentiment, for example, *Abi gezunt!* (The Main Thing: Good Health!, 1962) and his last show, *Doktoyrim heysn lakhn!* (Doctors Prescribe Laughter!, 1980).

must not only entertain but also serve as a doctor, treating the sadness of Jewish souls.[131] In an article, Dzigan discussed this function of the theater in the 1930s:

> From the day that we made it [the theater] into a stage for current political satire, the audience would come, as they say, to find comfort. Ararat became a kind of Western Wall for the Jews of Poland . . . there was a kind of unwritten oath between us, the actors, and the audience, to endure together, in partnership, the difficult and bitter times.[132]

Looking back on the duo's theater at the end of the 1930s, Dzigan saw it as a kind of Western Wall, a remnant of a world about to be destroyed, a place of catharsis for the soul. The performances emphasized liminal characteristics.[133] The theater strengthened the feeling of *communitas*, one of the characteristics of liminal situations, transforming hierarchy into equality, mainly among the audience, and cancelling established social roles. The breakdown of social barriers and borders creates a feeling of shared experience, enabling unmediated and spontaneous relations between people. A feeling of shared fate facilitates unity, and in its wake, structural social divides can be overcome. This feeling of *communitas* intensified in the years of crisis, and, as the calamity became more acute, the theater's significance as a spiritual center, as an arena for expressing the hope that it would be possible to rebuild the ruins, likewise increased.

131 Bashan, "Dzigan."
132 Bashan, "Monolog."
133 Gennep, *Rites of Passage*; Turner, *Forest of Symbols*.

Chapter 3
Tribulations of the Last Decade in Eastern Europe: 1939–1949

Dzigan and Shumacher's last performance in Poland before the outbreak of the Second World War – with the show *Nadir un veyn nisht!* (Take This and Don't Cry!) – took place in Kraków on August 23, 1939. The artists remained in Warsaw for around a month following the German invasion, and their status as theater stars helped them to contend with the difficult reality.[1] The producer Meyer Vinder encouraged them to use their names and status to obtain food and other necessities (according to Dzigan, Jewish merchants foresaw that the Germans would confiscate their goods and so preferred to give them to the artists). Life in occupied Poland became intolerable, and, after director and actor Jonas Turkow informed Dzigan that his name appeared on a Gestapo blacklist (apparently as a result of jokes and skits in which he spoke out against Hitler and the Nazis), the duo understood the gravity of their situation and began to plan their escape.[2] Dzigan succeeded in crossing the border to the Soviet Union at the end of September 1939, making his way to Białystok. Thus ended the period that Dzigan described as the happiest of his life – he was in his prime, his reputation preceded him, he made a respectable livelihood, and was friends with people from all political camps.[3] Shumacher left Warsaw for Białystok on October 23, 1939, together with Y. Sh. Goldshteyn and Moyshe Nudelman. The latter were also on a Gestapo blacklist because of the anti-Nazi skits they had written for Dzigan and Shumacher's theater. Celina Shumacher and Nudelman's wife remained in Warsaw, believing that the Nazis would not harm women and children.[4] Thanks to a telegram she received from her husband in March 1940, and with the help of a Polish official, Celina Shumacher later also succeeded in leaving Poland. She reached Białystok on May 13, 1940.

1 See Levin, Interview with Shimen Dzigan; Dzigan, *Der koyekh*, 145–50.

2 Dovid Lederman notes that Dzigan and Shumacher attended a meeting of actors in the Warsaw home of producer Meyer Vinder, at which those present discussed the need to leave the occupied city. Lederman, *Fun yener zayt*, 46.

3 Dzigan, *Der koyekh*, 124. For the story of Dzigan's crossing into the Soviet Union see ibid., 150–51.

4 Litvak, Interview with Celina Shumacher.

https://doi.org/10.1515/9783110717693-003

In the Soviet Union (1939–1947)

The Soviet chapter in the lives of Dzigan and Shumacher began with their arrival in Białystok and lasted for seven years.[5] Dzigan's autobiography testifies to the immense and traumatic effect that this period had on him: out of a total of 370 pages, 152 (more than forty percent of the book) are devoted to this short period in his life and artistic career. Likewise, the impact of this period is evident in extracts from many interviews conducted with Dzigan and Shumacher, as well as the numerous jokes and skits in their shows concerning the Soviet regime in general and its treatment of Jews in particular.[6] No recordings, scripts, or playbills of the performances from this period have survived; the only materials available concerning it are a number of newspaper reviews. Therefore, this chapter does not discuss in detail the content of the duo's performances in the Soviet Union.[7]

The unique development of Yiddish culture in the Soviet Union continued until after the end of the Second World War, although the oppression of Yiddish writers as part of Stalin's Great Purges began to intensify as early as 1936. This persecution eased somewhat during the war years.[8] At this stage, Jews believed that the continued existence of Yiddish-Jewish culture was assured because Stalin and the Communist Party recognized Yiddish as a national language of the Jewish minority.[9] In the first decades following the revolution, various Yiddish educational and cultural institutions flourished throughout the Soviet Union. Likewise, an organization of Yiddish writers was founded, as were publishing houses that produced Yiddish books and newspapers.

In the interwar period, Białystok was the second largest center of the textile industry (after Łódź) and boasted the greatest number of workers in Eastern Poland: a Jewish majority populated the city center, with a non-Jewish popula-

5 Turkow-Grudberg, *Af mayn veg*, 274.

6 Concerning the many skits performed by the artists later in Israel that criticized life in the Soviet Union, see ibid., 273–82.

7 The discussion in this chapter is based on the following materials: reviews of the performances; Dzigan's autobiography; the interview Dov Levin conducted with Dzigan in 1973; an interview conducted by Judith Brin Ingber with the dancer Felix Fibich (a member of Dzigan and Shumacher's theater troupe in Białystok) in 2010; Sara Bender's book concerning the Jews of Białystok during the World War II; and the autobiography of the actor Dovid Lederman, who resided in Białystok while Dzigan and Shumacher were consolidating their troupe and, following his release from prison, found refuge among its members. See also Estraikh, "The Missing Years."

8 Yiddish writers and cultural figures were arrested and murdered at various stages of Stalin's Great Purge, among them Moyshe Kulbak, Moyshe Litvakov, Esther Frumkin, Maks Erik, and many others. See Pinkus, *Yahadut brit hamo'atsot*.

9 Levin, *Teḳufa besograyim*, 136–37.

tion residing on its periphery. On August 23, 1939, the signing of the Ribbentrop-Molotov pact established the border between the lands annexed by the Soviet Union and those occupied by Germany; likewise, it delineated the transfer of populations between the two occupied areas. Upon the Nazi invasion of Poland in September 1939, masses of refugees, among them many Jews, fled to the Soviet Union. According to lists, in November 1939, there were 33,000 Jewish refugees in Białystok out of a total of some three to four hundred thousand Jews who had arrived in the Soviet Union by that time.[10] During the entire period of Soviet annexation, until the German invasion of the Soviet Union on June 22, 1941, Białystok was the capital city of the region officially designated as West Belorussia.

In the first months following the annexation of eastern Poland to the Soviet Union, the Soviet regime treated the refugees in the same manner as the local population. This situation changed in February 1940 when the authorities demanded that all residents, including refugees, accept Soviet citizenship. Many refugees still harbored hopes that they would be able to return to Poland and reunite with their families; thus, they refused to relinquish their Polish citizenship, even if this was likely to lead to their arrest.[11] On November 29, 1939, the Supreme Soviet published a decree granting Soviet citizenship to Polish citizens who had moved to western Ukraine and Belorussia. Subsequently, in February 1940, a "passportization" operation began.[12] Very few of the refugees seized the opportunity to apply for citizenship. Indeed, most opted not to submit a citizenship request in the hope that they would be able to return to their homes in the German occupied zone. Those without Soviet citizenship were subsequently placed on trains and exiled to work camps in the Russian Far East.[13] Similarly to other writers and artists, Dzigan and Shumacher submitted a request for Soviet citizenship, relinquishing their Polish citizenship. As Soviet citizens they were able to perform in theaters throughout the Soviet Union, as will be discussed in more detail below.

The process of Sovietizing Białystok caused deep-seated damage to the city's Jewish population. Unemployment rose, sources of income declined, and a process of economic and political oppression began: Jewish political parties and youth movements were outlawed. Jewish religious life, industry, and production suffered a great blow. The Soviet regime regarded education as the central tool in indoctrinating the population; consequently, Jewish schools were nationalized. The scarcity of food, the terrible sanitary standards, the housing shortage, and unemployment made the lives of the refugees especially difficult. As Sara Bender notes,

---

10 Bender, *Jews of Białystok*, 53.

11 Ibid., 52–59.

12 This provided an opportunity to test the refugees' loyalty. See Litvak, *Peliṭim* 112–18.

13 Levin, *Teḳufa besograyim*, 16–17, 205–9.

the Soviet authorities "spread fear and distrust through a policy of oppression and arrests," striking "a mortal blow to Jewish communal life. Nevertheless, Jewish life in the city appeared to proceed normally."[14] Despite these trends, cultural life in the city continued to blossom, although it too would eventually be extinguished.[15]

The Yiddish newspaper *Byalistoker shtern*, edited by Zelig Akselrod and Hersh Smolar, began to appear on a daily basis (it later become a weekly) in 1939. This was the only Yiddish paper in the entire territory of eastern Poland annexed by the Soviet Union, and it provided a platform for the Jewish intelligentsia and writers in the city.[16] A short time after the Soviets entered Białystok, the local authorities decided to authorize and even support the activities of two Yiddish theater troupes – a repertory theater and a revue theater – demonstrating the Soviet regime's tolerance of minority cultures. In addition to this motivation, theater also constituted a central means of indoctrination.

Local actor Yehuda Grinhoyz organized a theater troupe in Soviet Białystok, although it disintegrated a short time after staging its first play, Sholem Aleichem's *Amkho*. The authorities then called a meeting of actors, most of them refugees, which was chaired by the refugee-actor Avrom Morevski. This was the first step in the establishment of Der byalistoker melukhisher yidisher minyatur-teater (The Białystok National Jewish Miniature Theater), managed by Morevski, who, together with Ber Mark, was also responsible for its repertoire. Later, Morevski was replaced by the Soviet actor Yitskhok Rakitin.[17] The second troupe was a revue theater with Dzigan and Shumacher as its main actors.

In February 1940, a few months after arriving as refugees in Białystok,[18] Moyshe Broderzon was appointed as artistic manager of Der byalistoker melukhisher yidisher minyatur-teater, which was supported by the Minsk region's

---

14 Ibid., 101. See also 74–104.

15 Bender, *Jews of Białystok*, 70–83.

16 Concerning Jewish journalism in this period see Levin, *Tekufa besograyim*, 137–46. As Bender notes, "[Polish Jewish authors who had settled in Białystok] . . . hoped that publication in the *Bialystoker shtern* would confer on them the status of Soviet authors, with all that that implied – especially freedom from harassment by the secret police. Despite its limited circulation, the *Bialystoker shtern* became the mouthpiece of all Jews in former eastern Poland." Bender, *Jews of Białystok*, 71; see also Bender, 74–80.

17 The troupe included more than eighty people and was active until the German invasion, at which time it was in the midst of a tour of performances. Regarding the establishment of the theater and its repertoire, see Turkow-Grudberg, *Yidish teater*, 114; Lederman, *Fun yener zayt*; Levin, *Tekufa besograyim*, 162–76; Bender, *Jews of Białystok*, 81–82.

18 Regarding this period see Dzigan, *Der koyekh*, 152–56. As was noted, Celina Shumacher arrived in Białystok a few months after the actors. See Lederman, *Fun yener zayt*, 131–32; Litvak, Interview with Celina Shumacher (1978).

Ministry of Culture.[19] Dzigan and Shumacher were the troupe's directors, with Moyshe Broderzon as dramaturg. Adam Umansky, a member of the Communist Party, was appointed by the authorities as executive director.[20] Alongside Broderzon, the theater's main writers were Moyshe Nudelman and Y. Sh. Goldshteyn. The theater included refugee actors from Poland and an eight-piece orchestra: seven of the musicians were Jewish refugees and one was a Polish non-Jew.[21] Shaul Berezovsky was the main composer and conductor, and Dzigan's younger brother was the theater's costume maker. Until its dissolution in 1941, the theater succeeded in staging two shows: *Zingendik un tantsndik* (Singing and Dancing, 1940) and *Rozhinkes mit mandlen* (Raisins and Almonds, 1940).[22]

The first program the theater staged was comprised of two parts and included a total of fourteen segments: the songs "Zingendik un tantsndik" and "Karaganda" by Shaul Berezovsky;[23] "Aynshteyn-Vaynshteyn" by Y. Sh. Goldshteyn and Moyshe Nudelman;[24] "Der monolog fun Itshe-Meyer" (Itshe Meyer's Monologue);[25] "A briv fun a polet" (A Letter from a Refugee), performed by Shumacher, in which a refugee writes a letter to his brother describing the good life in "mother Russia with great ideological" enthusiasm; the dance "Shidukhim," starring Mina Bern; and the following acts, the original names of which have not survived:[26] "Cantor"

---

19 See Bender, *Jews of Białystok*, 82–83. A group of writers, actors, and journalists who were willing to integrate into the establishment received positive treatment. The actors helped to found four Yiddish theater troupes in western Belorussia. See Litvak, *Peliṭim*, 98–99.

20 According to Dzigan and some reviews in the Soviet press, the artistic directors were Dzigan and Shumacher and Moyshe Broderzon was literary director, see Dzigan, *Der koyekh*, 162–3, Н. ИВЛЕВ, "Еврейский театр миниатюр (К предстоящим гастролям)" [N. Ivlev, "Jewish Theatre of Miniatures (For the Upcoming Tour),"] BAA, file 153–03.

21 In addition to Dzigan and Shumacher, the members of the troupe were Yehudit Berg, Yoel Bergman, Mina Bern, Vladek Godik, Shmulik Goldshteyn, Hela Luksenberg, Lyublinskaya, Mark Morevski, Lola Folman, Felix Fibich, Kvanisberg, Yekusiel Rotenberg, Meytek Rotsheyn, and Shifer.

22 The details about the members of Dzigan and Shumacher's theater and Dzigan's brother, the theater's costume-maker, are based on press reviews and Lederman's book, Lederman, *Fun yener zayt*, 332. See also И. САМОЙЛОВ, "Напевая И Танцуя (Гастроли Белостокского Еврейского Театра Миниатюр)," Бакинский рабочий, September 10, 1940 [I. Samoilov, "Singing and Dancing (Tour by the Białystok Jewish Miniature Theater)," *Bakinski Rabochi* (Baku Workers)], BAA, file 153–03; И. Добрушин, "'ИЗЮМ И МИНДАЛЬ' – ГАСТРОЛИ БЕЛОСТОКСКОГО ЕВРЕЙСКОГО ТЕАТРА МИНИАТЮР," ПЯТИГОРСКАЯ ПРАВДА, September 27, 1940 [Yekhezkel Dobrushin, "'Raisins and Almonds' – Tour by the Białystok Jewish Miniature Theater," *Pyatigorsk Pravda* (Pyatigorsk Truth)], BAA, file 153–03.

23 See below, pp. 89–90.

24 See pp. 51–53.

25 See below, pp. 92–93.

26 These are my translations, based on the names noted by reviews in the Russian press.

and "The Theater Manager," in which Dzigan plays the role of a provincial theater manager trying to establish a theater troupe comprised of a disabled dancer, a stuttering singer, a deaf actor, and "Old Man," a skit based on Mordkhe Gebirtig's poem entitled "Ba'alei mum" (Cripples).

The Belorussian Ministry of Culture in Minsk arranged a tour during which the theater performed in many cities, some of them home to large Jewish populations. The troupe appeared in Soviet cities both within and outside the occupied zone, among them Moscow, Leningrad, Lvov, Odessa, Kiev, Kharkov, Minsk, Bobruisk, Nikolayev, Baku, Yerevan, and Tbilisi. Likewise, it staged performances at the school for pilots in Taganrog and various divisions of the Russian Army. The tour was received with great enthusiasm: for example, tickets for the troupe's first eight performances in Moscow's famous Hermitage Theater sold out.[27] In Nikolayev, the actors were met at the train station with applause and bouquets of flowers. Among those present were central figures from civil and political organizations, as well as local artists and journalists.

Theater as a Means of Indoctrination

At the reception for the artists in Nikolayev, the conductor of the local philharmonic orchestra began his welcoming speech by blessing "artists representing the liberated people who are now building a happy life, together with us, in a friendly Soviet family."[28] This rhetoric, replete with ideological enthusiasm and loyalty, emphasized the role that the Polish-Jewish-refugee artists were expected to play. A similar rhetoric characterized theater reviews published in the press. Indeed, reviewers considered the theater troupe as a symbol of the Red Army's victory over the Polish enemy and bourgeois society. The Jewish-Polish actors had not been liberated from the Germans (then allies of the Soviet Union) but rather from capitalist Polish society. They were "fulfilling a dream," becoming supporters of Communism and "part of the family of Soviet nations." The name of the theater (which included the word "Białystok") was not only a sign of its origin but testified that it was based in a city recently annexed by the Soviet Union: a symbol of Soviet victory and a reminder that this was a theater of Polish refugees.

27 Dzigan, *Der koyekh*, 174. See also Khantshin, "Di gastroln." A performance by a Yiddish theater group in Moscow or Leningrad was not rare. The Moscow Jewish State Theater (GOSET) also appeared in these cities with great success, including performances at the Narodni Dom, the Velikan cinema, and other locations. See Veidlinger, *Moscow State Yiddish Theater*.

28 The article, entitled "A Brotherly Meeting," was published in a local Nikolayev newspaper in October 1940, without the author's name. See BAA, file 153–03.

In the process of instrumentalizing the theater, the regime pressured members of the troupe to change the content of the shows, their appearance, and their cultural identity (although not the language in which they performed).[29]

Before it could perform, the theater needed to acquire permission from the local censorship – Jewish officials in the local cultural departments. Therefore, each show was performed especially for the censorship committee, before being staged publicly. This committee, for obvious reasons, had no interest in artistic elements, considering only the political aspects of the performance. According to Dovid Lederman, an actor and refugee who participated in the troupe's first rehearsals prior to his arrest by the Soviets, following the censorship's scrutiny the theater was able to present only neutral materials, mainly skits based on adaptations of folk songs.

The theater suited its repertoire to the new political system – it could no longer criticize the political, economic, and social reality.[30] Instead of political satire focusing on the "withered system," it necessarily highlighted the responsibility of other countries for the Soviet Union's sorrows. In such a regime, Dzigan summarized, a comedian must "shoot rubber bullets at false targets."[31] This also applied to the Germans, the allies of the Soviet Union: poking fun at them was forbidden. Thus, when writing skits, Moyshe Nudelman and Y. Sh. Goldshteyn could laugh only at the English, the French, the Americans, and at themselves, the Jewish refugees from "capitalist Poland." This resulted in shows comprised of patriotic Russian and Jewish songs. The name of the troupe's first show, *Zingendik un tantsndik* (Singing and Dancing) (September 1940), quotes Broderzon's song of the same name, which the artists included in a program they staged in Łódź after their return to Poland in October 1948, *Balebatish un demokratish* (Bourgeois and Democratic).[32] The song was adapted to suit the reigning ideology in the Soviet Union and Communist Poland, as the later version used in the Polish performance (which has survived) reveals:

> גענוג שוין זײַן צעבראָכענע, / צעווירענע, צעקראָכענע, / צו זײַן איין וויסטע קאַליקעס / אויף הפּקר און אויף שפּאַס / אויף כּסדר באַלעבאַטישן, / מכּלומרשט, דעמאָקראַטישן. / מיר ווילן מער קיין קאַליקעס, / מיר זײַנען אויף גאָטס באַראָט. // [רעפֿריין:] טאָ זינגענדיק פֿאָרויס מיר גייען / און טאַנצנדיק איז אונדזער גאַנג, / מיר גלויבן נאָר אין קעפּ געהויבענע, / נאָך דיר געבענקט מיר האָבן לאַנג. / געצונדענע / דורך זיבן זונען, / פֿאַרשוווּנדן ווערט / דער טרויער גאַנץ. / טאָ זינגט ברידער / דאָ גליק איז אויסגעפֿונען!, / כאַ־כאַ / לאַכט, / וואַכט, / גיט אַ טאַנץ![33]

29 Lederman, *Fun yener zayt*, 113; Bender, *Jews of Białystok*.

30 Dzigan, *Der koyekh*, 159–60.

31 Ibid., 185.

32 A copy of the poem, in an edition authorized by the Polish censorship, has survived, along with other texts bearing the censor's approval and seal. See BAA, file 149–01.

33 Ibid.

[Enough with being broken/ swollen, worn out, / being a miserable cripple / a subject of mockery, / dependent on the bourgeois, / those fake democrats. / We will no longer be cripples / we rely on God's providence. // [refrain:] Singing we go forwards / and dancing we make our way, / we believe only in heads held high, / we have longed for you for so long./ With the radiance / of seven suns, / sorrow will disappear. / Let us sing, brothers, / here happiness is to be found! / Ha-ha / laugh, / arise, / dance!]

The song expresses a desire to leave behind weakness and disintegration, replacing them with song and dance; a movement forward, toward a joyful life, following a period of fake democracy and bourgeois values. The song uses revolutionary rhetoric similar to that which characterized Broderzon's writing in the days of Ararat and Yung-Yidish, yet the message was adapted to Soviet ideological expectations. Presumably, this was also true of other skits performed by the troupe.

The Attitude of the Soviet Press

Cultural and theatrical figures published (supportive) reviews of the productions staged by Dzigan and Shumacher's theater in the local Soviet press. Indeed, reviewing the theater's performances in Rostow in March 1941, the journalist, poet, and playwright Gregory Katz wrote that the show demonstrated the actors' talent, wisdom, true love of life, and their refined artistic taste. As did many others, he praised their expressive abilities and the show's light tone: even theatergoers who were not fluent in Yiddish could enjoy the performance.[34] Likewise, in a review published in the local paper in Baku, a critic noted that the audience, two thirds of whom were Russians, Azerbaijanis, and Armenians without any knowledge of Yiddish, enjoyed the performance. "The true language of art is international," wrote I. Samoilov.[35] Similar comments were also made in the local newspaper in Yerevan.[36] According to critics, the general nature of it shows (they were not of a specifically Jewish character) united different cultures (or negated their differences). This process, which in a sense "globalized" the language and culture of a certain ethnic group, is an additional indicator of the cultural paral-

34 Григорий Кац, "ГАСТРОЛИ БЕЛОСТОКСКОГО ЕВРЕЙСКОГО ТЕАТРА МИНИАТЮР," МОЛОТ, March 22, 1941 (Gregory Katz, "A Tour of Performances by a Jewish Miniature Theater from Białystok," *Molot* [Hammer]), BAA, file 153–03. Gregory Katz was also a translator and the manager of a radio station in Rostow.

35 Above, note 23.

36 Н. Адамян, "Гастроли Белостокского – Театра Миниатюр В Ереване," КОММУНИСТ – ОРГАН ЦК КП АРМЕНИИ, December 4, 1941 (N. Adamian, "Tour of Performances by Białystok's Miniature Theater in Yerevan," *Komunist*), BAA, file 149–01.

ysis that afflicted the theater in this period. Indeed, the weight of the strict censorship and the pressure from critics in the press neutralized the piercing and critical Yiddish theater of Dzigan and Shumacher, which now found itself unable to impart condemnation or shoot its critical arrows. This was the paradox of the (conditional) freedom that allowed the artists to appear in their own language: Yiddish was a "kosher" (legitimate) theatrical language as long as performances could also be understood by those unfamiliar it.

Furthermore, Soviet theater critics expressed concern regarding the presentation of traditional Jewish stereotypes from the Eastern European traditional shtetl and the depictions of Polish "bourgeois life."[37] In the local newspaper in Vitebsk, critics commented that the show staged by the theater in Belarus was wise, talented, and brilliant, yet they regarded the portrayal of the old Jewish way of life as exposing the "ugly past" to the modern Soviet audience. They concluded by expressing their expectation that the theater would concentrate on the new Soviet reality.[38] A critic in Baku noted the audience's dissatisfaction with the theater's repertoire, "which is not suited to the demands of the Soviet audience."[39] N. Ivlev wrote, in a tone that was at once defensive and insistent, that in the theater's first tour of performances the actors had failed to rid themselves of Polish bourgeois characteristics, Moreover, he demanded that it change and update its repertoire.[40] M. Zhivov also argued that the artists needed to spurn the "superficial remnants of the past" in order to acclimate to the new reality.[41] In a review published in the newspaper *Pyatigorsk Pravda* (Pyatigorsk Truth), I. Dobrushin suggested including Jewish Soviet writers in the company in order to rejuvenate the repertoire and suit it to the Soviet reality.[42] N. Adamian declared that the theater presented "ugly pictures of the old Jewish life."[43]

---

37 According to the dancer Felix Fibich, a member of the troupe, not only critics but also theatergoers in small towns complained that the theater's subject matter was too religious, meaning too Jewish. See Brin Ingber, "The Unwitting *Gastrol.*"

38 І. Ісакаў, М. Марковіч, "МАИСТЕРСКІ СПЕКТАКЛЬ," ВІЦЕБСКІ РАБОЧЫ, December 30, 1940 (I. Isakov and M. Markovits, "Master Performance," *Vitebsk Rabochi* [Vitebsk Workers]). BAA file 153–03.

39 See above, note 35.

40 Н. ИВЛЕВ, "Еврейский театр миниатюр (К предстоящим гастролям)," (N. Ivlev, "Jewish Miniature Theater [For the Upcoming Tour])," BAA, file 153–03. Date and name of the newspaper unknown.

41 М. Живов, "Первые шаги," Советское искусство, August 3, 1940 (M. Zhivov, "First Steps," *Sovetskoye Iskusstvo* [Soviet Art]), BAA, file 153–03.

42 See above, note 23.

43 See above, note 36.

Thus, many believed that the theater of the Polish Jewish refugees harked back to an unwanted past. While, according to the duo's last skit in Poland, Jewish existence in Poland required the renunciation of human elements, their acceptance as Soviet artists necessitated the rejection of their Jewish-Polish identity – both civilian and cultural. They needed to divest themselves of the external signs of Polish Jewry, the substance of the bourgeois identity, merging with the Soviet model and refraining from critical expressions. The only way to survive was via silence – or by limiting themselves to "singing and dancing."[44]

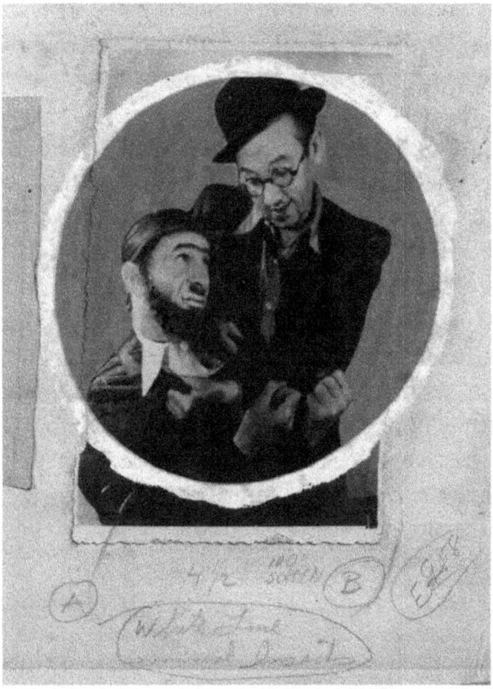

Figure 8: Shimen Dzigan (left) as Itshe-Meyer and Yisroel Shumacher as the bourgeois "refugee" (Lydia Shumacher-Ophir Collection).

In the Soviet Union, Dzigan and Shumacher endeavored to transform their Polish-Jewish identity from a cultural obstacle that isolated them from the Soviet audience into an artistic advantage. Soviet Jewry perceived the Hasidic Jew as an object of mockery and denigration. They ridiculed Polish Jewry's simplicity, dress, dialect, and way of life. The artists solved this problem by focusing on a

44 See Brin Ingber, "The Unwitting *Gastrol.*"

character diametrically opposed to the new Soviet Jew: the Polish Hasid. This character, whom they named "Itshe-Meyer," represented the negative stereotype of the Polish Hasid [See Figure 8].

The series of monologues (performed by Dzigan) devoted to Itshe-Meyer,[45] which depict the confrontation between a defenseless Hasid and modern Russian Jews (and non-Jews), were a great success. Outbursts of laughter were heard when the character of the Hasidic Jew, wearing a long kaftan, a traditional Jewish hat, and a red kerchief appeared on stage. According to Dzigan, the artists consciously made the decision to mold the Polish Hasidic Jew as a character to be mocked, a target of satire, which bordered on self-mockery, to create a connection with the Soviet audience, at least on the declarative, open level. This step differentiated the actors from the despised Polish Jews and included them in the majority, the "enlightened and liberated" Soviet audience.

Dzigan's Perception of the Theater's Role in the Soviet Period

Dzigan's memoirs include detailed depictions of the theater that he established together with Shumacher, alongside portraits of the harsh living conditions in the Soviet Union, the aggressive regime, the hunger, the artistic persecution, Soviet antisemitism, and his own personal experiences.[46] The actor recalls witticisms critiquing the lack of food, the ideological persecution of Jews, the Show Trials, and more, which he included in later performances in Communist Poland, after leaving the Soviet Union.[47] Likewise, he depicts emotional encounters with the Soviet audience, accompanied by a constant awareness that the Jewish collective in Soviet territories was disintegrating. Dzigan describes how he reacted to performing in a Minsk synagogue that had been converted into a theater, feeling that his theater was party to the desecration of a holy site.[48] In the context of the blurring boundaries of Jewish identity, Dzigan portrays the theater as simultaneously cooperating with the Soviet goal of obliterating this identity and actively striving

45 According to the only surviving script of one of these monologues, it was written by Dzigan and Shumacher. It is reasonable to presume that some of them were written by Moyshe Nudelman and Y. Sh. Goldshteyn. BAA, file 149–01.

46 Dzigan, *Der koyekh*, 153–69, 179–80.

47 Ibid., 156.

48 The Choral Synagogue in Minsk was inaugurated in September 1906 and was commandeered from the Jewish religious authority of Minsk in February 1923, at the instruction of the managing committee of the city's Communist Party. It was converted into a cultural center under the management of the municipal Ministry of Culture.

to strengthen it. As an example, he relates that one man in Yerevan bought a ticket for the first row not because this would give him the best seat, but rather so that he could ask to sit with the actors after the performance and be "among Jews." These words express the feeling of community characteristic of Dzigan and Shumacher's performances.[49] Dzigan's memoirs indicate that the theater was a place of catharsis for the audience. It compensated, at least fleetingly, for the damage to Jewish culture perpetrated by the Soviet regime. Likewise, it provided an opportunity for an ethnic-communal gathering, combined with artistic creativity, in a language and culture that were gradually being silenced and oppressed.

The Breakdown of the Theater

On June 22, 1941, while Dzigan and Shumacher were performing in Odessa, the Germans launched their invasion of the Soviet Union. The following day, Umansky, the theater's manager, decided that the troupe should leave Odessa (which was located in the battle zone). It proceeded to stage performances in Kharkov and Ashkhabad (Ashgabat) in central Asia, where it finally fell apart.[50] Upon receiving a new government directive requesting the artists to take part in the task entertaining the troops, Umansky disbanded the troupe: the musicians were dispatched to play Russian songs in a circus, the youngsters to dance, and the older actors to perform for the war-injured.[51] Dzigan and Shumacher prepared a repertoire in Russian to entertain injured soldiers. However, the duo's performances were not welcomed: the soldiers jeered at them, calling them "Jews, cowards." The actors became a target for the injured soldiers' anger: "Go to the Front! Fight like we fought! Don't come and sing us songs..."[52]

The war and the dissolution of the theater troupe had a detrimental effect on the artists' status and livelihood. Yet these developments also encouraged Dzigan and Shumacher to take an active role in the hostilities themselves.[53] The artists joined the seventh division of the Polish army, known as the Anders Army, which was established in the Soviet Union in August 1941 to fight against the Germans.[54] They were accepted on the recommendation of General Leopold Okulicki, Anders'

---

49 Dzigan, *Der koyekh*, 166–67.

50 Ibid., 193–95.

51 At the time, GOSET was undergoing managerial and artistic reorganization, transforming it into a propaganda tool for the war effort. See Veidlinger, *Moscow State Yiddish Theater*, 234.

52 Dzigan, *Der koyekh*, 203.

53 Ibid., 199–204.

54 Celina Shumacher also joined the cultural department of the Anders Army.

chief of staff. Like many other Jewish refugees, the actors intended to investigate the possibility of leaving the Soviet Union.[55] However, when the division was ready to depart, Polish soldiers arrested Dzigan and Shumacher, accusing them of deserting from the Red Army. Dzigan and Shumacher argued that they had been denounced by Polish informers in retaliation for relinquishing their Polish citizenship and as revenge for their satirical critiques of the prewar Polish regime.[56] According to Dzigan's memoirs, a few years later Umansky admitted that he had informed on them, hoping that they would be discharged from the Polish army and thus able to return to the theater.[57] The artists were imprisoned in Kermen, Uzbekistan, for three months, in separate cells. Dzigan relates that when they went out to the prison yard for the first time, he whistled the first part of Ararat's anthem. From the other side of the wall, Shumacher replied, continuing the tune. In this way, they were able to identify one another and confirm that they were both still alive.[58] Artists and friends tried to help secure their release, without success. Celina Shumacher met with General Anders, but she too was unable to influence the decision. The Polish Army departed for Iran, and the artists were

55 Ibid., 206–7. Following the Nazi invasion of the Soviet Union, the Soviets released Władysław Anders, allowing him to establish a Polish army that would fight alongside them. Anders was appointed as commander of the army, which was officially named the Second Polish Corps although, as noted, it was commonly referred to as the Anders Army. Dzigan relates that he and Shumacher met General Leopold Okulicki of the Seventh Division of the Polish Army on a train journey to a Polish army base and that he helped them, then Soviet citizens, to join the army. Regarding the status of Polish citizens who held Soviet citizenship, Yisrael Gutman writes: "The individuals in question had had Soviet citizenship imposed on them, but in accordance with the terms of the Polish-Soviet agreement, were still regarded as Polish citizens, and could in theory enlist in General Anders Armed Forces. The Soviets, however, regarded them as deserters from conscripted Soviet units, to be treated as such." See Gutman, "Jews in General Anders' Army," 16.

56 Ibid., 119. Dzigan and Shumacher made similar statements during their visit to Paris in 1949. Litvak claims that they were arrested for antisemitic reasons, using the justification that they were Soviet "citizens." See Litvak, Interview with Celina Shumacher (1978), 194.

57 In an interview with Rafael Bashan, Dzigan claimed that this was Umansky's revenge for the artists' criticism of the Polish government: they had staged a skit poking fun at the statement made by Polish Marshal Edward Rydz-Śmigły on August 6, 1939, following the threat of a German invasion, "Nie tylko nie damy całsukni, ale nawet guzika nie damy" [Not only will we refuse to give them the jacket; we won't give up even a single button]. See Bashan, "Dzigan." I would like to thank Karolina Szymaniak for this reference. In the satirical skit, Dzigan says: "You see? I have left everything behind, but you see? I brought the button with me." See Dzigan, *Der koyekh*, 211. Dzigan states that when the artists met Umansky at the Polish Embassy in Moscow in 1946, he admitted that this was his reason for denouncing them. See ibid., 210–12. Celina Shumacher related that they were accused of deserting from the Red Army. See Litvak, Interview with Celina Shumacher (1978).

58 Dzigan, *Der koyekh*, 214–19.

sent from Kermen to the town of Yangiyul. A few days later, they were transferred to the custody of the secret police (NKVD, The People's Commissariat for Internal Affairs) and imprisoned in Tashkent. Dzigan relates that in Tashkent they were asked to perform for prisoners and soldiers at a festive evening in honor of the October revolution:

איך האָב זיך געמאַכט קוראַזש, ארויף אויפֿן טיש, און כ'ווייס נישט פֿאַר וואָס, נאָר כ'האָב זיך צעזונגען מיט גרויס דבֿקות דעם חסידישן ניגון פֿון ש' אַנ־סקיס 'דיבוק'. און נישט אַזוי האָב איך זיך צעזונגען, ווי איך האָב זיך צעטאַנצט אין אַ ווילדן טאַנץ, אַ קונציקן גאַלאָפּ אויף איין אָרט; דערבײַ האָבן מײַנע הענט זיך געדרייט ווי די פֿליגל פֿון אַ ווינט מיל. די אייגענע התלהבות האָט מיך מיטגעריסן און כ'האָב פֿאַרגעסן וועגן אַלץ און אַלעם. די זעלנער זענען געוואָרן אָנגעצונדן. זיי האָבן געפּלעטשט מיט די הענט אין חסידישן טאַקט. ס'האָט זיי בלויז געפֿעלט קאַפּאָטעס, וואָלט עס אויסגעזען ווי אַ שימחה בײַם רבין.[59]

[I gathered up my courage, got up on the table and, I don't know why, but I began to sing the Hasidic tune from Sh. An-sky's *Dybbuk* with great enthusiasm. I didn't just dance; I danced a wild dance, a clever gallop on the spot; my hands moving around like the wings of a windmill. I was swept away by my enthusiasm, and I forgot about everything. The soldiers became excited. They began to clap their hands to a Hasidic beat. All that was missing were *kapotes* (long black coats) and it would have looked like a celebration around the Rebbe.]

Here Dzigan describes how his enthusiastic performance of a Hasidic tune succeeded in momentarily altering reality. Dzigan became a Hasid, or even a Hasidic leader, a Rebbe, while the Soviet soldiers were his Hasidim, his followers, dancing around him in his court. The performance was a short carnival as a result of which Dzigan gained an extra portion of food.

In Tashkent, Dzigan and Shumacher were interrogated separately and subsequently sentenced to four years in the labor camp for re-education in Aktyubinsk, Kazakhstan.[60] NKVD investigators added an accusation that the artists were sent to the Soviet Union to spy for the Germans. However, the prosecutor, a Soviet Jew, changed the political charge to a criminal one on his own authority.[61]

Upon their arrest, Dzigan and Shumacher disappeared from the Soviet public consciousness: "Until the arrest, they were the darlings of the Jewish cultural world in the Soviet Union," comments Yitskhok Turkow-Grudberg, "and suddenly – everyone turned their backs on them, as though they had never known them, as though they had never existed."[62] In March 1943, after spending nine months in prison in Tashkent, the artists were transferred to the camp in

59 Ibid., 239.
60 Ibid., 220–39.
61 See Litvak, *Peliṭim*, 194–95.
62 Turkow-Grudberg, *Af mayn veg*, 277.

Aktyubinsk.[63] Three months later, together with other prisoners in the camp, they established a theater, becoming its principal actors and directors. Dzigan recalls that the group performed mainly in Yiddish.[64] However, according to the memoirs of one prisoner they performed in Russian and only on rare occasions managed to integrate one or two Yiddish songs into the shows.[65] The group appeared three or four times each week, with great success. Jewish workers at a local factory and the director of the municipal philharmonic orchestra invited the group to perform in the city of Aktyubinsk, and the camp authorities permitted the actors to leave the camp for this purpose.[66]

Dzigan and Shumacher were released from the camp on August 19, 1946. They disposed of all the documents pertaining to their arrest. Upon arriving in Moscow, they contacted the committee for the repatriation of Polish citizens, which sent them to Lwów. There they were again arrested and interrogated by the NKVD[67] after a list of Zionist Jewish activists was found in their clothing.[68] Their identity documents were confiscated, they were forbidden to leave Lwów, and they were ordered to report daily to the NKVD offices. Their situation was worse than that of prisoners in a labor camp: they had no roof over their heads and their health deteriorated, as did their financial situation. They suspected that secret agents were following them, feared for their lives, and even doubted that they would survive. Dzigan and Shumacher lacked any official identity and began a period of personal and artistic silence. They sat in a park, waiting, in Dzigan's words, for a miracle. Help finally came, not from influential figures in the cultural world but rather, as Dzigan emphasizes in his book, from an "average person." One day, a "simple Jew" recognized them and came to their aid: he collected redemption money[69] from the members of his synagogue and used it to bribe to the NKVD

63 The prisoners in re-education camps worked at hard labor, lived in dreadful conditions, received little or no food, and suffered from disease and cold. See Litvak, *Peliṭim*, 86, 132–35.

64 Levin, Interview with Shimen Dzigan (1973).

65 Litvak remembers that the performances were in Russian and were open to audiences from outside the camp. See Litvak, *Peliṭim*, 200.

66 Dzigan, *Der koyekh*, 226–47, 259–60. See also Levin, Interview with Shimen Dzigan (1973). No evidence of the materials that were performed in the camp has survived, apart from one picture found in the archive of the City Museum of New York. See MNY, 264192.

67 Dzigan, *Der koyekh*, 262–66.

68 Concerning the reasons for their arrest and the NKVD's demand that the artists denounce the musician Edi Rozner and his wife, see ibid., 270–74.

69 Jewish law considers releasing a Jew from captivity a religious duty. This is known as *pidyon shevuim* or the redemption of captives. See, for example, Babylonian Talmud, Bava Batra 8b.

officials in Lwów.[70] The bribe was effective: the artists were arrested for one week and subsequently released in February 1947, without the return of their identity documents. Dzigan and Shumacher returned to the labor camp in Aktyubinsk to request new identity documents, and there they were recognized as citizens once again. On July 25, 1947, the two received permission to leave the Soviet Union for Poland.

Return to Poland (1947–1949)

קיין מאָל איז מען אָבער נישט געווען אַזוי אויסגעהונגערט נאָך אַ ביסל הומאָר, ווי נאָכן גרויזאַמען חורבן, נאָך די אַזוי טראַגישע איבערלעבונגען, נאָכן פֿאַרגיסן אַזוי פֿיל טרערן.

[We have never been so starved for a bit of humor as after the gruesome Holocaust, after such tragic experiences, after shedding so many tears.]

– Leneman, "Abi men zet zikh"

ש: שאַ, דאַכט זיך ס'גייט אַ ייִדישע פֿרוי.
ד: פֿון וואַנען ווייסטו אַז זי איז אַ ייִדישע?
ש: זעסט דאָך, זי גייט אַ צלם.

[Sh: Shush, that looks like a Jewish woman.
Dz: How do you know she's Jewish?
Sh: You can see, she's wearing a crucifix.]

– Yosl Cutler, "Spółdzielnia"

The period between January 1946 and February 1947 was one of the hardest in the lives of Jewish survivors in postwar Poland, as antisemitic attacks and killings occurred in towns across the country. Likewise, in the years 1947–1948 two historical events deeply affected the Polish Jews: the transition from a popular democracy to Communist rule in Poland and the establishment of the State of Israel.[71] These developments led to a breakdown of the separate and independent Jewish organization that had emerged following the liberation of the country. The most explicit expression of this process was the dissolution of the Central Committee of Polish Jews (CKZP) in spring 1949.[72]

In July 1947, after four years of wandering and performing in the Soviet Union and another four years of imprisonment in the labor camp in Aktyubinsk,

---

70 Ibid., 275–86. Litvak cites the financial help given to Dzigan and Shumacher as an example of Polish Jewish refugees supporting one another in the Soviet Union. See Litvak, *Peliṭim*, 200. A bribe of 1.5 million rubles was paid to the head of the NKVD. See Dzigan, *Der koyekh*, 286.

71 See Shlomi, "Hit'argenut," 532–38.

72 Ibid., 537–38.

Dzigan and Shumacher returned to Poland.[73] “My heart turned to stone,” thus Dzigan describes the day of their return to Warsaw. “Shumacher and I walked through the ruins in silence. There was nothing to talk about. We knew everything already.”[74] Upon their first encounter with the remains of the city of Warsaw and the remnants of Polish Jewry – with the evidence of the war – their voices and words disappeared. On their first day in postwar Poland, Dzigan and Shumacher arrived late at night at the offices of the Central Committee of Polish Jews.[75] The night guard welcomed them and suggested they spend the night in the office. By morning, the arrival of the famous satiric artists from prewar Poland was no longer a secret. Jews, thrilled to discover that both were alive and in Warsaw, flocked to the office to see them with their own eyes. Like miracle-workers or saints, Dzigan and Shumacher needed to offer material proof of their identity:

> מען האָט אונדז געטאַפּט צי מיר זענען אמתע. כ'האָב זיי געמוזט מכבד זײַן מיט אַ פּאָר פֿאַרמלחמהדיקע וויצן, זיי זאָלן זיך איבערצײַגן, אַז דאָס זענען מיר – דזשיגאַן און שומאַכער.[76]
>
> [They touched us in order to verify that we were real. I had to honor them with jokes from before the war to convince them that it was truly us – Dzigan and Shumacher.]

Telling Yiddish jokes from prewar Poland was, according to Dzigan, an identifying sign, a code confirming that teller and listener shared a common past, that they were alive, they remembered, and were still able to laugh. The joke became not only a humoristic interpretation of the present reality and a way to cope with it but also a document of the past.

The shows staged by Dzigan and Shumacher in postwar Poland, until their first performance in Israel, are characterized by two main elements: on the one hand, the transformation of their art into a “lieu de mémoire” of culture and language[77] and, on the other, reconstruction and recycling. Reconstruction is a gesture to a destroyed culture, as well as an endorsement of this culture’s con-

---

73 'דאָס האַרץ אין מיר איז געוווען פֿאַרשטיינערט . . . איך מיט שומאַכערן האָבן געשפּאַנט דורך די חורבֿות און געשוויגן. ס'איז נישט געוווען וועגן וואָס צו רעדן. מיר האָבן שוין אַל״ץ געוווּסט.'

Dzigan states that they arrived in Warsaw in June. According to reports in the press, it seems that they arrived in July. See Dos naye lebn, “Dzigan un Shumacher in Poyln”; Dzigan, Der koyekh, 288.

74 Dzigan, ibid.

75 The Committee was established in November 1944 to mediate between the state and the Jewish population. At first, it was headed by Dr. Emil Sommerstein and included representatives from most of the Jewish parties and organizations active at that time in Poland. See Redlich, *Life in Transit*, 29–52; Shlomi, “Hit’argenut,” 525–526, 542.

76 Dzigan, *Der koyekh*, 288.

77 This term was coined by Pierre Nora. See Nora, “Between Memory and History.”

tinued existence. Staging performances from the past is an inseparable part of theatrical art. Every mise-en-scène contains a new interpretation of a text or a mise-en-scène that has been performed previously. Even if interpretation remained unchanged in Dzigan and Shumacher's performances, the context of the performance – for example, presenting jokes from before the war – created new meaning, transforming it from a critical or humoristic performance into one of memory, including the memory of their own artistic activity. This added an auto-referential dimension that did not exist prior to the war. In the words of Hans Belting, "Artists . . . are performing art history as 'remake' with a mixture of nostalgia and freedom that rejects the historical authority of art."[78]

Only days after arriving in Warsaw, Dzigan and Shumacher relocated to Łódź, the city of their personal and professional births, which was in fact the capital of Poland and the center of Jewish culture in the early postwar years.[79] They spent the next two years in Poland – with Pavel Gornshteyn as their theater manager – during which time they staged four theater shows. The first, *Abi m'zet zikh!* (The Main Thing: We Meet Again!), was performed at the end of August 1947. The other three were produced with the support of the Central Committee of Jews in Poland, which subsidized the activities of two theater groups: one in lower Silesia – the destination of many refugees who had fled to the Soviet Union – that was managed by Ida Kaminska,[80] and the other in Łódź, the L.Y.T. (Łódź Yiddish Theater). In 1947, Dzigan and Shumacher were appointed managers of the latter, which until this point had performed classic plays of Yiddish popular theater such as *Di kishef-makherin* (The Witch) by Avrom Goldfaden and *Khasye di yesoyme* (Khasya the Orphan Girl) by Jacob Gordin. As was noted, in 1947, with the financial support of the Central Committee, the artists performed their second show, *Nu, un vos vayter?* (Nu, So What Now?), a rhetorical question concerning the future of their art and the Jews in Poland. In February 1948 they staged the *Zingendik un tantsndik*, which bore the same name as the show they had performed in the Soviet Union; and in October 1948 they performed their last show in Poland, *Balebatish un demokratish*, their first postwar show to include current satirical content [See Figure 10].[81] It is difficult to ascertain an exact number of

78 Belting, *Art History*, 10.

79 See Redlich, *Life in Transit*.

80 Moshe Lipman had returned from Russia a few months earlier and, in August 1946, successfully staged several plays in Łodz. Ida Kaminska and her husband, the actor Marian Melman, returned from Russia in December 1946. In January 1947 she began performing in the show *Mirele Efros*.

81 I have not found playbills for the performances or full descriptions of them. The following discussion is based on memoirs, reviews, and advertisements for the shows, in addition to the few scripts that have survived.

performances or audience numbers during these years. However, according to press reports the shows were performed between forty-five and fifty-nine times and were watched by 70,000– to 80,000 people.[82]

The first show, *Abi m'zet zikh!*, was staged at the end of August 1947 in the Roma Theater in Warsaw and marked Dzigan and Shumacher's reunion with their audience. The reviewer Yitskhok Bornshteyn noted that the performance was of great artistic, social, and cultural significance. He depicted the surprising appearance of Yiddish posters in the streets of Warsaw, which contributed to a feeling of a cultural revival, adding that eight years had passed since the Jews last laughed in this way.[83] Other critics commented on the public's high expectations, as well as the actors' immense success, talent, precision in constructing archetypal Jewish characters and creating a folk voice to connect with their audience. Further reviewers observed that the artists succeeded in generating a feeling of great intimacy and remarked on the Jewish characteristics of their performances, their Yiddishkeit.[84] One reviewer noted that the new show was similar to those performed by Ararat in the prewar period, although due to the recent events its content was deeper.[85]

Not only adult survivors who had attended Dzigan and Shumacher's prewar performances came to see them perform again. Rather, the shows were also attended by families with children, as well as "many Jews without Jewish names, who recently started attending Jewish events."[86] Some did not speak Yiddish and required explanations and translations during the performance.[87] The duo's target audience changed and expanded, influencing their choice of material, the level of their language, and its symbolic meaning in the audience's consciousness. In the months of September and October 1947, Dzigan and Shumacher embarked on their first tour in postwar Poland. They appeared everywhere that a Jewish population was to be found, and these Jews also brought their children

---

82 These statistics are based on the words of Yisroel Shumacher, quoted by M. Goldin, "Af a tsuzamentref." Redlich defines the Yiddish theater as one of the most impressive achievements of Jewish culture in Łodz and describes the city as a thriving center of Yiddish culture. See Redlich, *Life in Transit*, 71–73. Regarding the memory of the Holocaust in public ceremonies see ibid., 70–71.

83 Bornshteyn, "Akht yorn."

84 Bornshteyn, "Di ershte"; Sfard, "Tsum ershtn uftrit"; Av., "Dzigan un Shumacher"; *Unzer vort*, "Shturmisher."

85 Av., "Dzigan un Shumacher."

86 Bornshteyn, "Akht yorn."

87 Ibid.

to the theater.[88] The performances became exceptional cultural and social events that no Jew wanted to forego.[89]

Performing in the provinces was akin to acting in front of an audience of “dead people,” writes Dzigan. The jovial monologues sounded sad, and instead of words, he uttered the Kaddish, the mourners’ prayer. Every word evoked the past and those no longer alive; feelings of longing consumed audience and actors alike. “I told jokes and we all cried,” confesses Dzigan, revealing the emotional dimension that ruled in their theater. The performances became not only a reconstructed document of the past but also a cultural and linguistic eulogy.[90] The artists found it difficult to bear the disparity between their intention in telling jokes and their artistic expression and the audience’s reaction.

“Abi m’zet zikh!”: Between Silence and Speech, Death and Revival

Following the duo’s performance in Paris in September 1949, Leon Leneman described the skit “Abi m’zet zikh!” which was also the name of the entire show, as follows [See Figure 9]:

> ווען דער פֿאָרהאַנג האָט זיך אויפֿגעהויבן, זענען זיי ביידע, דזשיגאַן און שומאַכער, געשטאַנען אויף דער בינע און נישט רעדנדיק גאָרנישט, געקוקט אויפֿן עולם, וואָס האָט פֿאַרפֿולט דעם זאַל. לאַנג האָבן זיי אַזוי געקוקט אויפֿן עולם, אויף "זייער עולם", וועלכער איז געזעסן שטיל און גוט פֿאַרשטאַנען, וואָס דער שטומער בליק באַדײַט. ביז זיי האָבן ביידע צוזאַמען אַרויסגעזאָגט: אַבי מען זעט זיך... די דאָזיקע פֿיר ווערטער וועלכע פֿלעגן קומען נאָכן באַגריסן זיך מיט די בליקן, האָבן ממש עלעקטריזירט דעם עולם און אַ שטורעם פֿון אַפּלאָדיסמענטן האָט געגעבן צו פֿאַרשטיין, וויפֿל זין און אינהאַלט די געציילטע ווערטער פֿאַרמאָגן אין זיך . . . "איר זענט געראַטעוועט! מיר לעבן! . . . מיר זעען זיך, מיר לעבן, מיר וועלן לעבן!"[91]

88 Bornshteyn relates that the producer of the show gave all the children sweets so that they would not cry during the performance. See Bornshteyn, “Dzigan un Shumacher.”
89 These aspects were not unique to the theater of Dzigan and Shumacher. The theater played a similar social role in the cultural activities of survivors in DP camps. Although not professional theater, it created a sense of cultural revival, as was expressed in the newspapers published in the camps. Concerning theater in the DP camps see Florsheim, “Sipuro shel te’aṭron hayidish.”
90 Dzigan, *Der koyekh*, 291–92.
91 Leneman, “Abi men zet zikh.” Shmuel Atzmon-Wircer also described the impression that the performance left on its audience following the duo’s first performance in Israel: “Their first performance was in Ohel Shem. It made a great impression on me. To such an extent that Shimon Israeli and I did not go to bed. We remained in the theater. We went to sleep in the theater, because the next day there would be a rehearsal, and we got dressed in their clothes. The next morning, the workers came and said: ‘Dzigan and Shumacher have nowhere to sleep, they are sleeping in the theater.’” See Rotman, “Hadibuk ’einenu Moshe Sneh.”

> [When the curtain rose, both Dzigan and Shumacher were standing on the stage, not saying a word, looking at the audience, which filled the venue to capacity. For a long time, they remained watching the audience, "their audience," which sat quietly, understanding the significance of this silent look. Until they both pronounced in unison: Abi m'zet zikh. . . Those four words, following the greeting with their eyes, electrified the audience, and a storm of applause expressed how much content those words possess . . . "You are right! We are alive! . . . we meet again each other, we live, we will live!"]

The silence, which is mentioned in most descriptions of the performance, endowed the encounter between actors and audience with a ritual dimension. By drawing out the silence at the first postwar meeting with their audience, Dzigan and Shumacher emphasized the dimensions of the disaster and the gaping hole between past and present, between the reality of the war and its artistic representation. This was the artists' initial reaction to the disaster. David Roskies describes the Jewish inhabitants of Sholem Aleichem's world in the following manner: "I talk, therefore I am."[92] Inverting this statement, silence, or the representation of silence on stage, casts doubt upon existence.

Silence played an explicit and vital role in the dialogue after Auschwitz. Silence as a statement is an inseparable part of speech. Dzigan and Shumacher's silence signaled that no words could describe the catastrophe. The silence on stage was an aesthetic expression of an ethical perception, a symbolic representation of the impossibility – or the futility or lack of desire – of articulating something in words, an artistic representation of trauma. This silence, which characterized the initial encounter with their audience wherever they appeared in the years 1947–1952 (in Poland and throughout Europe, Israel, and South America), was a ceremony of joint introspection that encompassed both performers and audience, "'Their audience,' which sat quietly, understanding the significance of the silent look," as Leneman wrote.[93] The spectators watched Dzigan and Shumacher's silence in silence, a Yiddish silence, and it stretched out for a period that was difficult to bear.[94]

In those moments of silence, separating the tragedy from the continuity of life, history was split into two. These two mediators – for whom the Yiddish word and the Łódź dialect functioned as a bridge constructed from the Yiddish phrase "Abi m'zet zikh!" – floated over the abyss separating past from present, life from death, silence from speech. These words, beyond simply stressing the act of reunion, returned life to the stage, brought the audience back to the present, and rescued the listeners from the paralyzing abyss of the past.

---

92 Roskies, *Against the Apocalypse*, 163.

93 Leneman, "Abi men zet zikh."

94 After World War II, survivors feared speaking Yiddish publicly in Poland.

Figure 9: Advertisement for the program *Abi m'zet zikh!*, Roma theater in Warsaw. Dzigan and Shumacher's first performance after the war. BAA file 149–01.

Carol Kidron has examined the role that memory and silence played in conveying the traumatic story of the Holocaust among second-generation survivors. She notes that writing the history of genocide is complicated by the fact that the event is beyond words, beyond any narrative or possible representation.[95] Popular culture and science perceive personal or national silence negatively: this lack of speech stands in contrast to the reigning presumption that "making a sound" is a necessary condition for healthy "experience." However, Kidron

95 Kidron, "Ethnography of Silence," 5–7.

claims that silence itself is a means of expression, communication, and even a way to share knowledge: a legitimate narrative voice.[96] In their performance, silence and impotence became the main topics of Dzigan and Shumacher's dialogue. Indeed, the dialogue – action and speech – annulled the silence and the impotence, stressing the role of silence as a preliminary condition for the reunion of artists and audience:

ביידע: אַבי מ'זעט זיך!
ש: נו, וואָס רעדסטו נישט?
ד: פֿאַר וואָס רעדסטו נישט?
ש: ס'רעדט זיך נישט, אַ מאָדנער געפֿיל. אַלץ בלײַבט שטעקן אין האַלדז.
ד: ס'איז דען אַ ווּנדער?
ש: טאַקע נישט קיין ווּנדער, אַזוי לאַנג געוואַרט אויף דעם דאָזיקן מאָמענט. ווידער זײַן אין דער היים, אויף דער בינע. ווי אַ מאָל, האָבן פֿאַר זיך אַן עולם.
...
ש: איבעריקנס וואָס איז דאָ אַ סך צו זאָגן.
ביידע: אַבי מ׳זעט זיך... און שוין.[97]

[Both: The main thing: We meet again!
Sh: Nu, why aren't you talking?
Dz: Why aren't you talking?
Sh: I can't talk. A strange feeling. Everything gets stuck in my throat.
Dz: Is that a wonder?
Sh: It's actually no wonder at all. We waited so long for this moment. To be at home again, on the stage, like in the old days, with our audience.
...
Sh: Apart from that, what's left to say.
Together: The main thing: We meet again ... And that's it.]

Even after pronouncing the sentence "Abi m'zet zikh," the words stick in the actors' throats. Following the excitement at once again performing on stage, "at home," before an audience, words are redundant: the main thing is the encounter, not the performance. The actors afterwards continue with a dialogue concerning humor and art after the Holocaust:

ש: ניין, מײַנע פֿרײַנד. ס'איז נישטאָ פֿון וואָס צו לאַכן, פֿון וועמען צו לאַכן און פֿאַר וועמען. אַז איך קוק זיך אַרום און זע דעם חורבן וואָלט איך זיך באַגראָבן לעבעדיקערהייט. אַבֿרהם, אַ גלעזל ביר!

ד: הערט נישט וואָס דער מרה־שחורהניק רעדט. איך האַלט אַז מען דאַרף לאַכן און מען מוז לאַכן. אויב מען האָט דערלעבט אַ נקמה אין די שׂונאים דאַרף מען זײַן פֿריילעך. גיט מיר ווײַן, ווײַב, געזאַנג און מאַנע־קאַשע.

96 Ibid., 6–7.
97 BAA, file 149–02.

> [Sh: No, my friends, there's nothing to laugh about, no one to laugh about, and no one to laugh for. When I look around and see the destruction, I want to bury myself alive. Avrom, a glass of beer!
> Dz: Don't listen to the feelings of despair. I believe we must laugh, and we ought to laugh. And if one has lived to see revenge, one must be happy. Bring me wine, a woman, song, and kasha (buckwheat porridge).]

Shumacher disagrees, again arguing that they should don sack and ashes, mourn continuously, and renounce all life's pleasures. The dialogue concludes with an open question, outlining the infinite number of possibilities available to the Jews in Poland: to leave, to remain, to cry, to laugh, to take, to give, to act, or not to act:

ד: וואָס?
ש: איר פֿאָרט?
ד: ווען?
ש: איר בלײַבט?
ד: ווו?
ש: אויף דער ווײַט?
ד: ווער?
ש: אויף יענער זײַט?
ד: וואָס?
ש: מאַכט נישט קיין פּאַניק.
ד: ווער?
ש: איך בלײַב אויך.
ד: ווו?
ביידע: ווער? וואָס? ווען? ווו?

> [Dz: What?
> Sh: Are you going?
> Dz: When?
> Sh: Are you staying?
> Dz: Where?
> Sh: Far?
> Dz: Who?
> Sh: On that side?
> Dz: What?
> Sh: Don't cause a panic?
> Dz: Who?
> Sh: I'm staying too.
> Dz: Where?
> Both: Who? What? When? Where?]

This inability to act and a dialogue that borders on the absurd recall another central dialogue in the history of Western theater – that of Vladimir and Estragon in Beckett's play *Waiting for Godot*. The play was written in French (October

1948–January 1949)[98] and first performed in the Théâtre de Babylone in Paris on January 5, 1953, directed by Roger Blin, four years after Dzigan and Shumacher staged *Abi m'zet zikh!* in the same city:

> Vladimir: We can still part, if you think it would be better.
> Estragon: It's not worth while now.
> [*Silence.*]
> Vladimir: No, it's not worth while now.
> [*Silence.*]
> Estragon: Well, shall we go?
> Vladimir: Yes, let's go.
> [*They do not move.*][99]

It is difficult to determine with any certainty whether Beckett or Blin saw Dzigan and Shumacher's performance in Paris. However, the original name of Estragon's character was Levi, a name popular among French Jews.[100] Similarly to Estragon's statement that he is not a historian in the second scene of *Waiting for Godot*, Dzigan and Shumacher created a theater of the present, into which they artificially wove sections symbolically representing a past that no longer existed (such as *Kasrilevker-sreyfes* by Sholem Aleichem).[101] Isaac Janasowicz claimed in 1947 that this was not the time to experiment with artistic revolutions or to search for new means of expression. He believed that the priority was a return to the central and classic element of the theater – the actor – and the reconstruction of the world anew around this figure. The actor, according to Janasowicz, himself became a representation of the last refugee from a destroyed world, a world that needed rebuilding.[102]

The main difference between Dzigan and Shumacher, on the one hand, and Vladimir and Estragon, on the other, is that the Jewish actors transitioned from a status of passivity, expressing impotence, to debating the question of action and, immediately afterwards, to action itself. After voicing the existential questions publicly, and following the ritualized silent opening, after the main thing

---

98 Ackerly and Gontarski, *Samuel Beckett*, 620.

99 Beckett, *Dramatic Works*, 52.

100 Beckett began to take an interest in Jewish art while residing in Germany and even gave one of his poems a Yiddish title, "Ooftish." Since childhood, he was in contact with Jewish families and, following his friend Alfred Perron, even joined the French Resistance at a time when many Jewish refugees were members of this underground group.

101 Concerning *Kasrilevker sreyfes* see below pp. 130–134.

102 Janasowicz, "Der ershter program." An analysis of Dzigan and Shumacher's skit as a drama of eternal refugees, even in the State of Israel, reveals many points of overlap with the duo's skit from Łodz and Beckett's play. This topic requires a separate examination.

(meeting again), they can move on to the secondary matter – acting, speaking, and humor. This, in fact, was the main thing:[103]

ש: גאָלדענע ייִדן.
ד: האַרציקע ייִדן.
ש: וועגן זיי האָבן מיר געחלומט.
ד: נאָך זיי האָבן מיר געבענקט.
ש: און איצט אַז מיר זײַנען צוזאַמען...
ד: אין טעאַטער... אין שטוב...
ש: זאָל זײַן היימלעך. איר וועט עפּעס דערציילן, איך וועל זינגען.
ד: איך וועל שפּילן... כ'וועל שוין נישט שפּילן.
ש: און וואָס איז דאָ אײַך צו זאָגן:
ביידע: אַבי מ'זעט זיך...

[Sh: Dear Jews.
Dz: Beloved Jews.
Sh: We dreamed about them.
Dz: We missed them.
Sh: And now that we are together...
Dz: In the theater... at home...
Sh: To make it familiar. You say something, I'll sing.
Dz: I'll act... I won't act.
Sh: And what is left to tell you:
Together: The main thing: We meet again...]

Upon concluding the dialogue, the two began to sing a cabaret-like song – thus bringing the stalemate to an end.[104]

"A word does not start as a word," claims theater director Peter Brook, "it is an end product which begins as an impulse, stimulated by attitude and behavior which dictates the need for expression."[105] The silence in the post-Holocaust dialogue symbolizes the inability to express or to respond to the death, the loss, and the destruction. By contrast, the act of speaking, the word, and articulation

103 In their first show in postwar Poland, Dzigan and Shumacher also performed skits memorializing prewar Jewish life: monologues, lighthearted skits, folk songs, and dances.
104 It is possible that this structure was influenced by the show *Freylekhs*, performed by GOSET, which opened with a scene presenting the myth of creation: beginning with an empty stage, the light gradually reveals the forms of human beings. At first, the stage is silent, then thunder is heard, and suddenly a *badkhn* appears, endeavoring to brush the melancholy aside. See Veidlinger, *Moscow State Yiddish Theater*, 247–49.
105 Brook, *Empty Space*, 11–12.

symbolize existence, as in the Biblical process of creation. Dzigan notes in his memoirs:

> האָבן מיר אויפֿגעלעבט באַלוט מיט אונדזער לשון . . . דער עולם אין זאַל לאַכט, ער פֿרייט זיך מיט דעם באַקאַנטן ווערטערקלאַנג, וואָס גלעט אַזוי זײַן אויער . . . ווידער האָט דאָס ייִדישע וואָרט, דאָס ייִדישע ליד, דערמאָנט יעדערן זײַן סבֿיבֿה, זײַנע נאָענטע, זײַנע בעסטע יאָרן . . . נאָך איין רגע און מען האָט געקענט מיינען, אַז ס'איז גאָרנישט געשען; אַז דאָס אַלץ איז געווען אַ בייזער חלום. אָט האָבן מיר, איך און שומאַכער, זיך פֿונאַנדערגערעדט מיט דער לאָדזשער אויסשפּראַך.[106]
>
> [We revived (the neighborhood of) Bałuty with our language . . . the audience laughs in the theater hall, rejoices as the familiar-sounding words caress their ears . . . Again, the Yiddish word, the Yiddish song, reminded everyone of his surroundings, his relatives, the most beautiful years . . . for a moment you might think that nothing happened, that it was all a bad dream. Shumacher and I created this world using the Łódź dialect.]

The concept of revival became central in the postwar discourse, touching on the ideas of continuity, life, death, and survival. Following Dzigan and Shumacher's return to Poland, Isaac Janasowicz wrote:

> דאָס קלײנקונסט־טעאַטער איז בכּוח אילוזאָריש אויפֿצולעבן די פֿילעוודיקע שײנקייט פֿון אונדזער נאָענטן אַמאָל . . . אויב מיר טראַכטן וועגן המשך, מוזן מיר כּסדר האָבן פֿאַר די אויגן דאָס שיינע פֿון דער פֿאַרגאַנגענהייט.[107]
>
> [The kleynkunst-theater is able to revive in the imagination the evocative beauty of our recent past . . . when thinking about continuity, we must constantly hold before our eyes the beauty of that past.]

In this discourse regarding the resurrection of Jewish life in postwar Poland, the "new Jew" in Poland was, almost literally, "homeless." This is reflected in the phrase *heymloze Yidn* (homeless Jews), which was often used at this time to describe the Jewish state of being.[108] Using their language, dialect, and body language, Dzigan and Shumacher possessed the miraculous power to bring back to life the culture and the past, to create a temporary home at least for the duration of their performance. That was their way of creating or staging *Yiddishland*, temporary and independent sovereignties based on language, as defined by the social and political thinker and one of the ideologists of Yiddishism and diaspora nationalism, Haim Zhitlowski (1865–1943).[109]

---

106 Dzigan, *Der koyekh*, 291–92.

107 Janasowicz, "Vos far a kleynkunst."

108 See Efros, *Heymloze yidn*.

109 Before the First World War, Haim Zhitlowski (1865–1943) defined this concept, which connects between language (Yiddish) and land: "A national spiritual territory . . . whose atmosphere is the fresh and healthy air of the seashore, and in which every breath that is taken, every word that is spoken, upholds the living and their existence in the world as a nation." Zhitlowski, *Geklibene verk*, 321–22. Translation from Chaver, *What Must Be Forgotten*, xiv.

Deterritorialization

The murder of the great majority of Yiddish speakers and the destruction of the cultural center of European Jewry in the Holocaust, the persecutions in the Soviet Union and Poland after the Holocaust, and the negative policy toward Yiddish in the State of Israel, together with the migration of many survivors from Europe to Mandatory Palestine and America – all these led to a new understanding of Yiddish, both the culture and the language. "For Zhitlowski," argues American scholar Jeffrey Shandler, "the tautology of language and people embodied in this term . . . epitomizes the power of language to realize Jewish sovereignty in the face of the widespread perception of Jews as a people without a land."[110] According to Shandler, Yiddishland characterizes the linguistic practice of Yiddish after the Holocaust, when Yiddish acquired a symbolic dimension beyond that of a language of communication.[111] The act of speaking enabled the temporary existence of *Yiddishland*, similarly to the "temporary autonomous zones" defined by Hakim Bey, which are governed by unofficial speech, culture, and language.[112] Thus, Yiddishland is any space that is defined by speech in Yiddish.[113] While George Steiner regarded the text as the Heimat (Homeland), and Czesław Miłosz believed the mother tongue constitutes the native land, for Dzigan and Shumacher performing on stage the Yiddish word, and specifically the Łódź dialect, enabled them to reconstruct a home, a territory. For Dzigan and Shumacher, and for the Jewish survivors, postwar Łódź and Warsaw became non-places, or photographic negatives of the cities in their prewar state. In this reality, when the cities were no longer what they had been, their representations on stage became more real, or closer to the original, than the actual Łódź or Warsaw. Warsaw and the Jewish neighborhood of Bałuty in Łódź, as revived by Dzigan and Shumacher, became Foucauldian heterotopias: counter-spaces, negatives, or, better-expressed, positives of the other spaces. A heterotopia can juxtapose in one real place several

---

110 Shandler, *Yiddishland*, 37.

111 Ibid., 31–58, 126–153.

112 Bey, *T.A.Z.*, 96–97.

113 The political and national movement, Yiddishism, connected Yiddish language with the concept of nation: it sought to endow Jewish life in the diaspora, which centered on Eastern Europe, with legitimacy. The Jewish workers' movement, the Bund, a secular socialist movement established in 1897, claimed that the language spoken by most of the Jews in the diaspora created modern Jewish culture, distinguishing the Jews from their surroundings and justifying their existence wherever they lived. The central term in the movement's perception of nationalism was "hereness," a concept coined by Vladimir Medem.

spaces that are incompatible.[114] The Yiddish language and the Łódź dialect no longer belonged to an existing geographical place or landscape; they belonged to a group of dispersed speakers and survivors. The local place had disappeared. The dialect became a sound without a home, a dialect in danger of extinction, containing the memory of a city and a culture. As such, it was a means to revive, for the duration of the performance, a world that had ceased to exist. The dialect, the language, became the territory, the land, a faithful reconstruction of an original that no longer was.

Melech Ravitch described Dzigan and Shumacher as bearing a Łódź version of Menakhem-Mendl's music.[115] Arn Zeitlin also commented on their unique diction, their melodious Polish, and their folksy, spoken language.[116] In 1969, a few years after Shumacher's death, the poet and essayist Jacob Glatstein referred to the metonymic status of Dzigan's language after the Holocaust, noting that his spoken and body language, which were beyond any artistic and literary theory, represented not only the special pronunciation of Łódź but Polish Yiddish in general:

> ווען דזשיגאַן עפֿנט דאָס מויל, רעדט ער נישט נאָר לאָדזשער ייִדיש, נאָר ער דיסטילירט אין זײַן רעדן די גאַנצע מוזיק און דעם חן פֿון פּוילישן ייִדיש . . . דזשיגאַן רעדט דעם ייִדיש פֿון גאַנצן פּוילישן ייִדנטום . . . [ער] שפּילט אויס מיט זיין מויל די גאַנצע גאַמע פֿון פּוילישן ייִדיש. דערצו קומט נאָך זײַן קענטשאַפֿט פֿון פּויליש־ייִדישן קנייטש, פֿון די זשעסטן בײַם רעדן, פֿון די זשעסטן בעתן אומגעדולדיקן הערן יענעם און אפֿילו בײַם שווײַגן. דאָס פּוילישע ייִדיש האָט אין דזשיגאַנען געקראָגן איר גרויסן אַרויסריידער און צוריקרופֿער.[117]
>
> [When Dzigan opens his mouth, he is not only talking in Łódź Yiddish. In his speech, Dzigan concentrates the entire music of Polish Yiddish. Dzigan speaks the Yiddish of all Polish Jews . . . (He) performs with his mouth the entire range of Polish Yiddish. Furthermore, (we appreciate) his familiarity with all the nuances of Polish-Yiddish, the gestures while speaking, the gestures while listening impatiently to someone else, and even in silence. Dzigan offered the greatest contribution to reviving and expressing Polish Yiddish.]

Following the Holocaust, the hierarchy between signifier and signified, between representor and represented, altered. In a review of the show *Balebatish un demokratish*, the Jewish Polish theater critic J. Pinskier claimed that Dzigan's red kerchief, which before the war was a clear identifying sign of the artist, continued to arouse the same feelings also in the postwar period.[118] However, in the

---

114 Foucault, "Other Spaces."

115 Melech Ravitch, in the playbill for *Nadir un veyn nisht*.

116 Zeitlin, "Dzigans un Shumachers nign."

117 Glatstein, "Dzigan kumt."

118 Pinskier, "*Kuznia folkloru: Permiera zespolu Dzigana i Szumacher*," September 28, 1948, the name of the newspaper is not noted. See BAA, file 149–02.

new age the kerchief symbolized not only Dzigan specifically, and the Polish Jew in general, "the simple Jews," but also the red kerchief itself in its prewar role. Dzigan and Shumacher fulfilled a similar role: they were not only a theater of the present; they represented and carried with them the memory of Dzigan and Shumacher's prewar theater. It is fascinating that when performing, they sometimes appeared like an unreliable reproduction of themselves: "Following a performance at the beginning of the 1950s in Buenos Aires, an old Jewish woman approached us. She said to us: 'You were good, boys, but I know the real Dzigan and Shumacher from before the war.'"[119] In this postwar reincarnation of performance, text, language, and body language, the actor became a custodian of memory. All aspects of the actors' bodies and the duo's performance were not merely a performance of the present but also an expression of nostalgia, a means of connecting with the past. The theater, the red kerchief, and Dzigan and Shumacher became not only themselves but also a reminder of what they were before the Second World War, a *lieu de mémoire*, a human monument with the power to revive the past and renew or immortalize it, a (more or less faithful) copy of a lost original.

The first performance of Dzigan and Shumacher's second show in Poland (and their first show as managers of the L.Y.T.) took place on December 19, 1947, in Łódź. This was an important social event attended by central figures from the Jewish community in Poland.[120] The title of the show, *Nu, un vos vayter?* (Nu, So What Now?), articulated one of the pressing questions that the artists and Polish Jewry – survivors and refugees – faced after the Holocaust. On stage, Dzigan and Shumacher reflected on how individuals confronted the new reality, the question of re-creating Jewish identity, the issue of migration, and the difficulties of material survival.

So too, the monologue "Azoy zogt Itshe-Meyer" (So Says Itshe-Meyer), which Dzigan and Shumacher wrote and performed in 1947, centers on a character who had already appeared in their performances in the Soviet Union and became, in Poland, the last survivor of an extinct race (or the last representative of the Hasidic Jews). Itshe-Meyer raises existential questions and debates the renewal of the Jewish nomadic experience. His monologue describes the terrible conditions that the Jews endured in postwar Poland and the disappearance of the traditional

---

119 Y. L., "Shumacher – 'Einenu." They had previously been compared to themselves at performances in Polish provinces before the Second World War. However, in the context of the post-Holocaust narrative, this story (which may or may not be true) acquired a symbolic meaning.
120 *Dos naye lebn*, "Fayerlekhe premyere."

Jew.[121] The monologue begins with an existential declaration, illustrating that he (Itshe-Meyer) is a survivor, "Kh'bin do!" (I am here!), and immediately continues with two questions. The first casts doubt on the previous statement: "Kh'leb?" (Am I alive?), while the second raises doubts and difficulties concerning the near future: "Kh'vel hobn parnose?" (Will I make a livelihood?).

Changing Names, Changing Appearance: The New Jewish Identity

One of the central expressions of survivors' attempts to mold a new identity in the postwar reality, one of the ways to survive or be reborn, was to give up their Jewish names.[122] In the monologue "Baytn dem nomen oder nisht?" (To Change My Name or Not?, 1947), written by Celina Shumacher for her husband, the actor says: "I want to follow the trend, I want to change my name, because it sounds too Jewish, or the opposite, too German: Shumacher."[123] Shumacher continues, describing the complexities that the German (and Jewish) sound of his name caused him in post-war Poland:

> כ'וועל מוזן בײַטן דעם נאָמען און אויב שוין יאָ בײַטן, וועל איך דאָך מיר איצט נישט אַ נאָמען געבן ייִדיש. כ'ווייס מזוזה, אָדער חנוכּה־לײַכטער, אין פּויליש. אויפֿן האַרץ איז נעבעך שוואַרץ און ביטער, זאָל כאָטש דער נאָמען זײַן סימבאָליש. טשאַרני־נאָזשקעוויטש, אָדער גאָזשקאַ־טשאַרניעצקי. און דער נאָמען? ישׂראל גאָזשקאַ־טשאַרניעצקי. ס'איז גוט, אמת? ס'איז דאָך אַלץ בעסער, ווי מײַן באַקאַנטע זיסל זויערקרויט, הייסט איצט זענאָביאַ זקוואַסקאָווטקי־קאַפּושטשינסקאַ, אָדער בינעם שבתי־פֿײַנבערג הייסט: באָניפֿאַצי שוויאַטאָפּעלעק דאַבראָטאַ־גושינסקי . . . אַ כּלל ס'בלײַבט אַזוי, איך הייס: סרוליסלאַוו גאָזשקאַ־טשאַרניעצקי.

121 The script of the monologue, together with other scripts submitted to the Polish censor, survived.

122 The custom of changing names (personal or family names) was common among assimilated and enlightened Jews in both Western and Eastern Europe even before the Holocaust. A similar phenomenon occurred in the exchange of "diaspora" names for Hebrew ones among Zionist circles in the State of Israel. In her article on the mythological sabra and the Jewish past, Yael Zerubavel discusses the changing of names as one of the tactics used to replace the diasporic Jewish identity with a Zionist one. Zerubavel connects this with the ceremonial religious meaning of changing names in Jewish tradition. See Zerubavel, "Mythological Sabra," 117–18. The change of name in order to change identity or as an attempt to affect an individual's future was well known among the Conversos and is manifest in the Jewish belief that changing one's name can alter one's life. This practice derives from the Talmud, which states: "Four things annul the decree that seals a person's fate; namely, alms, prayer, change of name, and change of deeds" (Babylonian Talmud, Rosh Hashana 16b).

123 'אַז איך וויל מיטטאַנצן מיט דער מאָדע, אַז איך וויל טוישן מײַן נאָמען, ווײַל ער קלינגט צו ייִדיש, צי פֿאַרקערט, צו דײַטשיש: שומאַכער.'

> [I have to change my name and, if I'm already changing it, I won't give myself a Jewish name. I know, Mezuzah or Chanukah light in Polish. My poor heart is bitter, at least the name should be symbolic. Czarny-Noszkewic or Goszka-Czarniecki. And the name? Israel Goszka-Czarniecki. It's good, right? It's better than my acquaintance Zisl Zoyerkroyt who is now called Zenovia Zkváskový-Kapuścińska, or Binem Shasey-Faynberg, who is called Bonifacy Świętopełk Dobrota- Guszinsky . . . In short, it stays like this: Srulislaw Goszka-Czarnecki.]

Replacing one's Jewish name with a non-Jewish one was intended to signify the subject's re-birth, even if it was based on a translation of the original name. This change of name (and appearance, see below) expressed the person's hope that it would help protect him from persecution, that he would fade into the Polish human and semantic landscapes.

Polish Jews also attempted to alter their identities in other ways. The external appearance of the Hasidic Jew had been erased from the Polish landscape. Itshe-Meyer relates in the monologue that initially he looked for Jewish survivors "with a *kapote*, with a Jewish hat, with a beard. A Jew from Nowolipki Street."[124] However, considering the situation, he satisfied himself with finding a Jewish beard: "I went through half the city until I found a beard; it wasn't a beard but a tiny beard, and not the beard of a Jew, but (the beard) of a Billy goat."[125] In the new reality, the Jew changed, disguised himself, or disappeared. Most of the Polish Orthodox Jewish population perished in the Holocaust, and many of those that remained abandoned their faith. Therefore, according to the skit, the closest thing to a Jewish beard that one could find on the Polish street after the war was a Billy goat. The Billy goat's beard preserved the memory of the Jewish appearance.[126]

The support given to survivors and refugees by international Jewish aid organizations contributed to building the new Jewish identity. Dzigan and Shumacher critiqued certain aspects of these organizations' activities. For example, criticism of the American Joint Distribution Committee and the dependence it created

---

124 'מיט אַ קאַפּאָטע, מיט אַ ייִדיש היטל, מיט אַ באָרד. אַ ייִד פֿון דער נאָוואָליפּקי־גאַס.'

125 כ'בין דאָך אויסגעלאָפֿן אַ האַלבע שטאָט ביז כ'האָב געפּאַקט אַ באָרד, איז עס נישט געווען קיין באָרד נאָר אַ בערדל, און נישט פֿון קיין ייִד נאָר פֿון אַ קאָזע.'

126 The Billy goat's beard was a simile and idiomatic phrase that came to be linked with the description of the Hasidic Jew. Grafman writes about Dzigan's appearance on stage in 1937:

> 'ווען עס האָט זיך ווידער באַוויזן דאָס דזשיגאַנישע רויטע טיכעלע מיטן קאָזע־בערדל האָט דער זאַל אויפֿגעשטורמט.'

[When Dzigan returned to the stage with his red kerchief and a Billy goat's beard, a great storm ensued in the hall.] See Grafman, "Beys der hafsoke."

Figure 10: Yisroel Shumacher and Shimen Dzigan with puppets in the show *Balebatish un demokratish*, Łódź, 1948 (Lydia Shumacher-Ophir collection).

among the survivors appears in a monologue that was authorized by the Polish censor:

> כ'פֿאַרשטיי נישט, די אַמעריקאַנער ייִדן, זיי מיינען אַוודאי אַז די פּאָר פּוילישע ייִדן וואָס זײַנען געבליבן לעבן זײַנען משוגע פֿאַר פֿרייד, שיקן זיי זאַכן ווי פֿאַר משוגעים.[127]
>
> [I don't understand the American Jews, they must think that the pair of Polish Jews who are still alive are crazy with happiness, (because) they send things that only crazy people would want.]

The criticism intensifies over the course of the monologue: Itshe-Meyer believes that should he walk down the street wearing the (American style) clothes he received from the Joint, people will wish him a "Happy Purim" (believing he is celebrating Purim, a festival on which Jews traditionally dress up in costumes). The monologue, which was apparently written by Dzigan and Shumacher, reflects

---

127 BAA, file 194–04.

humorously on the tragic dimension of changing one's identity in the present reality: according to the artists, Polish Jews were involuntary participants in a carnival of fabricated identities.

Eternal Wandering

In 1923, Uri Zvi Greenberg published a text that expressed his feelings as he embarked on a life of nomadism. Such feelings were common among many European Jews, who felt threatened by the shadow of Ahasver, the wandering Jew:[128]

> ניִשט אַזוי לײַכט פֿאַרלאָזט מען אפילו אַזאַ ווייטיקן־היים, ווי די, ווו איך בין געבוירן און געוואַקסן, און מען פֿאַרפֿאָרט למרחקים מיטן גאַנצן ביסל ייִדן־אָרעמקייט און מיט דעם צעווייטיקטן מהות פֿון אַזאַ מין בן־אָדם ווי איך. קיין שום נײַ מזל באַגעגענט ניִשט, ווײַל דער שאָטן פֿון אַהאַסווער־זײַן ליגט דאָך ביזן טויט אויפֿן קאָפּ: קינס שוואַרצע גלאָריע.[129]
>
> [It's not so easy to leave even such a painful homeland as the one in which I was born and raised and traverse great distances, even with all the poverty of the Jews and with the painful essence of a person such as myself. No new fortune greets you, because the shadow of Ahasver hovers over you until the day of your death: Cain's black glory.]

The new Jew in postwar Poland was, as mentioned above, in a state of homelessness.[130] In such a situation, identity becomes deterritorialized or undergoes constant territorial changes.[131] This applied to the Austrian Jew whom Itshe-Meyer encountered in the offices of the Central Committee of Polish Jews. The former tells Itshe-Meyer:

> כ'וועל מיך אַרומקוקן און פֿאָרן ווײַטער . . . קיין סטראַליע . . . כ'וועל מיך [דאָרט] אַרומקוקן און פֿאָרן ווײַטער.[132]
>
> [I will look around and go on traveling . . . to Australia . . . I will look around (there) and then go on traveling.]

This feeling of existential homelessness accompanied many Jews for years. It was also the state in which the artists had found themselves since leaving their homes

---

128 The source of the name Ahasver is in the *Ahasver-bukh*, a booklet about Ahasver the wandering Jew that circulated in Germany in the seventeenth century. See Hasan-Rokem, "Carl Schmitt and Ahashver."

129 Uri Zvi Greenberg, "*Baym shlus:* veytikn-heym af slavisher," *Albatros* (1923), in Greenberg, *Gezamlte verk*, 473.

130 See, for example, the book by Yisroel Efros concerning Holocaust survivors (the remaining remnant), entitled *Heymloze yidn*.

131 Ferguson and Gupta, "Beyond 'Culture,'" 9–10, following Edward Said.

132 BAA, file 149–01.

in Warsaw in September 1939, and it persisted until they purchased homes in Tel Aviv nineteen years later. In the intervening period, the two lived in hotels or short-term rentals, preserving the feeling of constant wandering that was exemplified in the name of their first show in Israel *Vayis'u veyaḥanu* (And They Journeyed and They Encamped).[133] The stage was the home that they carried on their backs, the only territory to which Dzigan and Shumacher could cling for more than two decades. In these years, the stage became – almost literally – a place, a home, and a homeland with a language, culture, and laws of its own.

In the new political reality, it was also difficult to discern hope for a better future in the political parties. The song "Shumacherishe kupletn" (Shumacher-like Couplets), performed by Shumacher, directly criticizes the great proliferation of political parties, their platforms, and the validity of the solutions they offered for the existence of the Jewish people:

> די ציוניסטישע פּאַרטייען, / כ'מיין, איר מעגט זיי אַלע גלייבן, / וועקן, רופֿן, מאָנען, שרײַען, / אַז עס זאָל נישט קיינער בלײַבן – / אויף דער זײַט. // נאָר זיי אַליין, זיי בלײַבן היגע, / בעסער זיצן דאָ במנוחה, / איידער דאָרטן כאַפּן פֿליגן, / איידער וואַרטן אויף משיחן – /אויף יענער זײַט. // בלויז דער 'בונד' האָט אַ פּלאַטפֿאָרם: / זיצן דאָ, ווו מ'איז געזעסן! / וואָס מיר פֿאָרן, ווען מיר פֿאָרן, / צאַטס [צײַט] צו טרינקען, צאַטס [צײַט] צו עסן / אויף דער זאַט. // . . . אַ סוף נעמט צו די גלות־פּלאָגן, / צום פּראָבלעם פֿון פּאַלעסטינע. / מיר קאָנען נאָר געננוי נישט זאָגן, / צי מ'עט האָבן די מדינה – / אויף דער זײַט / און אויף יענער זײַט. . .[134]
>
> [The Zionist parties, / I think you can believe them all / awake, call, demand, cry / that no one should remain – / on this side. // But they themselves, they remain here, / better to sit here calmly, / than to catch flies there / than to wait for the Messiah – / on that side. // Only the Bund has a platform: / sit here, where we are! / Why leave? When should we go? / It's time to drink, time to eat / on this side. // . . . The end is in sight for the diaspora troubles / for the problems of Palestine. / We can't say exactly / whether we will have a country – / on this side / and [or] on that side . . .]

Memory, Monument, and Theater

At the center of the skit "Der albom" (The album) by Broderzon, which was first staged in 1929 and in a new adaptation in post-Holocaust Poland in 1948, is a stage prop in the form of a massive photo album. The actors flick through its pages,

133 This phrase recurs repeatedly in the biblical description of the Children of Israel traveling through the desert following the Exodus from Egypt (Numbers, chapter 33), during which the Children of Israel lived in temporary dwellings. Jews commemorate these journeys during the festival of Sukkot (Tabernacles) by living in temporary dwellings for seven days.

134 The text is found among the manuscripts from the Polish post-Holocaust period, BAA, file 149–01.

bringing to life personalities and pictures from prewar Poland.[135] Isaac Janasowicz claimed that this skit represented a mental condition common to all the Jewish survivors, adding that it should become a fixed model in Jewish theater to display the communal past. Following the Second World War, many saw Yiddish theater not only as art but also as a memorial to European Jewry before the Holocaust.

"When Jews now mourn in public," writes David Roskies, "they preserve the collective memory of the collective disaster, but in so doing fall back on symbolic constructs and ritual acts, which necessarily blur the specificity and the implacable contradictions of the event."[136] "Der albom" is an explicit example of this [See Figure 11].

We can examine the extent to which the act of remembering in the theater of Dzigan and Shumacher, and especially in this skit, influenced one member of the audience: Ann Szedlecki, who watched one of the duo's performances when she returned to Łódź after the war. In her memoirs, Szedlecki describes the skit as an "unforgettable experience, a portrait of a lost world, never to be regained."[137] She notes the range of distinctive characters still existing in the memories of the residents of Poland, although they had disappeared from the country's streets, and how they suddenly appeared once again on the stage before her eyes, played by Dzigan and Shumacher. At the end of the introduction to her book, she compares the act of writing her memoirs to the actors flicking through the massive album on stage and, in so doing, re-creating the past. Yiddish theater became, in theory, an archive of lost Jewish life (and of itself). She perceived the process of writing, inspired by the performance, as a process of embodying memory. In order to write her memoirs, she needed to embody the past, to reenact it, "page by page."[138]

In Dzigan and Shumacher's post-Holocaust performances, it seems that the old jokes (which were part of their repertoire), certain skits that were performed before the war, and even some of the actions, language, and pronunciation became an archival memory of a reality that no longer existed.[139] The repertoire embodied the memory by means of language and body language – performativity, gestures, voice, movement, dance, song – which were seemingly ephemeral, knowledge that cannot be reproduced.

135 Ibid.
136 Roskies, *Against the Apocalypse*, 4
137 Szedlecki, *Album*, 1–2.
138 Ibid.
139 Archival memory exists in documents, maps, literary texts, archaeological remains, and video recordings, which ostensibly do not change. What changes, according to Diana Taylor, is their value and relevancy, the meaning of the archive, the way in which it is interpreted, and even enacted. See Taylor, *Archive*, 19.

Figure 11: Dzigan and Shumacher's skits in Poland: "Der albom," "Shmendrik tsurik a Yid," and "Der monolog fun Itshe-Meyer". Source unknown (BAA, file 149–01).

The living performance cannot be transferred through an archive. Traditions are preserved in the body via mnemonic aids and transmitted to the audience live, in the present.[140] Artists define or emphasize a new role for performance: preserving and imparting cultural memory and, at the same time, renewing the repertoire. Performance (language and body language) acquires a further symbolic element: some of the materials obtain an additional archival dimension, others symbolize continuity or renewal. This is the battle between creating a document of the past and between its revival as an action of memory. Cultural memory is accorded a central place in the present-day performance that seeks to prevent a culture's disappearance.

Over many years, numerous shows performed by Dzigan and Shumacher integrated a skit or song concerning the lives of the Jews before the Holocaust. An obvious example of this is "Der monument fun di kemfer fun Varshever geto" (The Monument of the Warsaw Ghetto Fighters), written by Avrom Shulman and performed in the show *Sha, sha, der sholem geyt* (Shush, Shush, the Peace is Coming, 1969). In it, the figures in Nathan Rapaport's famous sculpture *Monument to the Ghetto Heroes*, located in Warsaw, come to life and discuss what Poland means for Jews after the Holocaust. The dialogue is filled with pathos. In artistic terms, it is more interesting to analyze Dzigan's introduction to the piece:

> ליבע פֿרײַנד, און איצט װעלן מיר אַװעקשטעלן דאָס געלעכטער אין אַ זײַט. מיר װעלן נאָך הײַנט אַזױ פֿיל לאַכן אַז מיר קאָנען זיך דערלױבן צו װערן אַ ביסל ערנסט. אמת, לאַכן איז טאַקע געזונט, אָבער מיר זענען עדות פֿון אַזעלכע גרױליקע פּאַסירונגען אַז מיר װילן נישט, און טאָרן אױך נישט אַריבערגײן איבער דעם מיט שװײַגן.[141]
>
> [Dear friends, and now we will put laughter aside. Today we will laugh so much that we can allow ourselves to be a little serious. Truly, laughing is healthy, but we are witnesses to such horrific events that we will not, and also must not, pass over them with silence.]

140 Ibid., 20–24. The division that Taylor creates recalls, as she herself argues, Nora's distinction between *lieux de memoire*, which are parallel to what Taylor terms archival memory – the artificial monuments by which national and ethnic memory are created in the modern age – and *milieux de memoire*, which parallel repertoire. In Nora's opinion, the milieu of memory is the initial place of "true" memory, unfiltered and spontaneous, while a memorial is its antithesis, the modern fiction. Modernity, according to Nora, is characterized by replacing the milieus of memory by monuments of memory, such as archives and memorials. Taylor argues that Nora's concepts do not distinguish between methods of imparting memory or between types of audience. He distinguishes between "before" and "after," between past (traditional, authentic, and lost) and present (which is depicted generally as modern and global, identified with mass culture). In opposition to Nora, who argues that in modern society textual memory has assumed the place of embodied memory, Taylor claims that the repertoire serves, either alone or together with the archive, to create and preserve cultural memory.

141 BAA, files 145–02, 171–04, 178–03.

Figure 12: Dzigan and Shumacher in the Soviet Union (1942?) or Poland (1948?) (Lydia Shumacher-Ophir collection).

Dzigan's opening makes a sharp and clear distinction between holy and profane, between the happiness of humor and life and the painful rituality of dealing with death and grief. In the new reality, the memorial ceremony was obligatory.

> דזשיגאַן: כ'האָב דאָ אין זינען דאָס איצטיקע פּוילן. טויזנט יאָר ייִדיש פּוילן און וואָס איז פֿון דעם געבליבן? טויזנט יאָר ייִדיש פּוילן איז ווי אין שטויב צעריבן. קאָן מען איבער דעם אַריבערגיין מיט שווײַגן? און אפֿשר... ווי האָט געזאָגט מײַן לערער דער פּאָעט משה בראָדערזאָן: – ווײ־געשוויגן קאָן העכער רופֿן ווי ווײ־געשריגן. איז זאָלן מיר איצט אויסשווײַגן אונדזער געשריי – טויזנט יאָר ייִדיש פּוילן איז אַוועק מיט רויך. געבליבן איז נאָר ווי אַ זכר – זעט, דער מאָנומענט פֿון די וואַרשעווער קעמפֿער אין געטאָ![142]

[Dzigan: I am thinking about present-day Poland. A thousand years of Jewish Poland, and what remains of it? A thousand years of Jewish Poland ground down to dust. Can we pass

142 Ibid.

> over this in silence? And maybe... As my teacher, the poet Moyshe Broderzon, said: The silence of pain can be louder than a cry of pain. So, we shall now silence our cry – a thousand years of Jewish Poland went up in smoke. Only a memory remains – look, the monument to the Warsaw ghetto fighters!]

It seems that Jewish theater, at least when tackling current events, could not be whole again. It needed the gaping hole. It required its mourning garb.

Ya'akov Zerubavel described Dzigan and Shumacher's artistic activities after the Holocaust as a cultural mission to establish a monument to a way of life and Jewish folklore through word and movement, speech, and jokes.[143] Zerubavel's metaphor interprets the performative dimension as embodying the memory of the culture and, at the same time, generating a new creation by reconstructing the archival memory.

The Film *Undzere Kinder* (1949)

Dzigan's memoirs do not mention the film *Undzere kinder* (Our Children), the fourth and final in the duo's artistic careers. The film's importance lies in its testimony to the artistic activities of the two actors in postwar Poland, and it likewise sheds light on Jewish responses, artistic and historiographic, to the Holocaust in the first years immediately following the war, in close geographic proximity to where the events occurred. Here the film is discussed in the context of Dzigan and Shumacher's artistic activities in Poland [Figure 12].[144]

Undzere kinder is the only full-length Yiddish feature film made in Poland after World War II. The film was produced at the same time as *Ulica Graniczna* (Border Street) by Alexander Ford (1948), which focused on life in Warsaw before the war from the perspective of children; *Ostatni Etap* (The Last Stage) by Wanda Yakobovsky (1948), a dramatization and testimony of the director's experiences in Auschwitz; *Lang ist der Weg* (Long is the Road), script by Karl Kolev (Polish, Yiddish, and German), directed by Herbert Fredersdorf and Mark Goldstein (1948); and the documentary film *Mir lebn-geblibene* (We Who Remain) directed by Natan Gross (1948), discussed below.

143 *Nay-velt*, "Dzigan–Shumacher." Concerning Yiddish theater after the Holocaust as a monument, see Rotman, "Language Politics."

144 The discussion is based on newly discovered documents, among them an initial sketch of the film, as well as newspaper articles from the period. For more on the film, see Finder, "Überlebende Kinder"; Langer, "Undzere Kinder"; Konigsberg, "Our Children."

In 1948, Natan Gross, the director of *Undzere kinder*, wrote that cinema had become an important tool for educating and distributing the ideas of freedom, brotherhood, and justice in the Soviet Union and popular democracies. Feature films produced in these countries, documentary or partially documentary in nature, guided people toward happiness and envisioned the world that they should aspire to create. According to Gross, the Jewish film produced after the war also needed to apply this perspective. Gross's words clearly demonstrate the ideological background to his cinematic endeavors:

> The Jewish cinema in Poland decided to delve deep into the history of this country of ours and has meaning if it connects to our revival. The tragedy of our people must be the starting point for Jewish art and today's Jewish struggle. Until now, the Jewish film in Poland has assumed documentary roles. It was concerned with capturing in real time the traces of the tragedy and the first steps toward rehabilitation, even though these important roles did not elicit the appropriate reaction from relevant Jewish elements and the Jewish press.[145]

In 1948, Natan Gross approached Shaul Goskind – whose production company Kinor had already produced the documentary film *Mir lebn-geblibene* – with a proposal for a film about the Holocaust starring Dzigan and Shumacher, mainly focusing on the so-called "Jewish revival." Goskind asked Gross a question similar to that posed by Dzigan and Shumacher in their first performances in postwar Poland: How can comedy talk about the Holocaust? In addition, he added a question of his own: How could Dzigan and Shumacher star in a film that would not be a comedy?[146] Gross's first response was that the film would be a musical about Jewish children after the war, but the idea changed as he worked on the script together with Dzigan and Shumacher.[147] Rokhl Oyerbakh, a writer, historian, Holocaust survivor, and one of the foremost figures involved in documenting and collecting material relating to the Holocaust, was also involved in writing the script.[148] The film contains elements similar to those that characterized Dzigan

145 Gross, *Toldot hakolno'a*, 98–101,

146 Ibid.

147 Natan Gross, "*Dwa lata filmu żydowskiego w Polsce*," 1949. The name of the newspaper is not noted. See BAA, file 149–01.

148 During the German occupation – at the initiative of Dr. Emanuel Ringelblum, director of Oyneg Shabes (Oneg Shabbat), the underground archive of the Warsaw Ghetto – Oyerbakh managed the kitchen at 40 Leszno Street, documenting for the archive many testimonies about the terrible hunger that Jews experienced in this period. After the war, she continued her work to preserve the memory of Polish Jewry during the German occupation. She immigrated to Israel and established the division for recording Holocaust survivors' testimonies at Yad Vashem. Concerning Oyerbakh, see Friedman-Cohen, "Rokhl Oyerbakh." Likewise, a historical voice is interwoven with that of the artists when they approach the children upon arriving in Helenówek. Dzigan and Shumacher's performances in the early post-Holocaust years and which are also reflected in Dzigan's memoirs: the silence after the Holocaust and its artistic representation, the ethical question concerning the representation of the Holocaust, the role of children in rehabilitating Jewish life, molding the memory of the past, and the continuation of the Jewish cultural and linguistic tradition.

Undzere kinder was filmed in the first months of 1949, after Dzigan and Shumacher finished a series of performances with their last show in Poland, *Balebatish un demokratish* (1948), and Niusia Gold, the actress who plays the director of the orphanage, completed a tour of performances in Poland.[149] The film was shown at two public screenings, on April 3, 1950, in Warsaw, and the following day in Łódź.[150] According to the popular version of events, the Communist regime banned the film because it was proscribed by the censor. The two screenings that I noted are not mentioned in academic articles written about the film, and until now it was commonly believed that there were no screenings of the film in Poland immediately following its production.[151] It is likely that the screenings in Poland were stopped, and perhaps even that the film was banned, because the leading actors, as well as many others that participated in the making of it, had already left Poland: a fact that contradicts its message.

The film begins with the scene of a group of children and their teacher standing in front of Rapoport's Monument to the Heroes of the Warsaw ghetto uprising. The scene is directly linked to the memorial ceremony that took place at the foot of the monument in April 1948, which "symbolized Jewish national unity and led to a spiritual elevation," in the words of Hanna Shlomi.[152] In the background is the narration written by Binem Heller, read by Jacob Rotbaum:[153]

> אונדזערע קינדער, אונדזערע קינדער, וויפֿל אינהאַלט ליגט אין אָט די צוויי פּשוטע ווערטער! דאָס זײַנען אונדזערע קינדער, וואָס די היטלעריסטישע תּלינים האָבן געטריבן אין די לאַגערן פֿון אומקום. קוקט אויף די ייִדישקע נפֿשות. זיי האָבן געוויס קיין אַנונג נישט געהאַט וועגן די גרוילן אין די פֿאַנטאַזיעס פֿון די פֿאַשיסטישע

and Shumacher tell the children that they did not come to teach the youngsters but rather to collect materials. Once again, the actors present themselves as collectors of historical testimonies.

149 Niusia Gold arrived in Poland in November 1948 and remained until April 1949 (a farewell party for the actress was held on April 15, 1949; Shumacher gave a speech at the party). Apparently, she became available for filming in January 1949. Concerning the actress's arrival, see Hon, "Tsu Niusia Golds kumen." Gold (Goldberg) was born in Warsaw in 1909 and moved to Russia with her family as a child. There she began to play the roles of children in the theater of Zina Rapel. After a number of years, she studied theater in Romania and appeared in different theater groups.

150 Lastik, "Undzere kinder."

151 See Bar-On, "Hayeladim."

152 Shlomi, "Hit'argenut," 538.

153 In the original idea for the film, as Gross described it, the teacher talks to his students about the lives and fates of children during the Holocaust as they stand by the monument. See Gross, above note 149.

וועלט־אונטערצינדער. אָט זעט איר זיי הינטער דראָטן, קינדער אָפּגעטיילט פֿון דער גרויסער, פֿרײַער וועלט, קינדער פֿאַרמישפּטע צו אונטערגאַנג. דאָ זײַנען זייערע שיכעלעך. די קינדער אַליין זײַנען שוין פֿאַרוואַנדלט אין אַש, אָבער זייערע שיכעלעך זײַנען געבליבן, זייערע ליאַלקעס. עס דאַכט זיך, זיי זײַנען נאָך נישט אויפֿגעקילט פֿון די וואַרעמע קינדערהענטעלעך. אָבער נישט בלויז אומקום איז געוועזן דער גורל פֿון אונדזערע קינדער. צווישן די קעמפֿער קעגן די אָקופּאַנטן זײַנען געוועזן נישט ווייניק קינדערהעלדן. אָט איז איינער פֿון זיי, אַ באַלוינטער מיט אָרדנס און מעדאַלן, ער שטייט אויפֿן פֿאָן פֿון דענקמאָל פֿאַר די געפֿאַלענע העלדן פֿון וואַרשעווער געטאָ. זיי אַליין זײַנען אומגעקומען אין קאַמף קעגן די פֿאַשיסטן, אָבער סײַ דער דענקמאָל, סײַ די געשטאַלטן פֿון קינדערהעלדן זאָגן עדות, אַז די זאַך פֿאַר וועלכע זיי האָבן [געקעמפּט] האָט אין אונדזער לעבן פֿאָרט געזיגט. אין דעם פֿײַער פֿון די מנורות וואָס ברענען צו זייער אייביקן אָנדענק, לעבן אויף אייביק זייערע געשטאַלטן. זיי זעען דעם נײַעם ייִדן־דור פֿון באַפֿרײַטן פֿאָלק אין פּוילן. דאָס איז דער דור וואָס האָט זיך באַפֿרײַט פֿון נעכטיקן קאָשמאַר.[154]

[*Undzere kinder*, our children, what a great burden those two simple words bear! These are our children that the Hitlerist executioners drove to the extermination camps. Look at the Jewish souls. Certainly, they had no idea of the horrors imagined by the Fascists who set the world aflame. Here, you see them behind wire, children who were separated from the great, free world; children sentenced to death. Here are their little shoes. The children themselves have already been turned to ashes, but their little shoes, their dolls, remain. It seems that they still retain the warmth of the warm, little childish hands. But not only death was the fate of our children. Among those who fought against the occupier were child-heroes. Here is one of them, decorated with awards and medals, he stands in the background of the monument to the fallen heroes of the Warsaw ghetto. They were murdered in the battle against the Fascists, but the monument and the figures of the child-heroes testify that the aim for which they battled was achieved in our lifetime. They live forever in the light of the lamps burning in their eternal memory. They see the new Jewish generation living freely in Poland. This is the generation that liberated itself from yesterday's nightmare.]

The images of the children standing before Rapoport's monument – integrated with documentary footage of the piles of shoes and dolls, the physical evidence of the murder that took place in the extermination camps – are immediately followed by footage of Jewish youth building Warsaw anew and of the Jewish orphanage in Helenówek, where children play outside, plant a garden, and "learn in their language," Yiddish; even though Yiddish was not the language that most of them spoke.[155] The film depicts a clear path from death to revival, with the children playing a fundamental role in this process.[156]

The children that Gross filmed and Heller described were not only those who were liberated from yesterday's nightmares. They were also the children

---

154 The deciphering of the Yiddish text and its translation here are mine. The roll of film is damaged and therefore the other extracts are based on the Hebrew translation, in the version distributed by Ya'akov Gross.

155 See above, note 154.

156 In the original script, this image was supposed to be staged in a theater, reconstructing on stage the Warsaw monument. The decision to film at the sites themselves – such as the monument, the streets in Łodz, and Helenówek – endow the film with a documentary dimension.

"walking in the joy of life toward the socialist future. The happy children. Look at their joyful faces . . . These children were as though reborn in order to live in this time." Indeed, only children can bring about revival, playing "happily and without worries in a free country," according to the words of the film's narrator. The depiction of the children as motivation and justification for a new life after the Holocaust likewise reflects the contemporary discourse in the Yiddish press.[157] This is also characteristic of many artworks concerning the Holocaust, which focus on the survivor child as a historical witness and a central force in cultural and physical renewal.[158] This discourse is similarly evident in Dzigan's memoirs, in his depiction of the physical and mental suffering that he discerned among many Jews in Łódź when he and Shumacher returned to the city: "Their health was weak. We did not have the power to make them happy. The catastrophe, the loneliness of the city depressed us." [159] In order to deal with this reality, and to "return to themselves," the duo decided to travel to Helenówek, a "children's home" established in 1945 by the Central Committee of Polish Jews. Until 1939, this had been the location of an orphanage managed by Khayim Mordkhe Rumkowski – who subsequently became the chairman of the Judenrat in the Łódź Ghetto. Dzigan describes this visit in his memoirs:

> כ'בין געשטאַנען אין אַ ווינקל, כ'האָב געקוקט אונדזערע משהלעך, שיינדעלעך, און דער טרויער האָט געגריזשעט מײַן געמיט. איינצלנע זענען זיי געבליבן פֿון משפּחות . . . כ'האָב געזען בײַ אַנדערע קינדער אַ מאָדנעם עצבֿות אין די אויגן בעת זייערע קונדסערײַען. אַן עצבֿות פֿון דערוואַקסענע; אָבער נישט קוקנדיק אויף דעם, האָב איך געפֿונען אַ טרייסט נעבן זיי. אָט די קינדער, האָב איך געטראַכט, זענען אונדזער המשך – אויף צו להכעיס די שׂונאים און פֿאַרטיליקער. פֿאַר זיי, די קינדער, איז כּדאַי ווײַטער ממשיך צו זײַן און בויען דאָס לעבן פֿון דאָס נײַ. דאָס קליינוואַרג האָט אונדז געגעבן כּוח אָפּשאַקלען פֿון זיך די אייגענע גרוילן, אויף וויפֿל דאָס האָט זיך געלאָזט.[160]

157 Among other sources, we can learn about the status of children within Jewish society in postwar Poland from two articles published on May 9, 1947, in the newspaper *Dos naye lebn*: "Undzere kinder tsu gast in Frankraykh" (Our Children Visit France) and "Undzere kinder farbindn di yishuvim" (Our Children Unite the Communities). The rhetoric in these articles adopts the survivor children as the nation's collective young (making them "our children") and notes the importance of the children's activities and their central role in rehabilitating Polish Jewry. In another article, ""Dos kind iz undzer tsukunft – Fragn un problemen fun kinderhoyz" (The Child Is Our Future – Questions and Problems in Children's Homes), the author depicts the children as the hope for the future. See Alter, "Undzer tsukunft."

158 Concerning the role of children in relating Holocaust experiences, in American culture in general and in works such as the book *Night* by Eli Wiesel, *The Diary of Anne Frank*, or the Jewish museum in Washington in particular, see Anderson, "The Child Victim as Witness." Regarding the establishment of children's orphanages in Poland after World War II, see Shlomi, "Hit'argenut," 531, 538.

159 Dzigan, *Der koyekh*, 289–90.

160 Ibid.

[I stood in a corner, I looked at our little Moysheles, Sheyndls, and the sadness ate away at me. They remained, single remnants of entire families . . . I saw in the eyes of some children a strange sadness while they were being mischievous. The sadness of adults: but regardless of this, I found comfort in being near them. These children, I thought, are our continuity – to spite the enemies and those who sought to destroy us. For them, the children, we must continue living and rebuild life. The little people gave us strength to shake off our own sadness, as far as this was possible.]

In Dzigan's narrative, which draws on the rhetoric characteristic of the contemporary discourse, the survivor children are a positive and healthy negative of the adult survivors, giving him and Shumacher the strength to cope with the horrors. The child survivors are the "Desert Generation," alluding to the post-Exodus generation who wandered for forty years in the desert and never reached Eretz Israel, in discussions of Jewish revival in Poland. Reading Dzigan's memoirs after watching the film raises the question of whether *Undzere kinder* was based on Dzigan and Shumacher's personal experiences or the opposite: the film molded the memories and description of the period in Dzigan's book. Personal memory, historical document, and the partially fictional script of the film became interwoven.

According to Gross, the film sought to reveal "the reality and problematic nature of Polish Jewry in artistic garb." In the original idea for the film, Dzigan and Shumacher were to play war refugees looking for work in various orphanages. During their search, the audience is introduced to "the lives of the children, integrated with songs and skits." The film was to offer a kind of survey of the orphanages, with Dzigan and Shumacher as narrators.[161] However, the final script was different: the children's homes and their inhabitants were filmed in the real orphanage at Helenówek, although the children in the film were not necessarily from that orphanage. The children starred in roles that were scripted in advance. Dzigan and Shumacher appeared as themselves: refugee actors performing their show *Balebatish un demokratish* in a theater in Łódź, as is evident from the posters seen hanging in the streets of Łódź in the film. When the actors perform the skit "Zamarei hageṭo" (The Ghetto Singers),[162] children from the orphanage of Helenówek, survivors watching the performance, feel that the skit does not reflect the reality of the ghetto and boycott the performance. After the show, they come to the actors' dressing room to apologize for their behavior, arriving just as Dzigan and Shumacher are discussing one of the film's central questions: How

---

161 Natan Gross, "*Dwa lata filmu żydowskiego w Polsce*," 1949. Newspaper not named. See BAA, file 149–01.

162 It is not clear whether the piece was actually performed in this particular show.

can the Holocaust be represented on the theatrical stage; indeed, is the Holocaust a subject for artistic representation? This question, which Konigsberg and Langer discussed many years later in their articles about the film,[163] is a cinematic representation of the question that Dzigan and Shumacher posed on stage in their first performance in postwar Poland, in the skit "Abi m'zet zikh!"

Discussing the legitimacy of representing the Holocaust artistically became an inseparable part of the artistic performance itself. At this time, it was impossible to deal with the Holocaust via artistic means without reflecting the divergent opinions on this topic, the ethical and aesthetic reservations.

In the actors' dressing room, in an attempt to correct the representation of the ghetto on stage, the children act out their roles during the war, and even the part of Hitler, in addition to singing songs from the ghetto. This is performative testimony of the past, an "objective"-artistic response to the unrealistic artistic representation offered by Dzigan and Shumacher. In the liminal space of the dressing room, the roles of the actor-refugee-adult and the audience-survivor-child-witness are reversed; the hierarchies of knowledge and lack thereof, of artistic representation of the past and its ostensibly objective presentation, are inverted. Through this acting-testimony, the survivor children lay claim to the responsibility for historical representation, questioning Dzigan and Shumacher's authority to offer a representation of the ghetto years.

Following the children's improvisations in the dressing room, Shumacher argues that these youngsters are a "treasure trove and source of knowledge," and, furthermore, that "it is necessary to learn from them how to describe the ghetto." It is reasonable to suppose that this reaction was less a reflection of the duo's attitude than an echo of Oyerbakh's voice.

After the meeting in the dressing room, the director of the institution, played by Niusia Gold, invites the duo to visit Helenówek, and they accept her invitation.[164] On the way to the orphanage, on a journey from the city into nature, a Jewish, Yiddish-speaking farmer, played by Yosef Videtsky, gives the pair a ride in his cart. "There are a lot of Jewish farmers here," he reveals to the surprised artists. "We were here in the concentration camps, and when the Red Army liberated us, we remained here. We received land, beasts, equipment. You see, it's all good," claims the farmer, enthusiastically expressing the ideology of revival characteristic of the film. In the midst of the journey on the wagon, comedians

163 Konigsberg, "Our Children," 14; Langer, "Undzere Kinder."

164 In the original script, the artists are invited to go to Helenówek to rest and perform for the children at Hanukkah, a choice that can be interpreted as a symbolic link between the children and the miraculous Jewish survival. See BAA, file 149–01.

and farmer begin to sing a popular song, "Dray zikh milekhl" (Let the Millstone Turn) which was written and composed by Goldfaden for the historical operetta *Bar Kokhba*. However, new words are woven into it:

> ווי לאַנג די זאַנג איז יינגער, / איז דער קאָרן – מאָגער, גרינגער, / ווי לאַנג די זאַנג איז יינגער, / קוקט מען זיך ניט צו / ווערט אָבער דער קאָרן דיקער, / גיט עס דער ראָד אַ קער, / ער ווערט צעריבן איוף שטיקער, / מען דערקענט אים שיון ניט מער. אַרבעטער, אַרבעטער, אַרבעט דאָס ווידער. איז דאָס נישט קיין שפּיל, / דריי זיך גוט, דריי זיך גוט, / רעדעלע, מילעכל! / צערײַב גוט דעם קאָרן – צעטייל! / נישטאָ שיון קיין זאַנגען– / צעריבן דער קאָרן. / די ערשטע געשטאַלט האָט ער שוין לאַנג פֿאַרלאָרן,/ צעמישן, צעריבן געוואָרן / אונטער דער ראָד איז צעריבן געוואָרן, / עס איז שיון גאָר ווײַס / און הייסט מעל! און הייסט מעל!
>
> [As long as the ear of corn is young / the corn is thin, light, / as long as the ear of corn is young / one doesn't touch it / however, when the corn becomes thick / the wheel begins to turn, / cutting it into pieces, / and it's impossible to identify it any more. Workers, workers, turn it again. It's no game! / Turn it well, turn it well, the wheel / the millstone! / Grind up the corn – separate it! Now there are no ears of corn here – / grind the corn. / It has long lost its original form, / it's been ground down completely. / It's no longer rye, it's already flour. / It's flour! It's flour!]

In the context of the narrative of revival and the socialist reality, the meaning of the song is self-evident. Interestingly, the song is so suited to the new reality that it is difficult to discern the addition to the original:

> ווי לאַנג דער ייִד האָט נישט געפּלאַקערט / האָט מען אים געלאָזט צו רו. // אָט האָט דער ייִד אָנגעהויבן האַנדלען וואַנדלען / האָט דאָס ראָד געגעבן אַ קער. / ראָזשינקעס מיט מאַנדלען, איך געדענק שוין נישט מער...[165]
>
> [As long as the Jew was invisible / they left him alone. // But when the Jew started to trade and wander, / the wheel turned. / Raisins and almonds, I don't remember any more...]

The anti-capitalist message is clear, and it accords textually with Goldfaden's song. If the Jew will change, leaving behind trade and returning to agricultural labor, he will hold the (socialist) future in his hands. The socialist-ideological thrust is evident not only in the farmer's song, but also in the scathing propaganda message at the end of the film. The journey to the orphanage is a journey from the old world (of the refugees) to the new, and the performance is the stage for the encounter with an audience of parentless children, who have no direct link to the traumatic past, symbolizing hope and re-birth.

The ideological message of the film's creators is expressed through the pastoral Polish landscapes that visually symbolize the ideal of returning to the land, to work, and to freedom. From this landscape, in a utopian picture, Polish farmers wave to the Jewish survivors. The landscape is an ideal vision of liberated Poland

---

165 I would like to thank Yitskhok Niborski for his help in deciphering the song.

filmed by Gross,[166] that same nostalgic Polish landscape of lost childhood days that Dzigan depicts in the story of his departure from Poland in 1949:

> כ'האָב נישט געוואָלט זען די פּוילישע לאַנדשאַפֿט, וואָס איז מיר געבליבן אַזוי נאָענט, אַזוי אויפֿגעגאָסן מיט די הײַטערסטע יאָרן פֿון מײַן לעבן. האַרט פֿאַר דער גרענעץ האָב איך יאָ אַרויסגעקוקט דורכן פֿענצטער, כ'האָב זיך נישט געקאָנט אײַנהאַלטן. כ'האָב געמוזט נעמען אָפּשייד פֿון די ביימער, די בלומען די פּוילישע . . . כ'האָב געמוזט זאָגן זײַ געזונט אַלץ, וואָס האָט בונט געפֿאַרבט מײַן יוגנט.[167]
>
> [I didn't want to see the Polish landscape, to which I was so attached, that merged with the happiest years of my life. Right by the border, I looked through the window, I could not stop myself. I had to bid farewell to the trees, the Polish flowers . . . I had to bid farewell to everything that colored my youth.]

The scenes of the visit and the performance for the children at the orphanage in Helenówek reconstruct the artists' activity directly after the war: their tours in rural cities, including performances for children in various institutions around Poland,[168] among them a Jewish school in Rychbach and an orphanage in Chorzów, Upper Silesia, close to Katowice.[169] In both places, happy children appeared before the two artists, and choirs sang "Mir kumen on" (We are Coming!), which was also sung by children in a 1936 promotional film of the same name depicting the sanitorium named after Vladimir Medem in Międzeszyn, near Warsaw. In Rychbach, the children performed short theatrical pieces and recited texts by classic Yiddish writers (similarly to the events of the film). In Chorzów, and presumably also in Rychbach, Dzigan and Shumacher staged a performance of "Kasrilevker sreyfes" (Kasrilevke Fires), an adaptation of Sholem Aleichem's story that the actors usually performed after the opening skit in their show *Abi m'zet zikh!* and which is performed for the children in Helenówek in the film

---

166 Shlomo Lastik wrote a scathing review of the film, noting that its main achievement is the landscape footage of Poland. See Lastik, "Undzere kinder."

167 Dzigan, *Der koyekh*, 295.

168 In the original script, in a scene omitted from the film, Dzigan and Shumacher arrive at a building that houses a nursery. They present the letter of invitation from the director of the orphanage to a nurse. While she is showing the letter to the director (off camera), they walk between the cots, excited by the sight of the babies, talk about the mothers these children will never know, and finally Shumacher takes one of the children into his arms, singing him a lullaby. Dzigan sits in an armchair, cradling a doll in his arms, his face dreamy, listening to Shumacher's song. In the midst of the lullaby, the nurse enters and informs them that they are in the wrong institution.

169 In Rychbach, Dzigan and Shumacher appeared at the institution for children run by T.O.Z. (Towarzystwo Ochrony Zdrowia Ludnosci Żydowskiej, The Company for Preserving the Health of the Jewish Community).

Undzere kinder.[170] Before the performance, they would ask the children: "Do you know Yiddish? Do you know who Sholem Aleichem was?" The questions highlight the presumed isolation of the children from Jewish tradition, cultural and linguistic, or alternatively the desire to strengthen their connection with this tradition. So too, the artists ask these questions when performing at Helenówek in the film.[171]

At Helenówek, the children welcome the artists with the song "Yugntlid" by Binem Heller, which opens with a quotation from the well-known partisan song by Hirsh Glik, in a paraphrase adapted to suit the current times.[172] Its performance by the children – with the well-known lines, "Never say that you are walking the final road," and the conclusion "we are here" – confirms that the partisans' path was not their final one. The children seem to say: We are here and we remember, the partisans light up our way in days of peace and war, guiding us. The children are beginning their life anew, in the liberated world.

The children possess a great deal of knowledge about the Holocaust and are the only ones able to represent and reconstruct what happened, in contrast to the refugee actors. Yet Dzigan and Shumacher are the custodians of tradition and can impart it to the new generation. "Kasrilevker sreyfes," the skit that they perform for the children, not only provides a fascinating and rare testimony of how Dzigan

170 Dzigan and Shumacher also performed this skit in Ararat before the war. It was first staged under the title "Sreyfes" (Fires) in the show *Mis yude'ye* (Miss Judea) in 1929. Concerning the skit, see Grafman, "Zmires mit lokhsn."

171 Bornshteyn, "Dzigan un Shumacher."

172 The words of the song "Yugntlid," as they appear in the film *Undzere kinder*:

"זאָגט נישט קיינמאָל אַז דו גייסט דעם לעצטן וועג" - / געזונגען האָבן זיי אין יענע גורל־טעג. / געקומען איז אַצינד די אויסגעבענקטע שעה: / הערט זיך איַין אין אונדזער טראָט: מיר זיַינען דאָ! // מיר וועלן קיין מאָל נישט פֿאַרגעסן יענע שלאַכט, / און אויך נישט אין די העלדן אין דער געטאָ־נאַכט, / ווען איַינגעוויקלט אין רויכן און אין בראַנד - / געדויערט מוטיק האָבן זיי אין ווידערשטאַנד. // ס'וועט זייער שיינער רום באַליַיכטן אונדז דעם וועג/ אין שווערע קאַמפֿן און אויך אין די שלום־טעג. / און סיַי אין אַרבעט, סיַי אויף פֿראָנטן פֿון דעם קריג, / זיי וועלן שטענדיק אונדז באַגייסטערן צום זיג. // מיר זענען יונג, די גאַנצע וועלט פֿאַר אונדז איז פֿריַי, / מיר הייבן אָן דאָס לעבן מונטער אויף דאָס ניַי. / זאָל קלינגען מוטיק איבער וואַלד און איבער פֿעלד / דאָס ליד פֿון ייִד און מענטש אין אַ באַפֿריַיטער וועלט.'

["Never say that you are walking the final road" – / so they sang in those fateful days. / Now the longed-for hour has come: / listen to our march: We are here! // We will never forget that battle, / and also not the heroes who, in the ghetto night, / covered in smoke and flames,– // they remained courageous in their resistance. // Their beautiful glory will light up our path. / In difficult days and also in times of peace. / Both in work, and at the battle front, / they will always elevate our spirit to victory. // We are young, the entire world is free before us, / we begin to live again with joy. / May it ring out courageously over forest and over field, / the song of Jew and man in the liberated world.]

and Shumacher performed texts by Sholem Aleichem. The skit also represents prewar Yiddish culture and theater in Poland, and at the same time, it becomes part of the cultural archival memory.

Testimonies given by children who starred in the film reveal that they were never asked at school about their wartime experiences. Eliezer Zelkind, one of these children, said: “We lived then in the present, in the everyday. That is what occupied us. We wanted to get back to normal, to have fun.”[173] However, the idea of confronting the experiences of the Holocaust through art as a means to process them was not new: on April 20, 1948, around eight months before filming began, at the initiative of their teachers, children from orphanages in Poland, including Helenówek, staged an artistic evening in Warsaw. A press report described it in the following manner:

> זיי [קינדער פֿון העלענאָוועק] פֿירן אויס אַ קאָמבינירטן געטאָ־מאָנטאַזש, מיט געפֿיל פֿאַר צער און ווייטאָג, האָבן די פּיצעלעך אויסגעפֿירט די גרויל סצענעס פֿון אונזער בלוטיקן עבר. דאַן באַווײַזן די קינדער אַ גוט אויסגערעזשיסירטן טאַנץ "דער טויט אין געטאָ" – דער טויט טאַנצט אַרום און לויערט אויף יעדן ייִד און טרײַבט טויזנטער ייִדן צו דער שחיטה. אין צווייטן טייל פֿון טאַנץ אָטעמט אָפּ דער פֿול געפּאַקטער זאַל, וואָס איז מיטגעריסן געוואָרן מיט דעם געטאָ־שוידער. מיט דער ליד 'זאָג נישט קיין מאָל', הייבט אָן דער 'טאַנץ פֿון נײַעם לעבן'.[174]
>
> [They (the children from Helenówek) presented a montage of ghetto life. With sensitivity to sadness and pain, the little ones portrayed horrific pictures of our bloody past. Then the children performed a dance, “Death in the Ghetto” – Death dances around and lies in wait for every Jew, driving thousands of them to the slaughter. In the second part of the dance, the fully packed hall, which was appalled by the horror of the ghetto, breathed a sigh of relief. With the song “Never Say,”[175] the “Dance of New Life” began.]

According to this article published in *Dos naye lebn*, which was entitled “We live! A Wonderful Show from the Polish Orphanages,” the dance succeeded in convincing the audience that “we have a new democratic, healthy Poland, with children that are growing up and devoted cultural figures and educators.” Even if this show was an exceptional case, art as therapy, as a way to deal with the experiences of the war, formed part of some educational and pedagogical programs in the orphanages during the postwar period. According to the classic school of psychoanalysis, talking about the horror is a vital stage in achieving release

173 Chitron, “Maba nadir.”

174 Y. V., “Mir lebn!”

175 “Zog nit keyn mol” (Never Say), a partisan song by Hirsh Glik. The first line of the song is “Never say that you are walking the final road.”

from trauma and the silence that accompanies it.[176] Presumably, the performance staged in Warsaw was a source of inspiration for the film.[177]

In their discussions of the film *Undzere kinder*, Gabriel Finder and Ira Konigsberg highlight the parallels with the song "S'brent" (It's Burning), written by Mordkhe Gebirtig for the skit "Kasrilevker sreyfes," which deals with a similar topic through humor.[178] The performance of Sholem Aleichem's story in the post-Holocaust film can be interpreted not only as a presentation of a literary and theatrical tradition identified with the past but also as the parable of a generation unable to prevent its own disaster.

In the film, immediately following the Sholem Aleichem skit, the actors draw a link between the fire in Kasrilevke and the recent past, asking the children: "Who has seen a fire?"[179] This is an additional moment when the voice of the historian (Oyerbakh) speaks through the characters. The actors suggest that the children hold a competition: who can best depict the fires that they saw in the ghetto? This exceptional proposal transforms the Holocaust into an ahistorical phenomenon, presenting it as merely "another fire" in the history of humanity. The competition, however, is not held because it is past the children's bedtime.

The idea of this competition is not surprising, particularly considering the documentary writing contests held in the days of the ghetto, for example that orga-

---

176 Kidron, "Ethnography of Silence."

177 Ira Konigsberg rightfully highlighted the possibility that the creators of this film were inspired by Alexander Ford's 1936 film, *Mir kumen on* (Children Must Laugh), which relates the history of the Medem Sanitorium in Międzeszyn. Konigsberg notes that not only the footage of children singing but also history connect the two films: on August 22, 1942, the children of the sanitorium were taken, along with their teachers, doctors, and nurses, to the gas chambers in Treblinka. In his opinion, the children in *Undzere kinder* symbolize the continuity of those children's lives. See Konigsberg, "Our Children," 12.

178 Konigsberg, "Our Children"; Finder, "Überlebende Kinder." Mordkhe Gebirtig's song was written in 1938 as a reaction to the pogrom in Przytyk and became one of the songs most frequently sung in the ghettos and concentration camps, and later at Holocaust memorial ceremonies.

179 The segue was not so sharp in the original script. After the Sholem Aleichem skit, the artists were supposed to sing a ballad about partisans' heroism in the ghetto. At a very serious moment in the ballad, the children would burst out laughing. This confuses the artists, who as a result stop singing. Shumacher asks the children why they are laughing. After some embarrassment, one of the children answers, "Because it wasn't like that." "How do you know that it wasn't like that?" asks Shumacher. "Because I was a partisan," answers another child. Subsequently each one of the children relates where he was during the war. Shumacher: "So you are wise, you need to teach us how it was. Maybe we will have a competition of plays about the days of the occupation." The children are amused, the director begs the artists to forgive the children's behavior, thanks them, and invites them to stay overnight at the orphanage.

nized by members of the Oyneg Shabes archives led by Emanuel Ringelblum in the Warsaw Ghetto, of which Oyerbakh was an active member. This was one way in which the Jews dealt with the horrors, both as they unfolded and later in the DP camps.[180] The director of the orphanage, who intervenes in the conversation between artists and children, argues in favor of the opposing view: the topic should not be spoken about in public. However, in the film, the performance of "Kasrilevker sreyfes" influences how the children deal with their own tragedy. Thanks to the performance and the actors-historians' suggestion that they reconstruct their experiences from the Holocaust – to release themselves from the nightmares of the past – the children tell one another about their experiences, and their stories are reconstructed in cinematic flashbacks. The children "dream" about the nightmares of yesterday while awake, sharing them with their peers, rather than the artists, who are adults and strangers.[181] However, the latter overhear the descriptions of the horrors from the stairway of the orphanage: an inversion of the well-known "spying" scene in which children try to eavesdrop on adults without being caught.

The next morning, the children laugh, reconstructing in their games the fire in the Sholem Aleichem skit, "acting out" the tradition of Yiddish theater, although they alter the tragic conclusion of the story. The children succeed where their predecessors failed – they heroically face the catastrophe and extinguish the fire. Thus, they re-write Sholem Aleichem's text through their performance.[182]

In the final scenes of the film, the children of Helenówek appear as "young workers." The girls sew and sing, the boys labor in a workshop, and everyone works together in a greenhouse. Dzigan and Shumacher walk among them, singing with them, seeing by the light of day the "rebirth" of those same children who at night related the horrors of the Holocaust. The recovery appears complete. The children sing the song "Zingt mit undz" (Sing with Us) by Binem Heller,

---

180 "Had those in the ghettos been convinced, as so many are today, that the war years stood outside history, that the Holocaust defied the literary imagination, and that all critical standards had therefore to be suspended, there would have been no contests for the best scholarly and literary works. When the Oyneg Shabes archive sponsored an essay contest on the topic 'Two-and-a-Half Years of War,' its purpose was to stimulate not only excellence but hope, as stated explicitly in the subtitle: 'Observations, Evaluations and Perspectives *for the Future*.'" Roskies, *Against the Apocalypse*, 200. Emphasis in the original.

181 Lastik, "Undzere kinder." Kidron notes that the stories about nightmares and crying at night were an explicit sign of the Holocaust survivors' suffering and identified as a central symptom of post-traumatic stress disorder in medical literature. See Kidron, "Ethnography of Silence," 5.

182 Lastik criticizes the "imperfect" idea of the film, its unclear structure, and the exaggerated degree of "psychologism." This reproach was perhaps influenced by the fact that, at the time of the film's screening, Dzigan and Shumacher, as well as others who appeared in the film, had already left Poland, suggesting a different solution for Polish Jewry. See Lastik, "Undzere kinder."

which glorifies the body and work for the sake of building the land, building the new socialist Poland after the war:

> Sing us a song of joy, / a young body does not tire. / Every young man will stretch out his hand / to realize the building of his land. / Sing to us a song of fun, / a young body does not tire. / Every young man will stretch out his hand / to realize the building of his land./ . . . Without needle and without string, / what is tailoring worth? / Add a bit here, take a bit from here / and the clothes are already finished! / It needs a little ironing, / there is no profession like that of a tailor. / We will work as fast as we can / and we will sing with all our hearts. / [refrain] / With plane and saw / sawdust flying in the workshop, / in a minute there will be a table. / When everything will be ready, / who will sit at the table? / We will put it in a hall, / and everyone will sit around it./ [refrain] / In a garden next to my house / I grew an ornamental rose, / sun, earth, and heat / nurtured here a red rose. / Rise, awaken, morning comes, / the toil, the work / drive the sorrows far away / and the roses come out pink. / [refrain].[183]

The border between documentary and fictional material in the film is blurred. Although Dzigan and Shumacher star as themselves, this is not true of the children. Only some of the children in the film were from Helenówek, and although some had survived the ghetto, in the film they did not relate their own stories but rather scripted ones, which were apparently based on testimonies gathered by Oyerbakh. Among the children who performed in the film were pupils from the Y. L. Peretz School and the Ghetto Fighters' Hebrew School from Łódź. Many of them did not know Yiddish and had to learn their lines using a Polish transliteration. This highlights the mixture of documentary and fictional material in the film, and gives an indication of the postwar linguistic reality.[184] Lydia Shumacher, who spent the war years in the Soviet Union and did not know Yiddish, played one of the children in the orphanage at Helenówek. She is the orphan who presents a bouquet of flowers to Shumacher, her real-life father [See Figure 13]. This fact, doubtless known to many people who saw the film at the time, strengthens the message that all the children are "our children."

Many survivors' stories conclude with their migration to Mandatory Palestine, sometimes a few years after the liberation. Indeed, this was often the survivors' final goal, in cinematic creations and in real life alike.[185] *Undzere kinder* concludes

---

183 This is based on the Hebrew translation from the copy distributed by Ya'akov Gross. The Yiddish is not sufficiently clear in this song. There is no printed version of the song and the name of the translator is unknown. In the original script, the children manage to make the artists want to continue living; subsequently, Dzigan and Shumacher organize a children's festival in Poland. The end of the film, according to this script, is a fast-paced montage of preparations for the festival.
184 See Finder, "Überlebende Kinder."
185 For example, in the film *David* by Peter Lilienthal (1979) or *Europa, Europa* (1990) by Agnieszka Holland. Margaret Olin also notes the film *Korczak* by Andrzej Wajda, in the last scene

Figure 13: Yisroel Shumacher with his wife Celina Stal and their daughter Lydia (Lydia Shumacher-Ophir collection).

with the actors leaving the children's home: the children accompany them on their way, even after they have bid farewell. This act seems to be a mistake in the script. The last scene can be interpreted, in light of Margaret Olin's comments, as the actors leaving for Israel or another destination. In reality, most of the children, as well as the creators of the film, indeed left Poland and reached the State of Israel.

The Screening in Israel: Translation and Ideology

The film was screened for the first time in Israel in July 1951 at the May Cinema, Haifa, and again in October 1952 on the intermediate days of Sukkot in the Eden Cinema, Tel Aviv. The name of the film was not translated literally to Hebrew,

---

of which children from orphanages are seen marching with white flags bearing a Star of David. She sees this as a symbol of the Israeli flag. See Olin, "Lanzmann's *Shoah*," 810.

but rather adapted to suit the Zionist narrative. The children were not "ours" but rather *Yaldei hasa'ar*, meaning "Children of the Storm." A subtitle was also added: "An Epos of Jewish Children's Heroism in the Period of Nazi Occupation." This addition highlights the distributors' commercial aims and the ideological subjugation of the film to the Zionist discourse on heroism, which preferred to avoid the trauma of the Holocaust.[186] The attempt to translate the film to the Israeli reality was likewise expressed in the addition of a ten-minute introduction entitled "Rejoicing and gladness," in which Dzigan and Shumacher are shown floating on carousel horses in a Tel Aviv fairground at Purim surrounded by Israeli children wearing costumes, including those children featured in the film who had subsequently immigrated to Israel. Due to the poor quality of the copy, the addition was archived after only a few screenings, and the film was later screened without it.[187]

A critic, who signed his name "Filma'i" (A film critic), described the film as a daring attempt to talk about the Holocaust from the perspective of children in an orphanage, combining humor with hope for the future. In his view, the film did not suit the Zionist narrative because it failed to highlight the establishment of the State of Israel as a solution for the diaspora Jews: "The special conditions in Poland led to denial. A characteristic detail: the Jewish children in Poland do not mention Palestine even once, although almost all these same children afterwards came to Israel. As a result, there is sometimes [an impression of] something forced, we are participating in a party of Conversos." Despite this, the reviewer saw the film as "documentary evidence" and regarded its ending as "encouraging": "The children are slowly liberated from the nightmares of the Holocaust, through a connection with the land and work. This section can be transplanted to the State of Israel." He concluded by placing the film in the same context that the Israeli public discourse consistently applied to Yiddish theater and culture: "The audience is impressed. Those watching it cry and laugh, as is usual for a melodrama."[188] This viewer's response to the film reflects the presiding negative and

---

186 *Yozma*, "Dzigan ṿeShumacher (*Yozma*, Magazine for Free Initiative of the General Organization of Merchants in Israel, was published from 1949 onwards); Z., "Undzere kinder"; Filma'i, "Yaldei hasa'ar."

187 The copy that was in the possession of the distributor Kantorovitz was used repeatedly. Eventually, it became so worn out that it was unusable, and the distributor destroyed it. He left the section "Kasrilevker sreyfes" for special distribution, although this was subsequently lost. In 1979, a copy with French subtitles was discovered in France. The Tel Aviv industrialist Bernard Turner purchased it and made a new copy to distribute in Israel.

188 Filma'i, "Yaldei hasa'ar."

stereotypical Israeli stance toward Yiddish culture, as was mentioned above.[189] According to Ya'akov Ben-On's article: "The failure was decisive. The proximity to the Holocaust bothered the audience. In the hall hysterical cries intermingled with silent weeping."[190]

After the screenings in Tel Aviv, the copies of the film were lost. As a metaphor for the negation of the exile, the evidence also disappeared from the Israeli-Jewish collective memory, until a copy was found in France in 1979. The film was screened again in Israel on April 29, 1980, in the Tel Aviv Museum of Art, as part of the Spring Time Festival in Tel Aviv. This screening was attended by children, now in their late 30s, who appeared in the film, together with producer Shaul Goskind, director Natan Gross, and Shimen Dzigan. In his remarks before the screening, Dzigan described the film as "an honest and true story of children who experienced on their flesh the horrors of the Holocaust, [it] seems to me more convincing than a thousand lectures. This is a film from real life."[191] The film and the memory were "restored," and the film was distributed on tape and then DVD, subsequently becoming the focus of studies and numerous discussions.[192] In 1999, Ya'akov Gross, the son of the film's director, finished editing a new version of the film that includes rare footage he discovered in the Israeli Film Archive at the Jerusalem Cinematheque.[193] This new version completes the partial picture provided by the version previously available and served as the basis for the discussion herein.

The film *Undzere kinder* reveals one of the ways in which artists and historians dealt with the Holocaust in its immediate aftermath and the cooperation between them. It reflects an attempt to unite two different perspectives – artistic and historiographic – in depicting the Holocaust, or more exactly in presenting ways to deal with it in the initial postwar years, considering the contemporary political reality in Poland and the creators' emotional limitations. The film combines documentary material, testimony, memory, reconstruction, humor, and fiction. It is the product of a period governed by hesitations and doubts.

---

189 See Rotman, "Yidish teater in Medines-Yisroel"; Rotman, "Language Politics".

190 Bar-On, "Hayeladim."

191 Ibid.

192 For example, the conference "Childhood Trauma in Film: *Undzere Kinder*," Institute for Psychoanalytic Training and Research, Center for Jewish History, YIVO Institute for Jewish Research, November 4, 2007. A special session devoted to the film, with the participation of Shimon Redlich, David Roskies, Gabriel Finder, Maurice Preter, and Diego Rotman, took place at the Fourteenth World Congress of Jewish Studies, Jerusalem, August 4, 2009.

193 Ya'akov Gross was a director of documentary films and was involved in preserving and restoring archival films. He died in Tel Aviv in 2017.

Departure from Poland

After the war, Jews began to leave Poland for various destinations, including France, Australia, and Argentina. However, many resided in the DP camps in Germany, later making their way to Mandatory Palestine with the help of Zionist organizations, because immigration was severely restricted by the British authorities. From the liberation until July 1946, 730,000 Jews left Poland. Following the pogrom in Kielce, between the months of July and September 1946, a further 52,000 Jews departed. Later, the flow of migrants dwindled. Dzigan and Shumacher, who arrived in Poland after large waves of migrants had already left the country, were among the intellectuals who remained there until 1949. In an article published in the Paris newspaper *Undzer vort* (Our Word) after they left Poland, the artists related that thousands of Jews were preparing to leave Poland for Mandatory Palestine, even though life there was peaceful. However, because there were so few Jews, it was impossible to establish a proper Jewish theater.[194] It is not clear whether the duo's lengthy stay in Poland was a result of their theatrical success, the filming of *Undzere kinder*, their belief that it was possible to build a normal life in Poland despite the Holocaust, or simply because they did not find a way to leave beforehand.

The historical reality of the destruction of Jewish life in Poland, the political and economic situation there, and the departure of colleagues and major writers of the artists' skits (Y. Sh. Goldshteyn and Moyshe Nudelman left for New York, Isaac Janasowicz and Asher Dorf for Paris) persuaded Dzigan and Shumacher that they too must leave Poland.[195] Thus began another decade of nomadism, moving between Israel, Europe, North America, and South America.[196]

During a tour of performances in Western Europe – organized by the well-known manager Henry Goldgran and en route to a tour in Israel – Dzigan and Shumacher staged adaptations of the four shows that they performed in postwar Poland, suited to their environs: they added one or two monologues concerning

---

194 N. Z., "Dzigan un Shumacher in Pariz."

195 Leneman, "Abi men zet zikh"; Shlomi, "Hit'argenut," 524–25.

196 Before departing, they reached an agreement with the Committee for Polish Jews in Israel according to which they would give a six-month long tour in Israel, having signed a contract with the theater manager Ze'ev Markovits. Initially, the Polish government refused to allow the artists to leave the country; the intervention of the Committee for Polish Jews was necessary in order for the government to agree to the request. See Raḥeli, "Ḳela'im." An article published in an Australian newspaper noted that the artists received an authorization from the Israeli government to perform in Yiddish. See N. Z., "Dzigan un Shumacher in Pariz"; Stutschinsky, "A shpatsir."

the local reality and replaced Polish political figures with local ones.[197] In August 1949, they performed the show *M'zet zikh? Shoyn?* (We Meet Again? So Be It!) in the Sarah Bernard Theater, Paris (today Théâtre de la ville). This was a light adaption of the first show they had performed in Poland after the war. Dzigan and Shumacher appeared together with the dancers Yehudit Berg and Felix Fibich (who were members of the theater troupe in Białystok; Berg also appeared in Ararat), and with the singer Sara Gorby, who sang Yiddish songs between the acts. After three performances in a hall with more than a thousand seats, three additional dates were set. More than 15,000 people saw their shows in Paris.[198]

Reviews in the Yiddish press oscillated between accolades for the actors' talents, noting the importance of their theater and praising it (in comparison to other Yiddish groups active in Paris at the time), and criticism regarding the quality of the content.[199] As in Poland, *Balebatish un demokratish* received more positive reviews than the other shows, although here too, according to Liberman, some parts were redundant.[200] A few texts related to the establishment of the

---

197 Goldin, "Revyu-spektakl." In Eastern Europe they always suited their programs to the local context, a principle that continued to guide them throughout their artistic careers. A clear example of this can be found in the review article by Yankev-Tsevi Lemel concerning local adaptations by Dzigan and Shumacher in their Argentinian performances: "It was truly a delight to see Dzigan and Shumacher in Argentinian colonial dress . . . and mainly the style of Jewish Gauchos, with the language of the provincial Jews, a piece of Jewish life from the colony." See Rivkes, "Der lakh-spektakl."

198 Concerning their performances in Europe see *Unzer shtime*, "Di artistn"; Yitskhoki, "Dzigan un Shumacher"; Lilienshteyn, "Dzigan un Shumacher"; *Naye prese*, "Shabes, zuntik un montik." On their performances in Paris see Goldgran, "Tsum yidishn teater-oylem"; N. Z., "Dzigan un Y. Shumacher in Pariz"; Goldin, "Af a tsuzamentref "; Dorf, "M'zet zikh?"; Borvin, "A kleyner shmues."

199 In the French *Kultur-yediyes*, a French reporter who signed his name with the initials S. K. wrote that some of the texts were not of the level expected from Dzigan and Shumacher. At the same time, he recommended watching the duo's performances because the audience would always enjoy the folk humor and good satire. See S. K., "A derfolg un a bavayz." In *Unzer vort*, A. Liberman criticized the quality of a number of the monologues but praised Dzigan and Shumacher's talents. Their performance, in his opinion, improved any text. See Liberman, "Men zet zikh?" See also: *Unzer vort*, "A bagegenish"; *Unzer vort*, "Dzigan un Shumacher in Pariz"; Goldin, "Af a tsuzamentref." According to a letter to the editor of the newspaper *Afn tsimbl*, the political criticism in one of Shumacher's monologues – claiming that there was no difference between fascism and democracy – succeeded in arousing whistles of scorn from the audience. The reader-writer noted that he expected the artists to remove political references from their works. See Strapontin-Tsushoyer, "Teater-notitsn."

200 Liberman, "Balebatish un demokratish." In a review of the program as it was performed in Poland, Sfard praised the tangible references to reality and the Jewish folk voice. See Sfard, "Af dem rikhtikn veg." Regarding Dzigan and Shumacher's performances of this program in Poland,

State of Israel. Pinskier wrote that Roza Rayske's beautiful rendition of the song "Kineretl" (Little Kinneret) made one feel that she was singing a song of praise to the State of Israel on behalf the entire Jewish public: the Kinneret is not only a point on a map but rather "a symbol of the newly born babe of our national sovereignty."[201] By contrast, Hortzy (Hirsh) Safrin argued that the show was a "musical-satirical performance" that lacked any echo of the enormous challenges facing the generation and its struggle for existence, national and official, apart from the song "Tel Aviv" by Isaac Janasowicz:[202]

> פֿון טרוים ביסטו ווירקלעכקייט געוואָרן / אין דער וואָר ביסטו נאָך אַלץ אַ טרוים. / און הערצער ציִען זיך צו דיר דורך יאָרן, / ווי ס'ציט זיך צו דער זון דער גרינער בוים . . .[רעפֿריין:] תּל־אָבֿיבֿ, תּל־אָבֿיבֿ / שטאָט פֿון פֿרילינג, פֿון האָפֿענונג און שײַן, / תּל־אָבֿיבֿ, תּל־אָבֿיבֿ / שטאָט פֿון ברידער און לידער וועסטו זײַן, / תּל־אָבֿיבֿ, דו מײַן טרוים, דו מײַן בענקשאַפֿט־ליד, / תּל־אָבֿיבֿ ווי מײַן האַרץ צו דיר ציט . . . / דערזעענדיק די סאַברעס יונג און שיין, / דו תּל־אָבֿיבֿ ביסט אונדזער טרוים געווען / און אונדזער שטאָלץ וועסטו אויך ווײַטער זײַן.[203]
>
> [From a dream you became reality / in reality you are still entirely a dream. / And hearts are drawn to you over the years, / just as the green tree is drawn to the sun . . . [refrain:] Tel Aviv, Tel Aviv, / city of spring, city of hope and beauty, / Tel Aviv, Tel Aviv, / you will be a city of brothers and poems, / Tel Aviv, you, my dream, you, my song of longing / Tel Aviv as my heart is drawn to you . . . / seeing the sabras young and beautiful, / you, Tel Aviv, were our dream / and you will continue to be our pride.]

Safrin praised the monologue "Shmendrik tsurik a Yid" (Shmendrik is a Jew Once Again) by Tsevi Stal (apparently the text was co-written by Celina Stal and Yisroel Shumacher), performed by Shumacher, in which a Jew reverts to his "Hebrew" name following events in Mandatory Palestine.[204] Other sections from the show which were praised by the critics include a parody of Romeo and Juliet (no documentation has survived); a puppet satire of politicians, among them Vyacheslav Molotov and Ernest Bevin (a picture of Dzigan and Shumacher with the puppets

---

see also Y. B., "Di ershte"; J. Pinskier, "Kuznia folklore: Permiera zespolu Dzigana i Szumacher," September 29, 1948. The name of the newspaper is not recorded. BAA, file 149–02.

201 Pinskier, "Kuznia folklore."

202 H. Safrin, "I cóż dalej Szary człowieku? (Na marginesie reqii Dzigana i Szumachera)," *Mosty*, undated, BAA, file 149–02. Safrin was a Polish poet, critic, author, and translator of Jewish origin. He translated Polish literature into Yiddish, as well as translating Yiddish and Hebrew literature into Polish.

203 BAA, file 194–04.

204 Safrin, who saw the performance in Poland, wrote that despite his esteem for the duo's talents and artistic effort, combined with his awareness of the technical difficulties, the program had two main drawbacks: it did not faithfully represent a cross section of the Polish Jewish reality, and it lacked a central thread linking its various parts together.

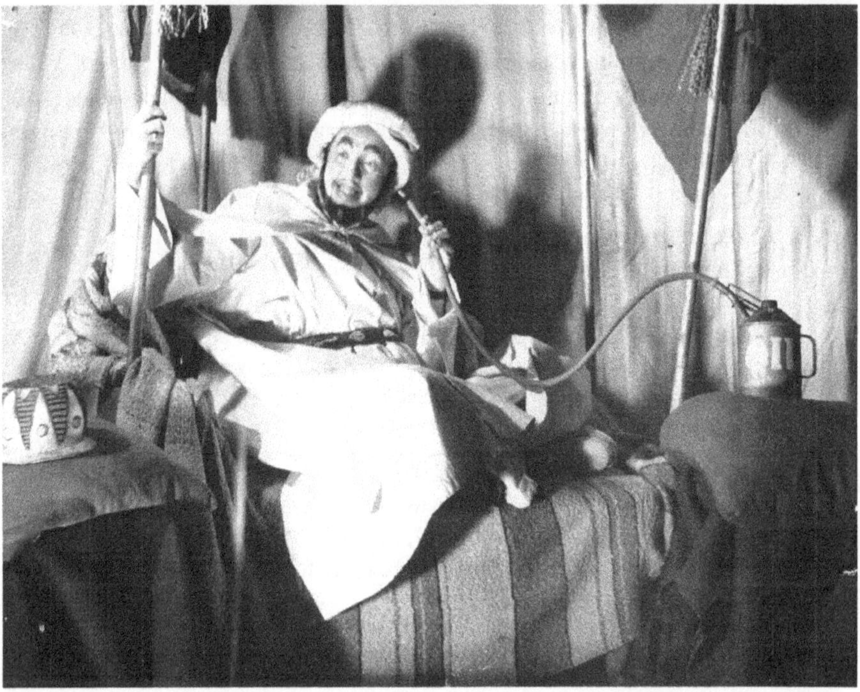

Figure 14: Yisroel Shumacher in the skit "Abdolas zmires" by Yisroel Shumacher, from the show *Balebatish and demokratish*, Łódź, 1948 (Lydia Shumacher-Ophir collection).

has survived) [See Figure 10]; and the satirical song "Abdolas zmires" (Abdullah's Songs), written and performed by Shumacher [See Figure 14].[205]

At a press conference held in Paris in 1949, Dzigan and Shumacher claimed that they remained faithful to their traditional genres: the revue and the miniature theater [Figure 15]. Their aim was, they stated, not to arouse laughter for the sake of laughter but to shed light on hazy sides of post-Holocaust Jewish life using humor. Furthermore, they regarded it as important to continue "the traditions of the Jewish people" and to immortalize the types of people that had populated the streets of Warsaw, Łódź, Białystok, Vilnius (Vilna), Kraków, and Lemberg (Lwów).[206] In so doing, the artists emphasized the central role of the theater in eternalizing pre-Holocaust Jewish life and its function as a tool in the act of remembering, as was discussed above.

205 Shumacher signed the song with his pen name, Y. Tsevi.

206 *Unzer vort,* "A bagegenish"; *Unzer vort,* "Dzigan un Shumacher in Pariz"; *Unzer vort,* "Shturmisher."

Figure 15: Dzigan and Shumacher in Europe (year unknown) (Lydia Shumacher-Ophir collection).

After performing in Paris, the artists appeared with great success in various European cities, among them Brussels, Antwerp, and Liège in Belgium. One of the most interesting and exceptional reviews concerns their tour of performances in the DP camps in Germany, which was preceded by a performance at the Deutsches Museum in Munich on November 3, 1949.[207] In *Vokhnblat* (Jewish Weekly), a newspaper published by survivors in the British zone, Meyer Bar Gutman published one of the most scathing reviews of Dzigan and Shumacher's theater ever printed. The show, in his eyes, was "much ado about nothing." Gutman complained about the great deal of banal and silly things that it was necessary to endure before

207 Ts. K. B., "Dzigan un Shumacher in Daytshland."

reaching one pearl in a monologue by Dzigan or Shumacher's appearance; he asked whether it was impossible to watch Yiddish theater without profanity and tasteless jokes. The opening of the show with the skit "Abi m'zet zikh!" – which moved many other reviewers – was in his eyes indescribably hackneyed.[208] After this series of performances in Europe, Dzigan and Shumacher made their way to Israel.

208 Gutman, "Shoyn?"

Chapter 4
“And They Journeyed and They Encamped”: Dzigan and Shumacher in Israel (1950–1980)

– געדענקסט, מיט דרײַסיק יאָר צוריק, ווען מיר זענען געווען עולים? מיר האָבן נישט געקענט קיין עברית; טויזנטער פֿון די נײַע עולים האָבן נישט געקענט קיין עברית און מיר האָבן געגעבן פֿאָרשטעלונגען אויף ייִדיש, מאַמע־לשון.

– און איצט? מיר רעדן אַלע עברית. ייִדיש האָט מען פֿאַרגעסן. איך אַליין האָב עס פֿאַרגעסן, אוי ווײ.

[– Do you remember, thirty years ago, when we were new immigrants? We didn’t know any Hebrew and we performed in Yiddish, in *mame-loshn*.

And now? We all talk Hebrew. Yiddish is being forgotten. I myself am forgetting. Oy vey.]

– “Dzigan un Shumacher in 1980” [Figure 16]

In the first half of the twentieth century, identity was a major concern for Jewish society in the *Yishuv*[1] and the State of Israel. In particular, language was considered the central foundation of a person’s identity. Anyone seeking to integrate into the local Jewish society needed to divest himself of all signs of diaspora, meaning, in the case of immigrants from Eastern Europe, first and foremost Yiddish.[2] Ya‘akov Zerubavel, the leader of the Po‘alei Zion Left Party and one of the founders of Mapam (United Workers Party), described the methods employed by Hebrew linguistic and cultural activists prior to the establishment of the State of Israel as a “methodical pogrom.” Following the founding of the state, the exclusion of Yiddish from the public arena became part of the regime’s official policy regarding the supervision and control of culture and language in the effort to confirm Hebrew as the sole national language of the Jewish nation in the State of Israel.[3]

---

1 *Yishuv*, which literally means “settlement,” refers to the body of Jewish residents in Palestine before the establishment of the State of Israel.

2 The idea that language defines nationality is a common phenomenon in the creation of modern nation states. Language – similarly to culture, race, or religion – was among the signs delineating the national identities of communities and enabling a distinction between national groups. The selection of a national language and the adoption of a stance vis-à-vis the languages of minority groups (whether to preserve them or to seek their eradication) touched not only upon the question of integration but also upon the legitimacy of the national culture and the ideology at the foundations of the political system. See Safran, “Language, Ideology, and State-Building”; Kedourie, “Nationalism and Self-Determination.”

3 Ya‘akov Zerubavel (1936), quoted in Fishman, *Never Say Die!*, 297–311. On the impassioned discussions among the leadership of the new *Yishuv* and the attitudes of various authors to the supremacy of Hebrew, see Pilowksy, *Tsvishn yo un neyn*. See also Lewy, *Hayeḳim*.

https://doi.org/10.1515/9783110717693-004

"The war of languages"[4] thus evolved into a bureaucratic struggle. Accordingly, in the early days of the State of Israel, many perceived Yiddish theater – in part due to its great popularity – as a threat to the nation's cultural and linguistic character. The state assumed the role previously played by various Zionist groups – defending the public against Yiddish culture in the name of the common good. In 1949, this battle acquired a legal dimension, when the Films and Plays Censorship Committee decided that Israeli actors would not be allowed to perform in Yiddish, only guest artists from abroad.[5] In this cultural reality, a Yiddish performance by local actors constituted an act of defiance, a cultural protest against the official policy.

Visiting Artists

Within this cultural and linguistic reality, on March 16, 1950, Dzigan and Shumacher staged their first performance as guest actors in Israel. The performance took place in the Ohel Shem Theater in Tel Aviv. The theatrical producers of their first performance were Ze'ev Markovits and Pavel Gornshteyn.[6] Their show, *Ṿayis'u ṿeyaḥanu* (And They Journeyed and They Encamped), was an adaptation of the earlier show *Abi m'zet zikh*, which they had staged in Poland in 1947. It also included some sections from other shows that the duo developed after World War II, suited to the Israeli reality via references to current Israeli affairs.[7]

As in the original show, Dzigan and Shumacher opened their performance with the skit "Abi m'zet zikh!" by Y. Shudzig (one of the pennames that they used when co-writing texts). The show was immensely successful with audiences – ticket sales broke the existing record in the Israeli theater – and was praised by theater critics in the Hebrew and Yiddish press.[8] Their rare and exceptional success intensified the establishment's perception of Yiddish theater as a threat to Hebrew theater and culture, even though the duo's theater was not yet based in

4 The "war of languages" erupted in 1913, in response to a decision by the Technion's Board of Trustees to use German as the institute's language of instruction.

5 This rule remained in force for two years. For details see Rotman, "Language Politics"; Rojanski, *Yiddish in Israel*, 104–13.

6 For the rest of their shows in Israel, Pavel Gornshteyn acted as agent. Dzigan's agent for his solo performances was Yitskhok Goskind, Shaul Goskind's brother.

7 See for example M. P., "Dzigan ṿeShumacher; *Haboker*, "Hofa'at habekhora."

8 "The duo Dzigan and Shumacher became a big 'hit' this season. Their 'takings' broke the record in the history of miniature theater in Israel. In the eighty performances given by Dzigan and Shumacher, every last ticket was sold, and the theaters would have filled up had there been more performances." See M., "Hasivuv hasheni." According to various reports in the press, in the first year of their performances in Israel, around 400,000 theatergoers attended their shows.

Israel. Dzigan and Shumacher clearly demonstrated the power of popular culture to protest against the consensus and the hegemony. Their success probably contributed to the government's efforts, in early May 1950, to limit or even forbid further performances by the duo in Yiddish.[9]

Figure 16: Yisroel Shumacher and Shimen Dzigan in the skit "Dzigan and Shumacher in 1980" (Lydia Shumacher-Ophir collection).

9 On March 13, 1950, the agent Ze'ev Markovits submitted a request to the Films and Plays Censorship Committee, requesting permission for Dzigan and Shumacher's performances, but the duo began performing before receiving the authorization. After three performances, the first of which took place on March 16 in Tel Aviv, the second in Haifa on March 22, and the third in Jerusalem on March 23, 1950, the committee decided to prohibit the duo's performances (letter dated March 26, 1950, from the head of the committee, Ya'akov Kisilov, to the Department for Criminal Identification and Investigation, Israeli police HQ). The head of the committee asked the police to stop the duo's performances (protocol of the meeting held on March 30, 1950). On April 9, 1950, the artists received a letter containing the longed for permission (no. 78), which noted that, as guest artists, they were allowed to perform the show until the end of April: "Further shows after this period will not be allowed." See Israel State Archive (ISA), file gimmel-3577/12.

As guest actors, Dzigan and Shumacher received outstanding encouragement from some central figures in the Hebrew press, in complete contrast to the general attitude toward Yiddish theater. Among their supporters was none other than Azriel Carlebach, editor of the newspaper *Maariv*, who tried to raise public awareness of the unjust Israeli cultural policy toward Yiddish theater:

> This evening Dzigan and Shumacher will give their last performance authorized by the State of Israel. From tomorrow onwards, such performances will be forbidden. The reasons that [the government] gives are highly significant and persuasive: these two people are – Jews. Even worse: they are Jewish refugees . . . In France and in other countries that they visit in Europe, the authorities received them with open arms and Holocaust survivors welcomed them enthusiastically. They thought that they would also be allowed to visit their thousands of veteran theatergoers in the State of Israel . . . [Yet] since they began performing in Israel – the police were sent after them.

Carlebach concluded his critical article in a sharp and ironic tone, highlighting that the artists were under pressure to perform in Hebrew: "Messrs. Dzigan and Shumacher aren't really in so much trouble. There's a simple solution: all they have to do is convert."[10]

Two official reasons were cited to justify the prohibition of their performances: first, the program had not been submitted to the Films and Plays Censorship Committee for review and approval (yet even after the material was submitted to the committee, permission was again denied); second, the same committee introduced a new restriction allowing guest actors to perform for a limited period of six weeks. This period, which was also applied retroactively, was probably motivated by Dzigan and Shumacher's success during the first six weeks of their stay.[11]

Thanks to the intervention of Carlebach and Yosef Heftman, chairman of the Journalists' Union who had served as editor of the Yiddish newspaper *Der moment* in prewar Poland,[12] and as a result of the duo's skillful negotiations with the authorities, a compromise was reached: further performances in Yiddish were permitted, on the condition that the duo include Hebrew sections amounting to at least one-third of the entire show.[13] In order to meet this stipulation, in typical

---

10 Carlebach, "Dzigan ṿeShumacher."

11 See ibid.; letter from the Films and Plays Censorship Committee to the duo, April 9, 1950, BAA, file 146–04.

12 The correspondence can be found in BAA, file 146–04. The minutes of the meeting of the Films and Plays Censorship Committee note the pressure applied by the press and the influence of Carlebach's article, which affected the decision in favor of granting permission. See ISA, file gimmel-3577/12.

13 See the letter from the Films and Plays Censorship Committee, dated May 15, 1950, sent to the artists at the Hotel Bristol in Tel Aviv and signed by Ya'akov Kisilov. BAA, file 146–04; *Hador*,

"trickster" fashion, Dzigan and Shumacher hired a female singer to perform Hebrew songs in the interludes between skits.[14]

Despite this permission to continue performing in Yiddish as guest actors, the policy of discrimination toward Yiddish theater in general, and the duo's theater in particular, continued to affect Dzigan and Shumacher. In a letter sent on October 19, 1950, to the agent Pavel Gornshteyn, who resided in Laḥir hotel,[15] the Films and Plays Censorship Committee authorized the performance of a second show by Dzigan and Shumacher, *Tate du lakhst!* (Father, You're Laughing!, 1950) [See Figure 17]. Although the decision was a result of public pressure, the Films and Plays Censorship Committee justified it on the grounds that after staging the show Dzigan and Shumacher were scheduled to leave the country.[16] The same letter informed the artists that after this the committee would not "continue to grant these artists the right, reserved for guest artists, to stage performances in languages other than Hebrew." In this way, the authorities sought to prevent appearances by the duo in Yiddish.[17]

The endeavors to censor Dzigan and Shumacher's activities were also mentioned in an anonymous article entitled "Hatslaḥatam shel Dzigan ṿeShumacher – 'Ein saṭira poliṭit beli ḥofesh ṿe'ein ḥofesh beli saṭira poliṭit" (The Success of Dzigan and Shumacher – There is No Political Satire Without Freedom and

"Dzigan ṿeShumacher be'ivrit"; *Yedioth Ahronoth*, "Minisṭer me'aḥorei haḳela'im"; *Ha'olam haze*, "Haḥoḳ hu' tseḥoḳ."

14 A trickster is, according to Daniel Boyarin, "that same folkloristic figure that exists in all the world, which represents the weak and whose wit can sometimes achieve controversial victories over the powerful." See Boyarin, "Ta'alulanim," 147. Boyarin relates to the term "trickster" as discussed by researchers of folklore, among them Paul Radin, *The Trickster* and Babcock-Abrahams, "Margin of Mess."

15 BAA, 146–04.

16 An article entitled "Sodot shel tsenzorim" (The Secrets of the Censors) claimed that the permission would not have been granted were the actors not about to leave for a tour of performances abroad. See M. D., "Tsenzorim." This is also evident from the protocol of the meeting of the Films and Plays Censorship Committee that took place on October 10, 1950. Seven days later (protocol of the meeting held on October 17, 1950), the council added a revision to permission no. 78, which was mentioned above: "The council expects their second show to include a significant Hebrew section . . . the council will not grant them further rights of guest actors and will not permit them to appear with a further show in Yiddish, not even partially." See ISA, file gimel-3577/70.

17 Yiddish performances were regarded as a threat. This was also the case also with other non-Yiddish plays, such as *Se'ara bayam* by the journalist and playwright Yehoshua Bar-Yosef: the Films and Plays Censorship Committee rejected a request by the Cameri Theater to perform this play in 1952, claiming that it would be "detrimental to the state's military effort." See Aderet, "Kevar be-1951."

11731 אב/130/15/6

ח׳ חשון תשי"א
19.10.50

1950 1.

לכבוד
ה׳ פ. גורנשטיין,
מלון "לחיר"
רח׳ מזא"ה 33,
תל-אביב.

א. נ.

הנידון:-הרשאה מס. 139.

בתשובה לבקשתך מיום 4.10.50, על מתן הרשאה להצגת
האמנים דז׳גאן ושמאכר בתכניה מעורבת בשם "טאטע דו לאכסט"?
(צחוק ולא יעכור) בהשתתפות האמנים רוזה ריסקין וחיה-לה
שיפר, הנני להודיעך כי המועצה החליטה להרשות הצגה זו, שהיא
הצגת-הפרידה של האמנים דז׳יגאן ושמאכר לפני צאתם לחו"ל.

2. יחד עם זה, הנני להודיעך כי המועצה החליטה לא
להוסיף ולהעניק לאמנים הללו הזכות הניתנת לאמנים אורחים לערוך
הצגות שלא בשפה העברית.

בכבוד רב,

י. קיסילוב
יו"ר המועצה.

העתק: לה"ה דז׳גאן ושומכר,
באמצעות ה׳ פ. גורנשטיין.

Figure 17: Letters from the Films and Plays Censorship Committee to Dzigan and Shumacher and the agent Pavel Gornshteyn (1950) (BAA, 146–04).

There Is No Freedom Without Political Satire), which was published in the Hebrew weekly *Yozma*:

> In our free country, the internal hidden censorship has taken control of political satire . . . the existing regime caresses rather than butting heads. In the provincial and stifling atmosphere of the *Yishuv*, Dzigan and Shumacher's satire is sorely needed. The efforts of several critics to impose indirect censorship on the artistic works of Dzigan and Shumacher will not succeed.[18]

18 *Yozma*, "Hatslaḥatam."

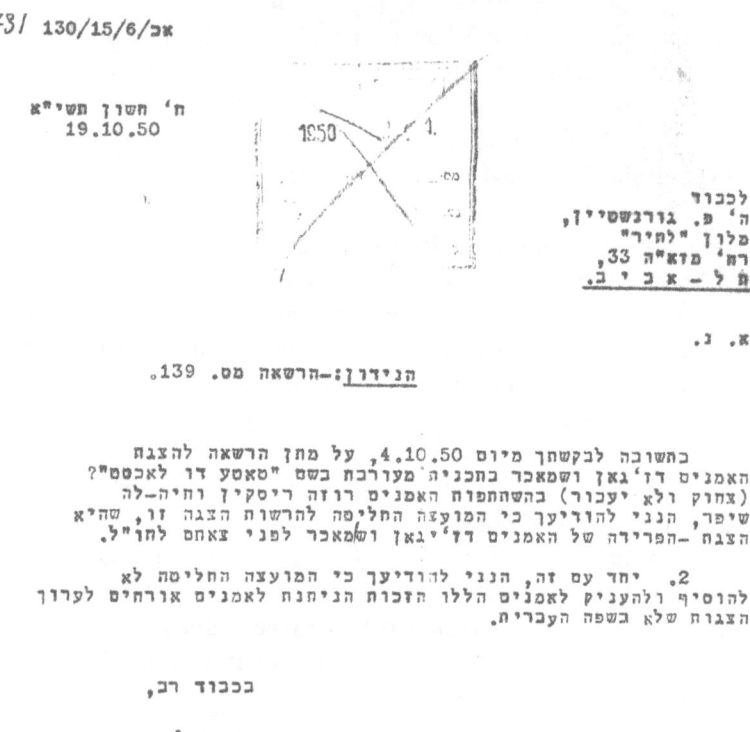

מדינת ישראל

בתשובה נא להזכיר
הענינים
המשרד
אכ/72/15/6
מספר

המועצה לבקרת סרטים
ומחזות.

כ'ב בניסן תשי
9 באפריל 1950.

לכבוד
דז'יגן ושומכר,
מלון בריסטון,
רחוב אליעזר בן יהודה,
תל אביב.

א.נ.

הנידון:– הרשאה מס.78 .

בתשובה לבקשתכם מיום ה–5 לאפריל, ש.ז.,
על מתן רשיון להצגות נוספות לפי החומר
באידיש שהגשתם, הנני לציין כי המועצה
לבקרת כרטים ומחזות נקטה עמדה שלילית
לגבי הצגותיכם שנעשו עד היום ללא רשיון
ונתנה הוראות שהאחראים על כך יובאו לדין.

2. בהתאם להחלטה כללית של המועצה, הנני
להודיעכם כי אתם רשאים כאמנים – אורחים
בישראל להמשיך בהצגותיכם לפי התכנית
"ויסעו – ויחנו" שהגשתם,עד לתקופה כוללת
של ששה שבועות מיום הצגתכם הראשונה,
דהיינו, עד סוף חודש אפריל ש.ז. הצגות
נוספות לאחר תקופה זו לא תורשינה.

בכבוד רב,

י.קיסלוב
יו"ר המועצה.

יק/בק.

Figure 17 (continued)

This prohibition on performing in Yiddish (and other non-Hebrew languages) remained in place for almost two years, during which time Yiddish theater in Israel entered a period of decline. The Avrom Goldfaden theater group – the first Israeli-based professional art theater troupe to perform in Yiddish, which openly opposed the prohibition on acting in Yiddish and performed illegally in Yiddish – was active from February 1951 until 1953. Among this theater's members were Nathan Wulfowitz (the troupe's director), Dovid Hart, Yiśra'el Segal, all of them new immigrants; Wulfowitz had performed with Dzigan and Shumacher's troupe in Warsaw and later appeared with them on stage in Israel. The theater succeeded in staging a number of shows, among them *Shulamis* and *Tsvey Kuni Leml* (Two Kuni Lemels) by Goldfaden, *Hershele Ostropoler* by Moyshe Gershenzon, *Di goldene keyt* (The Golden Chain) by Y. L. Peretz, *Mirele Efros* by Jacob Gordin, *Dos groyse gevins* (The Great Victory) by Sholem Aleichem, and *Grine felder* (Green Fields) by Perets Hirshbeyn, despite the challenging conditions in which it operated. Most of the performances took place in the Migdal-Or Garden in Givat Aliya, Jaffa. The police repeatedly sought to prevent these performances by fining the troupe and summoning its members to court appearances.[19] In this period various guest actors, among them Zygmunt and Roza Turkow, Maurice Schwartz, Joseph Buloff, Rokhl Holzer, and Avrom Morevski, performed in Israel. Likewise, local amateur groups, such as the Mapai (Workers' Party of Eretz Israel) group in Beit Shean, staged shows in Yiddish.

Due to the social and political pressure applied by Dzigan and Shumacher, as well as the efforts of the Avrom Goldfaden Theater, which performed in Yiddish despite the prohibitions, and appeals to the Supreme Court, the prohibition on local actors appearing in Yiddish was repealed at the end of 1951. The lifting of this ban led the establishment to pursue a more sophisticated cultural policy: from being "a language forbidden to Israelis" (at least in the theater), Yiddish became a "foreign language in Israel.[20] This was a further manifestation of the efforts to exile Yiddish from the local cultural scene. This policy was not only of rhetorical and cultural significance but also had financial ramifications: shows in Yiddish, performed in a foreign language, were subject to higher taxes than performances in Hebrew. This tax, and the refusal to grant state support to theaters that did not perform in Hebrew, were justified as a means to facilitate

19 Concerning Yiddish theater in the State of Israel see Rotman, "Yidish teater in Medines-Yisroel"; Rotman, "Language Politics."

20 Yiddish went from being "a forbidden language" in theater to a "foreign language," although in 1948 it was the first language of 46.8 percent of the Jewish population (166, 341), in the 1950s it was the first language of 33.3 percent (524,000), and in 1961 of 22.7 percent (446,200). See Fishman, *Yiddish*, 407.

the transition of Yiddish actors to the Hebrew stage.[21] Only in 1957 was Yiddish theater awarded a certain discount on this high entertainment tax, while the Hebrew Habima and Cameri theaters paid no taxes whatsoever.[22] In addition to this establishment policy, the Yiddish theater was also subject to general public pressure, in particular from critics. This applied especially to Dzigan and Shumacher, with reviewers repeatedly demanding that the actors perform in the Hebrew language.[23]

Dzigan and Shumacher staged ten shows together in the 1950s.[24] They worked with Yiddish theater actors as well as Yiddish-speaking actors active in the Hebrew theater, among them Yosef Oksenberg, Miriam Orit, Ḥayim Eynsman, Mikhael Grinshteyn, Miriam Valinska, Nathan Wulfowitz, Bronke Zaltsman, Shlomo Hermon, Garda Tauber, Esther Tovi, Eitan Lev, Adam Motil, Adam Morel, Yehudit Amid, Dalia Amihud, Rudi Frukhter, Avraham Karni, Gavriel Ravni, Raḥel Roden, Marian Shifman, and Lea Szlanger. They performed texts by Moyshe Broderzon, Sholem Aleichem, Isaac Janasowicz , Y. Tsevi (Yisroel Shumacher), Yosef Heiblum, Ḥaim

21 See Rotman, "Language Politics."

22 A tax of between fifteen and twenty percent was imposed on theaters that did not perform in Hebrew. Thus, Dzigan reports that he received a special discount only in 1968: "Because I act in Yiddish, I must pay an additional tax amounting to 10% of the ticket price. The Hebrew theater does not pay this tax. And I also need to be happy and to say thank you that they don't take 20% of the ticket price – like they do for all the other Yiddish theaters. This tax is a discriminatory tax in my perception." A. L., "Ba'ayotay."

23 Ibid. Dan Miron describes the effect of the ideological pressure on the attitude to Yiddish: "The person in the theater or at a gathering or a party who giggled upon hearing the first Yiddish word became, first and foremost, immediately and completely isolated, cut off from that group which was defined by the use of Yiddish, and [at the same time] joined another group, one defined negatively by the fact that its members did not use Yiddish. For this enjoyment, the person laughing mainly rewarded the actor, the storyteller, the artist of jokes, with laughter, applause, affection. The gratitude for the entertaining content of the specific Yiddish statement was secondary. The comedian and his crowd together celebrated their alienation from the abrogated human experience, and, in this way, through the negation, their membership in a respectable human group; this is the group that existed metonymically by laughing at itself." Miron, *Hatsad ha'afel*, 10.

24 Between April 1951 and December 1952, Dzigan and Shumacher gave a tour of performances in South America, appearing again in Israel in January 1953. Three months later, they left Israel again to perform in the US for the first time (supported by the Jewish National Fund) and continued on to other countries in North and South America. They returned to Israel only after almost two years, in February 1955. That same year they embarked on a tour that also included South Africa. In 1956, they performed again in Israel, before leaving for Europe. This wandering continued until 1958, when they finally decided to settle in Israel. However, even after doing so, they still traveled to the diaspora for performances.

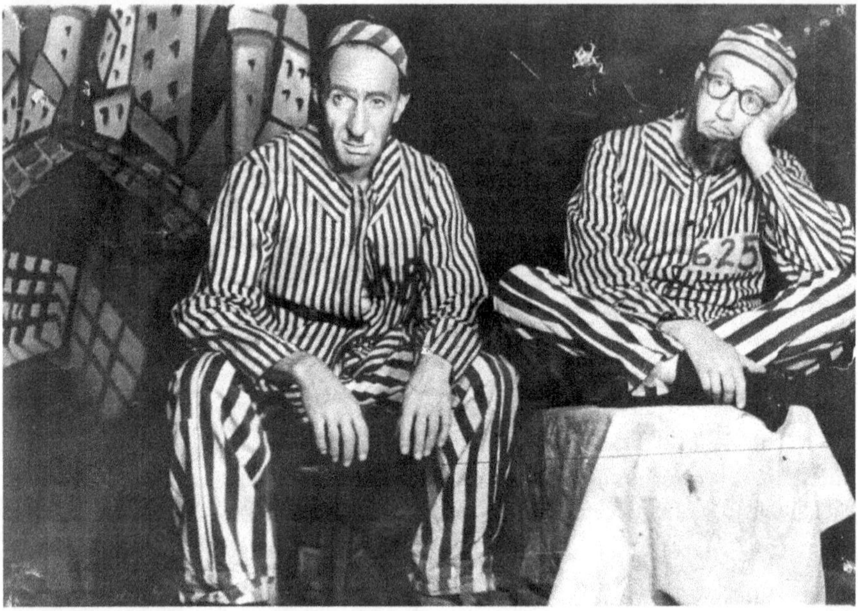

Figure 18: Shimen Dzigan and Yisroel Shumacher in the show *Di velt shoklt zikh!* (The World's Shaking!, 1953) (Lydia Shumacher-Ophir Collection).

Ritterman-Abir,[25] Moyshe Nudelman, many works that Dzigan and Shumacher composed themselves (and most of which were signed with the pen name "Shudzig") as well as translations of works by Hebrew writers such as Rafael Kletzkin and Efraim Kishon. The music was composed by Shaul Berezovsky, Dan Blitental, Henekh Kon, Hertz Rubin, and Shlomo Yafe [Figure 18].

In addition, Dzigan and Shumacher recorded selected skits from their performances. These recordings, which were released in Israel, Argentina, and France and sold all over the world, constitute an important documentation of their art.[26]

25 Haim (Henrik) Ritterman-Abir was born in 1906 in Poland and immigrated with his family to Palestine in 1940. He was a lawyer in the service of the British army and the author of satirical works. Before writing for Shimen Dzigan, he wrote for Hamatate Theater.

26 The records are sold over the internet to this day and new editions have been released. The importance of the recordings was expressed in an article published in 1968: "The indication of success that he [Dzigan] highlights with pride is not the existence of professional impersonators but rather the 'homemade' impersonators, those who buy his records and at home parties impersonate the person they refer to as 'Dzigman.' For him, they are the joyful proof that his humor penetrated life, becoming part of it." Boshes, "Hadevash hamar."

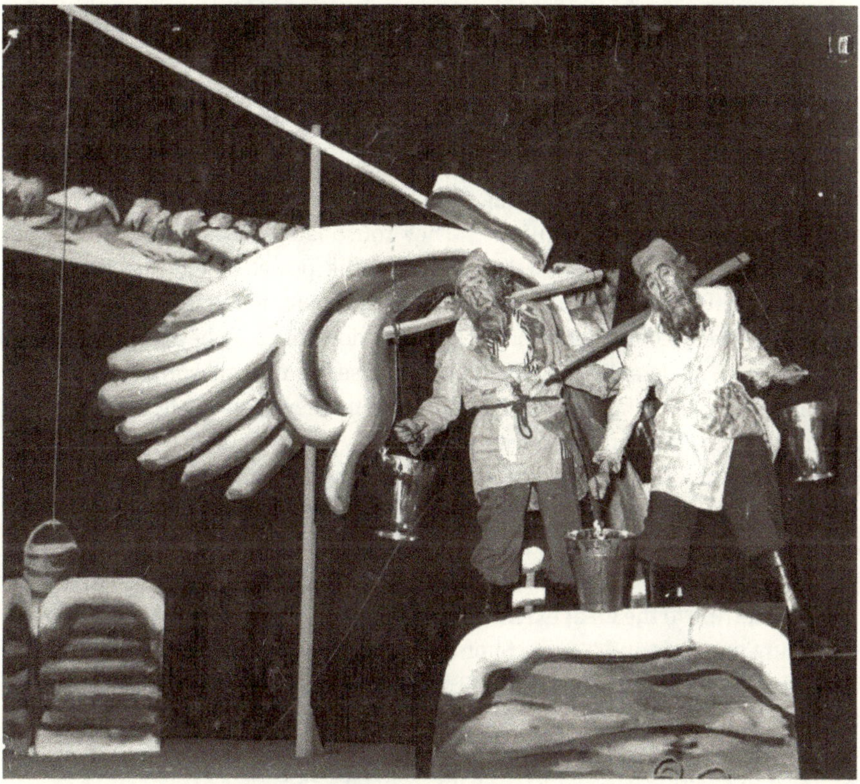

Figure 19: Yisroel Shumacher and Shimen Dzigan in the skit "Di vaser-treger" (The Water Carriers) by Moyshe Broderzon (Lydia Shumacher-Ophir collection).

The Yiddish Satirical Performance in the State of Israel: Between Admiration and Rejection

In addition to the acting talents of Dzigan and Shumacher, most Israeli theatergoers and journalists were fascinated by the duo's skillful decryption of the Israeli reality and its translation into critical and subversive political satire.[27]

27 Regarding the extent to which they tackled the Israeli reality, an article in *Maariv* noted: "Numerous comments reflected the sensitivity of the visiting artists to the changes that have taken place in Israel since their last visit here, in the economic field (tax, the cancellation of the 'austerity', the pig war), in the cultural field ('Porgy and Bess' . . .), and in party policy (Mapam and Sneh), elections and carnivals." *Maariv*, "'Ośim tseḥoḳ." However, some critics saw the references to Israel only as external clothing for the duo's theater: "The atmosphere on the stage and in the theater is similar to performances by the Yidishe Bande in Warsaw . . . and highly

Critics described the two actors as underground warriors, as "sniper artists"[28] with a "secret weapon,"[29] whose "arrows target not only the people and organizations in the headlines (the government, the Histadrut) but also the margins of the political landscape and our social experience."[30] They aim at "the rulers and the opposition," and "their arrows of jokes and jests hit the bullseye."[31] They "strike right and left"[32] with "daring satire that forces the audience to laugh, even when it cuts with a sharp knife."[33] "They rouse laughter as though they were using dynamite."[34] Emil Feuerstein depicted the power of the duo poetically, also using military rhetoric: "They dismantle in mere moments our weapons of opposition, we become their captives and they do with us as they please."[35] Thus, Hebrew-speaking Israelis could no longer oppose the Yiddish word, surrendering to the "enemy." As Y. M. Nayman concluded in the newspaper *Davar*, Dzigan and Shumacher "are dangerous comedians indeed . . . a sign should be placed on their backs: 'Take care! Explosive material!'"[36] Although Nayman wrote these words with affection and satisfaction, certain critics indeed viewed the political satire of Dzigan and Shumacher as powerful. In the newspaper *Hador* (Mapai's evening paper), for example, Y. Zonder warned his readers that their satire wielded great power, referring to the great extent of its influence.[37] "Dzigan and Shumacher are not acting underground," wrote Shmuel Svislotsky in the playbill for *Feter m'ken aykh!* (Uncle, We Know You!, 1959). "They act without fear and without pretense: they are not scared of the 'opposition' and they do not surrender to the 'coalition.'"[38] Likewise, Azaria Rapaport described them in similar terms, as quoted in the playbill for *Ze vi du geyst?!* (Look Where You're Going?!):

> Dzigan and Shumacher are the knights of Jewish laughter . . . they never hit "below the belt." They approach the material with justice, fairness, with nobility. When they decry ridiculous phenomena – they do not make themselves ridiculous. When they pull out their

characteristic of the diaspora are the singing sections in the show. Although they are beautiful in their own right, they do not sprout from our earth." Nahor, "Humor."

28 Avrahami, "Dzigan ṿeShumacher."

29 Gelbert, "Bintivei satira."

30 Avrahami, "Dzigan ṿeShumacher."

31 G. H., "Mima 'ata ḥai?"

32 Avrahami, "Dzigan ṿeShumacher." See also N., "Dzigan ṿeShumacher"; *Zemanim*, "'Eḥad miḳra"; Gamzu, "'Emesh bate'aṭron."

33 Sh. V., "Hatokhnit haḥadasha."

34 Roshanski, "A mayster-program."

35 Feuerstein, "'Eikh 'ta holekh."

36 Nayman, "Dzigan ṿeShumacher."

37 Zonder, "Tseḥoḳ."

38 Sh. Svislotsky, "Sod hatslaḥatam," playbill for *Feter, m'ken aykh!* (1959).

> hair – they do so with elegance. When they beat someone who deserves it with the broom of satire – they do so with the skill of expert swordsmen. Consequently, they are respected even by the targets of their laughter.[39]

In the newspaper *Morgn zhurnal*, which was published in New York, Shmuel Izban depicted Dzigan and Shumacher as leading the political opposition from the stage, noting that their criticism constituted bitter propaganda against the Israeli leadership.[40] Dzigan himself explained to Rafael Bashan why there was no political satire in Israel at this time: "If you write a neutral joke, 'parve' [neither milk nor meat], about an important person, you are digging yourself a grave. The Israeli humorists are scared of getting on the wrong side of a vengeful person and paying dearly for their jokes."[41] In 1959, Shlomo Nakdimon concluded his article in the introduction to the playbill for *Feter, m'ken aykh!* (Uncle, We Know You!): "A comic pearl from Dzigan and Shumacher: 'From Zion will go out Dicta-torah [dictatorship, a play on words dictatorship and Torah]."[42]

The reviews of the duo's shows were mainly positive, although negative sentiments were also voiced. The duo was reprimanded for not performing in Hebrew, for the differences in the quality of their various skits, and also – similarly to the criticism written in the Soviet Union – for concentrating too much on the "old world." A few reviewers argued that Dzigan and Shumacher allowed themselves to dwell on matters that did not accord with Israeli tastes. One journalist, who signed his article with the name Segol, was enraged by their jokes about the country's flag and the fact that one of them "scratches himself on stage." At the end of the review, the author proclaimed that there is a limit to what is allowed in the State of Israel.[43] Despite these negative responses, the critical voice of the artists, independent of any party or political platform, was received with enthusiasm and admiration against the background of the reserved Hebrew theater and the contemporary, ideologically driven Israeli journalism.

---

39 Azaria Rapaport, "'Abirei hatseḥok hayehudi," playbill for *Ze vi du geyst?!* (1958).
40 Izban, "Di grine aktyorn."
41 Bashan, "Dzigan."
42 Shlomo Nakdimon ("Ha'eṭ shemetaḳen"), identified with the duo's criticism of Mapai. Nakdimon was a senior journalist and political commentator and became a scholar of the history of the *Yishuv* in Erets Israel and the State of Israel.
43 Segol, "Dzigan ṿeShumacher."

The Israeli Audience

Throughout their careers, the audience played a central role in Dzigan and Shumacher's performances. Their Israeli audience in the 1950s was varied in terms of age, ideological identification, and social status. The spectators included young and old, journalists, government ministers, Knesset members, Orthodox Jews, and the leaders of Mapai.[44] Vera Levin noted that among the audience were Jews of Eastern European origin, for whom "every sentence, every expression, arouses a lot of different associations," as well as "people from the West, who grasped at Hebrew or German expressions from the Middle Ages in order to understand the words, and they too are affected by the grace of the diasporic language: its softness, its innocence, and mainly its folk humor." In addition, the performances were attended by "native Israelis, whose [knowledge of this way of life] – if they had any at all – came from family members or was acquired from literature."[45] Rapaport likewise emphasized the audience's diversity, stressing that theatergoers ranged from the higher socioeconomic echelons to butchers and "Jewish women wearing wigs."[46]

The audience composition underwent a change in the mid-1960s. According to B. Levin, who wrote in the American *Der tog–morgn zhurnal*, although the audience continued to be comprised of Yiddish speakers, many of them spoke Hebrew as their mother tongue.[47] Among the theatergoers were many tourists and a small group of Mizrahi Jews who understood Yiddish. At Dzigan's performance in Safed in 1964, Yehoshua Bar-Yosef discerned new immigrants from Romania, Hungary, and Poland, most of whom did not possess even basic Hebrew. Bar-Yosef defined them as "'*amkha*' [the masses] in the best sense of the word. Grocers, craftsmen, builders, workers of all kinds."[48] However, Dzigan claimed that the cream of his audience were members of the Israeli political and cultural elite, people who were abreast of "affairs," as he put it: they laughed heartily at his jokes. Although more demanding and critical, they understood his jokes and wisecracks properly, with the utmost enjoyment. Indeed, Dzigan endeavored to attract this audience in particular, seeing his theatrical path as "humorously-satirically molding Israeli life."[49] He wanted to perform to an audience that knew and understood

44 See Azar, "Dzigan un Shumacher"; *Maariv*, "Nim'as lehitlotsets."
45 Levin, "He lekha ye'al tivke."
46 Rapaport, "'Omanei hatseḥoḳ."
47 Levin, "Teaters in Yisroel."
48 Bar-Yosef, "Nivror le'idish."
49 Gilboa, "Holkhim bedarkam."

Yiddish yet was also intelligent and politically active: "I set my sights on a certain audience, the one that speaks and understands Yiddish but reads the daily Hebrew newspapers. An intelligent and discerning audience. The uneducated won't get anything out of my show and I don't feel their presence is necessary. I need an audience that knows how to laugh at the right time and won't kill the jokes."[50] Over the years, the number of young theatergoers dwindled.[51] The audience did not renew itself; rather it grew old and declined.[52]

Israel and the Diaspora

Although in the first half of the 1950s they expressed a desire to settle in Israel,[53] Dzigan and Shumacher made Israel their permanent home only in 1958, after purchasing two apartments in Tel Aviv. In this period, and in the subsequent years, they performed not only in Israel and continued to leave for long tours, visiting Yiddish-speaking audiences around the globe.

Their decision to perform as guest artists, thus excluding the possibility of settling permanently in Israel, was a consequence of the Israeli establishment's policy against Yiddish: in their Polish passports, the artists received a permit to enter Israel as *new ʻolim* (immigrants), yet they decided to enter the country as guest artists because, paradoxically, this was the only way that they could perform in Yiddish in Israel. Their extended absences were a consequence of the many challenges they encountered as Yiddish actors in Israel, the high taxes they were charged, as well as the existence of a large community in the diaspora that looked forward with great anticipation to the duo's performances. The successful tours in the diaspora also significantly improved the duo's financial situation. In the 1950s they performed at major locations – such as Carnegie Hall in New York [See Figure 20], the Corrientes Theater in Buenos Aires, and the Alhambra in Paris. Most of their performances were sold out,[54] arousing hopes for the future of artis-

50 Bar-On, "'Oy, Rabin."

51 A. L., "Baʻayotay."

52 Shem-Or, "Be'idish ze matsḥiḳ."

53 "We are fed up with wandering the world without a permanent home. Moreover, our wives are fed up of this. We have therefore decided to liquidate our property in Buenos Aires, to complete our tour of performances in South and Central America, in accordance with the contracts that were signed, to adapt and to repeat the material that we obtained in Israel in our new show, and to return to Israel, which will become our permanent base." See *Yedioth Ahronoth*, "Lanashim nim'as."

54 See, for example, A., "Mit Dzigan–Shumacher; A., "Di velt shoklt zikh"; Perelmuter, "Dzigan un Shumacher," 21; Zeitlin, "Dzigans un Shumachers nign"; *Keneder odler*, "Dzigan un Shumacher; Tsharnes, "Tsu der premyere."

tic Yiddish theater. The actors were honored and praised by the Yiddish press, and sometimes even by major local papers, such as *The Daily News* and *The New York Times*. In Argentina, where they remained for extended periods, they also tried their luck in the theater business: in November 1952 they entered a partnership to operate the Corrientes Theater as a permanent stage for Yiddish theater. This venture was unsuccessful, and the partnership was later dismantled.[55]

Figure 20: Posters advertising performances by Dzigan and Shumacher at Carnegie Hall, New York (Lydia Shumacher-Ophir Collection).

Their success in Jewish communities around the world led many to view Dzigan and Shumacher not only as emissaries of Yiddish culture but also as representatives of the State of Israel. Defining themselves in this way provided a "Zionist" justification for their extended absences from Israel. For the most part, the

55 BAA, file 146–03.

Israeli press interpreted their activities around the world positively. Dzigan saw himself – and many critics perceived and presented him as such also after Shumacher's death – as a social therapist, political commentator, state comptroller, and stage artist, and at the same time as building a bridge between "the islands of Yiddishkeit," the Yiddish-speaking Jewish communities scattered around the globe.

Dzigan and Shumacher themselves jokingly claimed that they were competing with the Jewish Agency's emissaries and the Israeli ambassadors serving all around the world. Numerous critics in the press in Israel and the diaspora shared this perception: Dzigan and Shumacher depicted the achievements of the State of Israel but also presented "an honest picture, real and critical" of the Israeli reality, with all its disadvantages. In the Hebrew newspaper *Hatzofe* (the newspaper of the National Religious Party), Emil Feuerstein defined Dzigan as the country's "greatest emissary," explaining that "there is no one else who can offer the enormous service to the state that Dzigan achieves in his frequent, habitual tours to all the large concentrations of Jews in the diaspora." Furthermore, he described Dzigan as a patriot who serves the State of Israel, "a kind of individual, personal propaganda center . . . distinguished from all the other emissaries by the fact that he himself funds his trips."[56] Yehoshua Bar-Yosef also attributed to Dzigan a didactic-Zionist role in the diaspora, bringing Zionism to the non-Hebrew speaking masses who could not understand the speeches given by Israeli officials. Bar-Yosef compared Dzigan's mission to the national educational mission of Hebrew theaters (Habima Theater and the Cameri Theater) in the diaspora and even suggested that the latter were less effective than Dzigan.[57] Likewise, the Yiddish newspaper *Folksblat* (Montevideo) portrayed the activities of Dzigan and Shumacher outside Israel as "a national mission."[58] Dzigan was humorously referred to as "the most dangerous Zionist emissary in the world."[59] In *Yedioth Ahronoth*, Yosef Nadava wrote: "For the most part they seem to be giving the State of Israel good propaganda, even if, toward the end of their show, they conclude piercingly: 'It's better for a Jew to sit in prison in Israel than next to bountifully-laid tables in America."[60]

Despite these many positive reviews, the extent of political criticism in the duo's shows (and later in Dzigan's solo shows), particularly at performances

56 Feuerstein, "Tokhnit ḥadasha."
57 Bar-Yosef, "Nivror le'idish."
58 *Folksblat*, "Dzigan un Shumacher."
59 Yehuda, "Dzigan vehaṭeliṿizya."
60 Nadava, "Ṭov kele' be'Yiśra'el."

outside Israel, led some journalists to voice reservations regarding freedom of speech and the power of their political satire, which was seen as opposition propaganda. Thus, for example, a critic, who signed with the name Avi-Miriam, wrote in Mapai's *Hador* newspaper:

> It gives the following impression to the theatergoer who does not know Israel: This country is Sodom, nothing more, nothing less, a nation that does nothing but ignore the weak, the new immigrant brothers, that aims only to cheat them and starve them, to steal the last remnants of their property and to deprive them of their rights. For three hours straight you do not hear even one positive word about Israel, its people, its endeavors; these artists saw nothing positive that was worthy of note in our country.[61]

Baruch Karo expressed similar thoughts in *Haboker* (the newspaper of the General Zionists):

> It seems that political satire, if it is to be staged at all, then it is preferable, according to a number of journalists, that this occur only within the borders of the state. Indeed, these artists are about to leave the country and bring to our brothers in America friendly "regards" from our life in Israel.[62]

The weekly *Di naye tsayt*, which was published in Buenos Aires by Mapai, discussed claims that Dzigan and Shumacher gave Israel a bad name by laughing about the country and its ministers.[63]

The artists – during their partnership and subsequently in Dzigan's solo career – offered the same critical picture of the Israeli reality at shows both inside the country and abroad. "The best proof of the positivity of the State of Israel," said Dzigan, "is the possibility of publicly criticizing its negative aspects, without the fear of having our mouths shut and being put in prison."[64]

In his memoirs, Dzigan recalls the opposition he encountered among the Jewish community in America when he voiced criticism of the State of Israel and

---

61 Avi-Miriam, "Kisui levush."

62 Karo, "Dzigan veShumacher." See also the words of Rapaport: "When they are abroad it was made clear to them once again that their only permanent and true home is the State of Israel . . . for a year and a half they plowed the settlements of the 'Jewish Empire" in South America . . . did they appear as artists from Israel? No, this was liable to cause them harm. As artists that had visited Israel? Yes, but this too was clear from the very [fact that the] show [was] comprised of material about Israel. In the show called *Ha'olam tsoḥeḳ* (The World Laughs), there were many pictures of life in Israel." See Rapaport, "Yehudim tsoḥaḳim."

63 N. M., "Dzigan – Shumacher."

64 Haim Gamzu, "Hate'aṭron hasa'ṭiri shel Dzigan," playbill for *Beser m'redt nisht* (Silence is Golden, 1976).

its political leaders – in his words, such criticism was regarded as “heresy” – versus his need to honestly critique certain aspects of the Israeli reality:

> מען האָט נישט געטאָרט לאָזן פֿאַלן אַ שטויבעלע אויף מדינת־ישׂראל . . . פֿאַר זיי דאַרף מדינת־ישׂראל שײַנען ווי אַן אויסגעשײַערטער סאַמאָוואַר לכּבֿוד יום־טובֿ – הייס און משפּחהדיק. און טאַקע אַזוי ווי אין אַ משפּחה פֿאַרגיט מען אַ קינד זײַנע זינד, אַזוי פֿאַרגיט דאָס אַמעריקאַנער ייִדנטום אַלע פֿעלערן, וואָס עס מאַכט די יונגע מדינה . . . מײַן רעפּערטואַר האָט געדאַרפֿט באַשטיין פֿון ריינעם לאַך־מאַטעריאַל, אָבער נישט פֿון סאַטירע. איך בין נישט געווען בשלמות מיט זיך אַליין . . . לסוף האָב איך זיך צעבונטעוועט און באַשלאָסן אַרײַננעמען אין מײַן פּראָגראַם אַ מאָנאָלאָג וועגן אַ ישׂראלדיקן מנחם־מענדל. דורך זײַן מויל האָב איך געמוזט אַ ביסל . . . מקטרג זײַן אויף געוויסע נעגאַטיווע דערשײַנונגען אין אונדזער עקאָנאָמיק, פֿאַרקריפּלטע אײַנשטעלונגען און בכלל – כ'האָב געדאַרפֿט אויף מײַן אופֿן דערציילן וועגן זאַכן, וואָס דאַרפֿן נישט זײַן אין מדינת־ישׂראל.[65]
>
> [It was forbidden to cast even a speck of dust on the State of Israel . . . for them, the State of Israel needed to shine like a polished samovar in honor of a festival – warm and homely. And indeed, just as in a family one forgives a child his sins, so the American Jews forgive all the mistakes made by the young state. . . . my repertoire needed to be comprised of purely humorous material, without satire. I was not content with this . . . eventually I rebelled and integrated into my show a monologue about an Israeli Menakhem-Mendl. Through him, I could denounce certain negative events of our economy, twisted perspectives . . . and in general – talk in my own way about things that should not happen in the State of Israel.]

After the war of 1967, with patriotic spirit reigning supreme in Israel, Dzigan chose to moderate his criticism and offer a special, “patriotic” show:

> איך האָב בײַגעשטײַערט צו דער זעקס־טאָקיגער־מלחמה מײַן אייגענעם געווער – הומאָר . . . כ'האָב זיך גענומען, ווי אַ טרײַער זעלנער, ברענגען אַ ביסל הײַטערקייט דעם ייִדן פֿון אַ גאַנץ יאָר, דעם פּשוטן ישׂראל־בירגער, וואָס קרעכצט בײַם צאָלן שטײַער און שיקט זײַן קינד אין פֿײַער אָן איין וואָרט.[66]
>
> [I contributed my own weapon to the Six Day War – humor . . . I took it upon myself, like a true soldier, to lift the spirits of the simple Jew, the Israeli citizen, who complains when he pays taxes but sends his son to the front lines without a word of protest].

In a show staged in 1968, Dzigan included segments that in his own words “broke the hearts” of Israelis who had left for America: he depicted the achievements of Israel after the Six Day War and offered “a successful closing picture of Jerusalem, colorful, vibrant, and uplifted.”[67] This was criticized by Mendel Kramer, who wrote in *The Gazette* that at the end of the show everything suddenly seemed like “Israeli propaganda” and a gesture to Israeli bravery during the war. He claimed that some of these sentimental sections detracted from the quality of the show.[68]

---

65 Dzigan, *Der koyekh*, 343–44.
66 Ibid., 351.
67 A. L., “Ba‘ayotay.”
68 Kramer, “Dzigan Headlines.”

In an interview with *Letste nayes*, Dzigan noted that had he presented in America sharp political satire in the same way as he did in Israel, he would have been lynched.[69] The show Dzigan referred to in this case was not regarded as particularly critical by Israelis.

In another interview, Dzigan stated: "I don't want to attack the government [while I am] abroad. So, I need to make it parve [bland] . . . but like I already told you, this doesn't interest me. In short, the situation is bad: I can't say whatever I want to and moreover I am forbidden to do so. They could kill me for being an antisemite. On the other hand, neutral humor is not for me."[70]

Figure 21: Yisroel Shumacher and Shimen Dzigan (Lydia Shumacher-Ophir collection).

Reception in Israel

During the decade in which they performed together in Israel, Dzigan and Shumacher succeeded in divesting themselves of the negative label usually attached to everything relating to "Yiddish theater." They won a central status in theatrical reviews in the Hebrew press (and, of course, in the Yiddish press), and at the same time they successfully battled the hostile cultural policy toward Yiddish theater in Israel, apart from the tax discrimination, which remained in place.

69 Brat, "Dzigan: Ikh vil nisht fargesn."

70 Shavit, "Lama 'ani 'atsuv."

Critics in the Hebrew press described Dzigan and Shumacher as "gifted,"[71] "excellent,"[72] "astounding,"[73] and "experienced"[74] comedians "with their own unique style,"[75] "flawless in the field of their art,"[76] with "exceptional talent,"[77] "a match made in heaven."[78] Others depicted them as "engineers of humor," "witty theatrical feuilletonists and talented directors," who knew how to "expose the ridiculous,"[79] "to serve political satire beautifully,"[80] "to tell a joke in a way few others can,"[81] who "understand the soul of the audience, know the secret of presentation, and the secret of minimalism,"[82] whose "professionalism is polished and cultured."[83] They were described as "excellent writers,"[84] and others noted that their humor was free from "vulgarity."[85] Among the innumerable similar depictions in the Yiddish press, Yiddish journalists noted that they were at once "comedians and the best satirical artists on both the Yiddish and Hebrew stages";[86] "a blessed and harmonious partnership";[87] "the last Mohicans" of Polish Jewry;[88] "a remedy" and, "more than theater, an institution that teaches laughter and [helps us] to see things differently."[89]

The criticism in the Hebrew press accorded Dzigan and Shumacher a central place in the local theatrical and cultural activity, not only with regard to Yiddish theater – which it almost completely ignored – but mainly in relation to the Hebrew satirical theater. Dzigan and Shumacher were, in the words of Yitsḥak Avrahami in the Progressive Party's newspaper *Zemanim*, "the best comedians on the Israeli stage." "As much as it may seem paradoxical," the journalist continued, "the best Israeli satirical theater is in fact the Yiddish stage of Dzigan and

71 Nahor, "Holekh."
72 Feuerstein, "Tish'a ḳabin."
73 Levin, "Teaters in Yisroel."
74 Gelbert, "Bintivei satira."
75 *Al hamishmar*, "Ḥadshot 'omanut ṿetarbut."
76 Avrahami, "Dzigan ṿeShumacher."
77 *Zemanim*, "'Eḥad miḳra'."
78 Nayman, "Dzigan ṿeShumacher"; Gan, "Dzigan ṿeShumacher be'ivrit."
79 Gelbert, "Bintivei satira."
80 G. H., "Mima 'ata ḥai?"
81 Ze'ev, "Makirim 'otkha."
82 Feuerstein, "'Eikh 'ta holekh."
83 Gelbert, " Bintivei satira."
84 Feuerstein, "Tish'a ḳabin."
85 Avrahami, "Dzigan ṿeShumacher."
86 Tsanin, "Tsu der premyere."
87 N. M., "Dzigan – Shumacher."
88 Faltitsky, "Di letste mohikaner."
89 M-m, "Dzigan un Shumacher"; Yuris, "Red tsu der zakh."

Shumacher."[90] The description of this cultural paradox reached its zenith in an article published by Asher Nahor in *Yedioth Ahronoth*:

> The shows performed in the Hebrew satirical theater for some reason evade the main thing—satire about current events. Batsal Yarok [Green Onion] wanders to the paths of the Music Hall, while Sambatyon still battles for artistic consolidation, and thus we have reached a paradox: the only ones to continue the tradition of Hamatate [The Broom] at present are Dzigan and Shumacher. In their style and in their specific Yiddish, the Łódź dialect, which is in no way the official literary Yiddish.[91]

The discourse in the Hebrew press depicted these "foreign heirs" as cultivating the genre of Hebrew satire, becoming a model for it.[92]

According to Mendel Kohansky, in the 1950s light entertainment flourished in the Israeli theater. Among the central troupes of the period, he notes the revue theater Li-La-Lo, which "performed revue performances of considerable dimensions, in the European style," and Do-Re-Mi, which at first staged operettas written before World War I, and in 1955 began to perform original Hebrew plays and later also American musicals, with little success. The third troupe mentioned by Kohansky is Sambatyon, which was established by Ze'ev Berlinksi and Mordechai Ben-Ze'ev. The satire of this troupe, according to Kohansky, was not sharp, and its political satire was characterized by direct and vulgar humor. The last troupe that Kohansky discusses is Batsal Yarok, which was founded in 1958. Shmuel Bunim served as its director, Haim Hefer was the songwriter, and Dan Ben-Amotz and Efraim Kishon wrote the troupe's texts. Its performances received negative reviews, the number of theatergoers declined, and it soon disappeared from the Israeli stage.[93]

90 Avrahami, "Ha'omanim"; see also Tsanin, "Tsu der premyere."

91 Nahor, "Dzigan ṿeShumacher." Similar comments were made by Nahor in the newspaper *Herut* (the daily paper of the Herut movement) in 1953: "Upon the foundation of the State [of Israel], [Hamatate Theater], which for many years cultivated social and political satire on its stage, abandoned the field of current humor and since then stages only comedies, which are mainly translated from foreign repertoires. The comic duo Dzigan and Shumacher captured the audience of their listeners during their first visit by reviving the satirical voice, which Hamatate and even Li-La-Lo neglected, the latter also made a sharp turn and became solely a revue theater." See Nahor, "'Erev 'im"; Feuerstein wrote: "Under their influence the sleeping Israeli humor awoke a little, and there is no doubt that the foundation of Sambatyon was inspired by them." See Feuerstein, "'Eikh 'ta holekh."

92 Yuris wrote in a Zionist spirit about the need to bridge between the two languages and even advised Dzigan and Shumacher to connect with "the remaining remnant" of the actors from Hamatate Theater in order to achieve a quality troupe. See Yuris, "Lakht gezunterheyt."

93 Kohansky, *Hate'aṭron ha'ivri*, 152–53.

Particularly interesting with regard to Dzigan and Shumacher's role in the field of Israeli satire are reviews by Haim Gamzu and Boaz Evron, which Kohansky quotes in his book. Indeed, Gamzu wrote in *Haaretz*:

> In the field of theater, we stand shamed and humiliated before the cultural poverty [of the young generation] and the superficiality of its intellectual demands. And now, here stands the young generation, satisfied with its amateur achievements, empty of the hopes that we hung upon it... Since HaTs'izbaṭron,[94] young men and women, likeable and suntanned, with scorching looks, have performed on our stages. This coarseness, which seems to herald the new "Israeliness," awakens the expectation of a new language, fresh gestures, to replace the normal Slavic-Jewish methods, which are at once quite pathetic and quite sentimental.... There is nothing easier than establishing a new theater troupe. There is nothing easier than transforming a nice amateur military troupe into a humorous and satirical troupe. A troupe without any ability to perform. Humor without a light comic gentleness. Satire without risk, without taking a stand ... Avigdor Hame'iri's "Haḳumḳum" had the right to exist. Yitskhok Nożyk and co.'s "Hamatate" also had that same right ... because they had an aim and they had substance ... Today's satirical troupes increasingly forget their role. They want to live in peace with everyone.[95]

In a review published in November 1959, also in *Haaretz*, Evron, a Canaanite[96] critic who categorically opposed Yiddish performances in Israel,[97] praised the "Israeli atmosphere" of the Batsal Yarok troupe, even if this atmosphere was "indistinct." He commended the local and authentic sounds. According to him, one did not feel that performative texts had been translated from Yiddish.[98]

Emil Feuerstein mentioned Israeli society's lack of humor and the dearth of a high quality miniature theater.[99] "Apart from exceptional cases," wrote another journalist anonymously in the newspaper *Zemanim*, "our public life and our publications are as serious as the graveyard."[100] In an article published in *Yedioth Ahronoth* in 1967, Yosef Shavit stated that the people of Israel are not only unhappy but lack a sense of humor.[101] In a piece entitled "Dzigan and Shumacher af eyn fus" (Dzigan and Shumacher on One Foot), which Feuerstein penned for the playbill for *Ze vi du geyst?!*, the writer discussed the disappearance of Jewish humor following the establishment of the State of Israel, highlighting Dzigan and

---

94 The entertainment troupe of the Palmach and IDF (Israel Defense Forces), which existed from 1948 until 1950.

95 Ibid., 154–55.

96 An ideological movement that arose in the 1940s in Palestine. See Klaus, "Canaanism."

97 See Rotman, "Yidish teater in Medines-Yisroel."

98 Kohansky, *Hate'aṭron ha'ivri*, 155–56.

99 Feuerstein, "Tish'a ḳabin."

100 *Zemanim*, "'Eḥad miḳra."

101 Shavit, "Lama 'ani 'atsuv."

Shumacher's central role as the guardians of "the last ember of humor on the Israeli street":

> There were two unique qualities characteristic of the Jews in the diaspora: generosity and humor. We lost both on the way to Israel. Gloomy seriousness permeated our lives and has continued to spread ever since the state was established . . . Thus, Israel became the classic land without humor. All the comic stages closed, one after another (apart from one miniature theater). In the sea of the press and journals, there is not even one humorous platform.

In 1955, the journalist Moshe Efrat wrote in *Hador*:

> But where is the Jewish humor? Where is the Israeli comedian who will voice the people's feelings? All the humoristic theaters in Israel have shut their doors, one after another. . . . "We succeeded" in finally bringing about the downfall of Hamatate Theater . . . We were able to close the doors of Li-La-Lo and to seal up this spring . . . and behold, suddenly, two artists appear, in great mercy, Shimon Dzigan and Yiśra'el Shumacher, and they begin a revolution. They make us laugh with the power of their juicy talent. Through their sharp vision and their spicy perspective, with their humor, which bursts forth with volcanic strength, they evoke waves of laughter. A miracle has occurred, and we are laughing at everything.[102]

The miracle was not only the appearance of comedians who spoke on behalf of the people but the fact that they did so in Łódź Yiddish. Efrat regarded the voice of Dzigan and Shumacher as a "dybbuk": it enabled the artists to express the collective subconscious or discuss topics that were taboo in Israeli society.

In an article regarding humor in Israeli literature, Esther Fuchs notes that irony, satire, and grotesque humor only began to enter the poetry of Yehuda Amichai, David Avidan, and Avot Yeshurun at the end of the 1950s, when the discord between the Zionist ideal and the reality in the State of Israel penetrated the Israeli consciousness and became a source of humor. By contrast, she argues, the Hebrew literature of the Palmach generation in the 1940s and 1950s almost completely lacked humor. Only one humoristic corpus was produced and published in that period, "Yalkuṭ hakazavim" (1956), the naïve humor of which is similar to the folk Jewish humor in stories of Chelm.[103]

This cultural void, the "humoristic vacuum," which was mentioned by many critics, was eventually filled by Dzigan and Shumacher. According to this rhetoric, their role was not subversive but rather pioneering-Zionist: they settled in the only area that remained empty – satire, humor, and self-criticism. The vacant space left by Israeli theater provided the ultimate site for Yiddish

---

102 Efrat, "Tseḥoḳ go'el."

103 See Oring, *Israeli Humor*; Fuchs, "Is There Humor." See also Noy, "Haḳayemet bediḥat 'am."

theater. Dzigan and Shumacher were "welcome rain in an arid land," "an oasis in the desert of gloomy Israeli seriousness," in the words of Feuerstein.[104]

Dzigan and Shumacher themselves also referred to the lack of humor in Israeli society on various occasions. At a meeting in 1969 between Dzigan and Amnon Zakov, a young and successful Israeli comedian, the two discussed Yiddish humor versus Hebrew's "lack of humor," in the words of Dzigan. Zakov, so Dzigan claimed, looked like a "non-Jew" and acts like a "non-Jew."[105] When Rafael Bashan asked Dzigan for his opinion on Israeli humor, the actor replied that there is something wrong with a people that cannot laugh at itself.[106] In an interview with Ami Shamir in 1965, Dzigan repeated these statements: Israel lacks humor and "a people that does not laugh – this is a national tragedy." In his opinion, although Israel provided a place for the ingathering of the exiles, this occurred only in the work environment, not at home. Therefore, there was no "opportunity for one to learn from his neighbor's humor." Likewise, he claimed that the Hebrew language was not musical but rather serious.[107]

It seems that Dzigan and Shumacher significantly influenced the public and political spheres in Israel, and their critical art generated reverberations among the public and in the media. The press frequently drew the readers' attention to the duo's jokes and jests,[108] sometimes describing their skits not only as humoristic segments but also as parables about Israeli society.[109]

Missing a performance by Dzigan and Shumacher was considered a great loss. In December 1958, the members of the Beer Sheva local council decided in unison to postpone their weekly meeting in order to attend the artists' performance in the city.[110] In the same month, two thieves were caught at the end of a show in Jerusalem, having stolen two tickets to a performance by Dzigan

104 Feuerstein, "Tish'a ḳabin."

105 Dzigan and Zakov, "The Duel."

106 Bashan, "Monolog."

107 Shamir, "'Inyan retsini."

108 See for example Rapaport, "Dzigan ṿeShumacher."

109 In a highly critical article concerning how the legal authorities dealt with an accident in which an old man of Yemenite origin was killed, Azriel Carlebach wrote: "The general public increasingly feels that they dealt with this just like the Jew (portrayed by Dzigan and Shumacher) sitting in prison in Jaffa and telling his friend how he got there." Carlebach summarizes the monologue: "So I brought cans of foods from abroad. And there were watches in the cans. And they caught me, and they brought me to court. And there was a lot of talking before the judge. And eventually the judge asks me what I prefer – a month in jail or [a fine of] fifty pounds. And so, I said to him, 'If that's the way it is, give me the fifty pounds.'" Immediately afterwards, his article concluded with the question: "And it's our choice?" See Carlebach, "Me'a lirot."

110 *Jerusalem Post*, "Beersheba Councillors."

and Shumacher among the contents of a house they had robbed in Jerusalem. Unable to resist the temptation, they used the stolen tickets to attend the show, which had designated seats, leading to their arrest.[111] Not only thieves but politicians, as well as Hebrew-speaking intellectuals, regularly attended performances by Dzigan and Shumacher.[112] According to the owner of the Knesset cafeteria, Knesset Members began to pay their debts after Shumacher performed a monologue in which he played the cafeteria owner, describing the debts the statesmen were amassing in the nation's cafeteria.[113] Ministers and politicians, among them Yitzhak Ben-Zvi, Zalman Shazar, Moshe Sharett, and Yosef Sprinzak waited for Dzigan and Shumacher after performances in order to congratulate them and have their picture taken with them (the latter may have been the artists' idea).[114] In 1955, Efraim Kishon recommended voting for the duo in the elections.[115] In the same year, Yosef Serlin, then serving as minister of health, humorously claimed – or worryingly confessed – that Dzigan and Shumacher "do more for 'health' with their humor than the Health Ministry does."[116] Dzigan himself attributed political influence to his shows and even claimed that his performances "contributed to the Likud's rise to power."[117] He reports that in 1977 he met Prime Minister Menachem Begin in the Knesset kiosk while visiting as the guest of Knesset Member Hillel Seidel. Begin asked the actor not to hold back in mocking him.

Language and Nationality

> The two comedians assimilated well into the theatrical landscape of our land, even though from birth they inherited [the traditions] of old Jewish theater and they continue to use Yiddish on stage. Some believe that the power of this handsome couple lies in their language, but it seems that this language alone would not have been sufficient for the two artists to succeed in Israel without the spiritual renewal that the free climate of our country facilitated. It is as though the Israeli milieu enabled their talent to sprout wings.
>
> – Gelbert, "Bintivei satira"

111 Avrahami, "Ze vi du geyst."
112 Shtshavinsky, "Ze vi du geyst?!"
113 *Yedioth Ahronoth*, "Humor yiśre'eli."
114 *Letste nayes*, "Prezident af der forshtelung"; *Yedioth Ahronoth*, "Hanaśi' ṿehaḳomiḳanim."
115 "Now it is up to you to decide, dear voter, how you want to shape the lives of the parties' leaders in the next four years . . . vote according to conscience, according to your feeling, according to a one-off payment [you received], or according to the note closest to hand. I myself – I wrote down: Dzigan and Shumacher for prime minister!" See Kishon, "Dzigan ṿeShumacher lashilṭon!"
116 Maariv, "Yad lapeh."
117 Bar-On, "Monolog mehurhar." On the influence that Dzigan attributed to the theater with regard to Israeli immigration policy, see Dzigan, *Der koyekh*, 310.

> The censor and members of the public committee went to investigate. Serious faces softened and that angry censor became their true friend. The same thing happened to the policemen who were to arrest the comedians . . . A few "laughter bombs" broke down the weapons of the police. One policeman, originally from Poland, said that if the duo were to be arrested, he would endeavor to accompany them to prison, because the prison was likely to become the most entertaining place in the country . . . The *mame-loshn* of Dzigan and Shumacher has the power to soften censors and ministers.
>
> – Nayman, "Dzigan ṿeShumacher"

Despite the exceptionally positive reception they received, Dzigan and Shumacher were continually forced to contend with the discriminatory policy against Yiddish theater and the repeated demands that they perform in Hebrew. Some critics understood that it would be impossible to translate their artistic language – doing so would distort their original meaning – and that "their power lay in their loyalty to themselves [and therefore] we must accept them [as they are] – or reject them."[118] However, with regard to language, the negative reactions outnumbered the supportive responses. Numerous reviews and articles about their performances expressed the need for a "Hebrew spirit," an urgent desire that the actors "immediately start acting in Yiddish," complaints about broken promises regarding Hebrew performances,[119] and disappointment at the "insufficient amount of Hebrew in the performances" and "their zealous attachment to Yiddish."[120] When Dzigan and Shumacher included Hebrew sections in their shows, the critics described these as attempts to fulfill an obligation, "not interesting . . . constructed on the basis of mistakes and misunderstandings."[121] "In the new show," wrote Asher Nahor in 1957 in *Herut*, "Dzigan and Shumacher permitted themselves to express scorn for the Hebrew language, and for this they will not be forgiven: they simply boycotted the Hebrew word throughout the entire performance."[122] In his review of the duo's second show in Israel, *Tate, du lakhst!* (which was given the Hebrew title ["Tseḥoḳ velo' ya'avor" [Laughter, Hard and Fast], drawing on the idiom "hard and fast law"),[123] Baruch Karo demanded that the actors increase the amount of Hebrew because "in Israel, we have the right to demand Hebrew dominance in

118 *Zemanim*, "'Eḥad miḳra."

119 See, for example, Efrat, "Tseḥoḳ go'el."

120 Ben-Meir, "'Makirim 'otkha dod." Ben-Meir is the penname of (Abba Ahimeir/ Abba Shaul Geisinovich).

121 A. Z., "Dzigan ṿeShumacher."

122 Nahor, "Ledarkam."

123 "Gentlemen! Because there are people that laugh at the law!/ Therefore we announce that laughter will be the law, / Our catchphrase: / Laughter is war! / It is healthy for the nation, what / oh, what, what?" From the concluding song of the show, "Finale," by Yechiel Hagiz, Shumacher's copy with notes in Hebrew, BAA, file 149–02.

art," proposing that they call their next show "Hebrew, Hard and Fast."[124] The same suggestion was sent to the artists in a friendly personal letter from the critic Arye Kinarti before their departure from Israel on March 29, 1951. In the letter, which was written on official stationary of the State of Israel, Kinarti wished them success and expressed the hope, in an entertaining tone, that their next show upon their return would be "Hebrew, Hard and Fast." In so doing, Kinarti in fact suggested placing Hebrew in the role of the law: a law not to be broken.[125]

Critics argued that Dzigan and Shumacher needed to "fulfil the duty to the language of the state in which they reside and are active," to be grateful for the leeway they had been given, and to prove their desire to be absorbed into the society by immediately translating their art, as Ben-Meir wrote in 1958.[126] Similarly, Asher Nahor commented in 1953: "The great leeway given to the two actors when they were still new immigrants was given conditionally . . . in the future, the State of Israel will also serve as a place of refuge for their art, if this art will divest itself of diaspora clothing and wear the Hebrew uniform in terms of sound and style."[127] Two years later, Nahor spoke out even more decisively:

> Dzigan and Shumacher do not understand that this matter is one of national, cultural, and even economic revolution, and therefore it is impossible to allow them to perform in Tel Aviv in the same way as they once performed in Łódź and Warsaw. If they will not be with us, in the end they will be against us, and a great part of the last show was against us . . . if after four or five years of living here the two comedians do not feel obliged to appear in even one Hebrew section, this is a sign that they remain foreign and want to be strangers.[128]

Around seven years after their first performance in Israel, Stefan Gelbert wrote an article in *Al hamishmar* praising the duo's acting talents, sharpness, and ability to understand the local reality. However, he commented on their foreignness, their "otherness":

> Why should this public artistic service be performed by others? Do we need to hear jokes from guests about the victory in the Sinai campaign, the retreat from Gaza, oil, immigration and absorption, the "religious" post, the growing wealth of careerists and parasites, and in general about our experience?[129]

---

124 Karo, "Dzigan ṿeShumacher."

125 Reports about the persecution of Yiddish in Israel in general and of Dzigan and Shumacher in particular were published in the contemporaneous Yiddish press. See, for example, Tsanin, "Der 'heyliker' tsorn"; regarding the government policy against the Yiddish theater and press, see B., "Di kontsertn."

126 Ben-Meir, "Dzigan un Shumacher."

127 Nahor, "'Erev 'im."

128 Nahor, "Humor."

129 Gelbert, "Miṭ'an tseḥoḳ."

In 1958, Dzigan and Shumacher were still seen as foreigners, albeit in a positive light:

> It is impossible to avoid noting that all the current pricks and bites – sharp satirical theatrical echoes of what is happening amongst us – are in fact served by Dzigan and Shumacher, who are part-guests, part-residents . . . They, the ostensible representatives of the diaspora, they are the best satirical marksmen hitting the most sensitive spots in the Israeli political and social arenas.[130]

The reception of Dzigan and Shumacher as Israeli artists thus depended, more than anything else, on their willingness to change their language. They needed to prove their place in the national revolution, or at least relate to it in polished Hebrew. In the rhetoric of the Hebrew press they remained, until the end of their days, cultural criminals – or at least linguistic criminals – out on bail. Dzigan and Shumacher eventually entered the canon of Israeli Hebrew theater in 2004, when an episode of a documentary series about Israeli humor by Anat Seltzer and Modi Bar-On (director: Avida Livni; investigative reporter: Asaf Galay) was dedicated to them.[131] They reappeared in internal Yiddish cultural discourse when the Yiddishpiel theater, which was established in 1988 at the initiative of Shmuel Atzmon-Wircer with government support,[132] devoted to them a show entitled *Di eybike Dzigan un Shumacher* (Dzigan and Shumacher Forever; 2004).[133] The play was reported on in the Hebrew press. In 2013, the theater staged a new play entitled *Dzigan un Shumacher knakn shoyn vider* (Dzigan and Shumacher Are At It Again), a musical comedy by B. Michael and Ephraim Sidon, starring Yaakov Bodo and Dovale (Dov) Glickman, and directed by Shmuel Atzmon-Wircer.[134]

---

130 Gilboa, "Holkhim bedarkam." On another occasion, a reviewer wrote: "Despite the fact that the two comedians are perhaps-new immigrants, perhaps-returnees, they have proved once again that they have their reasons and they are immersed in our reality." See *Haboker*, "Dzigan veShumacher."

131 Avida Livni, "Beyidish ze nishma' yoter tov." Producers: Anat Seltzer and Modi Bar-On. Third episode of "Bimdinat hayehudim," Channel 1, 2004.

132 Regarding the reception of Yiddishpiel and its role, which in the words of its manager was "to revive the tradition of Yiddish theater," see Rotman, "Yidish teater in Medines-Yisroel," 52–99.

133 The play was written by Kobi Luria and directed by Shmuel Atzmon-Wircer. Dzigan and Shumacher were played by Yaakov Bodo and Gadi Yagil.

134 The description of the play on Yiddishpiel's website is as follows: "Dzigan and Shumacher is another gesture to two giants of Jewish humor, who even from a distance of decades remain funny and hit the mark just as they did then – maybe even more so. B. Michael and Ephraim Sidon took the sketches that retained their vitality, renovated them in a modern setting and transferred Dzigan and Shumacher into our twenty-first century. Apparently the two are bored in the Garden of Eden. There's no 'evil instinct', no jokes, no cards, everything is serious and righteous and people saying Psalms. Therefore they ask God for a short break. A sabbatical year

Despite their refusal to perform in Hebrew, many saw the very fact that Dzigan and Shumacher tackled the Israeli reality and experiences as proof of their "Israeliness." Their Israeli identity did not manifest in an acquisition of the Hebrew language but rather in their talent for addressing the local, current experience, exposing the nation's weak spots. As Yehoshua Gilboa wrote: "In Yiddish, albeit, and at times with grimaces and gestures that recalled other landscapes – yet we can say with complete certainty: they are still the best on our stage in terms of their talent for humorously-satirically depicting Israeli life."[135] Azaria Rapaport explained how they became the artists of Israeli laughter by confronting the current reality and its figures:

> They arrived as artists of Jewish laughter and became the redeemers of Israeli laughter. Their performances are packed with the Israeli reality. Their skits hit the mark about what is happening on our streets. Their characters come from the office across the road, from the house around the corner, from the gallery of people involved in recent events. Dzigan and Shumacher became wizards of Israeli laughter, even when they are playing the man who runs the kiosk at the central bus station or the barber from Lilienblum Street, even when they place the "dybbuk" in the body of a new immigrant. . . . They have set down roots among us. This is not only because they purchased apartments here but because they made us the basis and the starting point for their activities.[136]

In an article that was partially reproduced in the playbill for *S'blaybt baym altn* (Just Like Old Times), the duo's last show together, Haim Shurer wrote:

> This is a theater of two that continuously assimilates further into our lives and into our world, that talks to us about our problems, our worries, our sorrows, our mistakes and our defects, our joys and our mishaps – and makes a laughingstock of our existence here. Dzigan and Shumacher are the flesh of our Israeli flesh. They live our lives and they pull us up [with their fishing rod] onto the stage using a language of grace and shining talent.[137]

---

back on earth. The Lord of the Worlds allows it, but for the sake of security He sends an angel after them who will report directly and make sure that the two do not behave as usual, getting into trouble." Website of Yiddishpiel, http://www.yiddishpiel.co.il/en/our-shows.html (visited August 2015).

135 Gilboa, "Holkhim bedarkam."

136 Azaria Rapaport, "'Abirei hatseḥoḳ hayehudi," playbill for *Ze vi du gesyt?!* (Look Where You're Going?!, 1958).

137 Shurer, "Dzigan ṿeShumacher." See also the words of Ron Ze'ev: "They come, and they keep coming – artists of the Yiddish theater from abroad. From the United States, from South America, and from Europe – they come to exploit the historical fact that here, in Israel, are concentrated all the Jews who did not learn Hebrew, and their thirst for the art of the stage will bring them to watch that same Yiddish theater that becomes – either accidentally or on purpose – one of the most serious blocks to consolidating a Hebrew culture in Israel. We do not write about these theaters. We do not go to see them. Apart from one that is unique, exceptional in every way,

Gamzu presented Dzigan's theater as a national cultural treasure: "The theater of Dzigan is a real Israeli satirical theater – if not in terms of its language, then in terms of contents. Here, Israel is spotlighted by means of its shadows."[138]

This ambivalent stance toward the Israeliness of Dzigan and Shumacher and their theater was prominent among reviewers and government officials alike. Many sought to adopt the talented, high quality, and popular artists as Israeli, yet simultaneously they found it difficult to accept that a Yiddish theater could constitute an inseparable part of the Israeli cultural reality.[139]

Ramifications of the Israeli Cultural Policy for Yiddish Artistic Activities

In their efforts to obtain a tax reduction, in 1958 Dzigan and Shumacher signed an agreement with the Pargod Theater, managed by Eliyahu Goldenberg, which began its way in Haifa and later relocated to Tel Aviv. In return for adding a number of members of the troupe to their performances, the duo would receive the tax discount that Pargod enjoyed as a Hebrew-speaking theater.[140] Despite this agreement, the extent of Hebrew material in their performances was less than expected. The Ministry of Education wrote to Goldenberg, complaining that in the duo's first performance in the Ohel Shem Theater on September 27, 1958,

---

not a theater of guests, but our stage, our national treasure: Dzigan and Shumacher." See Ze'ev, "Makirim 'otkha."

138 Haim Gamzu, "Hate'aṭron hasa'ṭiri shel Dzigan," playbill for *Beser m'redt nisht* (1976).

139 Examples of this discourse about the Israeli identity of the artists: "The show this time is entirely Israeli, apart from a few songs"; "This show, despite the fact that most of it was prepared abroad, is at any rate more Israeli than the earlier shows, which were devised in Israel, and this is praiseworthy from all perspectives." Nahor, "Sendvitsh." See also Karo, "Dzigan ṿeShumacher; *Al hamishmar*, "Ḥadshot 'omanut ṿetarbut"; Ben-Meir, "Dzigan un Shumacher"; Gelbert, "Bintivei satira." Concerning the perception of their activities as non-Israeli, Nahor wrote: "Despite the Israeli topics of the duets and monologues, for the most part (apart from the duet 'The Official's Funeral' by Y. Bar-Yosef), their humor is not local. The monologue 'Fishl the Sailor,' for example, is a very successful parody about a Jew who supervises the kosher food on a passenger ship. However, this ship is not necessarily Israeli, just as Fishl is not an Israeli Jew. In truth, it is more fitting for him, for Fishl, to organize prayer quorums for '*yortsayts*' and to check *mezuzot* on an Italian or American ship with a kosher kitchen for Jewish passengers than on an Israeli ship..." See Nahor, "Sendvitsh."

140 Eliyahu Goldenberg (1909–1976) was an actor, director, and announcer. At the beginning of the 1960s, Goldenberg was part of the original ensemble "The Three Shmuliks," with the actors Shmuel Rodansky and Shmulik Segal (after his death, he was replaced by Shmuel Atzmon-Wircer). The ensemble performed in Yiddish in various theaters in Israel and abroad.

"The first part, an hour and a half in length, included only two Hebrew songs lasting four minutes." The theater manager's lawyer dispatched a letter to the artists on October 5, 1958, reminding them that the aim of the partnership with Goldenberg, as agreed orally, was to integrate them "into the landscape of the Hebrew stage."[141] The letter claimed that Goldenberg had visited the Ministry of Education and Ministry of Finance "innumerable times" in order to receive authorization for the agreement, reminding them of Goldenberg's promise that the artists would gradually begin performing in Hebrew. The lawyer also mentioned "the great opposition in this respect among wide circles of artists from the Hebrew stage in Israel and the responsible figures in the government offices." Among the litany of complaints in the letter were allegations that the artists had failed to honor the agreement and that they omitted any mention of Pargod. In a letter dated December 28, 1958, Goldenberg himself wrote to the artists, apparently after settling the difficulties, stating that he had obtained permission to continue the Yiddish performances for another three months. However, to do so, he had promised "that in the coming shows the Hebrew component would be weightier." The newspaper *Haboker* published a section of the letter that was sent to Pargod by the Ministry of Education: "If you intend to draw artistic energies that will transition from Yiddish to Hebrew – we can only bless this."[142] Yet the extent of Hebrew in the artists' second show also failed to satisfy the authorities. Consequently, the tax discounts for Dzigan and Shumacher were cancelled because theirs was not "a Hebrew theater."[143]

The relationship between the parties became increasingly tense. The partnership disintegrated when Goldenberg submitted a legal case against Dzigan and Shumacher, with the latter submitting a counter claim.[144] Dzigan and Shumacher argued that it was immoral for Goldenberg to ask for money in return for helping them to obtain a tax exemption via cooperation with Pargod. Although Goldenberg's theater helped the duo receive tax deductions, they argued, he was exploiting the Israeli cultural policy of discrimination against the Yiddish theater and profiting from it.

141 BAA, file 141–04.

142 *Haboker*, "Shiḥrur mimas."

143 Regarding the Pargod episode and the artists' claims to Israeliness, see Dunevitz, "'Isḳei sha'ashu'im."; "Lo buṭal shiḥrur mimas"; *Yedioth Ahronoth*, "Shenei ba'alei miznon"; *Letste nayes*, "Mevatel"; Shin, "Dzigan ṿeShumacher"; Giora, "Pulmus so'er"; Yuris, "Dzigan un Shumachers mizug-galuyot."

144 The defense letter written by the attorney representing Dzigan and Shumacher, Eliezer Grosher, was received on May 16, 1959.

The Pargod episode sparked a renewed discussion of Dzigan and Shumacher's language and the status of Yiddish as a foreign tongue in Israel. The newspaper *Davar* portrayed the topic as "A problem named Dzigan and Shumacher." In *Yedioth Ahronoth*, the "problem" was phrased more simply and directly: "The main thing is: Will these two excellent comedians pay taxes to the government like foreign artists, or will they be exempt from taxes, as Hebrew theaters are?" Although eight years had passed since their first performance in Israel, opinions remained divided: Nahor claimed that Dzigan and Shumacher's association with a Hebrew theater, the name of which was written in Hebrew on the playbill, should lead them to perform in Hebrew and not only constitute a means to achieve a tax reduction. So too, other journalists opposed granting them a tax exemption. By contrast, some argued that Dzigan and Shumacher deserved tax reductions, regardless of the partnership with Pargod, based on the quality of their art, the eight years of performances in Israel, their cooperation with Israeli authors and writers, their discussion of the Israeli reality, and the fact they served as cultural emissaries in the diaspora. Dzigan and Shumacher also argued that they deserved a tax exemption in their own right.[145] They frequently argued that their theater was Israeli, albeit not in Hebrew, their performances abroad were inspired solely by the Israeli reality, and their scripts were written by local, popular writers.

On December 3, 1958, a public debate was held in Beit Sokolow, the Tel Aviv home of the Israel Journalists Association, with the intention of concluding this matter once and for all. The debate was entitled "Dzigan and Shumacher: In Yiddish or Hebrew?" The participants were Baruch Karo, journalist, writer, and translator; Pinchas Lender, writer and translator; Mordkhe Tsanin, editor of *Letste nayes*; Ya'akov Zerubavel, former leader of the Po'alei Zion Left and one of the founders of Mapam. Dzigan and Shumacher sat in the dock. The various arguments emphasized the relevance of the language question in Israeli public discourse ten years after the establishment of the state but did not contribute significantly to solving the specific question regarding Dzigan and Shumacher's performances. "This is the first time, I believe," wrote a journalist who signed his name A. I. in *Letste nayes*, "that there has been a public argument about an actor's professional activity, the first time that Hebrew journalists demanded that Yiddish artists, Dzigan and Shumacher, abandon the Yiddish stage and undergo

---

145 Dzigan and Shumacher added that the cancellation of the tax exemption would lead to the dissolution of the troupe, something that would not harm them "commercially" or detract from their popularity among Yiddish speakers, but it would force them to raise ticket prices for their shows.

'Hebraization.'"[146] Baruch Karo presented himself as "a Yiddish lover," someone who read in this language occasionally and spoke it with his mother, yet described it as a dead tongue connected to the Jewish past. Karo conceded that it would be acceptable to allocate ten minutes at events or in the theater for a Yiddish song, but he claimed that performances must be in the language of the future: Hebrew. Tsanin defended Yiddish and the art of Dzigan and Shumacher, arguing that it would be impossible to translate their humor and that forcing them to perform in Hebrew would constitute a death sentence for their art. According to H. Landau, theater should be performed for people with black hair, not grey. Zerubavel responded to the harsh criticism voiced by Landau, who also argued that Yiddish literature had moved too far away from the Jewish people, protesting at the denigration of Yiddish and its culture: he argued that the foreign language status accorded to Yiddish in Israel and its persecution constituted a "blood libel."[147]

Dzigan spoke for the "accused." As his defense statement, he related in Yiddish an anecdote about his visit to the studio of the artist Emmanuel Mané-Katz in Haifa:

> פֿאַראַן דאָרטן צוויי בילדער: 'ייִדן פֿרייען זיך אין שׂמחת־תּורה" און 'עם ישׂראל חי', אַ צײַכענונג פֿון ייִדישער פֿרייד אין מדינת־ישׂראל. 'ייִדן פֿרייען זיך אין שׂמחת־תּורה' ברענגט צום אויסדרוק לעבעדיקע, האַרציקע פֿרייד אויף די פּנימער פֿון ייִדן און 'עם ישׂראל חי' זענען אָנגעוואַרפֿענע מאָלערישע שטריכן אין וועלכע עס פֿעלט די פֿאַרבן־רײַכקייט פֿון קאַצס פּאַלעטע. פֿאַר וואָס איז אַזאַ אונטערשייד אין די צוויי בילדער – פֿרעגט דזשיגאַן און ענטפֿערט: ווײַל 'שׂמחת־תּורה' איז געמאָלן אויף ייִדיש און 'עם ישׂראל חי' אויף עברית... מאַנע קאַץ האָט אַנדערש נישט געקאָנט מאָלן דעם 'עם ישׂראל חי' און איך קאָן אויך נישט אַנדערש ווי שפּילן נאָר אויף ייִדיש. ווען איך זאָל שפּילן אויף עברית . . . וועט זײַן נאָך אַ שלעכטער אַרטיסט, וועלכע איר האָט דאָ גאַנץ גענוג. וואָס אַרט אײַך, אַז איך שפּיל גוט טעאַטער אויף ייִדיש?[148]
>
> [There are two pictures there [in the studio]: "Jews Celebrating Simḥat Torah" and "The Nation of Israel Lives," which depicts a scene of Jewish joy in the State of Israel. "Jews Celebrating Simḥat Torah" expresses the lively, heartfelt joy on the faces of the Jews, and "The Nation of Israel Lives" is sketched in artist's lines, without any of the rich colors typical of Katz's palette. Why is there such a difference between the two pictures? Dzigan asks, and then he answers: because "Simḥat Torah" is painted in Yiddish and "The Nation of Israel Lives" [is painted] in Hebrew... Mané-Katz could not paint "The Nation of Israel Lives" in any other way, and so too I cannot do anything but act in Yiddish. If I were to act in Hebrew . . . I would be a bad artist, and you have enough of them here. What does it matter to you that I perform good theater in Yiddish?]

After the partnership with Pargod collapsed, Dzigan and Shumacher approached the Ministry of Education and the Ministry of Finance to request a tax exemp-

---

146 Avrahami, "Dzigan un Shumacher."
147 Ibid.; *Maariv*, "Yode'a gam lin'om."
148 Avrahami, "Dzigan un Shumacher."

tion. In a letter dated November 2, 1958, they declared their intention "to settle in Israel for real [!] despite our evident success abroad in various countries, where we achieved not only great personal endorsement but also rallied support for Israel." The artists argued that they intended to stage bilingual shows as part of their efforts to set down roots in Israel and create a sustainable cultural asset. The letter concludes with a sophisticated argument highlighting the artists' political awareness and providing a characteristic example of their behavior vis-à-vis the authorities: "Let us just add that granting the requested exemption will generate a better impression throughout the wide Jewish world in the diaspora and will demonstrate the democratic character of our state and its true liberal spirit, and that it will put an end to the rumors that have spread in the diaspora regarding the discrimination against and oppression of Yiddish and Yiddish speakers in Israel."[149] Thanks to the pressure exerted by Levi Eshkol, the artists were granted an exemption from stamp tax for a period of nine months.

Even though the artists tackled the topic of Israeli identity extensively and defined themselves as "an Israeli theater that does not perform in Hebrew," and in spite of the recognition that the duo received from the political establishment, audiences, and critics, the Israeli critical discourse continued to view them – even at the end of the 1950s – as temporary guests, perhaps "returning residents", privileged citizens among the community of Yiddish speakers in Israel. From the perspective of Israeli culture, Dzigan and Shumacher were a wildflower in the local landscape. From the perspective of Yiddish theater in Israel, they were the peak before the abyss.[150]

The discrimination and the pressure to perform in Hebrew transformed Dzigan and Shumacher's natural performance in Yiddish into an act of linguistic opposition. This opposition was expressed in various ways. For example, they included performances of Hebrew songs between the Yiddish sections in order to meet the "Hebrew quota," as was noted above. Using the classic tactic employed by foreigners who wish to extend their visa and continue their stay in a foreign country, after six weeks of shows in Israel Dzigan and Shumacher visited Cyprus with their families, afterwards returning and once again receiving permission to appear on the Israeli stage as Yiddish-speaking guest artists.

149 Letter from Dzigan and Shumacher to the tax authorities, March 23, 1959. BAA, file 141–04.
150 Dzigan and Shumacher deemed it very important to emphasize their "Israeliness." For this purpose, they published in the playbills for their shows many texts that described their theater as a Yiddish-speaking Israeli theater, for example: A text by Azaria Rapaport in the playbill for *Ze vi du geyst?!* (see above, pp. 156–157.); a text by Shmuel Svislotsky in the playbill for *Feter m'ken aykh!* "Their performance is in Yiddish, but their theater is explicitly Israeli"; an entry by Haim Gamzu in the playbill for *Beser m'redt nisht* (1976), which was performed by Dzigan's theater.

An additional expression of this linguistic opposition was "reverse translation" – casting in an ironic light the demand that they perform in Hebrew. They "taught not only Oksenberg and Bronke Zaltsman from Hamatate, of blessed memory, to speak and sing in Yiddish, but also the Yemenite [singer] Sara Aviani."[151]

Inviting a Yemenite singer to sing Yiddish songs overturned Hebrew culture's representational model of the Yemenite woman through an act of "possession," causing her to speak a strange (diasporic) language. Thus, ironically, rather than simultaneously representing the old and new Hebrew cultures, she became a hybrid body reflecting the ingathering of the exiles.[152] This particular act was part of the battle to preserve in the State of Israel the multilingualism and multiculturalism that had characterized Jewish culture in the diaspora throughout the generations.

The End of the Partnership and the Establishment of Shimen Dzigan's Satirical Theater (1961–1980)

At the end of 1959, Dzigan and Shumacher quarreled.[153] Subsequently, at the end of January 1960, despite efforts by many public figures, audience members, artists, and friends to make peace between the two, their partnership was dismantled, each one continuing on his own path. The separation became a public affair, discussed by an endless stream of articles in the press. Dzigan chose to continue in the tradition of the satirical theater, while Shumacher – who had not performed dramatic roles since his youthful appearances in the amateur theater of the Hebrew gymnasium in Łódź[154] – accepted a role in a production of Sholem Asch's *Kidush Hashem*, staged by the Yidish Folksteater (Yiddish People's

151 Gamzu, "'Emesh bate'aṭron." Also, Dalia Amihud, who sang Israeli songs in the duo's shows for a few years, sang in Yiddish.

152 The reviving Hebrew culture in Mandatory Palestine regarded Yemenites as exotic and culturally primitive. Yael Guilat claims that the poetry, literature, plays, and songs written by members of the first and second *aliyot* testify to the role that the Yemenites' "otherness" played in the Hebrew national battle "to create a new Jew in the ancient Land of Israel." Hebrew culture saw the Yemenite woman as an agent of change and representative of the national revival (in contrast to the more conservative role assigned to the Yemenite man). Guilat, "Yemenite Jewish Women," 199.

153 As early as 1955, a disagreement between the artists was mentioned in the press: "Dzigan and Shumacher have fallen out. The two popular artists will continue to appear together and to cooperate in the artistic field, but they will cease to interact socially. They have stopped talking to each other." See *Hador*, "Ḥatul shaḥor."

154 Adler, "Benifrad."

Theater) and directed by Yosef Sheyn. The play was not particularly successful and did not receive positive reviews in the Hebrew press.[155]

In the words of Asher Nahor, this production of the play was "sentimental and folkloristic,"[156] and its deficiencies were clear, in particular when compared to the non-idealistic approach of the Hebrew version staged by Habima in 1947. Shumacher's talent as a dramatic actor was obvious in contrast to the other actors, and he was praised by many reviewers.[157] However, his decision to take a role in the Yiddish dramatic theater, which was considered low quality, sparked many negative comments and doubts were expressed regarding the wisdom of his split from Dzigan. Both the Hebrew and Yiddish press regarded his choice as a great loss for Israeli satirical theater. In his memoirs, Dzigan recalls his surprise at Shumacher's decision to perform in this play. He claimed that if Shumacher had chosen to stage a satirical show, both of them would have achieved great success and Israel would have profited, gaining an additional satirical theater.[158] Furthermore, Dzigan apparently anticipated that Shumacher would return to the partnership following the failure of this association with a new troupe. However, it is difficult to determine whether Dzigan truly desired such a reunion. The failure of this endeavor, in contrast to the success of his former partner, and Shumacher's subsequent illness, prevented a reunion. The part of the tailor in *Kidush Hashem* was Shumacher's last role on stage. He died after an extended illness, on May 21, 1961. His death was announced in the Hebrew and Yiddish newspapers in Israel, as well as in Yiddish papers around the world. The funeral procession, which set out from the national theater, Habima, a location symbolizing Hebrew culture, was accompanied by hundreds of mourners, among them central figures in Yiddish theater, actors from Habima, politicians, and Israeli cultural figures. Haim Gamzu and the Yiddish actor Joseph Buloff gave eulogies.[159]

Following Shumacher's death and the establishment of his new satirical troupe, Dzigan published a declaration of principles: his new satirical theater would perform in Yiddish, confront Israeli topics, reflect the daily reality in Israel, and continue to be faithful to the genre of miniature theater, while

155 Responses in the Yiddish press were more positive.

156 Nahor, "'Idilya."

157 See, for example, ibid; Y. A-g., "Shumacher be'Kidush Hashem.'"

158 Dzigan, *Der koyekh*, 327.

159 See, for example, *Davar*, "Met haśaḥḳan Shumacher"; *Yedioth Ahronoth*, "Haśaḥḳan Shumacher – Limnuḥot"; Y. L., "Shumacher – 'Einenu "; *Al hamishmar*, "Nifṭar haśaḥḳan Yiśra'el'el Shumacher"; Dunevitz, "Kama milim"; *Haaretz*, "Yiśra'el'el Shumacher – Limnuḥot"; Roshanski, "Yisroel Shumacher"; Feuerstein, "Ha'oman shehitsḥiḳ"; Tsanin, "Shumacher z"l"; Elboym, "Yisroel Shumacher"; Nudelman, "Shumacher z"l."

returning to his artistic and cultural roots. The name he gave to the theater also reflected this desire for a return to his cultural heritage: "The Moyshe Broderzon Satirical Theater, under the management of Shimen Dzigan."[160] The first performance staged by Dzigan's theater, *Frish, gezunt un meshuge!!!* (Fresh, Healthy, and Crazy!!!), which premiered in October 1960, achieved impressive success.[161] It was performed more than 160 times, viewed by 60,000 theatergoers, and reviewers praised both its artistic level and the degree of political satire.[162] After the closure of Sambatyon and Batsal Yarok in 1961, and until the end of the 1960s, Dzigan's was the only satirical theater active in Israel, and the press related to it as such.[163]

Dzigan staged twenty-two new shows following his split from Shumacher. The performances included texts by many authors, classic and modern, original works in Yiddish, adaptations and translations, as well as texts and adaptations by Dzigan himself.[164] The actors were new immigrants from Eastern Europe, veterans of the Yiddish theater, and Yiddish-speaking actors from the Hebrew theater.[165] The shows continued to tackle the same topics that had been at the heart of Dzigan and Shumacher's theater throughout the years of its existence, mainly political, economic, and social satire concerning the contemporary reality.

Changes and Influences: Dzigan's Theater at the End of the 1960s

Due to declining ticket sales, the lack of financial support, and the hefty taxes he was required to pay, Dzigan's theater began to suffer from economic difficulties in the mid-1960s. The actor referred to these topics repeatedly, both in skits and

160 See *Omer*, "Te'aṭron saṭiri"; "Artist Shimen Dzigan"; Horn, "Dzigan shaft"; A. Z., "Te'aṭron."
161 Lydia Shumacher-Ophir, Shumacher's daughter, saw the name of the performance as an insult to her deceased father. See Rotman, "Hadibuḳ 'einenu Moshe Sneh."
162 *Davar*, "Te'aṭron -ḳeva'"; *Lamerḥav*, "Dzigan mitkonen lehatsig"; *Letste nayes*, "Artist Shimen Dzigan"; Gelbert, "Te'aṭrono"; A-g. "'Ṭari, bari' umṭoraf"; Nahor, "Pegisha mera'anenet."
163 Gelbert, "Te'aṭrono"; Ben-Ami, "Ri'shon bein lo' shaḥim"; Keisari, "Kol Dzigan"; Feuerstein, "Hate'aṭron hasaṭiri."
164 Among the writers whose texts Dzigan staged in his shows were Sholem Aleichem, Moyshe Nudelman, Ḥaim Ritterman-Abir, Al. Akshteyn, Avrom Shulman, Yosef Vinitsky, Yosef Heiblum, and Efraim Kishon. See appendix A for the full list of shows.
165 Among the actors were Yaakov Alperin, Mikhael Grinshteyn, Yoel Zilber, Bronke Zaltsman, Karol Feldman, Yankev Reynglas, and Lea Szlanger. Among the directors were Daniel Gadron, Avraham Ninio, Shmuel Atzmon-Wircer, Shraga Fridman, Rafael Kletzkin, and Eli Sagi.

in the media.[166] Taxation led to a rise in ticket prices, and the theater found it difficult to stage its shows for long runs. At the beginning of the 1960s, Dzigan's shows were performed around 150 times during a period of six months. However, by the end of the decade, the running time for a show was three months at most. According to Dzigan, such a number of shows in Israel could not cover his costs, forcing him to rely on his tours abroad.[167] Likewise, the fact that Dzigan's theater possessed its own premises increased expenses.[168] In 1962, the declining number of theatergoers and significant financial losses forced Dzigan to reduce his troupe[169] as well as the number of times each show was performed.[170] Dzigan lost his economic independence and was losing his battle against the cultural policy that discriminated against him as a Yiddish actor.[171] However, in 1967, he claimed that even if he expected taxation at a similar rate to that of the Hebrew theater, he opposed government budgeting: "The fact that Yiddish culture and Yiddish theater need support from the establishment is not good. Good quality theater, real culture, can exist only if there are direct consumers."[172] At the end of the 1960s, as a result of Levi Eshkol's intervention, Dzigan was granted an exemption from paying entertainment tax, and in 1978 – two years before his death, at the age of seventy-three – Mayor of Tel Aviv Shlomo Lahat granted him an exemption from council tax.[173]

---

166 See "Sh. Dzigans satirish-teater"; Bar-Yosef, "Nivror le'idish"; Shmulevitsh, "Komiker Shimen Dzigan."

167 "For around three months Dzigan selects the material, puts together a new show, chooses suitable actors, and begins rehearsals. When the first performance premiers on stage he allots three months for it to run in the country. After three months, his audience in this country is used up. He makes changes to the show and makes a new version of it for export, made up of sections from the shows staged in Israel." See Na'aman, "'Ayin 'aḥat bokha." See also Rimon, "Dzigans uffirung."

168 Yasni, "Artist Shimen Dzigan redt zikh."

169 *Maariv*, "Hanof hapeḳiduti." Regarding the natural decline of the Yiddish-speaking audience in Israel due to age, and the learning of Hebrew, increased consumption of "Hebrew" culture, and detachment from Yiddish culture, see Janasowicz, "A shmues"; Sverdlin, "Shimen Dzigan farlirt."

170 Shavit, "Lama 'ani 'atsuv."

171 "Poland didn't finish me off. Russia didn't finish me off – but here, in the State of Israel, will the full stop be written? In the last three years in Israel I haven't covered even 50% of my expenses." Ohad, "Sheva' parotai."

172 Janasowicz, "A shmues." In another interview, Dzigan said: "I don't want them to give me money, subsidies. I'll be satisfied with them not taking it away from me." Har-Gil, "Gonvim mikol." See also Hon, "Dzigan kimvaḳer"; Har-Gil, "Humor yehudi."

173 Shofti, "Kol 'od neshama be'api."

"In what way are we better than Russia, Poland, or Romania? Quite the opposite!" Dzigan raged in an interview in 1978. "In Russia, Poland, and Romania there are theaters in Yiddish!!! There the governments fund the budgets of these theaters!!! And here, in Israel, the Yiddish theater is completely ignored! Doesn't it sound like a comedy?"[174] Dzigan, who feared that nothing had changed in Israel since the 1950s with regard to the discrimination against Yiddish, harshly opposed the establishment's only attempt to support a Yiddish theater. He questioned the intentions behind the foundation of the "Yidish kunst-teater" in 1975, supported by the Jewish Agency, the Ministry of Absorption, and the Ministry of Education, asking why the government chose to import artists from abroad rather than supporting those already active in Israel. "In every war, I am here," he claimed. "But when they want to pay someone and make a big star out of him, they bring Buloff from America, and now also Kaminska. What do they have to do with this country?"[175]

Another target of Dzigan's criticism in monologues and skits was Israeli television, which began broadcasting in 1967. He saw its attitude to Yiddish culture as a consolidation of the institutional mechanisms that discriminated against Yiddish theater and Yiddish culture in general. In September 1975, Dzigan was invited to create a one-hour long show for Israeli television.[176] The show was an impressive success – it was even screened again[177] – and Dzigan was invited to take part in a series of satirical shows about Yiddish humor. After making his second TV show, the management of the television station announced – without any explanation, according to Dzigan – that it was no longer interested in Dzigan's shows.[178] Dzigan threatened to embark on a hunger strike, and the affair

174 Oren, "'Ilu hayiti."

175 Na'aman, "'Ayin 'aḥat bokha." "They didn't go to experts, but to officials that make theater. They didn't come to me in particular." Ibid. In another interview, he said, "On the one hand, I welcome the fact that the Yiddish word and Yiddish cultural values have finally been remembered . . . but if the government and institutions have remembered the step-son and invested good money, why did they not bother to ensure for themselves a good play instead of a 'joke'? Whoever wants to stage *Amkha* needs at least four real actors who were raised in the Jewish tradition." See Ohad, "Sheva' parotai." For more about the establishment of an artistic Yiddish theater see Rotman, "Language Politics."

176 The show "Ha'erev im Shimon Dzigan" (Tonight with Shimen Dzigan) included sections from various performances staged by the theater and dealt with classic topics that he had tackled in the past (Israeli politics, the Jewish Agency, and bureaucracy) alongside jokes and songs.

177 See Tsanin, "Fun undzer televizye."

178 Ron, "Tsores fun der televizye"; Na'aman, "Dzigan 'ole." Apparently, the show was screened a year later. See Zohar, "Dzigan, Shalom Aleichem."

attracted media interest.[179] The actor regarded the cancellation of the show as an explicit expression of "discrimination against Ashkenazi Jews in this country. The Israeli television is 'discriminating' against me and against Yiddish."[180] Dzigan reported that Efraim Sten, head of the television drama department, was in favor of continuing with the shows and fought on Dzigan's behalf. However, he received a negative answer from the management: "Because in Yiddish it's a problem."[181]

As was noted, the journalists and theater critics did not remain apathetic, spreading the news publicly. G. Yehuda, who defined himself as "far from being a Yiddishist," discussed the tendency of Israeli culture "to turn its back on the treasures hidden in Yiddish culture and to sail toward the 'Canaanite' movement, which lacks historical basis and is isolated from our roots – including both the period of independence and the exile."[182] He praised Dzigan's shows, perceiving the actor as representing the richness of culture in the "exile." He complained that this culture does not reach the general public of Hebrew speakers, because the radio and television block their access to it. He also wrote, ironically, "Let us not provide ammunition for the rusty weapons of Israel's enemies, for plots of 'discrimination and oppression.'"[183] In the skit "Televizye-sho" (Television Hour, 1973), Dzigan addressed his audience as follows:

> ליבע צוהערער, נישט קענענדיק זיך דערוואַרטן ביז די ישׂראל־טעלעוויזיע וועט אַרײַננעמען אין איר פּראָגראַם אַ לעק ייִדיש, האָבן מיר פֿון אייגענע איניציאַטיוו, אָן דער הילף פֿון בילדונגס־מיניסטעריום, געשאַפֿן אַ טעלעוויזיע־שעה, וואָס וועט געוויזן ווערן יעדן אָוונט בײַ אונדז אין טעאַטער.
>
> [Dear viewers, because we cannot wait until Israeli television will include in its shows a drop of Yiddish, we have created, at our own initiative, without the help of the Ministry of Culture, "a television hour," which will be performed every evening here in our theater.]

Dzigan did not sit and wait for change. Rather, he sought to make the change himself.[184]

179 See for example, *Maariv*, "'Eshbot ra'av."
180 Na'aman, "Dzigan 'ole."
181 Ibid.
182 Yehuda, "Dzigan vehateleṿizya."
183 Ibid.
184 In the skit "Tele-reportazh" (TV interview), in the show *Tsurikgekumen besholem* (Back in One Piece; 1970), Dzigan is asked what he thinks about television shows and answers in gibberish. When asked what language he is talking, he responds that he is speaking Arabic, because it is forbidden to speak Yiddish on the television.

The Discourse of Sadness

וואָס וועט איר טאָן פּאַניע דזשיגאַן, אויף דער עלטער, אַז מען וועט מער נישט וועלן לאַכן פֿון אײַך? –פֿרעג איך.

–וועל איך ווערן אַ טראַגיקער.

–פֿאַר וואָס נישט קיין דראַמאַטיקער?

–ווײַל איך האַלט אָדער פֿון לאַכן אָדער פֿון וויינען, קיין מיטלוועג איז בײַ מיר נישטאָ.

[Mr. Dzigan, what will you do in your old age, when people no longer want to laugh at your jokes? – I ask.I will be a tragic actor.

Why not a dramatic actor?

Because I favor either laughing or crying, for me there is no middle road.]

– Goldshteyn, "Geshprekh mitn lets"

To mark the festival of Purim in 1967, Dzigan was invited to perform in a show staged at the Tel Aviv Committee House for Soldiers, which was also broadcast live on the IDF radio station. Dzigan was to perform a number of monologues to an audience of more than 1,000 soldiers. His slot followed a performance by a female singer, who sang a number of songs in English (her name was not mentioned in the newspapers), and the Burshteyn family's rendition of a few sections from *Megile-lider* by Itzik Manger in Yiddish. According to Dzigan, the applause for the Burshteyn family aroused his suspicions – it was not at the right time or of the correct duration. Despite this, Dzigan began his segment as planned. Suddenly, applause burst out in the middle of a joke, not in the right place. The applause continued, and Dzigan understood its meaning: the soldiers wanted him to leave the stage. Dzigan ceased his monologue and did so.

This incident deeply affected Dzigan and was discussed extensively in the media, which focused especially on the artist's response. Dzigan related that even when appearing before audiences of Russian soldiers in the Soviet Union who did not understand a word of Yiddish, he and Shumacher received a warm welcome. In his own country, he argued in astonishment, Jewish soldiers did not let him perform in his mother tongue.[185] This incident, indicative of the young generation's opposition to a performance in Yiddish, signified a turning point in Dzigan's media statements and the beginning of a change in his public image. He became a sad clown, a frustrated actor who was unable to affect the hostile cultural reality.

An article from 1967 entitled "Lama 'ani 'atsuv befurim ze" (Why I Am Sad this Purim), described Dzigan's loss of faith in the leaders of the state and complained

185 Zilberberg, "Vos Dzigan hot gezogt."

that young Israelis lacked manners and politeness.[186] Eliezer Wiesel claimed that Dzigan's monologue was interrupted by soldiers of Sephardi origin, to whom Yiddish was foreign. Without directly blaming their Mizrahi origin, Wiesel discussed the deterioration in morals among Israeli youth, their rude behavior, and the cynicism that had recently become widespread. Dzigan's sadness was, in Wiesel's words, a sign that the situation in Israel had significantly deteriorated.[187] According to him, and this sentiment was echoed by many other critics, this sadness also reflected the state of affairs in Israel. Around six years later, again during wartime, Gamzu noted the sadness characteristic of Dzigan's new performances, including the texts that he chose to stage. The critic argued that this was due to the Yom Kippur War, which left an imprint on his "understated and untheatrical" laughter, adding: "Dzigan's laughter has become sad. Very sad." The reasons for this included, in his opinion, seeing the world "without embellishment, as it is, a painful and disappointing reality."[188]

As early as 1963, Dzigan claimed that while he continued to "take aim" at politicians, they did not react to his words as they once had.[189] At the end of the 1970s, he recognized that his satire had lost its power, expressing his longing for the time when government ministers had asked him to mention them, even if he said "the worst possible things" about them.[190] From the end of the 1960s, Dzigan's personal prestige and the status of Yiddish satire in the Israeli reality underwent a shift. "The theater in Yiddish, both in the period of the Mapai government and also under the Likud government, is not the thing that interests the ruling elements."[191] Dzigan despaired, having lost faith in the ability of the political parties to prevent the decline in his personal status and that of Yiddish culture in general.

In 1974, Dzigan published his autobiographical work, *Der koyekh fun yidishn humor* (The Power of Jewish Humor), written with the help of Abraham Karpinovitz, Yitskhok Janasowicz, and Mendel Kohansky.[192] "Each one of them became

186 Shavit, "Lama 'ani 'atsuv."
187 Wiesel, "Der komiker Dzigan."
188 Gamzu, "Dzigan he'atsuv."
189 Gilboa, "Bekhol haretsinut."
190 Fuks, "Dzigan 'al hatsagato."
191 Bar-On, "Monolog mehurhar." Dzigan supported the Likud Party. Yet he argued that "really there is no difference between the regime of the Alignment [Hama'arakh party] and that of the Likud. With the first Yedlin made promises. With the second, it was Hammer . . . so, it's no surprise they say Yiddish theater is dying. Certainly, it is dying. The day it will die is not far off. Because, between us, what remains of it is comic. Of a low level, without culture!!!" Oren, "'Ilu hayiti."
192 Vedenyapin claims that it is difficult to determine who wrote Dzigan's book. Karpinovitz claimed that he wrote the entire book based on conversations with Dzigan, and the other two

Dzigan. They wrote exactly according to his character," the actor stated at an event marking the publication of the book.[193] Dzigan explained that his decision to write this book reflected his desire to shape his own memorial, especially considering how Shumacher was forgotten after his death.[194]

The book is divided into three parts, each one of which is devoted to a specific period and location in Dzigan creative's life: Poland, the Soviet Union, and the State of Israel. The chapter concerning the State of Israel deals with the longest period of his activities as an actor, yet it is the shortest: seventy-three pages in contrast to 124 pages devoted to Poland and 152 devoted to the Soviet Union. When asked why the section about Israel only describes his on-stage humor, without portraying the background and surrounding atmosphere, Dzigan answered: "I would lose half of my love for this country if I were to detail everything I have gone through here. Had I done so, after two weeks they wouldn't let me go on stage anymore, I would get into trouble with the police. These are things that must not be recorded on paper in such a book."[195]

The pain and frustration increased over the years. In a conversation with Amnon Zakov, published in 1969 in English in the El-Al magazine, Dzigan argued that he did not expect to be treated like a museum exhibit, to suffer persecution and discrimination and pay higher taxes because Yiddish was perceived as a foreign language in Israel, declaring: "Had I not been a fervent patriot, I would have long ago converted to Christianity and preached antisemitism all over the

only helped him. See Vedenyapin, *Doctors Prescribe Laughter.* Dzigan related that Moshe Ron played the central role in writing the book, although his name is not mentioned among the writers. See Shimen Dzigan, "Yotser ẏitsira," recording of an evening in honor of the publication of Dzigan's book *Der koyekh fun yidishn humor*, Tel Aviv Town Hall (1974). Hebrew University of Jerusalem, Institute of Contemporary Jewry, Oral History Department: 000279637.

193 Ibid.

194 Dzigan said that an additional motivation for writing the book was his desire "to gather the sources of Jewish humor [in one place], in order that people would have access to these sources and will know where to look . . . one day they will want to know – indeed, wisecracks and jokes pass from generation to generation, until they disappear at some point." See ibid.

195 Ibid. Dzigan also said, "Should I have related that in the twenty-four years I have been here I have not yet received one penny of support from the Ministry of Education? I would like to see one Hebrew theater that could exist without the extensive support from all kinds of institutions . . . perhaps, sadly, this is a reason that my theater has reached its end in Israel. To continue acting under such conditions – this is beyond my capacity. I tried to deal with the Hebrew theaters . . . but the expenses are so great that it became impossible to continue to exist. The critics reviewed, sometimes their negative reviews were also right. And then I saw that I must get out while I still have a little honor. And this too is one of the reasons that I wrote down my words." Ibid. Dzigan continued appearing until the last day of his life, six years after the book was published.

world."[196] In May 1978, he repeated his stinging declaration, this time in the Hebrew press: "You know what, if I were younger, I would convert to Christianity and get out of Israel. That's what is left to me at the end of the day . . . but what can I do when I love this country and this religion? My only choice is to stay and cry."[197] The provocative statement testifies both to Dzigan's bitterness and the feeling that he was trapped, with no way out. Such a statement was not exceptional in Dzigan's discourse of sadness, which developed in the 1970s. He began to refer to Jewish religious and national symbols when depicting his alienated state, honing and defining it. In the same article, Dzigan claimed that the two major political parties viewed Yiddish theater as equivalent to "a hostile Arab state."[198] After meeting with President Yitzhak Navon, he was convinced that the Sephardi president could remove "from Yiddish culture and language the 'yellow patch' that had been affixed to it [sic] in the State of Israel." [199] Using this concept, the controversial symbol of the yellow patch, Dzigan tried to impart the feeling of humiliation he felt due to the discrimination against Yiddish culture in Israel. Dzigan expressed the despair and identity crisis of an individual who, to the end of his days, refused "to convert" to Hebrew culture and language, in the words of Carlebach (see above), but rather chose to preserve his "diasporic identity."

At the end of the 1970s, Dzigan remarked that contemporary reviews about him in the press opened with "praise" and ended with "eulogies."[200] With characteristic sarcasm, the artist asked critics to refrain from eulogizing him, because "after one dies, it is no longer possible to still be dying." Dzigan presented himself as a ghost, adopting the rhetoric that described him as a "living memorial," the last symbol of an extinct culture: "Because what am I, still remaining after the war, one who survived Stalin and Hitler and Polish antisemitism, if not a memorial?"[201] In another interview, he even defined himself as a "Western Wall" – a memorial site and place of pilgrimage symbolizing the destroyed Temple.[202] Adopting the rhetoric of the press, Dzigan not only tried to draw attention to the cultural discrimination that he suffered in the State of Israel and receive "official recognition as a memorial site" but also to obtain official support – if not as a living body or institution, then at least as one of commemoration.

196 Dzigan and Zakov, "The Duel."
197 Oren, "'Ilu hayiti." On the response to this statement, see Fuks, "Dzigan 'al hatsagato."
198 Oren, "'Ilu hayiti."
199 Barash, "Hanaśi' Navon."
200 Fuks, "Dzigan 'al hatsagato."
201 Ibid.
202 Shem-Or, "Be'idish ze matsḥiḳ."

Dzigan did not capitulate to the demand that he "assimilate" into Israeli society by changing his language. He chose to retain his identity, and consequently his activities became acts of opposition, viewed as linguistic and cultural heresy. In the last decade of his life, Dzigan found only rhetorical solutions for this new reality, not practical ones. He lost his strength, or perhaps felt that his satirical weapon had become less powerful. The discourse about Dzigan moved between satire and tragedy. The artist remained alone in the territory of Yiddishland, which continued to shrink around him, until one of them – Dzigan or the territory – would disappear.

From the beginning of the 1970s, Dzigan's public expressions began to convey feelings of despair, even when this was not evident in his theater. The statement that had he been younger he would have converted to Christianity and left Israel, reflects deep frustration at his inability to change not only the future but also the present, for both himself and his culture.

Dzigan in the Press

In the Hebrew press, Dzigan was described as, among other things, "the artist of humor and jokes, champion of the folk monologues,"[203] who plays "with all distortions of speech and silence, entertains and saddens, is cruel and merciful, conquers his fear and overcomes his audience, leads us from hearty laughter to an embarrassed smile."[204] In the words of literary scholar Dov Sadan: "One grimace, one look, one word, is enough to reveal his entire portrait, a portrait of the great Jewish mimic, who spun the gold of his humor as every generation of Israel did in Poland, in the Soviet Union, and Eretz Israel."[205] Ze'ev Rav-Nof portrayed Dzigan as a figure of magnetic strength who did not seek to astound. Indeed, the best parts, in his words, "are those in which the text accords with Dzigan's power of expression – this combination creates a moment of elevation, of liberating laughter."[206]

Dzigan's performances, similarly to his joint shows with Shumacher, continued to constitute an artistic and social event. A new show by Dzigan was, in the words of Ya'akov Bar-On, a national and historic event, a "natural phenomenon,"[207] "a festival" as Shimen Kants noted.[208] Gamzu claimed that Dzigan was

203 Gelbert, "Beli kaḥal."
204 A. Z. "Te'aṭron."
205 Sadan, "Peras Manger."
206 Rav-Nof, "Yahalom."
207 Bar-On, "'Oy, Rabin."
208 Kants, "A simkhe."

unsurpassed in terms of his acting talent, possessing a rare and unique stage presence: he did not rely on speech to make people laugh.[209] In a piece included in the playbill for *Beser m'redt nisht* (Silence Is Golden), Gamzu wrote: "This wonderful artist, this unique talent, the prince of humor, irony, and satire . . . in my opinion the greatest humorist on our stage, he is the man with a face rich in mimicry, a voice wealthy in intonations, a true theatrical presence, even if he does not speak one word." Kants depicted Dzigan's theater as "theatrical-divine worship," conducted with great devotion and intention.[210] In the diaspora, Dzigan's performances were praised by both Yiddish journalists and major theater critics in the non-Jewish press. The most prominent examples are the articles by Richard Shepard (*The New York Times*), Lee Silver (*The Daily News*), and El Ellenberg (*The New York Post*).[211]

Dzigan was compared not only to actors from Yiddish theater, but also to other Israeli actors from Hebrew satiric troupes. Gamzu wrote:

> His extended profile, horse-like as it is, also includes in it life, more humanity, than that of most of the young actors, ostensibly masculine and handsome, with their Tarzan-like beauty, [yet] without the spices of humor and sharp satire which flow forth from Dzigan's old face. Just like the most well-known jesters at Jewish weddings [*badkhonim*], who combined all the arts.[212]

In Gamzu's words, Dzigan represented the traditional Jewish figure as a positive alternative to the masculine character of the new Hebrew theater, an example to be followed.[213] In 1980, after Dzigan's death, Ya'akov Bar-On published comments by the actor that juxtaposed Israeli military strength and Jewish humor in Eastern Europe:

> In the past, we used humor as a defense against our enemies. Our enemies caused us suffering, beat us, and persecuted us – and we fired jokes at them. Today, the Jews have an army, a "*vunderbar*" [wonderful] army, and, thank God, we don't lack ammunition, so now, apparently, we don't need jokes, and without jokes there's no humor...[214]

---

209 Gamzu, "'Al kanfei hahumor."

210 Kants, "A simkhe."

211 See Silver, "Israeli Revue"; Ellenberg, "Israel with Laughter"; Shepard, "Theater."

212 Gamzu, "Dzigan he'atsuv."

213 On the image of the diaspora Jew in contrast to the Zionist Jew, the new Hebrew, see for example Zerubavel, "Mythological Sabra." On the dominance of the Israeli image see Shavit, *Me'ivri 'ad kena'ani*. For a discussion of the body see below, pp. 252–256.

214 Bar-On, "Dzigan."

Despite the positive reviews of Dzigan's first show without Shumacher in 1960, some journalists began to criticize his troupe's performance methods. They claimed that it failed to fill the vacuum left by the Hebrew-speaking troupes on the one hand and by Yisroel Shumacher on the other.[215] Likewise, the lack of writers and the varying quality of the texts constituted major themes in reviews of his shows, mainly since Dzigan's second show without Shumacher. Dzigan and Shumacher had faced this problem in the past, yet it intensified over the years. Five or six writers were involved in constructing the shows for the miniature theaters in Poland, while in the 1960s the number of writers who could contribute a quality script for Dzigan in Yiddish, or even in Hebrew (after which it would be translated into Yiddish), had significantly declined. Dzigan claimed that the few good writers were occupied with writing for television or cinema. The texts in Dzigan's performances aroused opposing feelings. Yehoshua Bar-Yosef, for example, claimed that from an artistic perspective, some of them were "schmaltz," but they achieved cultural admiration because they evoked memories of the Jewish *shtetl*, nostalgia, and brought the Jewish culture closer to the Israeli audience.[216] Bar-Yosef attributed to the texts an educational, didactic, and emotional role. In Gamzu's words, the materials that Dzigan performed did not suit his singular qualities.[217] Repetition of materials from previous shows, skits that he himself composed, and the adaptation of classic materials, mainly by Sholem Aleichem, were the immediate solutions.

Dzigan's attempt to return to the theatrical language of Broderzon was unsuccessful. According to the newspaper *Folksblat*, despite declaring his loyalty to the tradition of Broderzon, Dzigan's show lacked the innovation that Broderzon brought to the theater, the cultural, folk, and linguistic treasure; likewise, the experimental language characteristic of Ararat was also lacking.[218] Dzigan himself recognized the impossibility of continuing theater in the tradition of Ararat in Israel and of making innovations in the theatrical language.[219]

---

215 Naḥman Ben-Ami, like many others, depicted Dzigan as a central element in the performance and noted that the quality varied: "Despite the heartfelt and enthusiastic laughter of the audience . . . the troupe cannot fill the hole left in the country after the disappearance of Hebrew satirical troupes." Ben-Ami, "Ri'shon bein lo' shaḥyim."

216 Bar-Yosef, "Nivror le'idish."

217 Gamzu, "Dzigan he'atsuv."

218 "Also lacking in the show are the Broderzon-like attempts to clothe the Jewish folk treasures in a new artistic dress. The experiments in form, which gave such grace to Ararat at the time, are likewise absent. So too, the poetry and word plays, so common in Broderzon's work, are missing." V. Gr., "Broderzon un Dzigan."

219 Keisari, " Dzigan beli 'ipur."

The Yiddish and Hebrew press crowned Dzigan the satirical historian of Jewish reality from the 1930s, and of Israeli reality since the 1950s, until the day of his death. "Each one of his creations and all of them together appear," wrote Uri Keisari, "like one big satirical embroidered tapestry depicting the Jewish experience."[220] "Through his gestures, his grimaces, his malleable expressions, Shimon Dzigan has, over the past twenty-eight years, written the history of this country in a twisted mirror, so funny it will make you cry," wrote Idit Na'aman, highlighting the development of an Israeli historiographical and interpretational narrative performed by Dzigan on the Yiddish stage.[221]

Dzigan was regarded as the embodiment of the treasury of Jewish humor and culture, as someone who gave Yiddish "regal pride, even when among us it is the queen of beggars."[222] Although he founded a troupe and performed alongside other actors, for reviewers in the press, Dzigan alone personified "the theater." All the actors around him, wrote Gamzu, added nothing to his glory. Dzigan himself was enough of a reason for theatergoers to "quietly sit through what they did not want to see or hear."[223] In this period, some criticism isolated Dzigan from both the human context in which he performed and from the textual context of his shows. The disparity between his qualities as an actor and all the other elements of his theatrical world gradually increased. In the Hebrew press, he was depicted as alienated from the surrounding reality, an actor still on stage even after his theatrical death.

Following the breakdown of his partnership with Shumacher and the latter's untimely death, Dzigan remained the last remnant of an extinct species. The press portrayed him as unique, one of a kind. He became a myth while still alive, via a rhetoric replete with compliments, and this myth simultaneously developed into a discourse about the death of Yiddish culture. In the words of Feuerstein, Dzigan was "the last remnant of a generation that has left this world, and he symbolizes it. The last Mohican, literally . . . a living monument to the Yiddish theater of the past, a kind of living and breathing museum exhibit regarding artistic style

220 Ibid.

221 Na'aman, "Monolog hapereda."

222 L. P., "Dzigan matslif."

223 Rav-Nof, "Yahalom." Gamzu wrote: "I go to them [Dzigan's shows] . . . because of three artists: Dzigan, Dzigan, and Dzigan." See Gamzu, "'Al timshekheni"; "His appearance alone is enough to fill the entire theater with laughter. We would have been satisfied with the appearance of Dzigan alone. But every actor needs a rest between one sketch and another." Gamzu, "'Al kanfei hahumor." Heda Boshes voiced a similar opinion: "In opposition to Dzigan, those who are called Israeli comedians seem clumsy, awkward, inarticulate, dismal, coarse, and rude. Dzigan's performance was funny, professional, and enjoyable, and they also arouse thoughts at the margins of things." See Boshes, "Be'idish – Hakol 'aḥeret."

in the field of acting."[224] Writing after Dzigan's death, Shmuel Schnitzer depicted the actor as a prayer leader without a community of devotees, refusing to accept the new reality after the Holocaust, the last and the greatest of the Jewish *badkhonim* (wedding jesters). Schnitzer described not only the death of a unique artist but of an entire tradition.[225] Like the last Jew in the skit performed by Dzigan and Shumacher in Poland in 1939, immediately prior to the Nazi invasion,[226] the existence of an entire culture – and in this case of Israeli satire in its entirety – was depicted as dependent on one man.

Despite Dzigan's central role in the local theatrical scene, and the feeling that the country had moved on, leaving the language war behind, the Israeli authorities continued to pursue a discriminatory policy toward Yiddish theater in the 1960s and 1970s. This policy was manifest, as was noted, in the high taxes imposed on Yiddish theater, the lack of financial support for Israeli theater in any language other than Hebrew, and the journalists' continued demands and expectations that the elderly actor abandon his mother tongue and perform in Hebrew.

The reviewers could not reconcile themselves to the fact that the highest quality satirical theater in Israel, at least until the end of the 1960s, was a Yiddish-speaking theater, which flourished as a local, living culture. Many theater critics and journalists repeatedly expressed their "great sorrow" at Dzigan's decision not to perform in Hebrew. A review in *Davar* portrayed Dzigan's theater as a "foreign stage," the theater of an "ethnic Ashkenazi group; its jokes and laughter are not likely to foster [national] unity"; Dzigan's humor "is Yiddish humor with a special genealogy and mentality, its roots lie in a particular Jewish collective."[227] "Dzigan," wrote Keisari, in a slightly threatening tone, "must find the path to Israeli Hebrew theater, because in so doing 'he will reach his goal and we will achieve ours.'"[228] At the end of 1960, Aharon Ze'ev Ben-Yishai suddenly declared that "the danger of the *la'az* [vernacular, Yiddish]" persisted. He criticized those who belittled this danger and expressed dissatisfaction at the establishment of Dzigan's satirical theater: "A non-Hebrew theater is even more dangerous than a non-Hebrew newspaper," he wrote. "Nothing disseminates language and conventionalizes it like theater does. A joke, a catchword, a rhyme in a certain language, in particular in a 'homely' language – they take wings and are absorbed more than reading that same language. And behold, these are the foundations of every

---

224 Feuerstein, "Tokhnit ḥadasha."
225 Schnitzer, "'Aḥaron habadḥanim."
226 See above, pp. 73–74.
227 A. Z., "Te'aṭron."
228 Keisari, "Kol Dzigan."

living language."[229] Ben-Yishai's words, expressing a rhetoric that borders on existential cultural anxiety in the face of the rich living folk culture embodied by Dzigan's theater, are a radical example of the contemporaneous press discourse, yet they evidently still carried weight among various circles in Israeli society.

Calls for Dzigan to perform in Hebrew continued to be voiced. Some anticipated this as one would "hope for a blessing,"[230] while others, humorously or impatiently, phrased their request as an "ultimatum." The establishment of Dzigan's new troupe sparked hope and expectations among many journalists that he would begin to perform in Hebrew. This was further enhanced when actors from the Hebrew theater joined the troupe, and it was fueled by Dzigan's own declarations – perhaps honest or perhaps an advertising strategy – that his troupe would also perform in Hebrew.[231] Dzigan justified the delay in the transfer to Hebrew in various ways, for example claiming that the level of the texts submitted to him in Hebrew was unsatisfactory. Indeed, Shimen Dzigan never performed in Hebrew and, as far as is known, only once expressed regret about this.[232]

For some reviewers, Dzigan's theater was a source of discomfort because it contradicted the anticipated cultural acclimatization: rather than Dzigan beginning to act in Hebrew, he succeeded in attracting to his private Yiddish theater major actors from the Hebrew stage, among them Mordechai Ben-Ze'ev and Hersh Hart. "The success of the satirical stage in Yiddish," wrote Ben-Yishai, "blocks the way for a permanent satirical stage in Hebrew at present, and it also crosses into the territory of the Hebrew theater in general."[233] Ben-Yishai depicted Dzigan's theater as competing with the important Hebrew theaters of the period and as a threat to them.[234]

229 Ben-Yishai, "Lefi sha'a."

230 *La'isha*, "'Al timshekheni."

231 On Dzigan's intention to appear in Hebrew, see *Omer*, "Te'aṭron satiri"; A., "Dzigan yasad"; *Davar*, "Te'aṭron-ḳeva'"; *Haaretz*, "Dzigan metakhnen"; *Hatzofe*, "Dzigan metakhnen hatsagot"; *Lamerḥav*, "Dzigan mitkonen lehatsig"; Nahor, "Pegisha mera'anent"; Kelai, "Hatsaga shelo"; Novak, "Yesh leDzigan"; Avidar, "Yesh li ma lomar."

232 "Z: . . . If I have one reproach to make to you Dzigan, it is that when you came over here twenty years ago you made no attempt to switch over so as to enrich Hebrew with your Yiddish music. D: It is a reproach I constantly make to myself. It was the mistake of my life. It'd have involved a tremendous effort, but I should have done it. I should have cultivated Hebrew without giving up Yiddish." See Dzigan and Zakov, "The Duel." In an interview in 1968, Dzigan cited reasons to support a transfer to Hebrew: lack of good materials in Yiddish and their high cost, lack of funding and support for Yiddish theater, payment of the additional fifteen percent above the ticket price because he was performing in Yiddish, and the growing distance from the young generation. See A. L., "Ba'ayotay."

233 Ben-Yishai, "Lefi sha'a."

234 Ibid.

Mordechai Ben-Ze'ev's decision to appear on the stage of the Yiddish theater was traumatic for both the actor himself and his critics. Giora Manor recalled nostalgically the glory days of the young Hebrew actor:

> We remember a period before this, in the 1930s. Then he recited so beautifully Ya'akov Cohen's "Biryonim" [Alliance of Strongmen][235] . . . and when he would come to the refrain, "In blood and fire shall Judah rise," it was difficult for even the most fertile imagination to believe that one day this young man would make a spade from the Yiddish language and dig with it . . . The facts show that instead of the Hebrew theater absorbing immigrants and helping them progress from Yiddish to Hebrew, immigrants create possibilities of existence for Hebrew actors.[236]

Manor explained Ben-Ze'ev's move to the Yiddish theater as financially motivated. He highlighted that the Yiddish theater supported the Hebrew theater, or more precisely supported many actors and other artists involved in the Hebrew stage.[237] He also expressed sorrow that the Do-Re-Mi theater had encountered financial difficulties and as a result had begun to stage *Tsvey Kuni Leml* in Yiddish.

Unsurprisingly, the Yiddish press welcomed the move of these actors, receiving them with wonder and enthusiasm:

> מרדכי בן־זאב איז אַ העברעיִשער אַקטיאָר, געבוירן אין לאַנד. און ווי אַזוי ער רעדט דאָס יִדיש און האָט זיך געשאַפֿן זײַנע אייגענע טשיקאַווע אַקצענטן און דער אויסשפּראַך, וואָס האָבן אַ באַזונדער חן.[238]
>
> [Mordechai Ben-Ze'ev is a Hebrew actor, a native Israeli. But he speaks Yiddish with his own unique accent and pronunciation, which have a special grace.]

The actor himself denied that his move to Dzigan's theater was motivated only by financial considerations. Rather, he depicted it as an artistic challenge:

> . . . indeed, this month, the past one, was the hardest and bitterest in my life. I do not have the words and it will be difficult to describe the extent of the deliberation, the emotional tension [I felt] every day, and the stubborn battle to conquer a language I have never

235 "We rose up, we returned, the strong youth, / We rose, we returned, we the strongmen, / To redeem our land in the storm of war, / We demand our legacy fearlessly. / In blood and fire Judah fell, / In blood and fire Judah will rise, it will rise." The poem was set to music and performed by Shimshon Bar-Noy, accompanied by a choir and orchestra conducted by Roman Messing, who also adapted it. The song was recorded on the record "Meshirei hamered," Alliance of the Etzel Soldiers, 862, 980 (1953). A recording of the song and its lyrics can be found at https://www.zemereshet.co.il/song.asp?id=1820 (accessed December 2016).

236 Giora, "Ben-Ze'ev."

237 Ibid.

238 G., "Dzigans satire."

> spoken, its sounds, and its special accent. On more than one occasion during the rehearsals, despairing, I said to myself: Run away! As fast as you can and as far as you can, because you won't be able to do it.[239]

However, Ben-Ze'ev argued, the desire to gain experience in the language and to perform what he described as excellent material inspired him to overcome the obstacles. Principally, he saw this as an opportunity not to be missed, both artistically and of course economically, but also a chance to act alongside an extremely talented actor. Shraga Friedman, an actor in Habima and one of those most closely identified with it, also contradicted the narrative dominant in the Hebrew press, relating that he learned more from his work with Dzigan than he did from all the other professional theaters in Israel.[240]

239 Kelai, "Ṿiduyaṿ."
240 In Avi., "Dzigan vegn."

Chapter 5
The Text, the Body, and the Stage

The texts Dzigan and Shumacher staged over the course of their careers were written by a range of authors, at different historical moments, and in diverse locations. Some were included in the duo's shows more than once, adapted and suited to the new conditions. The most prominent writers were Moyshe Broderzon, Yoysef-Shimen Goldshteyn, Der Tunkeler, Moyshe Nudelman, Yankev Oberzhanek, Yitskhok Brat, Yosef Heiblum, Ḥaim Ritterman-Abir, and Dzigan and Shumacher themselves. Most of the texts were penned especially for the artists, although some were translated from other languages (Russian, Hebrew, and French) or adapted for the satirical stage at the artists' request. As was noted, Dzigan and Shumacher also wrote and edited some of the texts themselves, usually signing with the penname "Shudzig" or "Y. Gizdush" (combinations of their two surnames), Shimsi (Dzigan), Y. Tsevi (Shumacher), but they also signed with their own names. In the postwar period, they often complained about the lack of high-quality writers with experience in their style of humor.

In Israel, the two actors endeavored to bridge the great cultural divide by staging Yiddish texts that responded to the contemporary Israeli reality and translations of works by Israeli authors, mainly Efraim Kishon. Avrom-Shmuel Yuris commented that Kishon's humor was more western than the comedy composed by Nudelman, who continued to write for the duo from the United States. According to Yuris, Nudelman's writing was characterized by an Eastern European, Polish-Yiddish style, which endowed it with a folkloristic grace and voice. According to the Hebrew press, Kishon's works were far superior to those of Nudelman.[1]

Sources of Humor

Most of Dzigan and Shumacher's jokes were adaptations of popular puns that the authors collected and incorporated into their various shows.[2] The two tended to claim that their repertoire was written by "reality itself"; that they "go out into

1 Yuris, "Dzigan–Shumacher."

2 Modern Yiddish theater drew extensively on folkloristic materials. Indeed, Avrom Goldfaden outlined his connection to popular songs and folklore, detailing the importance of folk singers (*folk zingers*) and the Jewish *badkhn* in his modern theatrical creations. He presented himself as a collector of songs and attributed an artistic value to the act of collecting. See Mayzel, *Yidishe tematik*, 66. See also Cohen, "Shir 'am."

https://doi.org/10.1515/9783110717693-005

real life and draw handfuls from the springs of humor gurgling among us in the reality of our renewed lives and afterwards present it on stage."[3] This process of collecting and adapting folkloristic materials is evident in Dzigan's notebooks, in which he recorded jokes that he heard orally and even copied jests from various folkloric anthologies, such as Immanuel Olsvanger's work *Rejte Pomeranzen: Ostjüdische Schwänke und Erzählungen.*[4]

Dzigan and Shumacher were collectors and performers of folk works, meaning works with collective and oral characteristics.[5] Moreover, one could argue that Dzigan and Shumacher contributed to the distribution, preservation, and renewal of folklore (jokes, idioms, proverbs) and even helped to generate new jokes and idioms, which became part of the folklore when they were adopted and spread by the audience. The process was not unidirectional: as was noted, the jokes that the duo created or adapted for the stage circulated in the Yiddish-speaking street after every premiere.[6] They adapted texts to suit the cultural and political context of their performances by including words in the local vernacular and replacing certain characters with central figures from the surrounding society. Sometimes songs in the vernacular were sung in the interludes between segments, performed by (female) singers in their mother tongue. According to theater critics and the artists themselves, it seems that even if they were not "folk performers" in the folkloristic sense of the term, Dzigan and Shumacher were frequently defined as the ultimate representatives of folk culture. Interestingly, such a designation juxtaposes the actors and their Yiddish with the canonical, hierarchical high culture, attributing to them the subversive and critical foundations often regarded as characteristic of folk culture in general.[7]

The entire spectrum of texts performed by the theater of Dzigan and Shumacher is here related to as one corpus that includes works by various writers and of varying quality yet share a common ground: the voice of Dzigan and Shumacher, who were the editors, adaptors, performers, and directors of the texts.[8] The writers' reputations contributed to the theater's good name (or vice versa), but the role played by Dzigan and Shumacher was no less important. In the process of the transfer from the written word to stage, the text was adapted and appropriated by the artists, even if this was not explicitly noted in the playbill.

3 *Devar hashavua*, "Mitsrakh ḥiyuni."
4 Olsvanger, *Rejte Pomeranzen*.
5 See the definition by Francis Atle in Hasan-Rokem, "Hatarbut ha'amamit," 6.
6 See above, pp. 56–57.
7 Hasan-Rokem, "Hatarbut ha'amamit"; Schrire, "Shivrei hagola."
8 After his split with Shumacher, Dzigan directed his first solo show. Subsequently, he worked with a range of directors.

An examination of manuscripts of the skits and their comparison with recorded versions reveals the punctilious work of Dzigan and Shumacher:[9] when adapting the texts, they made alterations, added or omitted entire lines or jokes, moderated or sharpened certain aspects, and during performances they often improvised. Thus, their adaptation, their emphasis, their intonation, and, of course, their acting made them not only coauthors but also the final artistic authority for almost every text they performed. In this sense, the textual and performative corpora of the duo merged, becoming one unique corpus that encompassed a variety of voices.

The central topics that Dzigan and Shumacher tackled in their theater over the years reflect the wide spectrum of issues that troubled the Jews of their generation: how to make a livelihood, the economy, world and local politics, married life, Jewish tradition, antisemitism, and other topical questions. After immigrating to Israel, some of these topics remained relevant, but new issues were also added, including the individual's encounters with Israeli bureaucracy, the question of Yiddish vs. Hebrew language and culture as opposed to Hebrew, immigration to Israel (aliya), social acclimatization, health, the Cold War, scientific discoveries, Israeli politics, the Arab-Jewish conflict, leaving Israel to live in the diaspora (*yerida)*, a Jew emigrating from Israel is known as a *yoyred*), the attitude of the Jews in the diaspora (particularly the United States) toward Israel and Zionism, and the memory of Eastern European Jewry and the Holocaust. The following sections examine these topics in more detail.

The Jewish and Israeli Reality on the Satirical Stage

Although Dzigan and Shumacher succeeded in adjusting their theater to suit different political, cultural, and social circumstances, they maintained a well-defined cultural identity, which was characterized by their language (Łódź Yiddish) and by their use of Eastern European (in particular Polish) Jewish images and cultural discourse. Since leaving Łódź, theirs was a theater of refugee culture. Every encounter with another culture brought to the fore the theater's unique perspective, which was rooted in Eastern European Jewish culture.

The ultimate character by means of which the theater of Dzigan and Shumacher voiced criticism of the Israeli reality was "Der yisroeldiker Menakhem-

9 From the mid-1950s, the duo recorded their rehearsals and shows for their own personal use, using home recording machines. These recordings can be found in the BAA archive.

Mendl" (the Israeli Menachem-Mendel), an Israeli oikotype[10] of Sholem Aleichem's Menakhem-Mendl, a wandering figure who is amazed to discover the abrupt change that the move to Israel generated in Jewish identity:

> עפּעס אַ פֿאַרדרייטע וועלט. כ'בין גאָר נישט קיין מבֿין אויף דער הײַנטיקער וועלט, אַלץ פֿאַרקערט. אַלץ קאַפּויער. נאָר איין אַ משל: די דײַטשן האַנדלען, מאַכן געשעפֿטן, און מיר ייִדן פֿירן מלחמות...[11]
>
> [What a strange world. I'm no expert about today's world. Everything is the opposite; everything has been turned on its head. Just one example: the Germans engage in trade, make deals, while we Jews are making war...]

In Israel, Dzigan and Shumacher's performances depicted the legendary fathers of the nation alongside Eastern European Jewish characters. In this way, they highlighted the contrast between the mythical period of Jewish history and the contemporaneous Israeli reality, commenting on the idealization of the return to the Jewish people's roots, which was accompanied by an attempt to erase the diasporic years. The main character in the monologue "Der yisroeldiker bitnik" (The Israeli Beatnik)[12] by Yitskhok Brat is an average Israeli citizen, who is inspired by the example of the patriarchs to become a beatnik:

> האָב איך אַלץ איבערגעלאָזט און געוואָרן אַ ביטניק . . . פֿאַר אונדזערע אבֿות איז עס געווען אַ גאַנץ גוט לאַנד
> . . . שווער אַרבעטן האָבן זיי נישט געוואָלט. אַ גאַנצע וואָך האָבן זיי גאָרנישט געטאָן, און שבת האָבן זיי גערוט
> . . . אין גאַנצן ווי אונדזערע פּקידים.[13]
>
> [I left everything behind and became a beatnik . . . for our forefathers this was a very good land . . . they did not want to work hard. All week long they did nothing, and on the Sabbath they rested . . . Exactly like our officials.]

The monologue criticizes the Israeli work ethic and economy, comparing the short life expectancy of the Israeli citizen to the longevity of biblical figures. Thus, for example, Methuselah was able to enjoy a long life – according to the beatnik – because he did not try to make a living in an economy run by Minister of Finance

---

10 "Oikotype" (ecotype, a kind of plant adapted to a specific environment) is a term used in folklore research. It was coined by the Swedish scholar Carl W. von Sydow, who drew an analogy between the way that folk art in general, and folk literature in particular, is suited to a location and the acclimatization of wandering plants to different geographical and climatic conditions. See Sydow, *Folklore*, 44–59. The oikotype of Menakhem-Mendl in Erets Yisroel appeared in Der Tunkeler's *Fort a yid*, written after his visit to Palestine in 1931.

11 "Menakhem-Mendl astronaut" by Shimen Dzigan, BAA, files 175–04, 175–02, 178–04.

12 During the 1950s and 1960s, beatniks were associated with a social movement that emphasized self-expression and threw off traditional social conventions.

13 "Der yisroeldiker bitnik," staged in the show *Arayngetsimblt* (Whipped, 1966), BAA, files 175–03, 175–04, 178–01, 178–03.

Pinchas Sapir, did not listen to the news on the radio, did not see Israel cinema, and did not have to rely on the Israeli health service for medical care. Israel's culture, politics, economy, and health system – all the institutions of the state – were presented as the antithesis of the mythical Jewish period in Eretz Israel.

Departure and Wandering as a Personal Solution

The Israeli reality, beset by economic difficulties, the challenges of acclimatization, and continuing military conflict, once again led Dzigan and Shumacher to discuss the longing to leave, to embark on a life of wandering:

> וואָס טוט מען דאָ? נאָר אַנטלויפֿן. אָבער ווו אַהין? קיין אַלזשיר? לאָמיר נישט ריידן. קיין לאַאָס? לאָמיר נישט ריידן. קיין קובאַ? לאָמיר נישט ריידן. רוסלאַנד? נו אַדרבא, פּרובירט יאָ צו ריידן ...[14]
>
> [What can we do here? Only run away. But where to? To Algiers? Let's not talk about it. To Laos? Let's not talk about it. To Cuba? Let's not talk about it. Russia? Nu, let's see you trying to talk...]

Yet with the great powers racing for nuclear armament, together with growing militarism and the tensions of the Cold War, there was no better place. This sentiment was expressed in the skit "A fli tsu der levone" (A Trip to the Moon), by Moyshe Nudelman, performed in the show *Abi gezunt!* (The Main Thing: Good Health!, 1962). The characters Zelik and Kopl part from the *oylem* (which in Hebrew means "world" and in Yiddish means "audience") in a letter that epitomizes the search for a better, quieter, more democratic, and more humane life – a utopian reality that is always somewhere else:

> צו אַלע ייִדן פֿון דער גאַנצער וועלט! שלום, שלום על ישׂראל! איך, זעליק, מעכאַניק פֿון זינגערס ניי מאַשינען, און קאָפּל דער שנײַדער־מײַסטער פֿון קינדער־קאָנפֿעקציאָן, קומען זיך מיט אײַך געזעגענען. ווען איר וועט לייענען דעם דאָזיקן בריוו, וועלן מיר שוין זײַן מיט אייבערשטנס הילף, אויף אַנדערע וועלטן. איר ווילט וויסן פֿאַר וואָס? פֿאַר דאָס. פֿאַר דאָס, ווײַל די מענטשן האָבן דערפֿירט די וועלט אויף וועלכער מיר לעבן צו אַזאַ מדרגה, ס'גייט זיך אונדז אָן אַ חלשות פֿאַר בײדע, ס'הייסט – פֿאַר דער וועלט און פֿאַר די מענטשן. איין מענטש וויל אויפֿפֿרעסן דעם צווייטן. מ'שלאָגט זיך, מ'קריגט זיך, מ'רײַסט זיך, מ'בײַסט זיך.[15]
>
> [To all Jews in the entire world! Farewell, farewell to the nation of Israel! I, Zelik, technician of Singer sewing machines, and Kopl, master tailor of children's clothing, have come to take our leave. When you read this letter, we will already be, with God's help, in other worlds.

14 "A fli tsu der levone" by Moyshe Nudelman, staged in the show *Abi gezunt!* (1962), BAA, file 149–01. The playbill mistakenly notes that it was written by Yosef Heiblum. In the show *Ze vi du geyst?!* (1958), the skit was attributed to Shudzig (Dzigan and Shumacher).

15 Ibid.

You want to know why? Because. Because the people have reduced the world in which we live to such a state that we are sick of both – the world and the people. Men want to consume each other. They beat each other, they fight each other, they scream at each other, they bite each other.]

The same desire to leave the world is also expressed in the monologue “Menakhem-Mendl astronaut” (Menakhem-Mendl the Astronaut), which was written by Dzigan and performed in the show *Tsurikgekumen besholem* (Back in One Piece, 1970). The local reincarnation of Sholem Aleichem’s Menakhem-Mendl criticizes the illogical rivalry between the United States and the Soviet Union vis-à-vis armament and space exploration:

ווען זיי [די רוסן און די אַמעריקאַנער] וואָלטן געוואָלט אַרײַנלייגן אַזוי פֿיל געלט צו ווײַזן אַז מען קאָן לעבן אויף דער ערד – וויפֿל געלט זיי האָבן ארײַנגעלייגט צו ווײַזן אַז מען קאָן לעבן אויף דער לבֿנה, וואָס וואָלט אונדז דאָ געפֿעלט? ווער וואָלט שוין געדאַרפֿט זוכן גליקן אויף דער לבֿנה . . . איך פֿלי. איך וועל נישט וואַרטן. אויף וואָס זאָל איך וואַרטן? אַן אַטאָם־באָמבע זאָל מיר עפֿענען דעם קאָפּ? . . . וואָס ווילן זיי אויבן די רוסן? כ'ווייס... אפֿשר ווילן זיי ווײַזן דער וועלט אַז אַחוץ אין רוסלאַנד איז דאָ נאָך אַן אָרט וווּ מ'קאָן נישט לעבן . . . איך פֿלי. כ'וויל שוין איין מאָל פֿאַר אַלע מאָל פּטור ווערן פֿון דער וועלט. פּטור ווערן פֿון די מלחמות, פֿון שלום־קאָנפֿערענצן . . . שלום! שלום! איך פֿלי ...[16]

[Had they (the Russians and the Americans) spent so much money in showing that one can live on the earth, the same amount of money as they’ve spent demonstrating that people can live on the moon, what would we be lacking here? Who would need to search for his fortune on the moon . . . I’m off. I won’t wait. For what should I wait? For an atom bomb to split my head open? . . . What do the Russians want to do up there? I know... maybe they want to show the world that apart from Russia, there’s another place where no one can live . . . I’m off. I want to be rid of this world once and for all, the wars, the peace conferences . . . Goodbye! Goodbye! I’m off...]

In the narrative of Dzigan and Shumacher, Israel, similarly to Poland at the end of the 1930s, was not a desirable destination. Rather the best option was somewhere else: on the moon, in the stratosphere, or in the temporary heterotopia that existed on the stage of their theater. In his book concerning the history of the term *luftmentsh* (man of air) in German and Jewish culture, Nicholas Berg traces the development of this metaphorical term in Eastern European Jewish culture and discusses its manifestations in the Zionist discourse and modern Jewish literature.[17] Berg highlights that the metaphor *luftmentsh*, which originally developed from ironic self-criticism, was cultivated by antisemitic theory, later becoming a Jewish stereotype. *Luftmentsh* is a person without roots, without a homeland.

16 “Menakhem-Mendl astronaut,” BAA, files 175–02, 175–04, 178–04. On each occasion, the skit was suited to the local surroundings.

17 Berg, *Luftmenschen.*

Figure 22: Dzigan and Shumacher, unknown skit (Lydia Shumacher-Ophir collection).

Thus, Dzigan and Shumacher played Zelik and Kopl, a pair of despondent wandering Jews who once again suggest that leaving for outer space is the ultimate (and utopian) solution for Jews and humans alike.

If the idea of leaving was not sufficiently persuasive or utopian, Dzigan offered another option in the form of ostensibly ironic criticism that also represented a practical solution for personal survival – disappearing: not hearing, not knowing; laughing at the world, and at contemporary society; and avoiding getting involved in other people's affairs:

> שטופּ נישט – נישט קיין זין. / מאַך זיך נישט ווייסנדיק, טויב און שטום. / נאָר גרויס זיך נישט – און שטויס זיך נישט. / שטעל זיך אַוועק אין אַ זײַט. / לאַך פֿון דער וועלט – פֿון דער צײַט. / ביסט דאָך אַ ייִד, נישט קיין נאַר אַ גוי. / טײַטש עס דיר אויס אַזוי... // קריך נישט ווו מ'דאַרף נישט. / קריך נישט ווו מ'דאַרף נישט.[18]

18 "Krikh nisht vu m'darf nisht," by Avrom Karpinovitz and Shimen Dzigan, BAA, file 171–05.

[Don't stick your nose in – there's no point in it. / Pretend that you don't know, (like you're) deaf and dumb. / Just don't be arrogant – and don't stand out. / Stand on the sidelines. / Laugh at the world – at the times. / You're a Jew, nevertheless, not a stupid goy (non-Jew), interpret it that way... // Don't stick your nose in where it isn't needed, / don't interfere where you don't need to.]

Economy and Livelihood

As was noted, the severe economic crisis between the two world wars forced many Jews to search for new sources of income or even plan (due to ideological or economic motivations) their emigration to North America, South America, Mandatory Palestine, or other destinations. The ways that the individual tackled the economic reality in a period of crisis constituted a central topic in the works of Dzigan and Shumacher from the very outset of their artistic activities in the Ararat theater in Łódź through songs offering social commentary in the style of the European cabaret [Figure 22]. In the Warsaw period, the volume of satirical and humoristic jokes and skits within their shows increased. The duo criticized not only the authorities, the regime, or external elements, but also highlighted negative phenomena within Jewish society, sometimes touching upon Jewish attitudes to money. One joke, for example, concerns a Jew who wants to acquire a guard dog. However, instead of buying a dog, he decides to transform himself into a dog, thus saving the expense. Another skit features a Jew talking about his son's marriage: the boy was married to the daughter of the matchmaker in order to save the agent's fee. On another occasion, the artists described how a Jew responds when asked to which tribe he belongs: he says that he is neither a Cohen nor a Levite. Rather he is a debtor: using one word, he transforms his social status as a debtor into the central characteristic of his identity as a Jew.

In the early postwar period, in Europe and in their first performances in Israel, Dzigan and Shumacher commented on the difficult economic reality, depicted the individual's efforts to tackle this new situation, and the Jews' dependence on institutions such as the Joint Distribution Committee. When they relocated to Israel, the artists' critique, targets, and humor changed: their new target was the state of the Israeli economic policy and the figures responsible for it.

Dzigan and Shumacher's narrative depicted Israel as an impoverished woman, pitied even by those who sought to exploit her. In the skit "In tfise" (In Prison), performed in the United States in a show comprised of skits adapted

Figure 23: Dzigan and Shumacher, unknown skit (Lydia Shumacher-Ophir collection).

from previous performances, *M'lakht zikh arop fun hartsn* (Laughing to Lighten the Soul), a thief relates how he broke into Israel's state coffers but was shocked to find them empty:

> איך האָב געאַרבעט בײַ דער הויפּטקאַסע פֿון פֿינאַנס־מיניסטעריום . . .אַ גאַנצע נאַכט. מיט אַ שווייסמאַשין קוים מיט צרות אויפֿגעבראָכן די קאַסע, איז מיר פֿינצטער געוואָרן פֿאַר די אויגן. דער גאַנצער דלות פֿון אונדזער מדינה איז געלעגן אין דער קאַסע. נאָר ישׂראל־פֿונטן. ערשט כ'האָב מיך אַזוי געשעמט, אַז כ'האָב אַרויסגענומען מײַנע אייגענע פֿופֿציק דאָלאַר און צוגעלייגט.[19]
>
> [I worked on the main coffers in the Ministry of Finance . . . for a whole night. With a welding machine. The moment I succeeded in breaking into the coffers, with great effort, I couldn't believe my eyes. I saw the entire poverty of our state laid out before me. Only Israeli pounds. I was so ashamed that I took out my own $50 (bill) and left it there.]

This subversive criticism is exceptionally biting: Israel not only lacks resources, placing it in a pitiful position at the bottom of the economic ladder, but its criminals are of high economic and moral caliber, wishing to help the weak – in this case, the country.

19 BAA, file 168–01.

Israel's economic dependency on external aid became a frequent theme in the duo's work: they presented Israel as a beggar (*shnorer*) asking for handouts and dependent on the good will of rich foreign nations.[20] According to the duo, because of the bureaucratic laziness, the country's main income source of income was handouts [Figure 23]. Indeed, they described this as "the only economic branch in the country to develop very well without government [financial] aid." Dzigan and Shumacher's criticism was harsh, but it was also perceived as innocent and good-hearted: "Although Dzigan and Shumacher take aim with their 'whip' . . . this is generally a 'whipping' given by a good mother who 'only' wants to educate her child, to teach him to be 'good,' not to deal 'murderous blows' for no reason," claimed Shmuel Svislotsky. "Dzigan and Shumacher are not 'troublemakers,' they are just 'burning the leaven' within us, in order that we will be 'kosher for Pesach.' [Dzigan and Shumacher] are not acting 'underground'; they perform without fear and without bias; they are not afraid of the 'opposition' and they do not give in to the 'coalition.'"[21] Many jokes expressed criticism via inversion. For example, one relates that a miracle took place under Begin's premiership, while Simcha Ehrlich was serving as minister of finance: carrying money on the Sabbath was suddenly permitted because Israeli currency had no value, a hint at the galloping inflation. Another joke described Israel as a land in which a person can become a millionaire in just two years: within this period, a billionaire can easily be reduced to a millionaire.[22] The duo not only portrayed Israel as economically weak but also as treating the average citizen mercilessly. The cruel economic policy was evidenced by the high taxes, which made it difficult for citizens to earn a living:[23]

> כ'קאָן גאָר נישט אַרויסקריכן פֿון דער בלאָטע. כ'פֿאַרשטיי נישט וואָס האָט דער סאַפּיר געמאַכט נײַע שטײַערן?
> די אַלטע האָט מען שוין באַצאָלט? דאַרף איך פֿירן ביכער? וואָס באַדאַרף איך פֿירן חשבונות? פֿון הײַנט אָן וועל
> איך נעמען דאָס גאַנצע געלט וואָס כ'וועל פֿאַרדינען און אַוועקשיקן עס אין דעם מס הכנסה – זאָלן זיי זיך נעמען
> וויפֿל זיי ווילן, – די רעשט זאָלן זיי מיר צוריקשיקן און שוין...[24]

> [I just can't seem to pull myself out of the mud. I don't understand why (Pinchas) Sapir instituted new taxes? Had the old ones already been paid? Must I manage my books? Why do I have to manage my accounts? From today onwards I will take all the money I earn and

20 See below for a discussion of the monologue "Goldenyu" and the monologue by Moyshe Nudelman "Der Yisroeldiker Menakhem-Mendl." See the discussion in Vedenyapin, *Doctors Prescribe Laughter*.

21 Shmuel Svislotsky, "Sod hatslaḥatam," playbill for *Feter m'ken aykh!* (Uncle, We Know You!, 1959).

22 From the prologue to Dzigan's performances in Argentina (1979).

23 The artists also expressed this idea in statements to the media.

24 "Der yisroeldiker Menakhem-Mendl" by Moyshe Nudelman, *Doktoyrim heysn lakhn!* (Doctors Prescribe Laughter!, 1980), BAA, file 175–02.

send it off to the tax authority – they will take however much they want and send the rest back to me, and that's that...]

Criticism of taxation policy and the damage it inflicted on individuals recurs frequently in jokes, skits, and even the impersonation of Minister of Finance Yehoshua Rabinovitz in the monologue "Der Minister Rabinovitz."[25] Similar criticism was also voiced in Hebrew satire in the 1970s.[26]

The economic situation, the discrimination against Yiddish theater, and heavy taxation, as was noted, affected Dzigan and Shumacher's theater financially. We find direct reference to this at the beginning of one of Dzigan's solo shows: standing on an empty stage, Dzigan informs the audience that due to the high taxes, the challenging economic circumstances, and the competition with television, he cannot afford scenery, costumes, or even other actors. This was the future that Dzigan foresaw for Yiddish theater in the State of Israel.

The New Immigrant vs. Israeli Bureaucracy

The new immigrant's encounter with the Israeli Hebrew-speaking environment and the country's bureaucratic system became one of the central themes in the duo's art in Israel. The status of the immigrant in a new society, how he tackled the problems of absorption, making a livelihood, finding a place to live, and learning a new language, were all among the topics to which the artists returned repeatedly.

---

25 Taxes and finance ministers were central themes in a humorous open letter that Dzigan sent to Levi Eshkol before the latter left the Finance Ministry to become prime minister:

'איר זענט דאָך פֿאַר מיר געווען אַ גאָלדגרוב. איך בין דאָך געווען דער איינציקער ייִד אין לאַנד, וואָס האָט אויף אײַך מער פֿאַרדינט, ווי איר אויף מיר. אַכט יאָר האָט איר אַליין מיר צוגעשטעלט מער מאַטעריאַל ווי אַלע הומאָריסטן אין לאַנד צוזאַמען . . . בײַ אײַך האָבן זיי געוויינט און געצאָלט. בײַ מיר האָבן זיי געלאַכט און געצאָלט.'

[You were a goldmine for me. Indeed, I was the only Jew in the country who made more from you than you made from me. For eight years you gave me more material than all the other writers of humoristic texts in Israel put together . . . for you, they cried, and they paid. For me, they laughed and they paid.] Dzigan, *Der koyekh*, 341–43.

26 See for example the words of the song "'Ovdim 'aleinu 'avoda 'ivrit" (They Cheat Us with Hebrew Work) (words: Yossi Banai; melody and adaptation: Yair Rosenblum), which was recorded on a record of the same name with songs from a show staged by Hagashash Haḥiver, first performed June 12, 1977: "And why do they say / that there will be no poverty, and no more disparities? / And people will be able to buy apartments really cheap? / And that justice will reign here till the end of time? / They're cheating us, cheating, summer and winter, in the afternoon, / they're cheating us right in front of our eyes. / They're cheating us right in our faces / and we don't learn, don't learn. / Yes, we don't learn, yes, we don't learn, don't learn."

Figure 24: Dzigan and Shumacher, unknown skit (Lydia Shumacher-Ophir collection).

The Israeli reality, as reflected in the theater of Dzigan and Shumacher, placed many obstacles before the new immigrant. In the show *Yontef in der vokhn* (A Festival Mid-Week; 1957) one of the characters explains why the country is not providing work for the immigrants: when a person works he is hungrier, and therefore the government, which does not want hungry immigrants, chooses not to find work for them [Figure 24]. Paradoxes, absurdities, exaggerations, and contradictions were among the means that the artistic duo from Łódź employed to denounce the economic and social reality new immigrants faced. The laughter exposed the contradiction between the idyllic Zionist national idea and the reality, serving as a means to tackle the situation. The tragic disparity between expectation and reality was expressed on the satirical stage. The monologue "Der heyser tsienist" (The Fervent Zionist), by Efraim Kishon,[27] which was staged in the show *Nayn mos gelekhter* (Nine Measures of Laughter; 1957), depicts the acclimatization of a new immigrant named Lazar Kaganovits (inspired by Lazar

27 The translator's name is not recorded in the playbill.

Moiseyevich Kaganovich, a senior Soviet politician of Jewish origin who served as the secretary of the Communist Party in the 1920s and as a minister in Stalin's government in the 1940s). In the skit, Lazar Semionovits Kaganovits, who becomes Leyzer-Moyshe, is a new immigrant living in a garbage heap in Tel Aviv. Dzigan-Kaganovits tells jokes about life in the Soviet Union, his past connections with Stalin, and the change in his status after Nikita Khrushchev rose to power. Indeed, Khrushchev informed him, with a "Ukrainian smile" on his face, "Kaganovits and Abramovits, it's all the same." From this Kaganovits understood that he needed to leave the Soviet Union, which he did, together with a group of members of Maki (the Israeli Communist Party). After relating how he fled the Soviet Union, he explains, in an absurd manner, that while the Israelis viewed him as an anti-Zionist, the authorities respected him, and all doors were open before him:

> אין פּאָרט האָט מען מיך אויפגענומען אויסערגעווײנטלעך. ס'האָט זיך אַרום מיר פֿאַרזאַמלט אַ ריזיקער עולם. בליץ שנעל האָט זיך פֿאַרשפּרייט די ידיעה, אַז ס'איז געקומען אַ געשוווירענער ייִדן־פֿײַנט, אַ פֿאַרברענטער אַנטי־ציוניסט. אַזוי, ווי דער עולם האָט דאָס געהערט, האָבן אַלע זיך אויף מיר געוואָרפֿן און מ'האָט מיך אָנגעהויבן צו... קושן און צו האַלדזן . . . מ'האָט מיר נישט קאָנטראָלירט אַפֿילו די וואַליזע . . . ס'האָט נישט געדויערט קיין פֿערטל שעה איז שוין געקומען די מאַשין פֿון 'ראש הממשלה' און מ'האָט מיך באַלד צו אים אַהין געפֿירט, דער פּרעמיער האָט אַלע געלאָזט זיצן און מיט מיר געשמועסט אַ שעה צײַט.[28]
>
> [At the harbor they welcomed me warmly. A great crowd gathered around me. Very quickly the news spread that a sworn enemy of the Jews had arrived, a committed anti-Zionist. So, as the crowd heard this, they all fell upon me and began to . . . kiss and hug me . . . they didn't even check my suitcase . . . not more than a quarter of an hour passed and the prime minister's car arrived and immediately took me to him, the premier dropped everything and spent an hour talking to me.]

However, when Kaganovits reveals, at a meal with the prime minister, that he has become a Zionist and will remain one, that he no longer hates Jews, silence reigns in the room. Then:

> 'אַ ציוניסט?' – האָט אײנער אויסגעשריגן – 'נישט קיין צורר־ישׂראל? שווינדלער!' ס'האָט נישט געדויערט קיין מינוט זענען אַלע פֿאַרשוווּנדן . . . די דירה אויף צפֿון האָט מען אַוועקגעגעבן עפּעס אַ פֿידלער, אַ שטיקל קאָמוניסטל פֿון פּוילן, און מיר האָט מען געגעבן צו ווינען דעם דאָזיקן מיסטקאַסטן. אַזוי באַציט מען זיך צו אַ ציוניסטישן פֿירער?[29]
>
> ["A Zionist?" – someone called out – "Not a bitter enemy of the Jews? Cheat!" After no more than a minute everyone disappeared . . . the apartment in the North [of Tel Aviv] was given to a violinist from Poland who had some Communist connections, and they left me to live in this rubbish heap. Is this how they treat a Zionist leader?]

---

28 Efraim Kishon named the skit: "A tsienistisher askan iz gekumen" (The Arrival of a Zionist Activist), BAA, file 149–03.

29 Ibid.

The difficulty of "living" in the State of Israel recurs in other skits. In "Aropgefaln fun himl" (Fallen from Heaven),[30] an immigrant who cannot find a place to live wanders between government offices, eventually deciding to mimic "the Zionist emissaries" who stay in the diaspora. In the skit "A turist fun Amerike" (An American Tourist), by Dzigan, an American Jew relates what his wife, a Zionist activist, told him: "I don't want to leave my Israel in America and come to Eretz Israel."[31] Dzigan and Shumacher emphasized how difficult it was for many to realize the Zionist dream, as the skit "Der dikhter mitn vegele" (The Poet with the Little Cart) depicts:

> דרײַסיק יאָר בין איך געווען אין רומעניע אַ ציוניסטישער פֿירער, אַ פּרעזעס פֿון מכּבי, און אַז איך בין דאָ אַהערגעקומען און דערזען דעם גרויסן ים, דעם הר הכּרמל, דוד המלכס קבֿר – האָב איך דאָך געוואָלט שרײַען געוואַלד אין די גאַסן, ווײַל דאָס איז דאָך אַלץ פֿאַר מײַן געלט, פֿאַר מײַן האָרעוואַניע, פֿאַר די מיליאָנען וואָס איך האָב דרײַסיק יאָר געזאַמלט פֿאַר קרן־היסוד און פֿאַר קרן־קיימת . . .נאָך דעם ווי איך האב דרײַסיק יאָר געבענקט נאָך ישׂראל, מעג איך דאָך זיצן אין ניו־יאָרק אַלס קאָנסול, יאָ צו ניין?[32]
>
> [For thirty years I was a Zionist leader in Romania, a president of Maccabi, and then I came here and saw the great sea [the Mediterranean sea], Mount Carmel, the tomb of King David – I wanted to scream "Gevald!" in the streets, because all this was accomplished with my money, my hard work, with the millions that I collected over thirty years for Keren Hayesod and Keren Kayemet . . . After longing for Israel for thirty years, I'm allowed to set myself up in New York as Consul, am I right or wrong?]

The artists were not only occupied with immigration and its challenges but also with the responses to this reality, such as the decision to leave Israel. "A modern-day immigrant veteran," says the Israeli Menakhem-Mendl in a monologue by Nudelman, "is someone who was once an *oyle khadash* (new immigrant) and who in the future will become a *yoyred* (one who leaves the country)." The State of Israel is a waystation: New York has more Israelis than Israel. According to Dzigan and Shumacher, the Israelis' territorial reality was fluid, just as it was for the Jews in the diaspora in previous generations.

Wars, Neighbors, and the Arab-Israeli Conflict

The skit "Yidn khapn fish" (Jews Catching Fish) by Moyshe Nudelman, performed in the show *Hot a yid a lendele* (A Jew Has a Little Land, 1968), concerns the new territorial reality in Israel following the Six Day War (1967).[33] The skit depicts a

---

30 The author's name is not noted on the manuscript. See BAA, file 168–01.

31 "A turist in Amerike," BAA, file 178–05.

32 "Der dikhter mitn vegele," name of the author not noted on the playbill, BAA, file 194–03.

33 The skit was staged in a show by Dzigan that was broadcast on Israeli TV in 1975.

meeting between two fishermen: Kalman (played by Dzigan) and Yisroel (played by Yitskhok Habis). Yisroel, the first to arrive, erects the scenery to create the backdrop. Both fishermen want the area for themselves, but Kalman proposes a paradoxical solution: "Nevertheless, we can sit together separately." Their dialogue and argument express the major ideological and political conflict in Israel regarding ownership of the land: "There isn't room for both of us here. It's either me or you," argues Yisroel. To this, Kalman responds, "Me," while Yisroel contradicts him: "This is my area." The dispute intensifies, and the claims regarding the right to fish in the area escalate, reaching back to the days of the patriarch Abraham. When it becomes clear to both that they share the same ancestral rights, based on the same claim, Yisroel argues that the place is his because he got there first. The dialogue, replete with jokes, subsequently turns to a new and more complex argument: should the lands conquered in the Six Day War be returned to the Arabs?

קאַלמאַן: וואָס מיינט איר? עפּעס וועט מען דאַרפֿן צוריקגעבן.
ישׂראל: שלאָגט אײַך אַרויס פֿון קאָפּ! מען גיט נישט צוריק! גאָרנישט!
קאַלמאַן: ניין, ניין, ניין. עפּעס וועט מען צוריקגעבן. איר זעט דאָך. די געפֿאַנגענע סאָלדאַטן מיט די גענעראַלן האָט מען צוריקגעגעבן. די רוסישע טעכניקער האָט מען באַלד צוריקגעגעבן. די שיפֿן וואָס זיי האָבן פֿאַרזונקען אין סועץ־קאַנאַל האָט מען שוין אויך געוואָלט צוריקגעבן. מ'עט צוריקגעבן. מ'עט צוריקגעבן.
ישׂראל: הערט נאָר, איר רעדט דאָך אין גאַנצן נישט ווי קיין ייִד . . . ווען איך ווייס נישט אַז איר זענט קאַלמאַן, וואָלט איך געשווירן אַז איר זענט אַן אַראַבער. וואָס הייסט איר זאָגט מ'עט צוריק געבן? הײַנט איז 68', נישט 56'. הײַנט גיט מען גאָרנישט צוריק. איר וועט עס בײַ מיר נישט פּועלן.[34]

[Kalman: What do you mean? We need to give something back.
Yisroel: Get that idea out of your head! We're not giving it back. Nothing!
Kalman: No, no, no. They'll give something back. Indeed, you see, the captured soldiers were given back with the generals; the Russian technicians were returned immediately; they wanted to give back the ships that were sunk in the Suez Canal. Things will be given back. Given back.
Yisroel: Now, listen up, because you're not talking like a Jew . . . if I didn't know that you're Kalman, I would swear you're an Arab. What do you mean by saying things will be given back? It's '68, not '56. Nothing is going to be given back now. You won't persuade me.]

The pair continue arguing, and Yisroel, who claims that there is no need to return anything, also talks about the need to increase the Jewish population. The dialogue becomes a political argument concerning the Jewish demographic war, the two discussing how many children a man can have with his wife and with other women. Finally, Kalman snatches a ten-pound note from Yisroel. When Yisroel asks him to return the money, Kalman refuses, adopting Yisroel's argument and

34 Based on the manuscript and not on the later version screened on television. See BAA, file 171–05.

turning it against him: "Don't talk like an Arab. I'm not giving back anything." By adopting Yisroel's aggressive rhetoric, Kalman becomes a "Jew" and "puts Yisroel in his place." Thus, forcible acquisition, trickery, and taking the law into one's own hands are depicted as the Israeli way. The skit, which moves from individual allegory to collective act, raises questions about Israeli justice and morality.

The fervor and lust for power that reigned in Israeli society following the Six Day War are also highlighted in other works. In the skit "Nisim" (Miracles), the artists declare that following the great military victory, it is only to be expected that they will go on to liberate Jewish holy sites in Europe: the "graves of Chabad" in Russia, the tomb of the Baal Shem Tov in the Ukraine, and the grave of the Maharal in Prague. This portrayal of the thirst for occupation in the name of liberating holy places critiques the feeling of superiority that reigned at the time.

After his separation from Shumacher, Dzigan frequently returned to the conflict with the Arabs, always a central issue in the Israeli political discourse. In the skit "Meores-hamakhpeyle (The Machpelah Cave)[35] by Yitskhok Brat, staged in the show *Az m'lebt, derlebt men* (Live and Let Live) in November 1973, close to the Yom Kippur War, an Arab and a Hasid meet in the Machpelah Cave and proceed to argue about territorial rights. The two then encounter the patriarch Abraham and Hagar, who relate different versions of the past. In one sentence, the biblical Jewish figure manages to summarize the contemporaneous Israeli reality and the place of the Arabs, when he describes himself as "an Arab like all the Arabs. Muslim. I was born in Hebron. I work. I build houses for new immigrants from Russia." The skit concludes with a sophisticated joke by the Hasid, offering a solution to the conflict: "The Arabs need to wait 2,000 years, like we Jews waited." This quick-witted Jew turns the conventional arguments on their head: the person who arrived first does not have rights to the land, rather these are reserved for the one who has waited longer.

Marriage

While the occupation with marriage and family life was not unique to the satire and humor of Dzigan and Shumacher, these were central and recurring topics in their works. Phillip Auslander argues that in traditional western society joke-telling was generally considered a masculine pursuit and was linked to power status; for this same reason, among others, women were targeted in numerous jokes.[36]

35 BAA, file 178–01.
36 Auslander, "Stand-up Comedy," 205.

The theater of Dzigan and Shumacher is no exception in this regard. Jokes about the institution of marriage, found in innumerable skits and monologues, reflect a male perspective, with woman serving as the target of the jest. Examples include the skit "Aynshteyn-Vaynshteyn"[37] and the dialogue "Yidn khapn fish."[38] In the latter, in a conversation about fishing, Kalman rudely says to Yisroel referring to his wife: "At home I don't have worms. At home, I have one big worm." Later, Yisroel tells him: "I have a wife – she's called Khaye..." and Kalman replies, "And I have a *khaye* [animal] – she's called Soreh (Sarah)."[39]

Coming Full Circle: The Soviet Union on Stage

The period of their imprisonment in the Soviet Union was a major trauma in the lives of Dzigan and Shumacher, and they revisited it often in their theater. In his memoirs, Dzigan claimed that while imprisoned he concentrated on one dream: "Standing on stage again, laughing and mocking, breaking apart this fossilized regime, loathsome with its blood and tears, with a good joke."[40] The artists exacted "revenge" for their incarceration via a series of skits and jokes that concerned (principally) the following topics: the persecution of the Jews and the system of lies that reigned in the Soviet regime;[41] critical depictions of the Soviet Union and satire about it;[42] and showcase trials of the regime's opponents, in particular Jews.[43]

---

37 See above, pp. 51–53.

38 See above, pp. 212–214.

39 For further discussion of gender in the skit "Der nayer dibek," see below, pp. 225–243.

40 "צוריק אויף דער בינע אויסלאַכן, אָפּחוזקן, צעברעכן מיט אַ גוטן וויץ אָט דעם שטיינערנעם רעזשים, אַ באַשפּריצטן מיט בלוט און טרערן". Dzigan, *Der koyekh*, 224.

41 See for example: "From Russia we now hear good news and bad news. The good news: they won't be shooting Jews any more for speculating. The bad news – it's not true, you can't believe them." Prologue for the show *Gut yontef!!!* (Happy Holidays!!!), theater of Shimen Dzigan, BAA, file 168–01.

42 For example: "Wherever the Soviet people get a foot in the door, the cows stop giving milk and the chickens stop laying eggs." Dzigan, *Der koyekh*, 178.

43 These trials were at the center of skits such as "Der protses in Leningrad" (The Trial in Leningrad) and "Yidisher protses fun a yid in Rusland" (Trial of a Jew in Russia), or, as it was also known, "Di oysforshung" (The Investigation) by Avrom Shulman, which were staged in the show *Men lakht a lebn* (Laughing at Life; 1971). In "Der protses in Leningrad," the accused is bullied into admitting that he hijacked a plane carrying comrades Brezhnev and Kosygin (prime minister of the Soviet Union in the years 1964 to 1980), demanding in return for their freedom that they allow three million Jews to leave for Israel [See Figure 25]. The general prosecutor explains to the accused that in Russia a man has yet to be born who can resist admitting something when ordered

Figure 25: Yisroel Shumacher and Shimen Dzigan in the skit "Der protses in Leningrad" [The Trial in Leningrad] by Avrom Shulman (Lydia Shumacher-Ophir Collection).

In the skit "Lozt undz aroys" (Let Us Go) by Yitskhok Brat, performed in the show *Men lakht a lebn* (Laughing at Life), an old couple, immigrants from the Soviet Union, arrive at an office of the Jewish Agency and declare a hunger strike,

to do so. At the end of the trial, the prosecution manages to persuade the Jew that he hijacked the plane by taking his words out of context. "Yidisher protses fun a yid in Rusland" is also based on linguistic and cultural misunderstandings. In this trial, a Jew is accused of espionage, speculating, and maintaining contact with an enemy state: indeed, he received a package from his aunt in Israel. The skit was a direct response to a trial held in Leningrad in December 1970, following an attempt by Zionist activists Edward Kuznetsov and the former fighter pilot Mark Dimshits to hijack a small passenger plane in Leningrad and fly to Sweden in June 1970. The action failed and many Zionist activists were arrested. A trial was held, and Kuznetsov and Dimshits were sentenced to execution by firing squad. The other activists were sentenced to a period of between ten and fifteen years in prison. After the first trial, other similar trials were held in Leningrad, Riga, Kishinev, Sverdlovsk, Odessa, Samarkand, and Lutsk. See Beizer, "Hama'avaḳ hayehudi."

demanding that they be returned to Russia. The shocked Israeli official tries to reason with them, reminding them that in Israel they do not need to wait in line for everything. The old couple argue that they do not know what to do with so much free time. They also complain, absurdly, that many aspects of their new life are unsatisfactory: there are no retirement homes full of writers and academics; when there is a knock at your door in the middle of the night, there is no need to panic (because it is just the neighbor from across the hall); every morning you wake up in the same bed that you fell asleep in, etc.[44] If the theater of Dzigan and Shumacher, and in particular the theater of Shimen Dzigan, performed a healing function, the skits about life in Soviet Russia were an expression of self-healing, enabling the artists to process their trauma, which was also shared by many others. The criticism of the Soviet Union was piercing.

However, when seeking to criticize the Israeli reality, the Soviet reality could suddenly be depicted in a positive light, as when IDF soldiers interrupted Dzigan's performance because he spoke in Yiddish.[45] The New York Yiddish newspaper *Forverts* published Dzigan's response:

> איך האָב אַפֿילו פֿאַר רוסישע זעלנער, ניט־ייִדן, געשפּילט אין ייִדיש, און זיי האָבן מיר וואַרעם באַלוינט. דערפֿאַר איז מיר שווער איבערצוטראָגן דעם בזיון, אַז אין מײַן אייגענער מדינה לאָזן מיר ייִדישע זעלנער ניט שפּילן אין דעם לשון, וואָס איז מײַן נשמה־לשון, מײַן נשמה־אינסטרומענט.[46]
>
> [I even performed for Russian soldiers, non-Jews, in Yiddish, and they responded warmly. Therefore, it was difficult for me to bear the shame, when, in my own country, Jewish soldiers will not let me play in the language of my soul, on the instrument of my soul.]

Freedom of speech and freedom of language are relative. In Dzigan's subversive discourse, the Soviet regime, with its censorship and oppression, serves not only as a target of criticism but also as a positive source of comparison when depicting

44 There are many other skits criticizing the Soviet Union: In the skit "Baym teleskop" (At the Telescope), Dzigan and Shumacher watch the moon, now deserted because two months earlier the Soviets arrived and emptied it. The Soviets, the artists claim, have advanced technology, but they do not have bread in Sverdlovsk or butter in Kiev (name of the writer unknown, BAA, 171–05). The skit "Arayngetsimblt" (Whipped) by Shmuel Fisher includes the comment: "In Russia they give out meat twice a week. Once on the radio and once in [the newspaper] *Pravda* [Truth]." In the show *Arayngetsimblt*, BAA, 175–03. In the monologue "A telefon geshprekh mit Brezhnev" (A Telephone Conversation with Brezhnev), Dzigan ("The one who sat in prison in Kazakhstan for five years!") calls Alexei Kosygin. Dzigan represents another victim of the Soviet regime who succeeded in moving to Israel. He accuses Kosygin of antisemitism and siding with the Arabs. In the same monologue, which he penned himself, Dzigan compares the relations between Kosygin and Saddam Hussein to the pact between Stalin and Hitler.

45 See above, pp. 186–187.

46 Zilberberg, "Vos Dzigan hot gezogt."

the linguistic and cultural censorship imposed by the State of Israel. Although the censorship in the latter was achieved using different means, implemented to a different extent, and based on a very different ideology. However, it is noteworthy that the disparity or contradiction in the artist's critical narrative is discernible only via a comparative examination of the artistic discourse on stage and his statements in the Hebrew press, which were intended for different audiences and spoken in different languages.

Criticism of Yiddish Theater

Dzigan and Shumacher did not limit their criticism to social and political issues. Two parodies that they staged in different periods highlight their piercing dialogue with their own artistic arena.[47] "Kelberne hispayles" (Blind Wonder) was written by Moyshe Broderzon in Poland and staged in the show *Moyshe-Kapoyer* (Moses the Contrary) in 1935. No recording or script has survived, only references to it in press reviews.[48] This was a parody of the theatrical play *Yoshe Kalb* (Joseph the Calf) by Israel Joshua Singer, in a version staged by Maurice Schwartz at the Kaminsky family theater in Warsaw. The target of the parody was not only Singer's text but mainly Schwartz' mise-en-scène: the music, the acting, and even the lighting effects. The inclusion of references to these aspects indicates that the audience of Dzigan and Shumacher also attended Schwartz' shows in Warsaw.

The power of the parody is evidenced by that fact that Schwartz endeavored to prevent its performance: he appealed to the National Union of Yiddish Actors

---

47 The duo also staged parodies with the Ararat theater and in their joint theater, although neither the texts nor comprehensive reviews have survived. A curious parody was staged in the show *Gut-morgn koze!* (Good Morning, Goat!) in 1927. Broderzon wrote the text, which has a lengthy title: "Gebrotene litvakes oder tayvediker golem geyt al kidesh-Hashem bay nakht afn grinem mark in der yidn-shtot Ostropoliye" (Grilled Lithuanians or the Impassioned Golem Becomes a Martyr at Night in the Green Market in the Jewish City of Ostropol). This parodied several works by Jewish writers, among them H. Leyvik, Y. L. Peretz, Sholem Asch, and folkloristic texts. Dzigan played the golem, Shumacher the "enchanted tailor," the *badkhn*, and the Maharal of Prague.

48 In 1938, some of the members of Ararat joined a new miniature theater troupe in Warsaw, of which Broderzon was also a member and one of the main writers. The name of the troupe was Balaganeydn. Its actors included Dovid Birnboym, Yoel Bergman, Shmulik Goldshteyn, Yankev Reynglas, Motl Kon, Chayele Shifer, Mashe Feterman, and Zisel Girl Gorlitska. See Pulaver, *Ararat*, 95–96.

and sent letters to his lawyer, Gustav Beylin. These steps were unsuccessful, and Dzigan and Shumacher continued to stage the parody with great success.[49] The second parody, discussed at length below, is "Der nayer dibek," a parody of the play *The Dybbuk* as staged by Habima Theater.[50]

Dzigan's Satire vs. Hebrew Satire

In a piece entitled "Te'aṭron saṭiri – Tena'ei haḥofesh" (Satirical Theater – Conditions for Freedom), which was included in the playbill for *Tsit mikh nisht bay der tsung!* (Don't Put Words in My Mouth, 1961), Yaakov Malkin wrote:

> One of the childhood illnesses from which every new state suffered is an exaggerated attitude of reverence toward its institutions, leaders, and principles, thanks to which, or with the help of which, the state was founded. The most severe of the childhood illnesses suffered by the State of Israel was seriousness. While there were English rulers, they [the Jews] waved the brooms of laughter against them. When we became the rulers – we put the broom in the broom closet. Instead . . . we patted ourselves on the shoulder until our shoulders began to ache. When we dared to stage satire – we restricted it: we laughed at the corrupt, at careerists, of those known as such, or, in the best scenario, we levelled accusations [at the leaders] according to the ancient tradition we inherited.[51]

Later, Malkin argued that "democracy is based on the right to question everything. Every holy thing, every institution, every ideal and principle. The only thing that must not to be questioned is a question itself." He concluded the piece by highlighting that the theater of Dzigan represented one of the best chances for establishing a permanent satirical theater: hatred and alienation from customs and leaders, he asserted, make it impossible to offer humorous satire that provokes laughter and only afterwards leads to anger and contemplation: "Satire that is not a political platform – but rather an expression of freedom, the festival of doubt, the essence and source of an artistic experience in the theater."

Prior to the Six Day War, Hebrew satire was mild, mainly targeting the Israeli bureaucratic system and public corruption.[52] David Alexander, whose historical study of political satire in the Israeli theater does not mention the satire of Dzigan and Shumacher, claims that there was no piercing political satire in Israel during

49 See Goldshteyn, "Moris Shvarts"; Grafman, "'Moyshe Kapoyer"; Kipnis, "Moyshe-Kapoyer."
50 See below, 225–242.
51 Yaakov Malkin, playbill for *Tsit mikh nisht bay der tsung!* 1961 (in Hebrew).
52 Shaked, *Sipurim umaḥazot.*

the first two decades of the state's existence. This began to develop only after the Six Day War,[53] when Hanoch Levin started composing satirical cabarets, *'At ye'ani vehamilḥama haba'a* (You, Me and the Next War, 1968), directed by Edna Shavit, *Ketshup* (Ketchup), directed by his brother David Levin (1969), and *Malkat ha'ambaṭya* (The Queen of the Bathtub), also directed by David Levin (1970). Following heavy public pressure, the Cameri Theater ceased performing the last of these. Two years later, in 1972, Ephraim Sidon, Hanoch Marmari, B. Michael (Michael Brizon), and Kobi Niv (the Sakhbak group, which published satire in the newspaper of the Student Union at The Hebrew University of Jerusalem, *Pi ha'aton* [The Ass' Mouth]), established a satirical cabaret in Jerusalem. Thanks to their success they were invited to write a show for theater director and manager Ya'akov Agmon, and together with him they staged *Hamilḥama ha'aḥarona (shem zemani)* (The Last War [Temporary Name]). In 1974, Moti Kirshenbaum invited the Sakhbak group to write for television, for the satirical and popular show *Niḳui rosh* (A Clear Head). The satire and its sharpness received wide attention in the press, in Knesset discussions, and Yitzhak Rabin, then serving as prime minister, stated that *Niḳui rosh* had crossed a red line.

Many critics in the Israeli press expressed their resentment of this satire and its style. Discussing the contemporaneous Hebrew satire, Naḥman Ben-Ami said that it reflected "a spirit of animosity toward the establishment and self-hatred."[54] In 1971, Uri Keisari declared that satire worthy of this name was to be found only on Dzigan's stage: "Our Hebrew satire is celebrating excessively, it's too cheerful, it goes wild with laughter . . . it is suffocating, really suffocating, [but] the seeds of satire are nevertheless to be found spread among us. I don't know how and why, but whoever wants to hear good satire must look for it not among the various [Hebrew] entertainment troupes but [in the shows of] Shimon Dzigan, who talks, thinks, and writes Yiddish and acts in Yiddish."[55]

The critical Hebrew satire that began to develop in the 1970s was no longer light entertainment; in its style and in its questioning of the Zionist hegemony, it was seen as crossing the boundaries of good taste and challenging the historical Jewish ethos. On the background of this change, Dzigan's Yiddish satire was depicted as critiquing the political, economic, and social reality in Israel "to the right extent." Indeed, as Yeshayahu Ben-Porat wrote in 1960, it was free of "pretentiousness and without unnecessarily destructive arrows."[56] According to the

53 Alexander, *Leitsan heḥatser.*
54 Ben-Ami, "Matsḥiḳ."
55 Keisari, "Hasaṭira."
56 Ben-Porat, "Hamofa' hamedake'."

critics in the press, Dzigan represented the exact opposite of the Hebrew satirical theater that developed after the Six Day War: instead of hatred he symbolized love – love of the State of Israel and love of one's fellow man.[57]

Figure 26: Yisroel Shumacher and Shimen Dzigan (Lydia Shumacher-Ophir collection).

The Israeli Political Leadership in the Satire of Dzigan and Shumacher

> איך וואָלט ליקווידירט אַלע מיניסטעריומס, וואָלטן געווען ווייניקער מיניסטאָרן. ווער דאַרף האָבן אַזויפֿיל מיניסטאָרן? אַ מאָל, פֿאַרשטייט איך, צו זײַן אַ מיניסטער אין ישׂראל, איז געווען אַ גרויסער כּבֿוד, אָבער הײַנט? הײַנט איז שוין דערגאַנגען צו דעם, אַז מ'זאָגט איינעם, אַז ער האָט אַ קאָפּ פֿון אַ מיניסטער, באַליידיקט ער זיך.

57 In his memoirs from the Six Day War, Dzigan depicts himself as a soldier using his only weapon, humor, to bring comfort to the citizens of Israel who pay taxes and send their sons into battle. See Dzigan, *Der koyekh*, 351.

> [I would get rid of all the government ministries, so there will be fewer ministers. Who needs so many ministers? Once, I understand, to be a minister in Israel was a great honor, but today? Today we've reached the point that if you tell someone that he "thinks like a minister," he's insulted.]
>
> – Moyshe Nudelman, "Der yisroeldiker Menakhem-Mendl"

> Satire requires courage and even a great degree of fortitude, in order to swim against the current and not fear the "anger" of those against whom the arrows of satire are aimed and upon whom the laughter of the audience "grates."
>
> – Shmuel Svislotsky, "Sod hatslahatam," playbill for *Feter, m'ken aykh!* (1959)

Their sharp reading of the Israeli reality and their extraordinary expertise in the genre of satire enabled Dzigan and Shumacher to touch upon a wide range of topics that were relevant to Israeli society in general, and to immigrants (especially Yiddish speakers) in particular. One of the main targets of their satirical criticism in Israel was the country's political leadership. In monologues, skits, songs, and jokes, the artists addressed political crises, corruption, the various parties, and leaders.

In the monologue "Futbol-metsh" (Football Match) by Ḥaim Ritterman-Abir, staged in the show *Gut yontef!!!!* (Happy Holidays!!!, 1963), Dzigan plays a radio football commentator. He is covering a game in the Ramat Gan stadium between a team representing the ruling party and one representing the opposition, which is trying to save itself from relegation. The description of the match begins with a portrait of the spectators, among whom are many central political figures: Mordechai Namir – who should be the goalkeeper, according to the biblical verse, "And Mordechai sat at the king's gate" (Esther 2:21) (using the rhetoric of biblical commentary characteristic of Sholem Aleichem), yet is watching the match together with African guests, members of the underworld, and government officials. The African guests are the friends of Reuven Barkat, who was director of the state department in the Histadrut in the 1950s and played an important role in establishing relations between the Histadrut and popular movements in Asia and Africa.[58] Barkat himself arrives at the stadium in a magnificent white limousine – direct criticism of the capital he amassed while apparently representing the workers. In attendance are also Barkat's rivals in the Histadrut: Pinchas Lavon, who was blamed for Israel's failed operation in Egypt (The Lavon Affair), and Amos Ben-Gurion, the son of the former prime minister. Nahum Goldman, among the founders of the World Jewish Congress and its president for many years, the initiator of the reparations agreement, arrives in a black Cadillac, accompanied by two beautiful young women. For Goldman, the commentator explains, Israel

58 Barkat was also speaker of the Knesset from 1969 until his death in 1972.

is sport, even if he mainly plays in Monte Carlo – reproaching Goldman's behavior and the fact that a Zionist leader spends so much of his time abroad.

Among the players for the government team are David Ben-Gurion, Golda Meir, and Levi Eshkol, who arrive by helicopter from Sde Boker, all in silk shirts and white shoes. The opposition players include Menachem Begin, Pinchas Rozen, Moshe Sneh, and others – almost naked and barefoot, each one of them dressed differently. The referee is Abba Eban, but he is not welcomed by the opposition, which demands that he be replaced by Chaim Levanon (mayor of Tel Aviv from 1953 to1959). A few minutes into the game, it becomes clear, unsurprisingly, that Ben-Gurion is playing alone:

> בן גוריון צילט אויפֿן טויער! עמרם בלוי שרײַט: ציוניסט! נאַצי! פֿאַשאָל וואָן! אַוועק פֿון מײַן טויער! שבת־גוי!
>
> [Ben-Gurion kicks to the goal! Amram Blau[59] cries: Zionist! Nazi! Get out of my goal! Shabes-goy[60]!]

At the close of the first half, no one has yet scored a goal: "Zero-zero, two zeros for the good of the population." The commentator emphasizes the inability of the statesmen to advance the political game.[61]

In another skit, entitled "Ariel Sharon,"[62] Dzigan encounters Sharon, a soldier who had recently entered politics. To identify him, Dzigan asks him if he is the general who destroyed the industry or the one who destroyed tourism. Sharon reveals his cards to Dzigan: he is planning a revolution against the ruling party:

> ס'וועט זײַן מלחמה – מ'וועט שיסן! / עזר וועט באָמבאַרדירן דעם פֿראָנט,/ איך וועל אַטאַקירן דעם אונטן./ בעגין וועט שפּריצן מיט פֿײַער, / להט 'טשיטש' וועט זיך שדכנען צו גאָלדע מאיר, / מיט משה דיין וועט נישט זײַן שווער / ער איז דער וואָס האַלט זיך מיטן מיליטער, / אין דער לעצטער מינוט וועט ער מאַכן אַ קונץ/ און אַריבער צו אונדז. / איך בין אַריק שרון! / כ'וועל זיי ווײַזן וואָס איך קאָן! / איך, אַז מ'דאַרף, בין איך אַ רוח![63]

59 Leader and founder of ultra-Orthodox Neturei Karta, known for his isolationist stance and opposition to Zionism and the State of Israel.

60 This term is used to describe a non-Jew employed by religious Jews to perform certain services that are forbidden on the Sabbath (for example, switching on lights). The term is placed in the mouth of Amram Blau, a strongly anti-Zionist rabbi, who by using it effectively defines Ben-Gurion as a non-Jew.

61 This claim recurs also in other skits, such as "A shif on a ruder" (A Ship without a Rudder, 1969) by Avrom Shulman, Yitskhok Brat, and Shimen Dzigan, in which Meir and Dayan are portrayed as helpless.

62 The script of the skit has survived, although the name of the author and year are not recorded. BAA, file 168–03.

63 Ibid.

[There will be war – there will be shooting! / Ezer will bombard the front, / I will attack the rear. / Begin will squirt fire, / Lahat "Tshitsh" will go with Golda Meir, / Moshe Dayan won't cause any problems / he's involved in military, / at the last moment he'll perform a trick / and come over to us./ I am Arik Sharon! I will show them what I can do! / When necessary, I can be a demon!]

In another skit Dzigan meets Yitzhak Rabin and debates with the prime ministerial candidate:

דזשיגאַן: דערלויבט נאָך איין פֿראַגע, מיסטער ראַבין, קאָנקרעט. מיט וואָס קומט איר איצט צו די ווילער?
ראַבין: אויפֿן ערשטן אָרט: דעמאָקראַטיע.
דזשיגאַן: מר ראַבין, די וויצן לאָזט איבער פֿאַר מיר. קריכט מיר נישט אין דער פּרנסה אַרײַן . . .
ראַבין: מיר ווילן קומען צו די בירגער מיט אַ שלום! פֿאַר אַ שלום זענען מיר גרייט אפּצוגעבן די אַראַבער מער
ווי אַלע פּאַרטייען צוזאַמען. מיר וועלן דעם שלום ברענגען טויטערהייט.[64]

[Dzigan: Allow me one more question, Mr. Rabin, a real one. What are you offering the voters?
Rabin: First of all: democracy
Dzigan: Mr. Rabin, leave the jokes to me. Don't interfere in my business . . .
Rabin: We offer the citizens peace! In return for peace, we are prepared to give to the Arabs more than all the other parties together. We will bring peace even at the price of death.]

Thus, the Israeli political leadership was a central mark for Dzigan's satirical bullets. In the monologue "Futbol-metsh" (1963), described above, the artist created a metaphor for both the inter-party and internal party hierarchies, discussed Ben-Gurion's dictatorial leadership of the ruling party (see also the next section), imparted satirical criticism of the relationship between capital and power and between capital and political activists, and directly critiqued specific figures. In other skits mentioned here, he "met" political figures on stage, criticizing them by means of a hypothetical unmediated meeting, and he even managed to foretell the political future of Ariel Sharon, who would become a major figure in the Israeli military and state leadership, as well as Yitzhak Rabin.

The theater of Dzigan and Shumacher, and Dzigan's solo theater, played a subversive and transformative role vis-à-vis the issue of Israeli political authority (to be discussed at greater length in the next section). For the average citizen, and even the successful actor, the only possible options were to laugh at the political leadership or, as in the monologue "Valn-valn" (Elections-Elections) from 1977, take their place. In this skit, Dzigan, not trusting the Israeli political leadership, suggests that

64 From the skit: "Valn-valn" [Elections-elections], BAA, file 168–01.

he will run for prime minister and thus cease being an eternal loser, "another one of the three million nothings that are being pulled along by their noses."[65]

"Der nayer dibek" (The New Dybbuk, 1957)

> Once again, the Israeli does not own his own home. His language of symbols and his world of values have lost their meaning, having been stripped of their validity and internal power. Another, different language is replacing the one that has passed away forever.
>
> – Shaked, "'Or yatsel."

To deepen the discussion of Dzigan and Shumacher's Israeli political satire and the changes in Dzigan's art following their separation, this section will focus on two pairs of skits concerning two different prime ministers: David Ben-Gurion in the skits "Der nayer dibek" (The New Dybbuk, 1957) and "In der yeshive fun Dovidl Plonsker" (In the Yeshiva of Dovid of Plonsk, 1961), and Golda Meir in the monologue "Goldenyu" (1971) and "Golde baym poypst" (Golda Visits the Pope, 1973).

The premiere of the show *Nayn mos gelekhter* (Nine Measures of Laughter) took place on October 8, 1957, in the Ohel Shem theater, Tel Aviv. The show included eight humorous skits by Moyshe Nudelman, Efraim Kishon, Moshe Hadar, and Y. Shudzig (Dzigan and Shumacher). Between the skits Chayele Shifer and Lea Szlanger performed songs and refrains in Hebrew and Yiddish.[66]

Like their previous shows, Dzigan and Shumacher's new production was widely covered in the press, on the radio, and even on newsreels in the cinema – testimony to the actors' central place in the Israeli discourse. A number of critics claimed that the show rehashed old materials from the duo's stock,[67] although most reviews were supportive, some even arguing that this was one of the duo's best shows since their first performance in Israel in 1950.[68] Others praised the high artistic level, the quality of the political satire, and, in particular, the actors'

---

65 As was noted, Efraim Kishon had suggested this jokingly in an article published in the press a few years earlier. See Kishon, "Dzigan veShumacher lashilṭon."

66 The refrains were written by A. Dror, Haim Hefer, and Haim Shalmoni, and the music was composed by Dan Blitental, Shaul Berezovsky, and Avraham Ferara. Leon Veiner wrote the music for the song by Shmerke Kaczerginski, and two folk songs were performed – "A nigundl" and "Sorele."

67 A. Z., "Tish'a ḳabin"; Y. Ḥ., "'Emesh bate'aṭron"; Yuris, "Dzigan–Shumacher"; Davidovitz, "Shopworn."

68 D., "Tokhnit ḥadasha"; Tsanin, "Nayn mos gelekhter."

understanding of Israeli life.[69] Nevertheless, the final skit in the show – a satirical parody by "Y. Shudzig" (Dzigan and Shumacher) and starring the comic duo, with music by Shaul Berezovsky, entitled "Der nayer dibek" – caused a certain amount of discomfort.[70]

The discussion here is based on the script, which was preserved among the artists' papers, a home recording of the show,[71] archival pictures of the performance, footage of short sections that were eternalized in one of the weekly Yomanei geva (Geva Diaries)[72] news broadcasts, and press reviews.

The skit "Der nayer dibek" was twenty-five minutes in length, accounting for approximately one sixth of the entire show. It is one of the longest skits that the duo ever performed. The text is seven pages long, printed on a typewriter, with handwritten comments and deletions. The letters "DZ" appear on the first page of the manuscript, suggesting that this was Dzigan's copy and that he himself wrote the comments. According to this script, the skit was composed in 1956. In that year, Habima celebrated 1,000 performances of *The Dybbuk* and the prestigious Israel Prize was awarded to actress Hanna Rovina, who played Leah in Habima's production, events that in all likelihood triggered the writing of this parody. Yet a further year passed before Dzigan and Shumacher performed the skit. Thus, presumably, the script does not reflect the final version of the text, which underwent additional revisions before it was actually staged (this is also supported by a comparison with the recorded version).

---

69 See, for example, Shtern, "'Oḳtsanut"; D., "Tokhnit ḥadasha"; Yuris, "Dzigan–Shumacher"; Feuerstein, "Tish'a ḳabin."

70 The music for the skit was composed by Shaul Berezovsky. The duo themselves wrote the texts for the songs. Concerning the distinction between parody and satire, I follow Ziva Ben-Porat's definitions. Ben-Porat defines parody as: "An alleged representation, usually comic, of a literary text or other artistic object – i.e., a representation of a 'modelled reality,' which is itself already a particular representation of an original 'reality.'" She defines satire as: "A critical representation, always comic and often caricatural, of 'non-modelled reality,' i.e., of the real objects (their reality may be mythical or hypothetical) which the receiver reconstructs as the referents of the message." Ben-Porat "Method in Madness," 247.

71 The text and home recording are in the Yehuda Gabbai Theatre Archive in Beit Ariela, Tel Aviv. My thanks to the staff at the archive.

72 The documentation by Yomanei geva (newsreel broadcast in movie theaters) is of great significance. These sections were filmed during the show *Nayn mos gelekhter*, among them twenty seconds of "Der nayer dibek," one of the few film recordings of Dzigan and Shumacher performing on the Israeli stage. Other raw materials were destroyed in a fire that broke out in the archive. It should be noted that Shaul Goskind, one of the founders of Yomanei geva, was a Yiddish film producer in Poland and produced three films starring Dzigan and Shumacher prior to World War II. I am grateful to the Spielberg Archive of Jewish Cinema at The Hebrew University of Jerusalem and Herzliya Studios for their help in locating these sections and enabling me to watch them.

The source for Dzigan and Shumacher's parody was Sh. An-sky's *The Dybbuk.* This modern classic of the Jewish and Israeli stage was written between 1912 and 1917, in Russian and Yiddish, inspired by the traditions and stories about dybbuks that An-sky gathered while heading the Baron David Goratsievich Gintsburg ethnographic mission (1912–1914) in Volhynia and Podolia. The play was first performed in Warsaw by the Vilner trupe in Yiddish (1920) and in Haim Nahman Bialik's Hebrew translation in 1922 by Habima (Moscow), directed by Evgeniĭ Vakhtangov. In addition to becoming a canonical work of Jewish theater and the focus of innumerable reviews, debates, and studies, it has also inspired many other original works.[73]

Dzigan mentioned these two stage versions of An-sky's play, both of which constituted part of the theatergoers' collective memory, in his words of introduction on the surviving recording. The Yiddish version staged by the Vilner trupe in 1920, directed by Dovid Herman, was exceptionally successful among both critics and audiences (in the year and a half following its premiere, the play was performed more than 300 times), increasing the troupe's prominence in artistic Yiddish theater. It also inspired the 1937 film, made in Poland, which was directed by Michał Waszyński. The second, the source for Dzigan and Shumacher's parody, was the Hebrew version mentioned above. This production had a vast effect on both Hebrew and Yiddish theater, and it directly influenced the two artists from Łódź.[74] In 1962, Habima was still performing the play without any change in the acting style, and it achieved symbolic and mythical status in modern Hebrew theater.[75]

Dzigan and Shumacher's version is a reframing of the original Dybbuk story in the Israeli context:[76] Ḥanan and Leah's unrealized love; the deceased Ḥanan's spirit possesses the body of his beloved; this spirit (dybbuk) is exorcised by Rebbe Azriel of Miropol; and finally Leah's death allows the lovers to realize their union, although not in the world of the living. The setting for the parody is the *bes-medresh* (study house) of Reb Dovidl, the Rebbe of Plonsk (the spiritual leader of the Jews of Plonsk, a town in north-central Poland, which was the birthplace of David Ben-Gurion). Reb Dovidl, in other words, is none other than the prime minister, played by Shumacher. "Zeyde Yisroel" (Grandpa Israel), with his

---

73 Freddie Rokem notes the unique quality of *The Dybbuk* in inspiring new texts and performances. This phenomenon is evidenced by the many plays based on other performances of the work. See Rokem, "'Hadibuḳ' be'erets Yiśrael." See also Zylbercweig, *Leksikon* vol. 1; Portnoy, "Puppet Theatre"; Steinlauf, "Dybbuks."

74 See above, p. 21.

75 Nahshon, "Habima's Production of 'The Dybbuk.'" On the perception of the work in the Zionist context see ibid; Kaynar, "National Theatre"; Rokem, "Hebrew Theater."

76 In the case of Dzigan and Shumacher, the text is a Yiddish parody of the Hebrew production.

daughter Medinele (a diminutive for *medina* [state]), played by Dzigan, arrives at Reb Dovidl's "court," begging the renowned master to exorcise the demon that has possessed her. During the exorcism ceremony, the dybbuk reveals that he is a new immigrant who, at the age of forty-one, is unable to find work and therefore cannot make a living in his new country. After a certain amount of negotiating, the Tsaddik succeeds in exorcising the spirit, promising him in exchange an exemption from income tax. This is accomplished by having the dybbuk move to Eilat – at the time, a small, backwater town in the south of Israel, where residents were exempt from paying taxes. On the way, however, the dybbuk makes a short detour to Germany to collect his reparations payments.[77] Meanwhile, Medinele, who is madly in love with the dybbuk, awaits his return, and the parody (unlike the original play, which ends tragically) concludes with his reappearance and a love song, performed by the entire ensemble.

In suiting An-sky's play to the local milieu, and in adapting the drama to the genres of parody and satire and to the Yiddish miniature stage, the central characters in the canonical version – the rabbi, the bride, the spirit of Ḥanan – are accorded new local and symbolic identities. The local-Israeli subject matter is dressed up in Eastern European Hasidic garb. The two central themes of the parody are the hierarchy within the ruling party (and primarily the place of the nation's leader, David Ben-Gurion) and the frustration felt by the new immigrant in his Kafkaesque encounters with Israeli bureaucracy.

The parodic foundation is evident in the scenery, acting style, music, and the character of Medinele. For instance, the scenery, designed by Erich Moses, incorporated two elements from the production by Habima (the synagogue table and the window looking out onto the shtetl courtyard), the scenery for which was designed by Nathan Altman. However, apart from this, it transformed Altman's expressionist setting into something more characteristic of the miniature stage. The short section preserved in Yomanei Geva reveals that the performance and the actors' sing-song-like speech parodied the stylized acting in Evgeniĭ Vakhtangov's version. The music that Yoel Engel composed for Habima's production of *The Dybbuk* was inspired by Hasidic sources. By contrast, when writing the music for "Der nayer dibek," Shaul Berezovsky only used a variation of the Hasidic *nign* (tune) "Mipnei ma" (see below),[78] while the remainder of the music

---

77 A controversial agreement with the Germans that David Ben-Gurion supported, despite harsh criticism from the political opposition and a large portion of the public.

78 Concerning the music that Engel wrote for Habima, see Dobrovetsky, "Hamuziḳa shel Yoel Engel." For a sound recording of the work see Habima, *Hadibuḳ* (The Dybbuk), sound recording, CBS 2 70012/13, recordings 1–2 (2003). The reviews barely mentioned the music written by Shaul Berezovsky for the parody. Only Davidovitz's review mentioned that the musical drew on popular songs from American musicals. The central motif is based on the song "Hernando's Hideaway," by Richard Adler and Jerry Ros, from the musical *Pajama Game* (1954), set to a Hasidic rhythm and in operetta style. The song performed by Ḥanan in the original play, based on verses from the Song of Songs, is replaced with an adaptation of the song "Rose-Marie" from the 1936 American movie of the same name. Berezovsky's music contributed greatly to recreating the spirit of contemporary political cabaret.

Ben-Gurion as the Hasidic Rebbe

One of the central figures in the "Der nayer dibek" is Reb Dovidl. In the first part of the skit, the Hasidim (played by the singers Chayele Shifer and Lea Szlanger) sing his praises, in the second part he speaks to his followers, and in the third he conducts the exorcism. Similarly to An-sky's *The Dybbuk*, "Der nayer dibek" opens with Hasidic singing to the tune of "Mipnei ma, mipnei ma, yoredet haneshama" (Why, oh why, does the soul descend?) and a discussion of one of the central questions in Hasidic thought – the reason that the soul descends from the upper spiritual worlds to the lower world. In An-sky's play, the song (which also recurs at the end) alludes to the soul of Ḥanan, his occupation with Kabbalah, and his deviation from social norms. In "Der nayer dibek," the song concerns leaving (descent from) Israel and the efforts of the Jewish Agency to bring new immigrants. In their tales about Reb Dovidl, the Hasidim portray the miracles and wonders he has already performed. He, Reb Dovidl of Plonsk, is termed "the greatest leader of the generation," extolled for his "wise" and "holy" words; it is said that he has all the answers, that he met the devil himself and defeated him. The Hasidim enter the stage with the beadle (*shamash*, Mikhael Grinshteyn) and sing in chorus a Hasidic melody with a political bent that utilizes the name of Ben-Gurion's political party: "Ay, ay, ay, Mapai [Workers' Party of Eretz Israel], ay!" Thus, the followers of Reb Dovidl glorify their omniscient and omnipotent leader according to the Hasidic tradition. Likewise, similarly to many other Rebbes in Hasidic stories, Reb Dovidl is able to invert natural phenomena and bypass the laws of nature, altering reality for his own needs:

ס'איז גאָר געווען שבת, פּרשת תזריע מצורע, דער רבי האָט געוואָלט גיין דאַווענען, מיט אַ מאָל האָט
אויסגעבראָכן אַ שלאַקסרעגן. וואָס טוט מען? גיין קאָן מען דאָך נישט, ס'איז דאָך סכּנות־נפשות, ווידער פּאָרן

accompaniment for this section was "what is expected of an amateur production." Davidovitz, "Shopworn."

> טאָר מען דאָך נישט, ס'איז דאָך שבת... האָט דער רבי אויסגעשטרעקט זײַנע ליכטיקע הענט און אַ זאָג געטאָן: שבת אַהין, שבת אַהער... איז אַ ביסל שבת געגאַנגען אַהין און אַ ביסל שבת געגאַנגען אַהער און דער רבי האָט זיך אַרײַנגעזעצט אין אַ שירות און אַוועקגעפֿאָרן.[79]
>
> [It was on the Sabbath, *parshat Tazri'a-metsora*, just as the Rebbe (Reb Dovidl) wanted to go to pray, when all at once there was a downpour. What was to be done? One can certainly not walk in such weather, it was dangerous, on the other hand one must not travel, it's the Sabbath... The Rebbe stretched forth his brilliant hands and said: Sabbath – go this way! Sabbath – go that way... A bit of the Sabbath went one way and a bit of the Sabbath went the other way, and the Rebbe got into a *sherut* (taxi) and drove off.]

In this story, Reb Dovidl is compared to Moses parting the Red Sea. Indeed, in response to this wonderful deed, the Hasidim sing in Hebrew: "What a wonder, what a wonder, if there are miracles such as these, how is it possible not to live in such a land..." (to the folk tune used in a song of the same name by Natan Alterman). The fact that the Hasidim interpret their leader's transgression as a miracle is an ironic allusion to Ben-Gurion's behavior and the innocent interpretations of it by his devoted Mapai followers. The deliberate use of erroneous interpretation to express criticism is a classic comic tactic, and it is employed at other points in the skit. For example, the Hasidim relate that Satan once grabbed Reb Dovidl by the lapel of his kaftan. In response, Reb Dovidl grabbed his stick and threw it, and then "the stick remained a stick."[80] They are so astonished precisely because there is no reason for wonder. It is ironic criticism of the leader's failure and his followers' erroneous interpretation of this failure. Throughout the parody, the halo of the leader is gradually deconstructed, his power questioned.

An important layer in interpreting the rhetorical question that the Hasidim ask – "How is it possible not to live in such a land as this?" – which was (and still is) central to the Israeli paradigm, concerns the status of Yiddish theater in general and that of Dzigan and Shumacher in particular. Despite their exceptional success and the recognition they received from important voices among both theater critics and the political establishment, the duo remained on the margins of Israeli culture until the end of their days. It is likely that this marginality in fact enabled Dzigan and Shumacher to see the reality clearly, to criticize Ben-Gurion's behavior, and even to present him on stage as a dictatorial ruler wielding excessive power. This criticism, the exception to the rule on the Israeli stage in those years, is evident when the Hasidim of Plonsk-Mapai respond to Reb Dovidl's decision to leave his rabbinical seat in order to settle in the fields

79 All the translations are my own. This story appears in the text but not the recording. The remainder of the passages appear in both, unless otherwise noted.
80 Here we also find in the manuscript: "And the Satan [remained] Satan."

and become a shepherd. This is, of course, a jibe at Ben-Gurion's retirement to Kibbutz Sde Boker in the Negev in December 1953, which took place during one of the stable periods of his rule and sent shockwaves through the political system in general and Mapai in particular. In the skit, the Hasidim sing to Reb Dovidl following his retirement:

> און וואָס זענען מיר? מער ווי שאָף, רינדער, אָקסן און בהמות? ער איז אונדזער פֿאָטער, / מיר זענען זײַנע קינדער, / ער איז אונדזער פּאַסטעך, / מיר זענען שאָף און רינדער. / ער פֿאַשעט אונדז מיט בלעטער, / ער פֿאַשעט אונדז מיט גראָז, / ער איז אונדזער פֿירער. / ער פֿירט אונדז בײַ דער נאָז. / מעעע! מעעע! מעעע!
>
> And what are we if not sheep, cattle, oxen, and cows? He is our father, / We are his children, / He is our shepherd, / We are his sheep and cattle, / He feeds us with leaves/ He feeds us with grass, / He is our leader, / He leads us by the nose. / Baa! Baa! Baa!

This cabaret-like song, full of self-mockery, reflects on the one hand Dzigan and Shumacher's interpretation of the weakness and dependence of the Hasidim on their leader and, on the other hand, Reb Dovidl's fatherly, patronizing, and even godlike attitude toward them. The song's subversive nature is further intensified (to a nearly blasphemous register) by its invocation of a well-known prayer recited on the High Holy Days, "Anu 'amekha."[81] The song evoked a range of reactions among theatergoers, in accordance with their political inclinations.

Ben-Gurion's public persona as an indispensable national father figure, as lampooned in this song, is well attested in both firsthand sources and historical studies. The historian Yechiam Weitz describes in the following manner the reaction of some party members to Ben-Gurion's decision to retire: "First – the almost physical sensation of orphanhood, of unbearable separation from someone that many saw as a father figure; second – admiration, at times almost flattery, and sometimes even more than that."[82] The similarity between the period's portrayal in the skit and in Weitz's study underscores the satirists' insight into contemporary reality and their ability to provide critical commentary on historical processes as they were unfolding. From another perspective, the editorial published in the newspaper *Davar* upon Ben-Gurion's retirement noted: "We are unable to give up, not at this hour, not in this time, and not in the future, on the immense power – galvanizing, motivating, guiding, familiar, and unifying – that is Ben-Gurion."[83]

---

81 "We are Thy people, and Thou art our God; / We are Thy children and Thou art our Father, / We are Thy servants, and Thou art our Father . . . We are Thy flock, and Thou art our Shepherd . . . We are Thy vineyard, and Thou art our Keeper." Thanks to Amy Simon for bringing to my attention the words of the piyyut.

82 Weitz, "Fanṭazya," 300.

83 *Davar*, "Devar hayom."

In performance, non-fundamental characteristics of the signifier are presented prominently. The moment that the audience accepts the consensus of a mise-en-scène, every detail of the world presented in the scene on stage is endowed with meaning.[84] The words are no longer simple signifiers, they do not relate only to the signified. Rather, they connect to other signifiers, to previous mise-en-scènes, to actors in other roles, and in this case to the characters of the original play and the actors who played them in the production by Habima, in particular Hanna Rovina.

It is clear from the sound recording of the skit that Shumacher's stage entrance as Reb Dovidl – he looked amazingly similar to Ben-Gurion – created a stir: there was an initial hush, followed by vigorous laughter. The followers of Reb Dovidl crown him King of Israel and reveal the secret whereabouts of the leader: "David, King of Israel, lives and is alive, lives in Mapai, is alive in Mapam." Reb Dovidl asks for a microphone and presents his version of Rebbe Azriel of Miropol's "holy speech," imitating the Hasidic tune used in Habima's production. In Reb Dovidl's text, the traditionally sanctified religious symbols are adjusted to Israeli-Zionist civic life. Tel Aviv, for instance, acquires the venerable sanctity of Jerusalem as the Jewish holy city; the Histadrut (Labor Federation) building in the heart of the "white city" takes on the role of the Temple in Jerusalem, while the political parties assume the function of the ancient Levites. In addition, the most sanctified letters in the holy Hebrew language are now *shin-bet*, the Hebrew acronym for the ISA (Israeli Security Agency).[85] The hidden secrets of the Shin Bet, ironically replacing the mysticism of the Kabbalah, are known to only two privileged figures: the Holy One and David Ben-Gurion. Indeed, what Rachel Elior terms "expertise in holy names and reciprocal relations between the revealed and the hidden"[86] enables Reb Dovidl to perform the exorcism ceremony successfully. Thus, Dzigan and Shumacher parodically compare Ben-Gurion with Yosef Karo, Haim Vital, and the Baal Shem Tov. Through the words of Rebbe Azriel, spoken by Reb Dovidl of Plonsk, the sacred symbols of the religious system are adapted

---

84 See Bennett, *Theatre Audiences*, 70.

85 Ben-Gurion himself connected the Israeli Security Agency (Shin Bet) with spiritual values, referring in his diary to the Ministry of Security as the "Ministry of the Spirit": "The Ministry of the Spirit – that is the Ministry of Security. One hundred thousand Jews fight for the freedom of their nation – this is the greatest human handiwork in our days, which will inspire literature and art in coming generations." See Shapira, *Yehudim ḥadashim*, 227.

86 Rachel Elior, "Hadibuḳ," 526.

to the Israeli civil system, reflecting the religious-political perspective of the nation's thinkers.[87]

This religio-political formulation of national values invites comparison with Carl Schmitt's *Political Theology* (1922), in which he argued that

> [a]ll of the most effective concepts underlying the modern state's political idea are in effect secularizations of theological concepts. That is so not only in terms of historical development, in that they were lfted from religion and reembedded in the political, as in the case of the omnipotence of God, which has become replaced by the all-powerful lawmaker; but rather, it is true, as well, of their systemic structure.[88]

Among many others, Dan Diner and David Ohana have commented on the relevance of Schmitt's categories to the Jewish political lexicon constructed by Ben-Gurion and other national Jewish leaders.[89] In the case at hand, the use of a theological frame of reference, emptied of its religious significance in order to serve an entirely different sphere, receives particular force when portrayed via parody. Dzigan and Shumacher used elements of the sacred in order to emphasize and simultaneously critique Ben-Gurion's style of quasi-sanctified, mythic leadership. The transition from the mystical discourse of theology to the political-secular plane lends (critical) force to the perceived enlargement of the political powers of the state, of the ruling party, and – first and foremost – of the unchallenged leader himself. Parodying the sanctimoniousness of the Israeli political system was a means of de-mystification that aimed to deconstruct its dominant rhetoric.

So too, in the words of Reb Dovidl himself, the Plonsk-Mapai Hasidic sect is depicted as a strict, hierarchal, and undemocratic system that conceals dark secrets. The rigidity of this system is evident in the exorcism, which is not only directed at the dybbuk but is also the punishment for party members who do not agree with the leader's opinions:

> רבי: איין מאָל אין יאָר, אין אַ באַשטימטן טאָג קומען זיך צונויף אויפֿן הייליקסטן אָרט, די הייליקסטע מענטשן פֿון דער הייליקסטער פּאַרטיי און הערן אויס דאָס הייליקע וואָרט פֿון הייליקסטן מענטש, און ווײ איז צו דעם וואָס איז נישט מסכּים מיט זײַן דעה. ס'ווערט חרובֿ זײַן וועלט, זײַן שטוב, זײַן בענקל, זײַן פּרנסה און ער איז נעבעך פֿאַרמישפּט צו זײַן נע־ונד, צו וואַנדערן צווישן אַזיאַטישע פֿעלקער און זיך באַקענען מיט זייערע זיטן ר"ל.[90]

87 On Ben-Gurion's use of the term "messianic vision" as an expression of Zionist ideology, see Shapira, *Yehudim ḥadashim*, 217–47. On the religious rhetoric of the Labor movement see ibid., 238–75.

88 Schmitt, *Political Theology*, 36.

89 Diner, "Ambiguous Semantics." See also Ohana, "Politics of Political Despair," 362–63.

90 This version is from the manuscript. The version on the recording is shorter and more moderate.

> [Reb Dovidl: Once a year, on a certain day, they gather in the holiest place, the holiest people of the holiest party, and they listen to the holy word of the holiest person, and woe to whoever disagrees with his opinion. His world, his home, his position, his livelihood will be destroyed and he, poor thing, is sentenced to become a wanderer, to wander among Asian peoples and to learn the nature of their customs, God forbid.]

As was noted, the duo's arrows of ridicule were aimed also at other politicians, among them Moshe Dayan, Levi Eshkol, and Yitzhak Rabin, but their attitude to Ben-Gurion was unique.[91]

In "Der nayer dibek," Reb Dovidl can be identified as Dovid Grin, the son of Sheyndl and Avigdor, David Ben-Gurion's parents. The Rebbe of Plonsk seamlessly blends with the father of the Hebrew nation, as portrayed by Yisroel Shumacher – complete with his Łódź Yiddish accent. Shumacher's Ben-Gurion persona is a key element in the deconstruction or distortion of the Ben-Gurion myth. This bending of the myth occurs first in the act of impersonation: Shumacher "possesses" Ben-Gurion's image, just as the dybbuk takes spiritual hold of a person's body. Second, taking into account Yechiam Weitz's dictum that "Ben-Gurion and the State of Israel seemed to be one and the same,"[92] not only does the new immigrant actor "displace" the prime minister, but the immigrant "Yisroel" (Yisroel Shumacher), the state of Israel, and the leader (Reb Dovidl/Ben-Gurion) all become one and the same.

A Portrait of the State

The climatic last scene in the skit opens when the beadle, Michael, reports that Grandpa Israel has arrived at Reb Dovidl's *bes-medresh*. Grandpa Israel wants Reb Dovidl to exorcise the dybbuk that has possessed his only daughter, Medinele. Reb Dovidl tries to evade the challenge, claiming that he does not have the power to tackle this problem. His argument is similar to that employed by An-sky's Reb Azriel of Miropol. Likewise, it echoes Ben-Gurion's justification of his retirement to Sde Boker in 1955, which the prime minister explained as due to weakness, exhaustion, and old age.[93] However, Reb Dovidl eventually agrees to try: Medinele-Dzigan then appears on stage, a distorted version of Hanna Rovina playing Leahle, her classic role in Habima.[94] Dzigan's "possession" of Rovina's

---

91 Dzigan, *Der koyekh*, 337.

92 Weitz, "Fanṭazya," 306–7.

93 Ibid.

94 According to the manuscript, after Reb Dovidl refuses to help, it is suggested that they seek aid from another rabbi, named Menachem (Begin), but Reb Dovidl strongly opposes the idea. This has been struck through.

mythical body is evident before he even opens his mouth. Regarding Leah-Rovina as a myth, Dorit Yerushalmi notes:

> She became a symbol, the mother of the nation . . . she stands for both the land and the nation and people, which she personified. Of course, clearly such an identification is a signifying technique that strips Rovina of her specific personhood as an actress, transferring her presence and its significance to the signified, namely, the nation.[95]

As with Shumacher's first appearance on stage as Ben-Gurion, the "possession" of the mythical body of Rovina by Dzigan is evident even before a single word of the script is spoken; indeed, prolonged laughter can be heard on the recording. Medinele-Dzigan is both a Yiddish version and a caricature of "the mother of the nation," "the beautiful nation" symbolized by Rovina, with only the braid and white bridal dress remaining unchanged, a version that reveals the image of the nation in all its diasporic complexity. An interloper, a dybbuk seeking refuge, has taken over the state, invading its body, attaching itself to it and speaking from the state's throat in a masculine voice (and in the Łódź Yiddish dialect). Thus, this is essentially a compounded case of possession: Leah (and by extension, Rovina and the state, Medinele) has been possessed by Dzigan; while, on another level, the state itself has been taken over by the Rebbe (Ben-Gurion/Shumacher), who is responsible for exorcising the dybbuk. This is a grotesque version of the encounter between two Zionist symbols, between the father and mother of the nation, who speak about their troubles in *mame-loshn* (Yiddish).

As in the traditional exorcism ceremony, so too the "new dybbuk" must first be identified.[96] Here, rather than a young lover, he is an immigrant from the bottom of the social ladder, unemployed and homeless; not, as Reb Dovidl first guesses, a politician from the opposition or even Moshe Sneh.[97] Following the identification of the dybbuk, Reb Dovidl demands that he confess his sins, and this is followed by a lengthy negotiation that culminates in his agreement to leave Medinele's body. The dybbuk relates his adventures as a new immigrant and his failed attempts to navigate the Israeli bureaucracy, complaining that he does not

---

95 Yerushalmi, "Betsila shel Hanna Rovina." See also in L. F., "Perasei Yiśra'el": "[Rovina] is also the symbol of the Hebrew Woman."

96 Regarding the development of the traditional ceremony for the exorcism of a dybbuk see Bilu, "Hadibuķ bayahadut."

97 Moshe Sneh was at the time a Member of the Knesset for the Israeli Communist Party (Maki) and was considered a gifted speaker. Rumor had it that Ben-Gurion tried to avoid debates with him in the Knesset at all costs. The possibility that he is the dybbuk depicts him, and perhaps Communism in general, as an alien element in the state. Indeed, when the Tsaddik suggests the name Sneh, Medinele responds: "Moshe Sneh himself has been possessed by a dybbuk."

want to live on a Kibbutz or in the Negev but rather in north Tel Aviv, because he is "not a Zionist."[98] Unable to obtain a place to live or employment, his only option was to find himself a resting place in the state as a dybbuk. "In Israel," the invader justifies himself, "whoever grabs onto a place doesn't leave it." This is a hint at the leader's extended period in office and also the Israeli character, to which Dzigan and Shumacher had already alluded in the past. When Reb Dovidl threatens to use all his power to expel the dybbuk, the interloper responds sarcastically:

> מדינהלע: איך ווייס, אַז איר קאָנט מאַכן פֿון גאָרנישט מיניסטאָרן און פֿון מיניסטאָרן גאָרנישט . . . וואָס קען מיר שוין פּאַסירן? כ'האָב שוין אַלץ פֿאַרלוירן. כ'בין אַראָפּ פֿון דער שיף האָב איך פֿאַרלוירן דעם קאָפּ, אין סוכנות האָב איך פֿאַרלוירן די פֿיס, אין לשכּת־[ה]עבֿודה האָב איך פֿאַרלוירן דאָס האַרץ, אין פּאָרט האָב איך פֿאַרלוירן דעם באַגאַזש... וואָס קען איך נאָך יעצט פֿאַרלירן?
> רבי: וועסט פֿאַרלירן עולם־הבא.
> מדינהלע: דערווײַל דאַרף איך עולם־הזה.
>
> Medinele: I know that you can make ministers out of nothings and make nothings out of ministers . . . what else can happen to me? I've already lost everything. When I got off the ship, I lost my head, in the Jewish Agency, I lost my feet, in the employment agency, I lost my heart, at the port I lost my luggage... What else can I lose?
> Reb Dovidl: Do you want to lose the next life?
> Medinele: In the meantime, I need this one.]

Reb Dovidl and the dybbuk then embark upon negotiations, trying to find terms that will satisfy the new immigrant: he is willing to live in a place where he will be exempt from taxes. Reb Dovidl-Ben-Gurion suggests exile to Eilat, meaning the end of the world.[99]

This episode echoes the personal woes of Dzigan and Shumacher. Indeed, the payment of taxes was one of the most frequent topics in their works and a central issue in contemporaneous public discourse. It also signals a progression in the skit, from sharp political satire to light parody. Reb Dovidl succeeds in stopping the new immigrant's symbolic conquest of the state: using his stick, he marks a circle around Medinele and orders her to stay within this boundary until he instructs her otherwise. At that moment, the dybbuk leaves, descends (*yoyred*, leaves Israel) – he departs from Medinele. Echoing Leah in An-sky's play,

---

98 The answer "I am not a Zionist" is absent from the recording. Presumably, the artists chose to omit it.

99 At that time, Eilat was a regional council with only around 700 inhabitants. The film "'Ir sheshema 'Eilat" (A City Named Eilat, 1963), made by Keren Hayesod to improve the city's image and highlight its development from the mid-1950s until 1963, begins with the sentence that perfectly defines the attitude to Eilat in the 1950s: "That's – some say – the end of the world."

Medinele calls out to the dybbuk-immigrant, asking him to return to her, and in the final sentence she gives in and declares, in his voice: "Oy, immigrant, I can't go on without you." At this point (unlike in the original play), the dybbuk returns and once again takes control of Medinele. It is impossible to determine based on the script and recording whether Medinele breaks out of the circle, as Leah does in the original play. The entire ensemble then sings a love song.

Figure 27: Picture from the skit "Der nayer dibek" (Lydia Shumacher-Ophir collection).

The parody casts the new immigrant, who is "in love" with Medinele, in the role of Ḥanan the Torah scholar. This unnamed new immigrant represents the anonymous collective of new immigrants. Likewise, this immigrant, who loses his way while trying to realize his love for the state, can be seen as the alter-ego of Dzigan and Shumacher themselves. They are of a similar status and similar age to the new immigrant in their parody. They cannot realize their love for the state because they lack the cultural pedigree, the language, the financial support, and the tax exemption needed to do so. Similarly to the dybbuk, they cannot find a place to rest: when the parody was staged, they had not yet purchased a home in Israel, they were living temporarily in the Bristol Hotel, and suffering from the cultural and economic policies that discriminated against Yiddish theater. Just as the dybbuk departs from Leah only to return to her, the new dybbuk, as well as Dzigan and Shumacher, left Israel time after time in order to return to it (see below).

The gender reversal found in "Der nayer dibek" is a tactic commonly used in parodies – a central tool in discrediting conventions and myths. Following Naomi Seidman's lead in discussing An-sky's work from a gender perspective,[100] we can pursue this element further. The use of female actors to portray Reb Dovidl's Hasidim, for instance, highlights the inclusion of women in the body politic and its "male"-dominated discourse. Seidman discusses the ambiguous identity of the dybbuk, moving as it does between life and death, masculine and feminine, transcendental and grotesque, and hence the ambivalence inherent in the interpretation of the character and of An-Sky's play. The dybbuk is beyond physical desires and reformulates the heterosexual gesture – penetration and bonding, pregnancy and birth. Therefore, the decision to cast female actors as Hasidic characters in the parody may signify that women had penetrated the "male" terrain of religious or political knowledge.[101] In his drag performance, Dzigan, in turn, added another layer of physical gender reversal to this mix, emphasizing the hyper-masculine or transsexual profile of "the nation."

Critical Response

The political, social, and cultural criticism voiced in "Der nayer dibek" is sharp but not crude, softened by humor and music. Likewise, a comparison between the two versions (the text from 1956 and the recording from 1957) reveals that the artists chose to temper the skit as they prepared it for performance. Yet the discussions of the parody in the press demonstrate that many still understood its cutting criticism.

Such exposure of the sensitive points in Israeli society and politics had no parallel in other contemporaneous satirical theaters. Reviews of "Der nayer dibek" reveal the tensions that the parody awakened, the varied interpretations that the performance elicited, and, from a wider perspective, the sense of threat

100 Seidman, "Ghost of Queer Loves Past."
101 It should be noted that the casting also resulted from other considerations, among them the limitations of a small troupe and the possibility of the female actors also performing as singers.

that every good satire can arouse. Some reviews were positive, highlighting its excellence and sharpness,[102] noting that it facilitated "a new look at what is happening in the country."[103] One journalist declared that the artists' love of Israel was evident in the skit,[104] and Shumacher's impersonation of Ben-Gurion was an indication of his great admiration for the political leader.[105] However, most reviews considered the skit distasteful, going beyond the boundaries of the allowed and the acceptable. Some negative remarks also referred to the literary merits of the script or alleged that the parody was in poor taste. The newspaper *Haboker*, the mouthpiece of the organization of General Zionists, commented:

> The final part does not fit well with the general level of the show. Despite the talented acting and humorous tone, which is on the mark, this part is in poor taste; a kind of imitation of things that are sacred in Jewish tradition, [things] that many fine actors refrain from mocking.[106]

Al hamishmar noted that the segments "Ha'asḳan hatsioni" (The Zionist Activist) and "Der nayer dibek" "often exceeded the boundaries of [good] taste and the special genre of Dzigan and Shumacher. Until now, their humor was usually more heartwarming than stinging."[107] An article in *Davar* stated:

> Portraying the figure of the prime minister on the satirical stage is not to be forbidden on the grounds of honor and taste. In a democratic country, humor can choose its victim anywhere. It is rather a question of taste and wisdom, of choosing between high-level humor and artificial parody, not without signs of intentional foolishness. This is not a defense of the prime minister's honor, but rather our own honor, the honor of the humor that we enjoy, or which disgusts us.[108]

Perhaps the harshest reaction was penned by Avrom-Shmuel Yuris, who claimed that the artists presumed too much in trying to deal with high politics, and this attempt resulted in failure:

> This time Dzigan and Shumacher failed. They lost their way because they tried to deal with high politics. This is not a parody or a satire. My conclusion: even the best work by Shudzig should be "corrected" and even censored by its most "professional" authors.[109]

102 Y. Ḥ., "'Emesh bate'aṭron"; Shtern, "'Oḳtsanut."
103 Feuerstein, "Tish'a ḳabin."
104 Shtern, "'Oḳtsanut."
105 Y. Ḥ., "'Emesh bate'aṭron."
106 D., "Tokhnit ḥadasha."
107 *Al hamishmar*, "Ḥadshot 'omanut ṿetarbut."
108 A. Z., "Tish'a ḳabin."
109 Yuris, "Dzigan–Shumacher."

This was the not the first time that critics had condemned the acidity of the duo's satire. Indeed, as early as 1950 (see chapter 4), a journalist who signed with the pen name "Segol" wrote that their shows sometimes went beyond the bounds of good taste: "We, for example, are disgusted by the fact that they joke at the expense of a flag, even if it is the flag of another nation . . . interestingly, in the history of humor, the Christian church defended such comedy for reasons of acclimation. We cannot become so acclimatized." Furthermore, he added, "For an Israeli audience, the stage is not the same as it is for others, there is a limit to what is permissible."[110] In the case of "Der nayer dibek," some of the negative reviews focused on the literary quality of the text or the poor taste of the parody. Yet it seems that these aspects were not the real reason for the critics' discomfort.[111] Rather, the actors' parodic and satirical-critical portrayal of the sacred cows of Israeli politics and culture, as well as Jewish tradition, made them uneasy. The words of Yuris and others reveal the threatening dimension of Dzigan and Shumacher's parody. Indeed, according to those reviewers, the artists had strayed too far beyond the limits of freedom of speech, even for satirical theater.

Between Imitation and Criticism

Irony, which is an inseparable part of parody, is a discursive strategy that depends on the content of the text, the identity of the person using it, and the audience and their ideological positions. It exists on an axis between conservatism and revolutionary change. Irony is not only a means to oppose authority but can also to interpret reality.[112] Unsurprisingly, in the contemporaneous Israeli reality, not everyone construed "Der nayer dibek" in the same manner. The various understandings of the skit indicate not only the fundamental ambivalence to the genres of parody and satire but also the significance of the context in which this specific skit was performed and the extent to which it was subversive.

According to Linda Hutcheon, parody can be defined as "a form of repetition with ironic critical distance."[113] The tension between imitation and criticism, essential parts of parody, reflects the complexity of the genre and its capacity to elicit different interpretations. In this case, if the social role of an exorcism is to preserve the social order, and if An-sky's play was intended to preserve Jewish

110 Segol, "Dzigan ṿeShumacher."

111 The performance received enthusiastic responses from reviewers and, as we can hear on the recording, exceptional praise from the audience.

112 Hutcheon, *Theory of Parody*.

113 Ibid.

life, "Der nayer dibek" constituted an attempt to influence the interpretation of the social order.[114] The skit could potentially cast doubt upon the monolithic understanding of the contemporary national narrative; more precisely, it could publicly present an alternative reading, one that had never before been presented on the satirical stage in Israel, and breach, rhetorically and symbolically, the political and ideological status quo.

From their first public performances in Israel in the 1950s, Dzigan and Shumacher's art conformed more or less to the topics and standards of contemporaneous Israeli satire, mostly critiquing bureaucracy and corruption. However, it also incorporated sharp political satire – a novelty on the newly independent Israeli scene. In "Der nayer dibek," the comedians pushed beyond their previous satirical boundaries, embracing a blunter form of political commentary. In this sense, they took on the role that Yochai Oppenheimer attributed to the early works of the playwright Hanoch Levin in the late 1960s, who was active during the earliest stages of Hebrew-language political satire in the Israeli theater. Preceding Levin's early work by a decade, "Der nayer dibek" desecrated sacred cows and questioned the underlying ideological foundations of Israeli society, seeking to persuade the audience that "the accepted shibboleths are nothing but rhetoric."[115] The "shibboleths" at stake in this case in fact delegitimized any alternative mode of thinking about the country, its policies, or its social forms (such as a hypothetically multilingual and multicultural social sphere) – that is, any perspective not hegemonically enshrined by the powers-that-be. The satirical revisionism worked toward undoing the state's established rhetorical canon.

According to Leonard Feinberg, the satirist does not really expect moral change or correction, nor does he propose any realistic alternative.[116] The alternative that Dzigan and Shumacher suggested was not at the national level but rather at the level of the individual. They presented a survival tactic – a guide for coping with the Kafkaesque system that the individual faced, a tactic that Michel de Certeau defines as a practice of daily resistance: taking advantage of every opportunity that the system offers and every loophole within it, while constantly struggling and negotiating with it.[117] If these tactics ultimately fail, the option of holding fast to the state, capturing and conquering it in the form of a dybbuk, still remains.

---

114 Bilu, "Hadibuḳ bayahadut," 554–58. An-Sky himself claimed that the play was intended to contribute to maintaining the national existence. See An-Sky, "Vegen dem dibek."

115 Oppenheimer, "Hanoch Levin."

116 Feinberg, *The Satirist*, 35, 83.

117 Certeau, *Everyday Life*.

A Foreign and Grating Voice

In "Der nayer dibek," Dzigan and Shumacher strove to demystify national myths – Habima's *The Dybbuk* (by means of parody)[118] and David Ben-Gurion (via satire).[119] Habima continued to perform the classic version of this central work in its repertoire and was declared Israel's national theater in 1958 – one year after the performance of Dzigan and Shumacher's parody; David Ben-Gurion likewise served as prime minister until he finally (and permanently) stepped down in 1963. This demystification was accomplished through a process of linguistic, ethical, and cultural translation and the displacement of key myths from the Hebraic-Zionist iconography (Ben-Gurion, Rovina, and Habima), replanting them in the mythic world of Jewish Eastern Europe, or, in other words, adapting them to the Yiddish heritage.

A reading of "Der nayer dibek" in the context of scholarship on the dybbuk in Jewish culture places the new immigrant (as portrayed in the parody) alongside apostates, heretics, and other sinners, especially informers, murderers, and suicides.[120] According to tradition, the dybbuk is the spirit of a dead person who takes over a living body. In Dzigan and Shumacher's social-political metaphor, this is the status of the new immigrant in Israel and, by the same token, of the immigrant Yiddish actor. According to Rachel Elior and Yoram Bilu, the dybbuk has the power to reveal dark secrets from the community's past and voice aggressive, sexual, and anti-religious urges that are taboo in any other context. Indeed, the dybbuk had the capacity to challenge the traditional Jewish way of life.[121] In this sense, Dzigan and Shumacher were like a dybbuk in Israel: they were separated from the body of the community and the social consensus, liberated from the established norms dictating the rights of speech and silence. They demanded the voice that was denied to them and those they represented in Israel – the "diasporic" Yiddish-speaking Jews whose voice "speaks from the mouths" of Dzigan and Shumacher.[122] With characteristic humor, they revealed "secrets" and opinions that were repressed and excluded from the public Hebrew

118 Another attempt to demystify the classic version of *The Dybbuk* was the play staged by Habima in 1997, directed by Hanan Snir, forty years after "Der nayer dibek." See Yerushalmi, "The Habimah 'Dybbuk.'"

119 "A foreign and grating voice" were Ben-Gurion's words following a Yiddish speech given by Rozka Korczak, who was one the leaders of the Jewish organization of fighters in the Vilna ghetto, at the Histadrut convention, December 12, 1944, see Rachel Rojanski, *Yiddish in Israel*, 30. These words aroused a commotion in the hall and Ben-Gurion's speech was interrupted.

120 Elior, "Hadibuḳ," 519–20.

121 Elior, "Hadibuḳ"; Bilu, "Hadibuḳ bayahadut."

122 Efrat, "Tseḥoḳ go'el."

discourse using the body of their victim, which was also the body responsible for their oppression: the social, cultural, and political body that was at once beloved and alien.

In the language of the theater, "Der nayer dibek" paved a path to create a parallel universe, a counter-territory to the regnant reality. As the masters-of-ceremony in a rite of reversal, Dzigan and Shumacher established a state within a state, wherein language is not just a cultural aspect, an attribute of the individual's singular or corporate (ethno-national) identity, and also not a negative aspect or a symbol of difference. Rather, for Dzigan and Shumacher, language, as in the phenomenon of the dybbuk, was a strategic weapon in the fight for free cultural expression.

A literary analysis of the skit would designate it as a metaphor for Yiddish theater in Israel, or at least for the theater of Dzigan and Shumacher. The liminality deployed in "Der nayer dibek" is multidimensional, allowing for the expression not only of the "alien and discordant" rejected voice but also of the unresolved tensions between the living body and the dead spirit, between the immigrant and the national leader, between Yiddish and the Yiddish-speaking citizens of Israel. The new immigrant and the Yiddish language take possession of the state and express its unconscious, repressed urges. This constituted an attempt at cultural revolution, as Yiddish speakers demanded their rightful place in this new world order.

In the Plonsker Rebbe's Yeshiva

The critical discourse regarding the Israeli leadership continued in Dzigan's theatrical work after he and Shumacher parted ways. In 1961, four years after "Der nayer dibek" was performed, Dzigan staged a revue entitled *Tsit mikh nisht bay der tsung!* (Don't Put Words in My Mouth!), directed by Shraga Fridman. One skit in this show returned to the Rebbe of Plonsk: "In der yeshive fun Dovidl Plonsker" (In the Plonsker Rebbe's Yeshiva). This was an abbreviated adaptation of a Hebrew text originally written by Yosef Vinitsky (Y. Nets) for Dzigan and Shumacher, entitled "Shi'urei hatanakh shel Ben-Gurion" (Ben-Gurion's Bible Lessons) [See Figure 28].[123]

123 According to the manuscript, the text was adapted in the years 1957–1959. Apparently, Dzigan and Shumacher planned to perform the skit together, but the dissolution of their partnership made this impossible. Yosef Vinitsky (1914–1965), known by his pen name Y. Nets or Yosef Levi, was a journalist, publicist, author, and translator, whose writing often demonstrated satirical characteristics. He published a column in the weekly *La'isha* (the women's weekly, part of *Yedioth Ahronoth*) and wrote articles for *Letste nayes*.

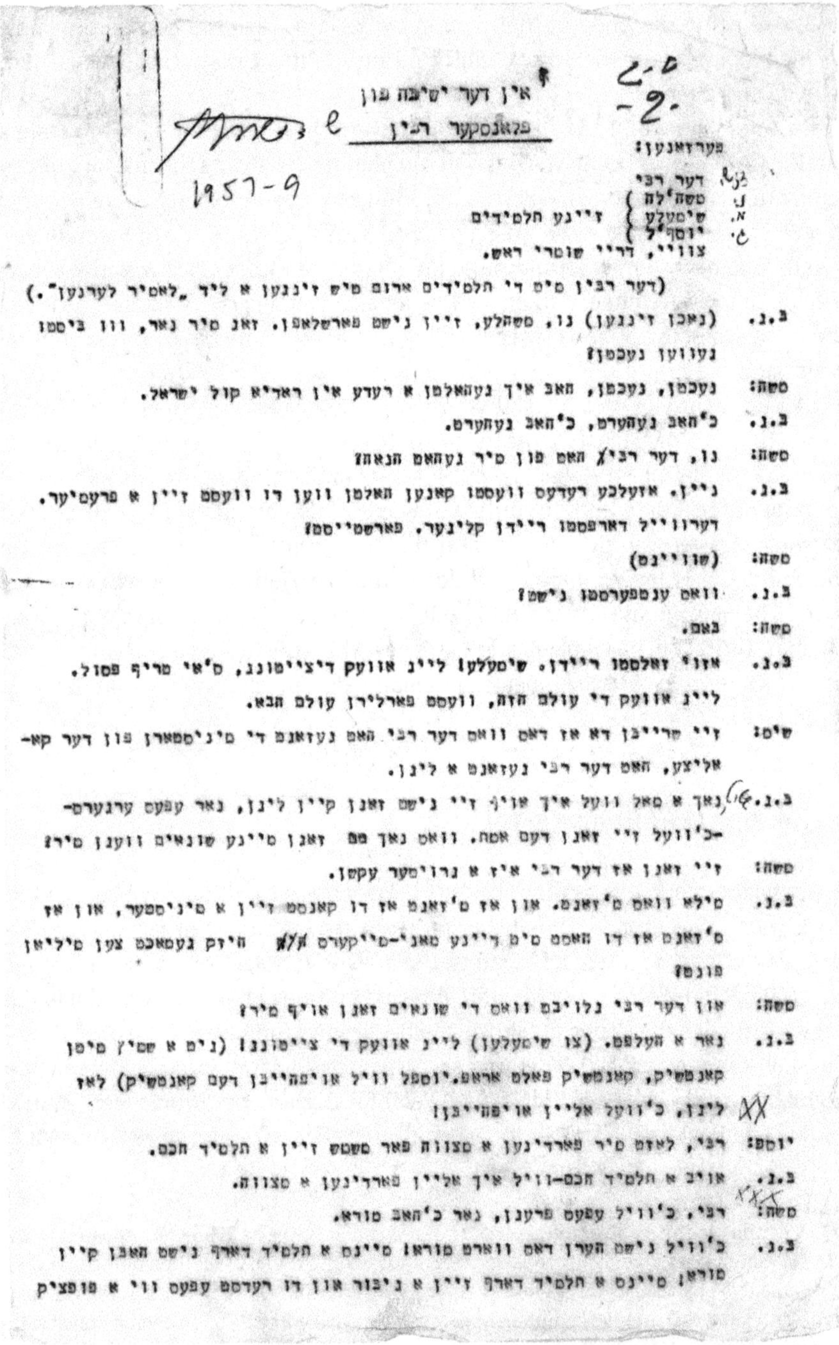

Figure 28: Script of the skit "In der yeshive fun Dovidl Plonsker" (BAA, file 177–04).

In this skit, Reb Dovidl once again displays an uncanny resemblance to David Ben-Gurion. As in "Der nayer dibek," he is an all-knowing rabbi whose students stand in awe of him.[124] However, this time the audience watches as he gives a bible lesson to four of his Hasidim. Unlike the anonymous Hasidim in "Der nayer dibek," these characters are clearly identified: Moyshele (Moshe Dayan), Shimele (Shimon Peres), Yosele (Yosef Almogi, secretary of Mapai), and Abale (Abba Eban). Thus, the satire is directed not only at the leader of the nation (and the party) but also at the entire leadership of Israel's ruling party.

The lesson itself is a satire on the dynamics, hierarchy, and power relations among the senior echelons of the leading party. For instance, Reb Dovidl criticizes an interview that Moyshele (Dayan) gave on Kol Yiśra'el (Israel Radio). He explains to his disciple that since he is not yet prime minister, he is allowed to say a few intelligent things and there was therefore no reason to completely avoid saying anything sensible in the radio interview. Reb Dovidl also forbids Shimele (Peres) to read the newspaper. He is an aggressive and impatient teacher. Furthermore, he demands that fearless: "A student of mine must be a hero," he says to Shimele, "and you are talking like a five-year-old child." In response, Shimele argues that nothing frightens him apart from one man – his historic political rival:

> אַלע ווייסן אַז איך האָב נישט קיין מורא, נישט פֿאַר קיין פֿײַער נישט פֿאַר קיין וואַסער, כ'האָב נישט מורא פֿאַר קיין באָמבעס און האַרמאַטן, כ'האָב נישט מורא פֿאַר 40 מיליאָן אַראַבער. נאָר אַז כ'זיץ נעבן [יצחק] ראַבין, ציטער איך.
>
> [Everyone knows that I'm not afraid (of anything), not of fire and not of water, I'm not afraid of bombs or cannon-fire, I'm not afraid of forty million Arabs. But when I sit next to (Yitzhak) Rabin, I quake.]

This joke not only emphasized one of the central rivalries in Mapai, dating back to the 1960s, but also prioritized internal Jewish conflicts and party rivalries over the conflict with the Arabs.

Meanwhile, in response to every sentence Reb Dovidl says, the Hasidim intone "bim-bom," signifying their blind faith in him. When Reb Dovidl asks for a stronger endorsement, they say it louder: "Bim-bom!" "That's the way I like it. That's clear," declares Reb Dovidl.

---

124 This also applies to other skits, such as "Futbol-metsh," mentioned above, and the monologue "Itshe balegole" written by Yosef Heiblum: "Ben-Gurion was also my passenger. He wasn't an easy passenger. He was a difficult one. He didn't like it that someone else was holding the reins." BAA, file 178–02.

Ben-Gurion, Reb Dovidl, has the power and authority to change and rewrite the law, to interpret the Bible anew, and he even compares himself with the Creator of the Universe: Ben-Gurion created the earth of Israel, or more accurately improved it:

> גאָט האָט באַשאַפֿן די הימלען. גוט, מסכּים . . . אָבער די ערד? וועלכע ערד? די ערד פֿון אונדזער לאַנד? אַ שיין פּנים האָט געהאַט דאָס לאַנד איידער איך בין אַהערגעקומען. אַ שיין פּנים. שטיינער, זאַמדן, זומפּן.
>
> [God created the sky. Good, I agree . . . but the earth? What earth? The earth of our Land? What a dump this place was before I got here, what a sight! Stones, sands, swamps.]

Ben-Gurion, the national and divine contractor, contacts Yosef Almogi, a Mapai Knesset Member, asking him to alter the biblical text so that only the creation of the heavens is left to the Almighty. The lesson continues with a series of new biblical interpretations and explanations of various miracles performed by Reb Dovidl.

The skit made waves not only among critics and the audience but also among members of the government. Following the premiere, which was staged during the run-up to elections, Dzigan met with Yosef Almogi in Café Lilit in Tel Aviv. According to Dzigan's account of this meeting, the politician informed him that there was "serious concern among Mapai's election staff that the skit might influence the voter to vote against the ruling party."[125] However, Ben-Gurion and Mapai were ultimately victorious in the closely contested elections for the fifth Knesset. While Dzigan's influence was not sufficient to alter the political order, he was nonetheless perceived as affecting the public pre-election discourse.

For many years, David Ben-Gurion constituted a central target of the artists' satirical criticism, in monologues and jokes on stage, and sometimes in media statements. In particular, they often referred to his lengthy term as prime minister:

> ווען אַ קינד ווערט געבוירן, קושט אים אַ מלאַך. גיט ער אים אַ קוש אין קאָפּ, וואַקסט עס אויס אַ דענקער. קושט ער אים אויף די ליפּן, וועט ער זײַן אַ רעדנער. פֿאַלט זײַן קוש אויף די הענט, וועט ער זײַן אַ פּיאַניסט. ווו האָט דער מלאַך אַ קוש געטאָן בן־גוריונען, אַז ער זיצט שוין אַזוי לאַנג אויף זײַן פּאָסטן...?[126]

125 Ben-Shlomo, "'Almogi biḳesh." Ben-Gurion openly stated (in 1957) that he felt a connection with the Bible but negated the Talmud and everything deriving from it that was created during the two thousand years of exile. This ignited a sharp controversy, and he was even accused of adopting a Canaanite stance toward diasporic Jewish culture. See Shapira, "Ben-Gurion ṿeha-Tanakh." The polemic was advanced aggressively by the writer and journalist Mordkhe Strigler, a Holocaust survivor, in a serious of articles against Ben-Gurion. See Szeintuch, "Mordkhe Strigler"; compare the opposition of the writer Haim Hazaz to Ben-Gurion's opinions on the importance of the Bible and the negation of the Talmud and the culture of the exile. See Bodenheimer, *Heḥaver miPlonsḳ*.

126 Dzigan, *Der koyekh*, 337.

[When a child is born, an angel kisses him. If he gives him a kiss on the head, he grows up a thinker. If he gives him a kiss on the lips, he grows up a good speaker. If the kiss falls on the hands, he will be a pianist. Where did the angel kiss Ben-Gurion, that he has held on to his post for so long?...]

A similar motif recurs in the dialogue "Dzigan ṿeShumacher be1980" (Dzigan and Shumacher in 1980), which was performed in the show *Tate, du lakhst!* (Father, You're Laughing!, 1950). In the imaginary conversation between the two in 1980, Ben-Gurion is still the only ruler: "Today we have only one party, one chair, one minister, one comedian, everything is done by one man: Ben-Gurion."

"Goldenyu" (1971) and "Golde baym poypst" (1973)

In the monologue "Goldenyu" (Our Dear Golda), which Dzigan wrote and staged in 1971 as part of his revue *Men lakht a lebn* (Laughing at Life), Dzigan played Prime Minister Golda Meir speaking to "the citizens of the nation." In the skit, she describes her meeting with American President Richard Nixon in Washington D.C., which had taken place a few months earlier. At the time, this meeting was considered a diplomatic coup; in its wake, Israel received American loans, and, according to political folklore, the two leaders also reached an agreement regarding both the purchase of American weaponry and the willingness of the American government to look the other way while Israel developed nuclear weapons.[127]

Dzigan's monologue did not focus on the nuclear issue, but rather on Golda's success in raising money and the gossip surrounding the journey. The Israeli prime minister speaks in folksy Yiddish. She depicts her successful trip to the United States in a manner that combines gossip, jokes, and ironic comments concerning various Israeli political figures. She tells stories about the increasingly friendly relationship between the two countries, using the metaphor of a couple in love; she confesses her fear of Communism (despite being a socialist), and eventually admits the real reason for her trip: *shnorering*, begging for handouts.

Both the content and narrative structure of "Goldenyu" draw liberally upon Yiddish cultural and literary traditions. Political-national discourse mixes indiscriminately with intimate household affairs. The journey to a world power in order to obtain financial support, weapons, and agreements is presented as a story about a Jewish mother who goes begging to the *porets* (Polish landowner).

---

127 The discussion of "Goldenyu" is based on the manuscript, BAA/Dz, 179–01, as well as the commercial recording of the monologue filmed by Israeli television in 1975. The discussion of "Golde baym poypst" is based on transcripts, BAA/Dz, 178–02.

By means of language and performance, Golda (the public personage) becomes "Goldenyu" (the lady from next door). In Dzigan's words, the prime minister is "the mother of the Jewish state." The dissonance between mother figure and state leader is exaggerated in the script as the audience hears about her reception in America: [Yiddish] "When we reached New York, the military band played *Hatikvah*, and afterwards, in my honor, they played a bit from *Mayn yidishe mame.*" Thus, Dzigan's Israel is one expanded Jewish family, and its prime minister is universally recognized as the quintessential Jewish mother.

Dzigan was not the only one to connect between the political and the domestic levels of discourse. The Israeli media regularly referred to Golda using gendered stereotypes – for instance, her inner forum of close advisers was nicknamed "Golda's kitchen." According to Dalia Gavrieli Nuri, this metaphor was meant to convey a secretive, nondemocratic method of fundamental decision-making, often in the realm of state security.[128] Another popular term among journalists was "Golda's shopping basket," which was used to refer to the prime minister's trips for security purchasing – the phantom jets, tanks, and missiles that she obtained at her meetings with President Richard Nixon.[129] Dzigan hints at this shopping basket, alluding mysteriously to the suitcases Goldenyu brings home from her trip.

In his monologue, Dzigan emphasized diametrically opposing elements in Golda Meir's image, such as the tension between her feminine and masculine attributes. This tension is expressed in both the text and the performance: a man plays the role of a woman who was sometimes perceived as "masculine." In the stage directions, Dzigan noted that Golda was to wave to the audience "with her hand up, in the masculine way." In the script, Golda-Dzigan says: "I spoke to the President . . . man to man" – a reference to Ben-Gurion's famous quip that Golda "is the only man in the government." This gender reversal – or crossdressing – recalls another figure: Yente, the heroine of Sholem Aleichem's monologue "Dos tepl" (The Pot), in which an independent woman copes with the challenges of her family's livelihood after the death of her husband. "In incautious moments," writes Dan Miron of Yente, "she [Yente] even speaks about herself in the masculine form, as if she were a man, and not just a man but an experienced man of the world."[130]

In contrast to the reviews of "Der nayer dibek," in which theater critics expressed their aversion to playing fast and loose with the "holy of holies" of

---

128 Gavrieli-Nuri, "Hamitbaḥ shel Golda."
129 Ibid.
130 Miron, *Hatsad ha'afel*, 26.

Israeli politics, "Goldenyu" received no such overt criticism. Dzigan's role-playing was not perceived as threatening. The critics even praised the verisimilitude of his imitation and noted that an underlying admiration for Golda was evident despite the satire. Indeed, Dzigan's impersonation of Golda was considered a tour de force, picture-perfect (both in the physical sense and in the spirit of the characterization) as well as soft-edged. He had studied her body language and speech patterns carefully, paid close attention to her television and public appearances, and even visited her privately at home. In his memoirs, Dzigan claimed that his imitation was incredibly accurate: so much so, that at the first performance of this skit, the audience was taken back, believing that the prime minister herself was standing on stage.[131] "When an impressionist, as talented as he may be, impersonates Abba Eban or Ben-Gurion, his work focuses on the technical-external side, in terms of pronunciation and intonation," wrote Naḥman Ben-Ami. "However, when Dzigan impersonates, for example... Golda – the moment he appears on stage . . . before even opening his mouth, in an impersonation so considered and so accurate, so spiritual-physical and so close to the mark, he already sends his audience into an extended commotion of laughter."[132]

Another skit, "Golde baym poypst" (Golda Visits the Pope), written by Mark Sidonia Sidon and adapted by Dzigan, is characterized by comparable satirical qualities and a similar tone. This skit offers a "reconstruction" of Golda Meir's visit to Pope Paul VI in the Vatican on January 16, 1973. Golda Meir's memoirs describe the encounter as a meeting of opposites: between a simple Jewish woman, albeit the prime minister of Israel, and the head of the Catholic Church.[133] Dzigan, once again playing Golda, exaggerated these differences for their comedic effect, highlighting the inappropriate behavior of the "simple" visitor, who enters the Pope's presence bareheaded, turns her back on him, and refuses to eat the food he offers her.

At the real meeting, Golda Meir responded to the papal criticism of how Israel treated Palestinian detainees, describing the terror attacks perpetrated by these "terrorists" against the Israeli population. Ex post facto she stated: "It may not have been a conventional way of talking to the pope, but I felt that I was speaking for all Jews everywhere, for those who were alive and those who had perished . . ."[134]

Golda-Dzigan refuses to reach a peace agreement with the Arabs, as the Pope requests, because peace can only be made, she argues, within secure borders. Golda-Dzigan also invites the Pope to speak in Yiddish, explaining that she can

131 Dzigan, *Der koyekh*, 362.
132 Ben-Ami, "Matsḥiḳ."
133 Meir, *My Life*, 406–10.
134 Meir, *My Life*, 408.

Figure 29: Dzigan playing Golda Meir (BAA, file 146–04).

grant him this courtesy since they are not on Israeli (Hebrew) television [Figure 29]. Thus, the ceremonious meeting takes place in a familiar and intimate tone that could never have been achieved in real life. The two try to reach a mutual understanding with regard to the inauguration of diplomatic relations (at the time, the Vatican did not recognize the State of Israel); at the end of the skit, before they part, the two dance a hora together. Golda, with her Jewish sharp-wittedness, makes her agreement dependent on her friend Nixon:

> . . . אַז יעזוס איז געבוירן געוואָרן, קאָן איך גלויבן; אַז פֿון הייליקן גײַסט – זאָל ער גלויבן. אַז יעזוס איז געשטאָרבן – דאָס קען איך גלויבן; אַז ער איז נאָך דרײַ טעג אויפֿגעשטאַנען תּחית־המתים, זאָל ער גלויבן. אַז ר'האָט צעטיילט צוויי ברויט פֿאַר זעכציק מענטשן, קאָן איך גלויבן; אַז זיי זענען געוואָרן זאַט, זאָל ער גלויבן.
>
> [. . . That Jesus was born, I can believe; that he was born from the Holy Spirit – let him believe it. That Jesus died – I can believe; that he rose from the dead after three days – let him believe it. That he divided two loaves of bread between sixty people, I can believe it; that they all had enough to eat – let him believe it.]

When the Pope comments that he would like to live in Jerusalem, however his job does not allow it, Golda responds that he is talking just like Dr. Nahum Goldman, the president of the World Jewish Congress, who lives in the diaspora. Golda asks to borrow Michelangelo's sculpture *Moses*, which the Pope describes as a treasure, offering in exchange "our Moses" (Moshe Dayan), also a "treasure." When they part, Golda distributes presents: to the Pope she presents the shofar that Rabbi Shlomo Goren[135] blew after the liberation of the Western Wall, and to the cardinal she gives a scarf – a present for his wife (he responds by reminding her that his religion forbids him to marry a woman). The Pope gives Golda "a dove of peace," and Golda thanks him and expresses hope that in Israel the dove will not become deaf (a play on the Yiddish word *toyb* which means both dove and deaf) [See Figure 30].

Figure 30: Dzigan playing "Golde baym poypst" (BAA, file 146–04).

The monologue "Goldenyu" and the skit "Golde baym poypst" are by no means literary masterpieces. They are less critical and less incisive than the political satires that Dzigan and Shumacher performed together. They do not reproach Golda Meir or her policies as they did Ben-Gurion. Despite the gender inversion, which in a way intensifies the subversive nature of the skits, the imitation of

135 Chief Rabbi of the Israel Defense Forces and the third Ashkenazi Chief Rabbi of Israel.

Golda reflects a certain intimacy with its subject and even arouses empathy. In the eyes of the critics, the inoffensive style compensated for the satirical representation of the prime minister in a language that was not the state's official tongue. (In this regard, it is noteworthy that Golda Meir, unlike Ben-Gurion, displayed an affinity for Yiddish; among other things, she attended performances by Dzigan and Shumacher.)

Slavoj Žižek has posited that those hostile to the ruling power may use a "critical tactic of over-identification" as a ploy: they demonstrate an obsessive fascination with the dominant ideology instead of preserving a proper distance from it, thus adopting a position that is too close for comfort.[136] This critical tactic was employed consciously by Dzigan and Shumacher in "Der nayer dibek." Conversely, in "Goldenyu," the exaggerated identification does not succeed in conveying criticism or even cause discomfort. Rather, it creates a "parallel reality": Dzigan offers himself as the double of both Golda and the state, leading a parallel nation that conducts its matters in a different language and with a generous sprinkling of humor.

Dzigan was reputedly delighted by (and spread) a joke that was popular among Yiddish speakers: according to this joke, when the pope met Golda Meir in 1973 (two years after "Goldenyu" was staged), he greeted her with the words: "Pleased to meet you, Mr. Dzigan."[137] When the mimic turns into the original, or the original turns into the imitator, the duplication creates a parallel reality. In his memoirs, Dzigan relates that the actor who suggested he impersonate Golda Meir said to him, "Look at your nose. It looks as though you took it right off her face." "You mean," answered Dzigan, "that thanks to my nose I can replace her as prime minister?"[138] Dzigan claimed that, for a certain period of time, there were, in a sense, two prime ministers in Israel – two states, two Goldas – and the boundary between them had become so blurred that the theatergoers could not only see Golda in Dzigan (as noted by reviewers) but also Dzigan in Golda.

The Poetics of the Diasporic Body and the Zionist Appearance

The process of approaching and figuratively blemishing the sanctified image of mythic figures begins with the body. In "Der nayer dibek," as we saw, Ben-Gurion, portrayed by Yisroel Shumacher, became a satiric icon of the diaspora figure who

136 Žižek, *Plague*.

137 There were a few versions of this joke involving other international characters: "Golda met the king of Sweden, and he shook her hand and said: It's nice to meet you, Mr. Dzigan!"

138 Dzigan, *Der koyekh*, 361.

speaks *mame-loshn* with a Łódź accent. The actor's body, claims John Rouse, can be interpreted as a text in which cultural norms are written, embroidered, or formed via stylistic codes of performative behavior.[139] In their theater, Dzigan and Shumacher presented their acclimatization to the Israeli reality not only via language but also through their body and their appearance. The only alternative available to the Polish Jew in Israel was to translate and adapt to the local milieu. However, a symbolic detail from his own past remained – the red kerchief became a *lieu de mémoire* to the diasporic Jew:

> כ'האָב געזוכט פֿאַרטרעטער פֿון מײַן פּוילישן ייִד מיט דער רויטער פֿאַטשיילע . . . כ'האָב אים, מײַן ייִד מיט דער קאַפּאָטע און דאָס קליינע היטעלע, געוואָלט איבערפֿלאַנצן אַהער, אויף דעם ישׂראלדיקן באָדן. כ'האָב געזוכט און געפֿונען. כ'האָב גענומען דעם שטאָטישן פּרנסה־זוכער און אַרויפֿגעצויגן אויף אים אַ דאָרפֿישע הויט. כ'האָב מײַן ייִד אויסגעטאָן די קאַפּאָטע און אים געגעבן א כאַקי־בלוזע מיט קורצע הײזלעך. אויפֿן קאָפּ האָב איך אים אַרויפֿגעטאָן אַ טעמבעל . . . בלויז די רויטע פֿאַטשיילע האָב איך איבערגעלאָזט אין זײַן האַנט ווי אַ סימבאָל פֿון המשכדיקייט . . . : שלום תּל־אָבֿיבֿער! עץ דערקאָנט מיך? כ'זע שוין אויס ווי אַ סאַברע, נײַן? כ'האָב אַראָפּגעוואָרפֿן פֿון זיך דעם גלות, אויס קאַפּאָטע, בלויז מיט דער פֿאַטשיילע קאָן איך מיך נישט שיידן. צוואַנציק יאָר איז זי געווען מיט מיר, געדינט צו דער נאָז, דערנאָך בײַ די נאַציס, צו די אויגן . . . אין ראַטן־פֿאַרבאַנד האָב איך די פֿאַטשיילע גענוצט פֿאַר אַ פֿאָן. דאָ, אין ישׂראל, נוצט זי מיר קעגן שווייס... איך אַרבעט אויפֿן דאָרף. כ'בין אַ קיבוצניק.[140]

> [I looked for a substitute for my Polish Jew with his red kerchief . . . I wanted to replant him here, in Israel, my Jew with the kaftan and the little hat. I searched and I found what I was looking for: I took the urban jobseeker and dressed him up in village garb. I removed from my Jew the kaftan and dressed him in a khaki shirt and short trousers. On his head I placed a *tembel* hat [a round brimless hat that became a national symbol] . . . but I left the red kerchief in his hand as a symbol of continuity . . . Shalom, people of Tel Aviv! Do you recognize me? I look like a sabra, no? I have divested myself of the diaspora, the kaftan, but I cannot take leave of the red kerchief. It has been with me for twenty years, wiping my nose, afterwards, with the Nazis, it wiped my eyes. . . . In the Soviet Union, I used the kerchief as a flag. Here, in Israel, I use it to wipe my brow... I work in the village. I am a kibbutznik.]

"Der kibbutsnik" (The Monologue of the Kibbutznik) written by Dzigan and Shumacher, created tension between the Jewish body and its clothes, between the language (Yiddish) and the process of becoming a sabra. Although the character's clothing undergoes a process of cultural translation, his language remains the same. The body and language remain alien to the clothing. The new Jew cannot hide the fact that he is unable to abandon his previous identity. It is not only the Yiddish language that symbolizes continuity but also the red kerchief and the (fake) beard. The kibbutznik claims that he is ridding himself of his diasporic persona, but at the same time he is still cleaving to the typical beard, the red

---

139 Rouse, "Textuality," 155.
140 Dzigan, *Der koyekh*, 310–13.

kerchief, the language (Yiddish), and his Jewish diasporic body language. Dzigan himself reveals in this monologue his desire "to take root," leaving in the past his Jew with the kaftan and his little hat, but it is unclear whether the Polish Jew becomes a sabra or rather, by contrast, an East European Jewish dybbuk possesses the kibbutznik, causing him to undergo an opposing process of adaptation – bodily, linguistic, and cultural.

This monologue expresses the complex process of cultural adaptation that Dzigan, and by extension the Polish Jew, experienced as he tried to adapt to the local reality. The acclimatization is not complete. Dzigan's kibbutznik reveals himself to be a hybrid of sabra and diasporic Jew who carries diaspora Jewry's traumatic memory, mediated by language and by the symbol of the red kerchief.

Dzigan and Shumacher took over Israeli bodies for the purpose of interpreting them, criticizing them, or identifying with them. For the duration of the performance, they took possession of local characters and created distorted interpretations of the Israeli sabra, as viewed through the eyes of the Eastern European Jew. Dzigan and Shumacher did not want to become sabras and did not do so; they dressed themselves up as sabras in carnivals of Yiddishland, of Dzigan and Shumacher's state, wherein the symbol of Eastern European Jewish culture became at once an expression of their consolidated and deconstructed identity.

In "Der nayer dibek," for instance, the diaspora body and the Zionist body merged in the figure of Reb Dovidl from Plonsk. In both "In der yeshive fun Dovidl Plonsker" and in "Goldenyu," the Yiddish actor is also in a state of *hefker* (lawlessness), as defined by Der Tunkeler, and consequently freely parodies religious texts and traditions.[141] Finally, Dzigan's personification of Medinele in "Der nayer dibek" and of Golda Meir in the two skits discussed added an element of gender reversal, addressing the masculinity that was considered a key aspect in the formation of the nation. As such, it served to deride some of the accepted portrayals of Israel and Israelis: if Golda Meir is the only real "man" in the Israeli government, then the government is a carnival. This metaphorical reality was realized when Dzigan played Golda and essentially took possession of her. Similarly to the original *The Dybbuk*, from the lover's perspective, the dybbuk symbolizes "the ultimate romantic gesture, a union of their souls in the absence of any possibility for earthly marriage."[142] Reb Dovidl-Shumacher, Medinele-Dzigan, and Golda-Dzigan are different expressions of the impossible love relationship between the Hebrew state and the Yiddish actor.

---

141 Tunkeler, *Sefer hahumoresḳot*, 71–83.
142 Seidman, "Ghost of Queer Loves Past."

In his book *Haguf hatsioni* (The Zionist Body), Michael Gluzman highlights that from the 1970s, "Hebrew literature began to generate a multifaceted discourse about the imperfection of the Jewish body. This literature – which was at the center of national thought – depicted the Jewish male as someone exiled not only from his land but also from his body and his masculinity."[143] The diasporic Jew is depicted as lacking roots, manipulative and cowardly, old and sick, without hope and with no protection against persecution, in contrast to the new Hebrew, later known as the sabra, who is young, strong, brave and resourceful.[144]

When the new immigrant – a male, Yiddish-speaking Jew from the diaspora – takes over the body of the Hebrew-speaking sabra virgin (Rovina-Leahle-Medinele), and even of Israeli prime ministers, David Ben-Gurion and Golda Meir, this constitutes a performative act of bodily merging that creates an alternative body image. It is a vengeful act of possession, bordering on rape, offering a different model of body, of beauty, and of language. At the end of the nineteenth century, the relationship between Yiddish and Hebrew was commonly compared to the relations between a servant girl and her master;[145] therefore, this metaphor for power relations was not an innovation. Rather, the innovation lay in presenting Medinele-Dzigan as a national Cinderella, a servant girl who stole the nation's wedding dress and desecrated the symbolic purity of the national actress, the national theater, and the state.

These moments on stage, in which Medinele-Dzigan performs as a drag queen, enabled a reconsideration of "the possible," according to Judith Butler's comments on drag culture.[146] If Dzigan is the body that interprets, personifies, and expresses the Israeli reality, as Haim Gamzu wrote,[147] when he played Medinele-Rovina, the kibbutznik, Menakhem-Mendl, and Golda Meir, or when Shumacher impersonated Ben-Gurion, they were presenting an alternative to the body, the visual, and the language imposed by the Hebrew nation.

---

143 Gluzman, *Haguf hatsioni*, 12–13.

144 Zerubavel, "Mythological Sabra." Moshe Dayan defined the ethos of the new Hebrew in his well-known eulogy for the soldier Roi Rotberg, given on April 30, 1956: "The choice of our lives – to live ready and armed, strong and stubborn, or the sword will be struck from our fists and our lives will be cut off." Quoted in Kimmerling, "Miliṭarizm," 123.

145 Seidman, *Marriage Made in Heaven*.

146 Butler, *Gender Trouble*, xx.

147 Gamzu, "Dzigan he'atsuv."

Conclusion

The Yiddish Stage as a Temporary Home

Throughout the years of its existence and using the tools of humor and satire, the theater of Dzigan and Shumacher played an important role in cultivating hope and expectation for change and in creating a critical frame in times of political oppression and economic crisis. In their texts and performances, the comic duo laughed at topics that were considered taboo, emphasized the weaknesses of the ruling groups, and buttressed the spirit of the minority group to which they belonged. The duo's theater highlighted the attempts of others (the censor) to silence them, expressed opposition to the social order in poetic ways, renewed the possibility of laughing at the enemy, and aroused hopes that change was possible. All this was achieved by means of an artistic satirical theater in Yiddish and via acts of cultural revival and memory.

Dzigan and Shumacher chose to be minor. By remaining loyal to the Łódź Yiddish dialect, they created cultural and linguistic opposition. In the concepts of Gilles Deleuze and Félix Guattari,[1] they deterritorialized the language, suggesting an alternative to the ruling language and its culture, and by means of language they carved out a linguistic autonomy, a strip of Yiddishland (or Łódźland), states without territory. In so doing, they depicted a mirror image of reality and created territories based on language, enabling an imagined community to become real, at least for the duration of their performance. In these temporary territories – their performances, wherein language was of central importance – the Yiddish of Łódź that the duo spoke became a "land," while Hebrew and the other languages of their surroundings constituted a sea bordering the linguistic and cultural territory, the mythical sea in which the young sabra from Tel Aviv feared that he may encounter the Leviathan.[2] The Bristol Hotel in Tel Aviv, where the artists resided until 1958, formed a kind of island, a tangible expression of Jewish wandering, alienation, and ephemerality, which the two princes of the exile sought to maintain and preserve. Ironically, the Bristol Hotel was located on Eliezer Ben Yehuda Street, which is named after the man who spearheaded the renewal of the Hebrew language.

This temporary deterritorialization was achieved not only via language. The duo tackled practical or hypothetical questions that touched on the simple Jew's

1 Deleuze and Guattari, *Kafka*.
2 In the skit "Politsyantn in Tel-Aviv" (Police in Tel Aviv), 1935.

https://doi.org/10.1515/9783110717693-006

efforts to improve his situation or change the surrounding reality by transplanting the individual or the collective to an existing social order in another place. In skits performed in both Poland, "Di koymen-kerers" (The Chimneysweeps, 1934) or "Yidn flien in der stratosfer" (Jews Flying in the Stratosphere, 1935), and in Israel, for example, the monologue "Menakhem-Mendl Astronaut" (Menakhem-Mendl the Astronaut, 1970), they depicted a temporary and elective exile.[3]

After the Holocaust, as expressed in the dialogue "Abi m'zet zikh" (The Main Thing: We Meet Again, 1947), the artists and their audience became refugees. Isaac Janasowicz argued that the actors were a metonymy of a refugee in a decimated world.[4] This definition should be expanded to view Dzigan and Shumacher as a metonymy of the Polish Jewish community, of a disappearing language, a metonymy of survival or eternal wandering in the face of the Hebrew revival, which itself was a metonymy of the nation's revival.[5]

For Dzigan, the story of voluntary exile and its artistic representation began when he decided to pursue a theatrical career, choosing to exclude the possibility of a normative life and instead live like the "wandering stars," actors in the Jewish theater. Dzigan was punished for this choice, banished from his father's home. The expulsion from his family home signified the beginning of a life of wandering, both on stage and off, which continued with his voluntary departure from the Ararat collective and from the city of his birth when the duo moved to the capital city, Warsaw. Later, after the German invasion of Poland, the political circumstances of the period made exile a necessity, and the duo embarked on a long series of wanderings. The narrative of exile and forced migrations characterized both the period and the personal stories of Dzigan and Shumacher, who were refugees, exiles, deportees, wandering Jews.

Continuing to speak Yiddish after leaving Poland indicated that the actors did not belong to any specific place and at the same time created an alternative space in which they and their audience felt at home. Performing in Yiddish became an obvious expression of voluntary exile in the State of Israel, which sought to "negate the exile" and viewed Yiddish linguistic and cultural activities as a form of protest against the Zionist endeavor. Performing in Yiddish became a kind of exile, an expression of speaking as wandering. It signified the existence of a diaspora within the very place from which the Jewish people had been exiled and countered the central component of the national Zionist endeavor – Hebrew revival. If I speak Yiddish, I am an exile.

3 On elective exiles, see Biemann, Cohen, and Wobick-Segev, *Spiritual Homelands*.
4 Janasowicz, "Der ershter program."
5 Chaver, *What Must Be Forgotten*, 13–18.

If nationality means belonging to a place, a people, a tradition, and is a confirmation of a home created via a community of language, culture, and customs,[6] then linguistic activity in another language, in another culture, establishes a home belonging to a different community and tradition. For Dzigan and Shumacher, performing and speaking in Yiddish created the possibility of a home, of a homeland. In the face of a hostile reality, Dzigan and Shumacher proposed using the tactics of laughter and language as a politics of opposition and a survival technique. The central object of this resistance, the targets of the satirical arrows fired on stage, were symbolic individuals-others such as statesmen, military officials, and iconic public figures who threatened the existence of the Jews in Poland, and later activists, ministers, military personnel, and government figures in Israel, whom the duo held responsible for their financial and health problems, the high taxes they were required to pay, and the cultural and linguistic discrimination from which they suffered. Confronting these negative characters stood two Jews, satirical artists who performed in Yiddish, representing the "I" of the collective of simple Jews, craftsmen, new immigrants, and the intelligentsia – two regular individuals, normal, everyday Jews. Dzigan and Shumacher's unique perspective focused on the individual, presenting a picture of unsuccessful national and political solutions. Their hope for change concentrated on the individuals' subversive act vis-à-vis reality and the battle against unjust systems of law and order: from the period of antisemitism in Poland to dealing with the Israeli bureaucracy, from the difficult economic situation in Eastern Europe to the heavy taxes imposed by the nascent State of Israel.

An examination of their artistic and public-civil activities locates the theater of Dzigan and Shumacher in the concurrent cultural context and emphasizes their artistic practice not merely as entertainment but as cultural endeavors with a critical and sharp character. A contemporary example demonstrating the extent to which they influenced the Israeli discourse concerning the boundaries of democracy can be found in a High Court ruling issued in March 2016, which used their satirical, humorous voice to criticize the Israeli government. In its ruling in a case brought against the planned gas pipeline, a project spearheaded by Prime Minister Benjamin Netanyahu, Deputy President of the Supreme Court Eliakim Rubinstein wrote: "The Yiddish comedians and satirists Dzigan and Shumacher explain in one of their skits the difference between democracy and dictatorship: 'Dictatorship is when the people can't say anything and the government does what it wants, and democracy is when the people can say what it wants – and the government still does whatever it likes.'" This was quoted by central media

6 Said, "Reflections on Exile."

outlets, and one article claimed that this was an excellent "summary" of the comprehensive ruling (180 pages), which had ramifications for maintaining the boundaries of Israel's democracy.[7]

In the various contexts in which they were active over the years, since their artistic intervention in the IPS café in Warsaw in 1939 dressed as orthodox Jews, Dzigan and Shumacher employed a range of strategies to realize the potential of "subordinate" groups, as they are described by James Scott,[8] using discourse to develop, to encourage, and to arouse revolutionary thought in opposition to the cultural hegemony. The duo's theater influenced the public arena not only in terms of the content it presented but also via its methods. This was achieved in a variety of ways: making the Łódź dialect the official language of the theater and continuing to use Yiddish instead of the local vernacular; presenting satire concerning political or public figures – from Göring to Ben-Gurion, from the priest Trzeciak to Moshe Dayan; inviting major actors from the Hebrew stage to appear with them in Yiddish, despite the government's demand that Yiddish actors begin to perform in Hebrew; filling the "Hebrew quota" that they were obliged to meet not by translating parts of the program but by including Hebrew songs – thus making Hebrew an "entertaining" interlude; and inviting Yemenite singers to sing in Yiddish.

In their shows in Poland, and later in Israel, the power relations between the ruling echelons and the subordinate group that the artists represented, Jews in Poland and Yiddish-speaking Jews in the State of Israel, temporarily changed; for two or three hours, Dzigan and Shumacher succeeded in creating an alternative time and space that was ruled by artistic culture in Yiddish, despite the political, economic, and ideological repression. Their performances were a temporary alternative to the reigning cultural and linguistic order.

Dzigan and Shumacher's theater successfully reflected and criticized the complex reality and the cultural discrimination that the Jews or the theater suffered in various periods. It also overcame these obstacles, building a time and space in which it was possible to imagine a different reality. The theater's artistic achievements were significant. The talent of the two stars caught the attention of many theatergoers and critics, as did the topical satirical content. Yet over the years, the theater failed to find new writers able to create quality satirical texts in Yiddish or new talented Yiddish actors. From the 1970s, the theater found renewal increasingly difficult. The audience too declined, as did the influence of Yiddish satirical theater in Israel.

---

7 *Levy-Weinrib*, "Pesaḳ hadin shel bagats"; see also Yahav, "Drama bebagats"; Gorali, "Ha'olam hashelishi." The quote in the ruling is apparently based on the skit "Aynshteyn-Vaynshteyn."
8 Scott, *Domination.*

From the end of the 1950s, the theater of Dzigan and Shumacher, and later Dzigan's solo theater, developed a practice that moved between innovation, reconstruction, and recycling, yet the extent of innovation continually declined. Indeed, certain sections of the shows became a commemorative performance of Dzigan and his work, albeit unintentionally. The desire for personal preservation also motivated Dzigan to write his memoirs, which he composed in Yiddish, assuming that Israeli culture would not accord him the attention he deserved.

Dzigan and Shumacher acted as mediators in an encounter between the Jewish and the Polish experiences, and later between the Hebrew Israeli reality and Yiddish as a language and culture. In Israel, the two existed in a liminal state. It is likely that this enabled them to bridge between the two cultures and to voice harsh and stinging criticism on the Israeli stage. They contributed greatly to liberating Yiddish-speakers from Hebrew domination. Likewise, they helped to free Hebrew speakers from their solemnity, from fear of criticism, and from internal censorship. In the context of the Israeli theater, the statement "it sounds better in Yiddish" appears to mean that it is possible to say in Yiddish that which cannot be articulated in Hebrew. For Dzigan and Shumacher, Yiddish was *taytsh*, a language by which they interpreted, translated, and appraised the Israeli experience.

In 1980, in the midst of the show *Doktoyrim heysn lakhn*! (Doctors Prescribe Laughter!), after the actress Eni Liton performed a text in which she parted from Dzigan with the words, "Leave in peace," life and theater merged. Dzigan collapsed on stage. This epic collapse symbolized the downfall of the culture that he, together with Shumacher and Moyshe Broderzon, had transformed from a peripheral dialect into a representative language, giving glory to the wider Yiddish culture connected to it.[9] Dzigan was theater, culture, language, and a memorial site, an embodiment of a cultural memory living through body and language, a museum of culture, of the theatrical institution of "Dzigan and Shumacher," and of the Jewish satirical theater. His status as representative of Yiddish culture and Yiddish theater in Israel at the end of the 1970s caused many to interpret his physical collapse as a metaphorical downfall of the Yiddish theater and of Polish Yiddish in its entirety. This was the only moment at which reality penetrated the stage not as an object of satire but as Dzigan's ultimate tragic performative act on the theatrical stage.

9 Regarding Dzigan's death see, Gross, "Kaze haya"; Kliger, "'Ish matsḥiḳ"; Ron, "Hofa'ato ha'aḥarona"; Schnitzer, "'Aḥaron habadḥanim."

Appendix A – Names of Spectacles and Shows

Ararat, Artistic Manager Moyshe Broderzon, Łódź (1927–1929)

1. *Glat kosher* (Glatt Kosher), October 1927, directed by the Ararat collective.
2. *Gut-morgn, koze!* (Good Morning, Goat!),[1] November 1927, directed by Moyshe Pulaver and Shimen Dzigan.
3. *Nisim min hashomayim* (Miracles from Heaven), December 1927, directed by Moyshe Pulaver.
4. *Salem-Aleykum*, January 1928, directed by Moyshe Pulaver.
5. *Melave-malke*,[2] March 1928, directed by Wilhelm Falek.
6. *Shneym asar mi yode'a*? (Who Knows Twelve?),[3] April 1928.
7. *Shoshanes-Yankev* (The Lily of Jacob),[4] May 1928.
8. *Yidishe tekhterlekh* (Jewish Girls), May 1928.
9. *Hotel terkalya* (Terkalya Hotel), September 1928, directed by the Ararat collective.
10. *Meshiekh geyt* (Messiah's Coming), September 1928, directed by the Ararat collective.
11. *Alts tantst* (All Dancing), November 1928, directed by the Ararat collective.
12. *Latkes* (Potato Pancakes),[5] December 1928, directed by the Ararat collective.
13. *Maskarad* (Masquerade), January 1929, directed by the Ararat collective.
14. *Mis yude'a* (Miss Yude'a), March 1929.
15. *Matse-bray* (Fried Matzah), April 1929.
16. *Yidishe klezmorimlekh* (Jewish Klezmer Musicians), 1929, directed by Moyshe Pulaver.

---

1 A mixed program of the same name was performed in 1930.
2 A meal eaten following the end of the Sabbath.
3 A song sung at the end of the Passover Seder service.
4 Customarily recited after the reading of the Megillah on Purim.
5 Traditionally eaten at the festival of Hanukkah.

Note: The information in these appendices is based on the collection of playbills of the performances in the archives of BAA (Beit Ariela Archives), ICDP (Israeli Center for the Documentation of the Performing Arts), and IGTAM (The Israel Goor Theatre Archives and Museum). Additional data was collected from the reviews primarily published in the Yiddish and Hebrew press. The different names give to the shows in different countries are not listed here.

https://doi.org/10.1515/9783110717693-007

Ararat, Artistic Manager Roman Rozental, Vilna (1929–1930)

17. *Yidn shmidn* (Jewish Blacksmiths), December 1929, directed by the Ararat collective.
18. *Der vayser maskarad* (The White Masquerade), January 1930, directed by the Ararat collective.
19. *A moyd a tsimes (gemisht program)* (A First-Class Girl (mixed program)), January 1930, directed by the Ararat collective.
20. *Hulyet!* (Rejoice!), February 1930, directed by the Ararat collective.
21. *Sosn-vesimkhe* (Happiness and Rejoicing), March 1930, directed by the Ararat collective.

Ararat, Artistic Manager Moyshe Broderzon, Łódź (1929–1930)

22. *Koym mit tsores* (With Great Difficulty), December 1929, directed by Yoysef Strugatsh.[6]
23. *Geklibene perl (gemisht program)* (Choice Pearls (mixed program)), January 1930, directed by Yoysef Strugatsh.
24. *Khay-gelebt!* (What a Wonderful Life!), January 1930, directed by Yoysef Strugatsh.
25. *On a kop* (Headless), January 1930, directed by Yoysef Strugatsh.
26. *Vekhol ma'aminim shehu! (gemisht program)* (And All Who Believe that He! (mixed program)),[7] March 1930, directed by Yoysef Strugatsh.
27. *Gold un zilber (gemisht program)* (Gold and Silver (mixed program)), March 1930, directed by Yoysef Strugatsh.
28. *Tshakedik un knakedik* (Spectacular and Festive), April 1930, directed by Yoysef Strugatsh.

Nayer Ararat, Artistic Manager Moyshe Broderzon, Lodz, (1930–1932)

29. *Gut-morgn, koze!* (Good Morning, Goat!), October 1930, directed by Dzigan and Shumacher.

---

6 According to Dzigan the show *Bronks expres* (Bronx express), a play by Osip Dimov in a version for miniature stage directed by Dovid Herman, premiered in 1930. See Bashan, "Monolog shel Shimon Dzigan."

7 From a liturgical poem recited on the High Holy Days.

30. *Afn himl a yarid!* (Much Ado about Nothing!), November 1930, directed by Dzigan and Shumacher.
31. *Ver mir guts gint* (My Best Wishes for My Well-Wishers), December 1930, directed by Dzigan and Shumacher.
32. *S'redl dreyt zikh* (Business is Going Well), January 1931, directed by Avrom Stokfeder.
33. *Yontef in der vokhn* (A Festival Mid-Week) March 1931, directed by Dzigan and Shumacher.
34. *M'lakht fun der velt!* (Laughing at the World!), February 1932, directed by Dzigan and Shumacher.
35. *Simkhes bay yidn!* (Happy Occasions for Jews!), March 1932, directed by Dzigan and Shumacher.
36. *Bay tog afn nayem mark* (Daytime at the New Market), March 1932, directed by Dzigan and Shumacher.
37. *Feygl in der luftn* (Birds in the Air), April 1932, directed by Dzigan and Shumacher.
38. *In Pintshev togt shoyn!* (Day Is Dawning in Pińczów!), December 1932, directed by Dzigan and Shumacher.

Di yidishe bande and the Ararat troupe, Warsaw (1933)

39. *"Tantst yidelekh!" un "Lakht fun der velt! "* ("Dance Jews!" and "Laugh at the World!"), October 1933.

Di yidishe bande (1933–1934)

40. *Nisht geshtoygn, nisht gefloygn* (Totally Ludicrous), November 1933.
41. *Himl efn zikh!* (Gates of Heaven, Open Up!), January 1934.

Ararat, Artistic Manager Moyshe Broderzon, Warsaw (1934–1936)

42. *A gdule af der bobe* (A Fat Lot of Good That'll Do), September 1934, directed by Dzigan and Shumacher.
43. *Zmires mit lokhsn* (Sabbath Hymns with Noodles), December 1934, directed by Dzigan and Shumacher.

44. *Khsidish, negidish, mamzerish* (Hasidic, Wealthy, and Sly), February 1935, directed by Dzigan and Shumacher.
45. *Ararat fort avek* (Ararat is Departing), March 1935, directed by Dzigan and Shumacher.
46. *Lekoved dem heylikn bim-bam!* (In Honor of the Holy Bim-Bam),[8] 1935, directed by Shimen Dzigan.
47. *A velt mit nisim* (A World with Miracles), October 1935, directed by Dzigan and Shumacher.
48. *Moyshe-kapoyer* (Moses the Contrary), February 1935, directed by Dzigan and Shumacher.
49. *A nakhes tsu kukn* (A Pleasure to Look), February 1936, directed by Dzigan and Shumacher.

Dzigan and Shumacher, Warsaw (1937–1939)

50. *Afn varshever yarid* (At the Warsaw Fair), March 1937, directed by Dzigan and Shumacher.
51. *Hot di velt a yidele!* (There's a Nice Little Jew in the World!), December 1937, directed by Dzigan and Shumacher.
52. *Tate, du lakhst!* (Father, You're Laughing!), March 1938, directed by Dzigan and Shumacher.
53. *A sho tsum lakhn* (Time to Laugh), January 1939, directed by Dzigan and Shumacher.
54. *Nadir un veyn nisht!* (Take This and Don't Cry!), April 1939, directed by Dzigan and Shumacher.

Der byalistoker melukhisher yidisher minyatur-teater (The Białystok National Jewish Miniature Theater), Soviet Union (1940–1941)

55. *Zingendik un tansndik* (Singing and Dancing), September 1940, directed by Dzigan and Shumacher.
56. *Rozhinkes mit mandlen* (Raisins and Almonds), March 1941, directed by Dzigan and Shumacher.

8 Sounds often made when singing Hasidic tunes (a *nign*).

Dzigan and Shumacher, Poland (1947)

57. *Abi m'zet zikh!* (The Main Thing: We Meet Again!), August 1947, directed by Dzigan and Shumacher.

L.Y.T. (Lodzsher yidisher teater) (1947–1948)

58. *Nu, un vos vayter?* (Nu, So What Now?), December 1947, directed by Dzigan and Shumacher.
59. *Zingendik un tantsndik* (Singing and Dancing), February 1948, directed by Dzigan and Shumacher.
60. *Balebatish un demokratish* (Bourgeois and Democratic), October 1948, directed by Dzigan and Shumacher.

Dzigan and Shumacher, Paris (1949)

61. *M'zet zikh? Shoyn?* (We Meet Again? So Be It!), August 1949, directed by Dzigan and Shumacher.

Dzigan and Shumacher, Israel (1950–1959)[9]

62. *Ṿayis'u ṿeyaḥanu* (And They Journeyed and They Encamped), March 1950, directed by Dzigan and Shumacher
63. *Tate, du lakhst!* (Father, You're Laughing!), October 1950, directed by Dzigan and Shumacher.
64. *Di velt shoklt zikh!* (The World's Shaking!), October 1953, directed by Dzigan and Shumacher.
65. *Nadir un veyn nisht!* (Take This and Don't Cry!), October 1955, directed by Dzigan and Shumacher.
66. *Toyznt un eyn lakh!* (A Thousand and One Laughs!), March 1956, directed by Dzigan and Shumacher.
67. *Yontef in der vokhn* (A Festival Mid-Week), April 1957, directed by Dzigan and Shumacher.

---

9 The shows had different names in Yiddish.

68. *Nayn mos gelekhter* (Nine Measures of Laughter), October 1957, directed by Dzigan and Shumacher.
69. *Ze vi du geyst?!* (Look Where You're Going?!), September 1958, directed by Dzigan and Shumacher
70. *Feter m'ken aykh!* (Uncle, We Know You!), April 1959, directed by Dzigan and Shumacher
71. *S'blaybt baym altn* (Just Like Old Times), directed by Dzigan and Shumacher.

The Moyshe Broderzon Satirical Theater under the management of Shimen Dzigan (1960–1980)[10]

72. *Frish, gezunt un meshuge!!!* (Fresh, Healthy, and Crazy!!!), October 1960, directed by Shimen Dzigan and Shraga Fridman.
73. *Tsit mikh nisht bay der tsung!* (Don't Put Words in My Mouth!), April 1961, directed by Shimen Dzigan and Shraga Fridman.
74. *Abi gezunt!* (The Main Thing: Good Health!), March 1962, directed by Shimen Dzigan.
75. *Red tsu der zakh!* (Get to the Point!), April 1963, directed by David Licht.
76. *Gut yontef!!!* (Happy Holidays!!!), February 1964, directed by Yoel Zilber.
77. *Zol sayn tsum gutn!* (It's for the Best!), February 1965, directed by Yoel Zilber.
78. *Sholem-Aleichem-yidn* (Sholem Aleichem's Jews), October 1966, directed by Yoel Zilber.
79. *Arayngetsimblt* (Whipped) March 1966, directed by Shraga Fridman.
80. *Hot a yid a lendele* (A Jew Has a Little Land), March 1968, directed by Avraham Ninio.
81. *Sha, sha, der sholem geyt* (Shush, Shush, the Peace is Coming), March 1969, directed by Avraham Ninio.
82. *Tsurikgekumen besholem* (Back in One Piece), April 1970, directed by Shraga Fridman.
83. *Men lakht a lebn* (Laughing at Life), March 1971, directed by Raphael Klatskin.
84. *Shimen Dzigan – 40 yor tetikeyt af der yidisher bine* (Celebratory Performance: Shimen Dzigan, 40 Years on the Jewish Stage), January 1972, directed by Yoel Zilber.
85. *Krikh nisht vu m'darf nisht!* (Don't Stick Your Nose In Where It Doesn't Belong!), March 1972, directed by Shmuel Atzmon-Wircer.

10 Later the name was changed to "The Satirical Theater under the management of Shimen Dzigan" and other similar names

86. *Elimelekh instalator* (Elimelech the Plumber), September 1973, directed by Shmuel Atzmon-Wircer
87. *Az m'lebt, derlebt men* (Live and Let Live), November 1973, directed by Niko Nitai.
88. *Tate, du lakhst*! (Father, You're Laughing!), May 1974, directed by Shmuel Atzmon-Wircer.
89. *Vu zenen mayne zibn gute yorn* (Where Are My Seven Good Years?), April 1975, directed by Daniel Gordon.
90. *Beser m'redt nisht* (Silence Is Golden), April 1976, directed by Eli Sagi.
91. *Men lekt nisht keyn honik* (We're Going through Rough Times), April 1977, directed by Dani Litai.
92. *Vu s'makht zikh – koydem lakht zikh*! (Laughter First!), May 1978, directed by Leo Filer.
93. *Doktoyrim heysn lakhn!* (Doctors Prescribe Laughter!), April 1980, directed by Avraham Ninio.

Appendix B – Movies Starring Dzigan and Shumacher

Al khet (For the Sins), Poland, 1936. Directed by Aleksander Marten.
Freylekhe kaptsonim (Jolly Paupers), Poland, 1937. Directed by Leon Jeannot.
On a heym (Without a Home), Poland, 1939. Directed by Aleksander Marten.
Undzere kinder (Our Children), Poland, 1949. Directed by Natan Gross.

https://doi.org/10.1515/9783110717693-008

Appendix C – Television Programs in Israel Starring Shimen Dzigan

Ha'erev 'im Shimon Dzigan (Tonight with Shimen Dzigan), 1975. Directed by Irv Kaplan.

Hamofa' shel Shimon Dzigan (Shimen Dzigan's Performance), 1976. Directed by Irv Kaplan. Never broadcast.

https://doi.org/10.1515/9783110717693-009

Appendix D – List of Artists and the Shows in Which They Participated

Alma, Ina: 44
Alperin, Yaakov: 75–77, 82, 83, 86, 91, 92
Amihud, Dalia: 69–73
Amir, Yehudit: 65
Anabela (Ya'akov-Kelner): 78, 80, 81, 83, 84, 86, 91, 93
Arditti, Karolina: 77
Armian R.: 48
Atzmon-Wircer, Shmuel: 85, 86, 88
Avni, Gavriel: 71
Barnash: 46
Barska-Fisher, Liza: 48
Ben-Ze'ev, Mordechai: 72
Berg, Yehudit (Iza Harari): 3, 55, 56, 61
Bergman, Yoel: 30, 38, 42–48, 50–52, 55, 56
Berman, Leyb: 13
Bern, Mina: 12–14, 17, 18, 20, 54–56
Bilkovitsh, Ḥanna (Rozentsvayg): 55, 58
Birnboym, Dovid (David): 30, 38, 44–47
Boker, Aliza: 82
Breyzblat, Avraham: 77
Brikan, A.: 2, 3, 5
Brin, Max: 41–45, 47, 50–52, 54
Broderzon, Sheyne-Miriam: 1–5, 9, 10, 12, 13, 22, 24, 25, 28–39, 33, 34, 38, 44–46
Cohen, Nurit: 82
Cohen, Uri: 82, 84, 89
Dimant, A.: 18, 20
Dolska, Maria (Miriam): 2, 22, 25, 28, 34
Dovin, Eni: 44
Dzigan, Shimen: 1–16, 22–93
Efron, K.: 55, 58
Feld, Fela: 66
Feldman, Betty: 91
Feldman, Karol: 84, 99–93
Fenigshteyn, H: 41
Feterman, Mashe: 2–5, 9, 10, 13, 14, 17, 18, 20, 29, 44–46
Fibich, Felix: 55, 56, 61

https://doi.org/10.1515/9783110717693-010

Fisher, L.: 47
Folman, Lola: 40–43, 51, 52, 55, 56
Frid: 14
Gershteyn, Larisa: 93
Glosek, Ofira: 90, 92
Godik, Vladek: 42–46, 55, 56
Goland, Yosef: 74
Goldshteyn, Shmulik: 2, 4, 5, 9, 12, 14, 16–18, 20, 24, 29, 33, 38, 41–48, 55, 56, 58
Gorby, Sara: 61
Gorlitska, Zise Girl: 2, 3, 5, 9, 10, 12, 16–18, 20, 29, 33, 60, 51
Grinhoyz-Turkow, Shura: 84, 88
Grinshteyn, Mikhael: 55, 58, 68, 70, 73, 91
Gronovsky, Alexander: 72, 73, 75, 76
Grosberg, Hanna: 41, 47, 48
Gutman, Kalmen: 54
Halmatan, Ḥ: 33
Halpern, Dina: 42, 43
Harari (Vainberg), Iza, see Berg, Yehudit
Harari, Kokhava: 77, 79, 80, 84, 89
Harison, Bebi: 46
Hart, Hersh: 22
Hermon, Shlomo: 65
Ḥen, Aliza: 91
Holzer, Rokhl: 40–43, 50–52
Hoyer, Sh.: 1, 2, 4, 5
Insman, Haim: 69–71
Kaminsky, M.: 72, 73
Karni, Avraham: 69, 70
Karta, Naḥum: 76
Katz, Zishe: 41–43
Kazanover (Moyshe Kosman): 1–3, 5
Kehaniṭ: 47, 48
Kenig, Haim: 65
Kenig, Leo: 84
Kerman, Peysakh: 41
Khabianka: 44
Kleyn, Jerry: 80, 81
Kowalska Esther: 58
Konisberg: 55, 56
Korman: 14

Kurlender, Ya'akov: 84, 85
Kurts, Avraham: 44
Latovtis, Karol: 88
Lederman, Dovid: 41–43, 47, 48
Lemberg: G.: 47, 48
Lerer, Shifra: 74
Lev, Eitan: 71
Levy, Yona: 71
Librovska: 46
Liebgold, Leon: 24, 43
Liliana, Lili (Ziyelińska): 30, 38, 40–43, 45
Liton, Eni: 93
Liviu, Dorothea: 88
Lora, F.: 30, 38, 45
Luca, Geta: 73
Lucianu, Bella: 81, 84
Luksenburg, Hela: 55, 56
Lutska: 52
Lyublaskaya: 55, 56
Maimon, Ruth: 66
Mandelbilt, Yankev: 22, 24, 25, 28
Marmer: 84
Maron, Hanna: 84
Marsalov, R. (Reuven Mandelboym): 47
Medinger, Mikhael: 81
Meged, Pnina: 77–79, 83
Melman, Meir, 55, 58
Moravsky, Mark: 41–43, 55, 56, 75
Morel, Adam: 69
Motil, Adam: 69
Nathan, Misha, 72, 73, 78–80, 89, 90, 93
Nelken, Moyshe: 1–5, 9, 10, 12, 13, 16–18
Oksenberg, Yosef: 69, 70
Openheym, Moyshe: 41–45, 50–52
Orit, Miriam: 65, 73, 84
Paver, Yael: 84
Peri, Lili: 9, 10, 12, 13
Polani, Chaim: 77
Potashinski, Moyshe: 22, 28
Pulaver, Moyshe: 1, 3–5, 9, 10, 12, 16–18, 20, 42–45, 54

Rappel, Malvina: 22, 24, 25, 40, 41
Reynglas, Yankev: 1–5, 9, 10, 12, 13, 16–18, 20, 22, 29, 33, 50, 51, 74, 79
Reysko, Roza: 55–58
Reyzer, Anita: 54
Rieber, Ḥanna: 90, 92
Rikhnberg, Natan: 24, 25, 28
Rodan, Raḥel: 69
Rodensky, Meir: 83
Rodensky, Shmuel: 84
Rotman, Ayzik: 41
Rotenberg, Yekusel: 54–56
Rotsheyn, Meytek: 55, 56
Rozen, Esther: 12, 29
Rozenberg, Liyuva: 22, 24, 25, 18
Rozenberg, Sh.: 51
Rubin: 75
Rubina, Fania: 47, 48, 54
Sarina: 84
Segal, Betti: 86
Segal, Roni: 84
Segalovitsh, Clara: 45
Send, M.: 55, 58
Sheftel, Sonya: 55, 58, 76, 77, 80–83, 86
Shidlovksi: 44
Shifman, Marian: 70
Shifer: 55, 56
Shifer, Chayele: 68
Shlifkovitsh, Ala: 46
Shoham, Yonit: 73, 84
Shternfeld, S.: 55, 56, 58
Shtruhl, Ophelia: 80
Shumacher, Yisroel: 1–5, 9, 10, 12–14, 17, 18, 20, 29, 33, 34, 40–70
Shvartshteyn, B.: 47, 51, 54
Siona: 62
Solo, Moshe: 80
Son, S.: 55
Strugatsh, Yoysef: 22, 34
Suvits, Zigmund: 81
Sve, Sh.: 58
Szlanger, Lea: 68–70, 72, 74

Tafner: 78, 80
Tantser, Ḥanna: 83
Taroni, Tsefrira: 76
Tauber, Garda: 46, 70
Tilbor, S.: 55
Tovi, Esther: 71
Toper, Ino: 47, 82, 91
Tsuznovits: 22
Urikh, Perl: 22, 24, 25, 28
Valinska, Miriam: 71
Varshavsky, Menashe: 82, 83
Vered-Tal, Miriam: 82
Verska, M.: 3
Videtsky, Yosef: 71, 86
Vinter, Frida: 86
Wulfowitz, Nathan (Nosen): 55, 58, 65, 76
Zahor, Miriam: 84
Zaltsman, Bronke: 65, 66, 69–71, 89
Zilberman, Leah (Lola): 1–5, 9, 10, 12, 14, 16, 18, 20, 25, 29, 33, 41
Zilska, Natalia: 75, 76
Zustanvits, Yankev: 28

Bibliography

Archives

Yehuda Gabbai Theatre Archive in the Beit Ariela Library in Tel Aviv (BAA)
Esther-Rachel Kaminska Theater Museum Collection, YIVO, New York
Israeli Center for the Documentation of the Performing Arts at Tel Aviv University (ICDPA)
Israel State Archives (ISA)
The Israel Goor Theatre Archives and Museum at The Hebrew University of Jerusalem (IGTA)
Yad Vashem Archives (YVA)
Yidisher Artistn Fareyn (1919–1939), YIVO, New York

Interviews, Recordings, and Television Programs

Dzigan, Shimen. "Yotser yitsira." An evening in honor of the publication of Shimen Dzigan's book, *Der koyekh fun yidishn humor*, Tel Aviv Town Hall. Hebrew University of Jerusalem, Institute of Contemporary Jewry, Oral History Department: 000279637 (1974).

Habima, *Hadibuk* [The Dybbuk], sound recording, CBS 2 70012/13, recordings 1–2 (2003).

Levin, Interview with Shimen Dzigan

Levin, Dov. Interview with Shimen Dzigan (recording), The Hebrew University of Jerusalem, Avraham Harman Institute of Contemporary Jewry, Oral History Division: 19 (85) (1973) [Yiddish]. National Library of Israel catalogue no. 990044219500205171.

Litvak, Interview with Celina Shumacher

Litvak, Yosef. Interview with Celina (Stal) Shumacher, part of the project "Jewish Refugees in the areas of Poland occupied by the Soviet Union," The Hebrew University of Jerusalem, Institute for Contemporary Jewry, Oral History Department, 1978: 9 (20) [Hebrew]. National Library of Israel catalogue no. 990044174460205 17.

Livni, Avida. "Beyidish ze nishma' yoter tov." Producers: Anat Seltzer and Modi Bar-On. Third episode of "Bimdinat hayehudim," Channel 1, 2004.

Rotman, Diego. Personal interview with Lydia Shumacher-Ophir (2009).

Rotman, Diego. Personal interview with Shmuel Atzmon-Wircer (2009).

A., "Mit Dzigan–Shumacher"

A. "Mit Dzigan–Shumacher (kemo-intervyu)." *Idishe-tsaytung* (Buenos Aires), July 10, 1952.

A., "Di velt shoklt zikh"

A. "Di velt shoklt zikh." *Di naye tsayt* (Buenos Aires), October 2, 1952.

A., "Dzigan yasad"

A. "Dzigan yasad te'aṭron ḥadash." *Al hamishmar*, October 2, 1960.

Abeliovich, *Possessed Voices*

Abeliovich, Ruthie. *Possessed Voices: Aural Remains from Modernist Hebrew Theater*. New York: SUNY Press, 2019.

Note: Newspapers printed in Israel do not note a city of publication.

https://doi.org/10.1515/9783110717693-011

Ackerly and Gontarski, *Samuel Beckett*
Ackerly, Chris J., and Stanley E. Gontarski, editors. *The Faber Companion to Samuel Beckett*. London: Faber and Faber, 2006.
Aderet, "Kevar be-1951"
Aderet, Ofer. "Kevar be-1951 pasla hatsenzura maḥaze miṭa'amei biṭaḥon." *Haaretz*, January 29, 2016.
Adler, "Benifrad"
Adler, B. "Dzigan ṿeShumacher – Benifrad." *Hatzofe*, September 15, 1960.
A-g, "Shumacher be'Kidush Hashem'"
A-g, Y. "Shumacher be'Kidush Hashem.'" *Haboker*, September 30, 1960.
A-g, "Ṭari, bari' umṭoraf"
A-g, Y. "'Ṭari, bari' umṭoraf,' – Bevitsu'a hate'aṭron hasaṭiri 'al shem Broderzon." *Haboker*, October 21, 1960
Agamben, *Homo Sacer*
Agamben, Giorgio. *Homo Sacer: Sovereign Power and Bare Life*. Translated by Daniel Heller-Roazen. Stanford: Stanford University Press, 1998.
A. L., "Ba'ayotaṿ"
A. L. "Ba'ayotaṿ shel Dzigan." *Davar*, May 24, 1968.
Al hamishmar, "Ḥadshot 'omanut ṿetarbut"
"Ḥadshot 'omanut ṿetarbut." *Al hamishmar*, October 18, 1957.
Al hamishmar, "Nifṭar haśaḥḳan Yiśra'el Shumacher"
"Nifṭar haśaḥḳan Yiśra'el Shumacher." *Al hamishmar*, May 22, 1961.
Alexander, *Leitsan heḥatser*
Alexander, David. *Leitsan heḥatser ṿehashaliṭ: Saṭira poliṭit beYiśra'el; sikum beinayim: 1948–1984*. Tel Aviv: Sifriat Poalim, 1985.
Alter, "Undzer tsukunft"
Alter, Sh. "Dos kind iz undzer tsukunft – Fragn un problemen fun kinderhoyz." *Dos naye lebn* (Łódź), September 8, 1948.
Anderson, "The Child Victim as Witness"
Anderson, Mark M. "The Child Victim as Witness to the Holocaust: An American Story?" *Jewish Social Studies* 14, no. 1 (2007): 1–22.
An-Sky, "Vegn dem dibek"
An-Sky, Sh. "Sh. An-sky vegn 'Dem dibek': A briv fun An-sky tsu doktor Haim Zhitlowski." *Literarishe bleter 1* (Warsaw), July 18, 1924, 2.
Appenszlak, "Nadir un Wejn Niszt"
Appenszlak, Jakub. "Nadir un Wejn Niszt." *Nasz Przeglad 131* (1939), S 13. Reproduced in Tomasz Moscicki (ed.), *Teatry Warszawy 1939: Kronika* (Warsaw: Bellona, 2009), 219–220.
Appignanesi, *Cabaret*
Appignanesi, Lisa. *The Cabaret*. Revised edition. New Haven: Yale University Press, 2004.
Auslander, "Stand-up Comedy"
Auslander, Philip. "Comedy about the Failure of Comedy: Stand-up Comedy and Postmodernism." In *Critical Theory and Performance*. Edited by Janelle G. Reinelt and Joseph R. Roach, 196–207. Ann Arbor: University of Michigan Press, 1992.
Austin, *Things with Words*
John L. Austin, *How to Do Things with Words*. Oxford: Clarendon Press, 1975.
Av., "Dzigan un Shumacher"
Av., Y., "Dzigan un Shumacher in Poyln." *Folkstsaytung* (Warsaw), September 20, 1947.

Avi., "Dzigan vegn"
Avi. "Sh. Dzigan vegn zayn nayem program – 'Tsit mikh nisht bay der tsung.'" *Letste nayes* (Tel Aviv), March 29, 1961.
Avi-Miriam, "Kisui levush"
Avi-Miriam, M. "Kisui levush 'omanuti." *Hador*, November 5, 1950.
Avidar, "Yesh li ma lomar"
Avidar, Tamar. "Dzigan: Yesh li ma lomar lano'ar." *Maariv*, July 2, 1968.
Avrahami, "Dzigan un Shumacher"
Avrahami, Yitsḥak (A. Y.). "Dzigan un Shumacher – Af yidish oder hebreyish." *Letste nayes* (Tel Aviv), December 5, 1958.
Avrahami, "Dzigan ṿeShumacher"
Avrahami, Yitsḥak. "Dzigan ṿeShumacher." *Zemanim*, March 18, 1955.
Avrahami, "Ha'omanim"
Avrahami, Yitsḥak. "Ha'omanim hatsalafim." *Maariv*, May 5, 1959.
Avrahami, "Ze vi du geyst"
Avrahami, Yitsḥak. "Ze vi du geyst." *Maariv*, December 31, 1958.
Avrekh, "Hanashim megalot"
Avrekh, Mira. "Hanashim megalot sodot ba'aleihen...." *Yedioth Ahronoth*, March 4, 1955.
A. Z., "Dzigan ṿeShumacher"
A. Z. "Dzigan ṿeShumacher betokhnit ḥadasha." *Davar*, October 14, 1955.
A. Z., "Te'aṭron"
A. Z. "Te'aṭron 'al shem Moyshe Broderzon." *Davar*, October 14, 1960.
A. Z., "Tish'a ḳabin"
A. Z. "Tish'a ḳabin." *Davar*, October 11, 1957.
Azar, "Dzigan un Shumacher"
Azar, Y. "Dzigan un Shumacher – A brokhe farn land." *Letste nayes* (Tel Aviv), October 10, 1955.
B., "Di kontsertn"
B. "Di kontsertn fun Dzigan un Shumacher in Yisroel – A geshprekh mitn impresaryo Goldgran." *Unzer shtime* (Paris), June 7, 1950.
Babcock-Abrahams, "Margin of Mess"
Babcock-Abrahams, Barbara. "'A Tolerated Margin of Mess': The Trickster and His Tales Reconsidered." *Journal of Folklore Institute* 11, no. 4 (1975): 147–186.
Bakhtin, *Rabelais*
Bakhtin, Mikhail Mikhailovich. *Rabelais and His World.* Translated by Hélène Iswolsky. Bloomington: Indiana University Press, 1984.
Barash, "Hanaśi' Navon"
Barash, Menachem. "Hanaśi' Navon ṿeha'oman Dzigan śoḥaḥu be'idish." *Yedioth Ahronoth*, June 9, 1978.
Bar-On, "Dzigan"
Bar-On, Ya'akov. "Dzigan." *Davar*, May 22, 1980.
Bar-On, "Hayeladim"
Bar-On, Ya'akov. "Hayeladim shel Goskind." *Maariv*, March 2, 1980.
Bar-On, "Monolog mehurhar"
Bar-On, Ya'akov. "Monolog mehurhar shel ḳomiḳa'i ṿatiḳ," *Maariv*, May 9, 1979.
Bar-On, "'Oy, Rabin"
Bar-On, Ya'akov. "'Oy, Rabin, 'eikh baraḥta li mehayadayim." *La'isha*, May 9, 1977.

Bar-Yosef, "Nivror le'idish"
Bar-Yosef, Yehoshua. "Nivror le'idish mita yafa," *Yedioth Ahronoth*, February 11, 1964.
Bashan, "Dzigan"
Bashan, Rafael. "Dzigan: Dyoḳano shel ḳomiḳ'ai ke'adam 'atsuv." *Maariv*, January 3, 1972.
Bashan, "Monolog"
Bashan, Rafael. "Monolog shel Shimon Dzigan." *Maariv*, January 31, 1964.
Bauman, "Performance"
Bauman, Richard. "Performance." In *Folklore, Cultural Performances, and Popular Entertainments: A Communications-Centered Handbook*. Edited by Richard Bauman, 41–49. New York: Oxford University Press, 1992.
Beckett, *Dramatic Works*
Beckett, Samuel. *The Complete Dramatic Works*. London: Faber and Faber, 1990.
Beizer, "Hama'avaḳ hayehudi"
Beizer, Michael. "Hama'avaḳ hayehudi: Hatenu'a hale'umit shel yehudei Brit haMo'atsot bashanim 1969–1989." Beit Hatfutsot (2007), available at: http://lib.cet.ac.il/pages/item.asp?item=17276&source=949 (Accessed October 13, 2015).
Belkin, *Hapurim-shpil*
Belkin, Ahuva. *Hapurim-shpil: 'Iyunim bate'aṭron hayehudi ha'amami*. Jerusalem: Bialik, 2003.
Belting, *Art History*
Belting, Hans. *Art History after Modernism*. Translated by Caroline Saltzwedel and Mitch Cohen. Chicago and London: The University of Chicago Press, 2003.
Ben-Ami, "Matsḥiḳ"
Ben-Ami, Naḥman. "Matsḥiḳ ṿelo' maḥṭi'." *Davar*, April 7, 1971.
Ben-Ami, "Ri'shon bein lo' shaṿim"
Ben-Ami, Naḥman. "Ri'shon bein lo' shaṿim – Shimon Dzigan be 'tari, bari' umṭoraf.'" *Maariv*, October 18, 1960.
Bender, *Jews of Białystok*
Sara Bender, *The Jews of Białystok during World War II and the Holocaust*. Translated by Yaffa Murciano. Waltham, MA: Brandeis University Press, 2008
Ben-Meir, "Dzigan un Shumacher"
Ben-Meir, A. (Abba Ahimeir [Abba Shaul Geisinovich]). "Dzigan un Shumacher betokhnit ḥadasha." *Herut*, October 17, 1958.
Ben-Meir, "Makirim 'otkha dod"
Ben-Meir, A. (Abba Ahimeir [Abba Shaul Geisinovich]). "'Makirim 'otkha dod' – Tokhnit ḥadasha shel Dzigan ṿeShumacher." *Herut*, May 22, 1959.
Bennett, *Theatre Audiences*
Bennett, Susan. *Theatre Audiences: A Theory of Production and Reception*. London, New York: Routledge, 1990.
Ben-Porat, "Hamofa' hamedake'"
Ben-Porat, Yesha'yahu. "Hamofa' hamedake' shemiḥuts la'ulamot." *La'isha*, October 23, 1960.
Ben-Porat, "Method in Madness"
Ben-Porat, Ziva. "Method in Madness: Notes on the Structure of Parody, Based on MAD TV Satires." *Poetics Today* 1, no.1/2, (Special Issue: Literature, Interpretation, Communication), (Autumn, 1979): 245–272.
Ben-Shlomo, "'Almogi biḳesh"
Ben-Shlomo, M. "'Almogi biḳesh miDzigan leḳatser balashon batokhnit ''Al timshekheni.'" *Hatsofe*, April 26, 1961.

Ben-Yishai, "Lefi sha'a"
Ben-Yishai, Aharon-Ze'ev. "'Lefi sha'a' – 'Ad sheyavo' 'Eliyahu (leva'yat ha'itonut vehate'atron halo' 'ivriyim be'Yiśra'el)." *Davar*, October 21, 1960.
Berg, *Luftmenschen*
Berg, Nicolas. *Luftmenschen: Zur Geschichte einer Metapher.* Göttingen: Vandenhoeck and Ruprecht, 2008.
Berkowitz, "Writing the History of Yiddish Theatre"
Berkowitz, Joel. "Introduction: Writing the History of Yiddish Theatre." In *Yiddish Theatre: New Approaches*. Edited by Joel Berkowitz, 1–25. Oxford: Littman Library of Jewish Civilization, 2003.
Bey, *T.A.Z.*
Bey, Hakim. *T.A.Z.: The Temporary Autonomous Zone, Ontological Anarchy, Poetic Terrorism*. 2nd edition with new preface. Brooklyn, NY: Autonoedia, 2003.
Biemann, Cohen, and Wobick-Segev, *Spiritual Homelands*
Biemann, Asher D., Richard I. Cohen, and Sarah E. Wobick-Segev, eds. *Spiritual Homelands: The Cultural Experience of Exile, Place and Displacement among Jews and Others*. Berlin, Boston: De Gruyter, 2019.
Bilu, "Hadibuķ bayahadut"
Bilu, Yoram. "Hadibuķ bayahadut: Hafra'a nafshit kemash'av tarbuti." *Meḥķarei Yerushalayim bemaḥshevet yiśra'el* bet (1983): 529–563.
Bodenheimer *Heḥaver miPlonsk*
Bodenheimer, Arie. *Bizkhut heḥaver miPlonsķ: Mas'otai 'im Shlomo Tsemaḥ veDavid Ben-Gurion*. Tel Aviv: Hakibbutz Hameuchad, 2010.
Bornshteyn, "Akht yorn"
Bornshteyn, Yitskhok. "Akht yorn hot men shoyn azoy nisht gelakht – Vi azoy di varshever yidn hobn ufgenumen Dzigan un Shumacher." *Dos naye lebn* (Łódź), October 4, 1947.
Bornshteyn, "Di ershte"
Bornshteyn, Yitskhok (Y. B). "Di ershte forshtelungen fun Dzigan un Shumacher in Lodzh." *Dos naye lebn* (Łódź). September 5, 1948.
Bornshteyn, "Dzigan un Shumacher"
Bornshteyn, Yitskhok. "Dzigan un Shumacher dertseyln." *Dos naye lebn* (Łódź), November 21, 1948.
Borvin, "A kleyner shmues"
Borvin. "A kleyner shmues mit Dzigan un Shumacher." *Unzer shtime* (Paris), January 22, 1950.
Boshes, "Hadevash hamar"
Boshes, Heda. "Hadevash hamar shel Shimon Dzigan." *Haaretz*, February 9, 1968.
Boshes, "Be'idish – Hakol 'aḥeret"
Boshes, Heda. "Be'idish – Hakol 'aḥeret." *Haaretz*, September 25, 1973.
Botoshansky, "Tsvishn yo un neyn"
Botoshansky, Yankev. "Tsvishn yo un neyn – Di mayse mit dem ferd un mit dem rayter un di tsvey vos zaynen eyn gantskeyt." *Di prese* (Buenos Aires), October 10, 1952.
Boyarin, "Ta'alulanim"
Boyarin, Daniel. "Ta'alulanim, meķadshei Hashem ufayśanim – 'Tasriṭim nistarim' umeyumanuyot hahitnagdut shel hapzura." *Te'orya ubiķoret* 10 (1997): 145–162.
Brat, "Dzigan: Ikh vil nisht fargesn"
Brat, Yitskhok. "Dzigan: Ikh vil nisht fargesn fun vos far a dor ikh shtam." *Letste nayes* (Tel Aviv), December 12, 1969.

Brat, "40 yor"
Brat, Yitzhok. "40 yor Dziganisher kinstler-nusekh – Tsu der groyser fayerung in 'Heikhal hatarbut.'" *Letste nayes* (Tel Aviv), December 31, 1971.
Bresler, "Epizodn"
Bresler, Zev-Volf. "Epizodn fun yidishn teater-lebn in Lodzh." In *Yidisher teater in Eyrope tsvishn beyde velt-milkhomes (Materialn tsu der geshikhte fun yidishn teater)*. Edited by Itzik Manger, Jonas Turkow, and Moyshe Perenson, 265–275. New York: Alveltlekher yidisher kultur-kongres, 1968.
Brin Ingber, "The Unwitting *Gastrol*"
Brin Ingber, Judith. "The Unwitting *Gastrol*: Excerpts from an Oral History Interview with Felix Fibich," http://www.jbriningber.com/Fibich_Apr_18_07.pdf. Accessed June 10, 2020.
Broderzon, "Di farshtendikung"
Broderzon, Moyshe. "Di farshtendikung." *Der moment* (Warsaw), July 7, 1925.
Broderzon, "Dos gesheftl"
Broderzon, Moyshe. "Dos gesheftl." *Der moment* (Warsaw), July 17, 1925.
Broderzon, "Purim-shpiler"
Broderzon, Moyshe. "Ikh – A purim-shpiler." *Yung-Yidish (*Yung-Idish*)* (Łódź, 1919): 7–5.
Broderzon, "Vegn Ararat"
Broderzon, Moyshe. "Vegn Ararat." *Literarishe bleter* (Warsaw) 7 (February 21, 1930), 146.
Broderzon, *Mayn leydns-veg*
Broderzon, Sheyne-Miriam. *Mayn leydns-veg mit Moyshe Broderzon: Di milkhome hot gedoyert far undz zibetsn yor*. Buenos Aires: Tsentral-farband fun poylishe yidn in Argentine, 1960.
Brook, *Empty Space*
Brook, Peter. *The Empty Space*. New York: Touchstone, 1996.
Bułat, "Kleynkunst"
Bułat Mirosława M. "Kleynkunst," The YIVO Encyclopedia of Jews in Eastern Europe, http://www.yivoencyclopedia.org/article.aspx/Kleynkunst2010.
Butler, *Gender Trouble*
Butler, Judith. *Gender Trouble: Feminism and the Subversion of Identity*. New York and London, Routledge, 1999.
Caplan, *Yiddish Empire*
Caplan, Debra. *Yiddish Empire: The Vilna Troupe, Jewish Theater, and the Art of Itinerancy*. Michigan: University of Michigan Press, 2018.
Carlebach, "Dzigan ṿeShumacher"
Carlebach, Azriel. "Dzigan ṿeShumacher." *Maariv*, May 2, 1950.
Carlebach, "Me'a lirot"
Carlebach, Azriel. "Me'a lirot." *Maariv*, March 27, 1953.
Carlson, *Haunted Stage*
Carlson, Marvin. *The Haunted Stage: The Theatre as Memory Machine*. Ann Arbor: University of Michigan Press. 2002.
Certau, *Everyday Life*
Certeau, Michel de. *The Practice of Everyday Life*. Translated by Steven Rendall. Berkeley: University of California Press, 2011.
Chaver, *What Must Be Forgotten*
Chaver, Yael. *What Must Be Forgotten: The Survival of Yiddish in Zionist Palestine*. Syracuse: Syracuse University Press, 2004.

Chitron, "Mabaṭ nadir"
Chitron, Chagai. "Mabaṭ nadir 'el 'olam sheḥarav." *Haaretz*, September 20, 2006.
Cohen, *Sefer, sofer ṿe'iton*
Cohen, Nathan. *Sefer, sofer ṿe'iton: Merkaz hatarbut hayehudit beṾarsha, 1918–1942*. Jerusalem: Magnes Press, 2003.
Cohen, "Shir 'am"
Cohen, Yehuda Leib. "Shir 'am ṿeshir 'amami." *Meḥḳarei Yerushalayim befolḳlor yehudi* 1 (1980): 146–152.
D., "Tokhnit ḥadasha"
D., "Dzigan ṿeShumacher betokhnit ḥadasha." *Haboker*, October 23, 1957.
Davar, "Devar hayom"
"Devar hayom." *Davar*, November 5, 1953.
Davar, "Met haśaḥḳan Shumacher"
"Met haśaḥḳan Yiśra'el Shumacher." *Davar*, May 22, 1961.
Davar, "Te'aṭron-ḳeva'"
"Dzigan yaḳim te'aṭron-ḳeva' – Meḳaṿe la'avor lehatsagot be'ivrit." *Davar*, October 3, 1960.
Davidovitz, "Shopworn"
Davidovitz, Ida. "Shopworn Comic Material." *Jerusalem Post*, October 23, 1957.
Deleuze and Guattari, *Kafka*
Deleuze, Gilles, and Félix Guattari. *Kafka: pour une littérature mineure*. Paris: Les Éditions de Minuit: 2016.
Devar hashavua, "Mitsrakh ḥiyuni"
"Hem mesapḳim mitsrakh ḥiyuni – Tseḥoḳ." *Devar hashavua*, February 5, 1953.
Diner, "Ambiguous Semantics"
Diner, Dan. "Ambiguous Semantics: Reflections on Jewish Political Concepts." *Jewish Quarterly Review* 98 (2008): 89–102.
Dobrovetsky, "Yoel Engel"
Dobrovetsky, Eda. "Hamuziḳa shel Yoel Engel lehatsagat 'Hadibuḳ' shel Evgeniĭ Vakhtangov," *Bama* 153–154 (1999): 99–110.
Dorf, "M'zet zikh?"
Dorf, Asher. "M'zet zikh? Shoyn!" *Unzer shtime* (Paris), September 14, 1949.
Dos naye lebn, "Dzigan un Shumacher in Poyln"
"Sh. Dzigan un Y. Shumacher tsurik in Poyln." *Dos naye lebn* (Łódź), August 1, 1947.
Dos naye lebn, "Fayerlekhe premyere'
"Fayerlekhe premyere in lodzher yidishn teater." *Dos naye lebn* (Łódź), December 28, 1947.
Dos naye lebn, "Undzere kinder farbindn"
"Undzere kinder farbindn di yishuvim." *Dos naye lebn* (Łódź), May 9, 1947.
Dos naye lebn, "Undzere kinder tsu gast"
"Undzere kinder tsu gast in Frankraykh." *Dos naye lebn* (Łódź), May 9, 1947.
Dunevitz, "'Isḳei sha'ashu'im"
Dunevitz, Nathan. "'Isḳei sha'ashu'im." *Haaretz*, September 25, 1958.
Dunevitz, "Kama milim"
Dunevitz, Nathan. "Kama milim 'al Shumacher." *Haaretz*, May 23, 1961.
Dwyer and Marinis, "Dramaturgy"
Dwyer, Paul and Marinis, Marcos De. "Dramaturgy of the Spectator." *The Drama Review* 31 (1987): 100–114.

Dzigan, *Der koyekh*
Dzigan, Shimen. *Der koyekh fun yidishn humor*. Tel Aviv: Gezelshaftlekhn komitet tsu fayern 40yor tetikeyt fun Shimen Dzigan af der yidisher bine, 1974.
Dzigan, *Dzigan-albom*
Dzigan, Shimen. *Dzigan-albom in vort un bild: 35yor stsenishe tetikeyt fun Shimen Dzigan*. Tel Aviv, 1964.
Dzigan and Zakov, "The Duel"
Dzigan, Shimon, and Amnon Zakov. "The Duel." *Israel Magazine – The Israeli Independent Monthly* 2, No. 4 (1969): 22–27.
Edwards, *Stanislavsky Heritage*
Edwards, Christine. *The Stanislavsky Heritage: Its Contribution to the Russian and American Theatre*. New York: New York University Press, 1965.
Efrat, "Tseḥoḳ go'el"
Efrat, Moshe. "Shenayim hamevi'im lanu tseḥoḳ go'el – Dzigan veShumacher betokhnitam haḥadasha 'Nadir un veyn nisht.'" *Hador*, May 7, 1955.
Efron, "From Łódź to Tel Aviv"
Efron, John D. "From Łódź to Tel Aviv": The Yiddish Political Satire of Shimen Dzigan and Yisroel Shumacher." *The Jewish Quarterly Review* 102 (2012): 50–79.
Efros, *Heymloze yidn*
Efros, Yisroel. *Heymloze yidn: A bazukh in di yidishe lagern in Daytshland*. Buenos Aires: Tsenṭral-farband fun poylishe yidn in Argentine, 1947.
Elam, *Semiotics*
Elam, Keir. *The Semiotics of Theatre and Drama*. 2nd edition. London: Routledge, 2002.
Elboym, "Yisroel Shumacher"
Elboym, Moyshe. "Yisroel Shumacher." *Forverts* (New York), June 16, 1961.
Elior, "Hadibuḳ"
Elior, Rachel. "Hadibuḳ – Bein ha'olam hanigle la'olam hanistar: Ḳolot medabrim, 'olamot shotḳim veḳolot mushtaḳim." In *Derekh haruaḥ: Sefer hayovel le'Eli'ezer Schweid*. Edited by Yehoyada Amir, 499–536. Jerusalem: The Hebrew University of Jerusalem and the Van Leer Institute, 2005.
Ellenberg, "Israel with Laughter"
Ellenberg, Al. "Israel with Laughter – Settles into The Barbizon." *New York Post*, October 18, 1969.
Epelberg, *Dovid in der viste*
Epelberg, Heshel. *Dovid in der viste, oder, Goliat ha-plishti: Historishe operete in aktn* [David in the Desert, or Goliath the Philistine: Historical Opera in Acts] (Warsaw: Defus Y. Alapin), 1888.
Erik, *Di komedyes*
Erik, Maks. *Di komedyes fun der berliner ufklerung*. Kiev: Melukhe-farlag far di natsyonale minderheytn in USSR, 1933.
Ertel, *Khaliastra*
Ertel, Rachel. *Khaliastra, Revue Littéraire Varsovie 1922–Paris 1924*. Paris: Lachenal & Ritter, 1989.
Estraikh, *In Harness*
Estraikh, Gennadii. *In Harness: Yiddish Writers' Romance with Communism*. Syracuse, NY: Syracuse University Press, 2005.

Estraikh, "The Missing Years"
Estraikh, Genadii. "The Missing Years: Yiddish Writers in Soviet Białystok", 1939–41, East European Jewish Affairs, 46:2, 2016, 176–191.
Faltitsky, "Di letste mohikaner"
Faltitsky, Yankev. "Di letste mohikaner fun poylish-yidish eygntum." *Der nayer moment* (San Paulo), April 4, 1952.
Fater, *Musiḳa yehudit*
Fater, Issachar. *Musiḳa yehudit bePolin bein shetei milḥamot ʻolam*. Tel Aviv: Hakibbutz Hameuchad, 1992.
Feinberg, *The Satirist*
Feinberg, Leonard. *The Satirist: His Temperament, Motivation and Influence*. Ames: Iowa State University Press, 1963.
Ferguson and Gupta, "Beyond 'Culture'"
Ferguson, James and Akhil Gupta. "Beyond 'Culture': Space, Identity, and the Politics of Difference." *Cultural Anthropology* 7, no. 1 (1992): 6–23.
Fertreter, "Nadir un veyn nisht!
A fertreter, "Nadir un veyn nisht!" *Haynt* (Warsaw), May 10, 1939.
Feuerstein, "'Eikh 'ta holekh"
Feuerstein, Emil. "'Eikh 'ta holekh." *Hatzofe*, November 7, 1958.
Feuerstein, "Ha'oman shehitsḥiḳ"
Feuerstein, Emil. "Ha'oman shehitsḥiḳ beli ma'amats (ʻal Yiśra'el Shumacher)." *Hatzofe*, May 26, 1961.
Feuerstein, "Hate'aṭron hasaṭiri"
Feuerstein, Emil. "Hate'aṭron hasaṭiri shel Sh. Dzigan." *Hatzofe*, October 28, 1960.
Feuerstein, "Tishʻa ḳabin"
Feuerstein, Emil. "Tishʻa ḳabin shel tseḥoḳ." *Hatzofe*, October 27, 1957.
Feuerstein, "Tokhnit ḥadasha"
Feuerstein, Emil. "Shimon Dzigan betokhnit ḥadasha." *Hatzofe*, May 19, 1969.
Filma'i, "Yaldei hasa'ar"
N.Filma'i. "Seraṭim – 'Yaldei hasaʻar,' Eden." *Davar*, October 24, 1952.
Finder, "Überlebende Kinder"
Finder, Gabriel N. "Überlebende Kinder im kollektiven Gedächtnis der polnischen Jüdinnen und Juden nach dem Holocaust: Der Beispiel 'Undzere Kinder.'" In *"Welchen der Steine du hebst": Filmische Erinnerung an den Holocaust*. Edited by Claudia Bruns, Asal Dardan, and Anette Dietrich, 47–64. Berlin: Bert and Fischer, 2012.
Finkin, "Jewish Jokes"
Finkin, Jordan. "Jewish Jokes, Yiddish Storytelling, and Sholem Aleichem: A Discursive Approach." *Jewish Social Studies* 16, no. 1 (2009): 85–110.
Fishman, *Never Say Die!*
Fishman, Joshua. *Never Say Die! A Thousand Years of Yiddish in Jewish Life and Letters*. The Hague: Mouton, 1981.
Fishman, *Yiddish*
Fishman, Joshua. *Yiddish: Turning to Life*. Amsterdam: John Benjamins Publishing Company, 1991.
Florsheim, "Sipuro shel te'aṭron hayidish"
Florsheim, Ella. "'Un vi durkh a kishef vert yidish teater' (Ukhmo bekhishuf notsar te'aṭron yidish) – Sipuro shel te'aṭron hayidish bemaḥane haʻaḳurim Bergen Belzen." *Bishevilei hazikaron* 4 (2009): 12–19.

Folksblat, "Dzigan un Shumacher"
"Dzigan un Shumacher gefinen zikh shoyn ba undz in shtot." *Folksblat* (Monteviedo), November 29, 1953.
Foucault, "Other Spaces"
Foucault, Michel. "Of Other Spaces." *Diacritics* 16, no. 1 (1986): 22–27.
Friedman-Cohen "Rokhl Oyerbakh"
Friedman-Cohen, Carrie. "Rokhl Oyerbakh: Ra'shei peraḳim leḥeker ḥayeha yitsirata." *Ḥulyot* 9 (2005): 297–304.
Freud, *Jokes*
Freud, Sigmund. *Jokes and Their Relation to the Unconscious*. Edited by James Strachey. London: Vintage, 2001.
Fuchs, "Is There Humor"
Fuchs, Esther. "Is There Humor in Israeli Literature and If Not, Why Are We Laughing?" In *Jewish Wry: Essays on Jewish Humor*. Edited by Sarah Blacher Cohen, 213–233. Bloomington: Indiana University Press, 1987.
Fuks, "Dzigan 'al hatsagato"
Fuks, Sarit. "Dzigan 'al hatsagato: 'Keshe'ani kan, tihye simḥa." *Maariv*, May 25, 1978.
Fuks, "Zikhere trit"
Fuks, Khayim-Leyb. "Zikhere trit – Dos drite Ararat-program." *Lodzher veker* (Łódź), January 30, 1928
G., "Dzigans satire"
G. [Moshe Grosman] "Dzigans satire kon helfn farklenern di 'yordim'-bavegung." *Heymish* (Tel Aviv), October 17, 1960.
Gamzu, "'Al kanfei hahumor"
Gamzu, Haim. "Dzigan – 'Al kanfei hahumor hayehudi." *Haaretz*, May 21, 1970.
Gamzu, "'Al timshekheni"
Gamzu, Haim. "'Al timshekheni balashon." *Haaretz*, April 13, 1961.
Gamzu, "Dzigan he'atsuv"
Gamzu, Haim. "Dzigan he'atsuv." *Haaretz*, June 4, 1974.
Gamzu, "'Emesh bate'aṭron"
Gamzu, Haim. "'Emesh bate'aṭron – Dzigan ṿeShumacher batokhnit ''Eikh 'ta holekh.''" *Haaretz*, October 12, 1958.
Gan, "Dzigan ṿeShumacher be'ivrit"
Gan, Shimon. "Dzigan ṿeShumacher be'ivrit." *Omer*, October 14, 1955.
Gavrieli-Nuri, "Hamitbaḥ shel Golda"
Gavrieli-Nuri, Dalia. "'Hamitbaḥ shel Golda': Meṭaforot milḥama ke'isḳei nashim." *Panim 56* (2011).
Gelbert, "Beli kaḥal"
Gelbert, Stefan. "Dzigan beli kaḥal ṿesaraḳ." *Davar*, June 16, 1960.
Gelbert, "Bintivei satira"
Gelbert, Stefan. "Bintivei satira 'aliza." *Al Hamishmar*, October 23, 1958.
Gelbert, "Miṭ'an tseḥoḳ"
Gelbert, Stefan. "Miṭ'an tseḥoḳ ṿehumor." *Al Hamishmar*, April 17, 1957.
Gelbert, "Te'aṭrono"
Gelbert, Stefan. "Te'aṭrono shel Dzigan." *Davar*, November 2, 1960.

Gennep, *Rites of Passage*
Gennep, Arnold van. *The Rites of Passage*. Translated by Monika B. Vizedom and Garbrielle L. Caffee. Chicago: University of Chicago Press, 1960.
G. H., "Mima 'ata ḥai?"
G. H. "Mima 'ata ḥai?" *Haboker*, May 22, 1959.
Gilboa, *David Frishman*
Gilboa, Menucha, editor. *David Frishman: Mivḥar ma'amrei biḳoret 'al yetsirato*. Tel Aviv: Hakibbutz Hameuchad, 1988.
Gilboa, "Bekhol haretsinut"
Gilboa, Yehoshua. "Dzigan – Bekhol haretsinut." *Maariv*, April 19, 1963.
Gilboa, "Holkhim bedarkam"
Gilboa, Yehoshua. "Hem holkhim bedarkam: 'Im hatokhnit haḥadasha shel Dzigan–Shumacher." *Maariv*, October 2, 1958.
Gilula, *Hate'aṭron hakameri*
Gilula, Leah. *Hate'aṭron hakameri (1945–1961): Haśigśug, hamashber ṿetiḳuno*. Jerusalem: Ben Zvi Institute, 2014.
Giora, "Ben-Ze'ev"
Giora, M. [Giora Manor] "Ben-Ze'ev 'over leyidish." *Haboker*, August 23, 1960.
Giora, "Pulmus so'er"
Giora, M. [Giora Manor] "Pulmus so'er sviv heskem 'Pargod' – Dzigan–Shumacher." *Haboker*, October 21, 1958.
Glatstein, "Dzigan kumt"
Glatstein, Jacob. "Dzigan kumt mit gelekhter." *Der tog-morgn zhurnal* (New York), October 10, 1969.
Gluzman, *Haguf hatsioni*
Gluzman, Michael. *Haguf hatsioni: Le'umiut, migdar uminiut basifrut hayiśre'elit hayiśra'elit haḥadasha*. Tel Aviv: Hakibbutz Hameuchad, 2007.
Goldin, "Af a tsuzamentref"
Goldin, M. "Af a tsuzamentref mit Dzigan un Shumachern di barimte folks-artistn." *Naye prese* (Paris), September 1, 1949.
Goldin, "Revyu-spektakl"
Goldin, M. "Der revyu-spektakl fun Dzigan un Shumacher." *Naye prese* (Paris), September 23, 1949.
Goldgran, "Yidishn teater-oylem"
Goldgran, Henry. "Tsum yidishn teater-oylem in Pariz." *Unzer vort* (Paris), August 12, 1949.
Goldshteyn, "Dzigan un Shumacher"
Goldshteyn, Yosef-Shimen. "Dzigan un Shumacher vegn lodzher un varshever yidn." *Haynt* (Warsaw), May 16, 1938.
Goldshteyn, "Geshprekh mitn lets"
Goldshteyn, Yosef-Shimen. "Geshprekh mitn lets fun 'Ararat' Shimen Dzigan." *Haynt* (Warsaw), October 31, 1932.
Goldshteyn, "Moris Shvarts"
Goldshteyn, Yoysef-Shimen [Der lustiker pessimist]. "Moris Shvarts farfirt a protses kegn 'Ararat.'" *Haynt* (Warsaw), December 6, 1935.
Goldshteyn, "Nokh der premyere"
Goldshteyn, Yoysef-Shimen [Der lustiker pessimist]. "Nokh der premyere fun 'Al khet.'" *Haynt* (Waraw), May 8, 1936.

Gorali, "Ha'olam hashelishi"
Gorali, Moshe. "Yerushalayim shel ha'olam hashelishi." *Calcalist*, March 29, 2016. http://www.calcalist.co.il/local/articles/0,7340,L-3684692,00.html.
Grafman, "Beys der hafsoke"
Grafman, Avrom-Yitskhok. "Beys der hafsoke. Groyser Dzigan–Shumacher-revyu in 'Novoshtshi.'" *Der moment* (Warsaw), February 21, 1937.
Grafman, "Moyshe Kapoyer"
Grafman, Avrom-Yitskhok. "'Moyshe Kapoyer – Di frishe premyere in 'Ararat.'" *Der moment* (Warsaw), December 11, 1935.
Grafman, "Yidish teater"
Grafman, Avrom-Yitskhok. "Yidish teater." *Der moment* (Warsaw), September 25, 1932.
Grafman, "Zmires mit lokshn"
Grafman, Avrom-Yitskhok. "Zmires mit lokshn – Notitsn fun yidishn teater." *Der moment* (Warsaw), December 21, 1934.
Greenberg, "Amalek"
Greenberg, Uri Zvi. "Ven Amalek hot geredt." *Der moment* (Warsaw), May 2, 1939.
Greenberg, *Gezamlte verk*
Greenberg, Uri Zvi. *Gezamlte verk I-II*. Edited by Chone Shmeruk. Jerusalem: Magnes Press, 1979.
Greenberg, "Tsu tsar"
Greenberg, Uri Zvi. "Tsu tsar un tsu tsorn." *Der moment* (Warsaw), May 4, 1939.
Gross, "Kaze haya"
Gross, Natan. "Kaze haya Dzigan 'al habama." *Al hamishmar*, April 22, 1980.
Gross, *Toldot hak̩olno'a*
Gross, Natan. *Toldot hak̩olno'a hayehudi bePolin, 1910–1950*. Jerusalem: Magnes Press, 1990.
Guilat, "Yemenite Jewish Women"
Guilat, Yael. "Yemenite Jewish Women." *Nashim: A Journal of Jewish Women's Studies & Gender Issues* 11 (2006): 198–223.
Guralnik, Krempel, and Ładnowska, *Yankl Adler*
Guralnik, Nechama, Ulrich Krempel, and Janina Ładnowska, editors. *Yankl Adler 1895–1945*. [Hebrew] Tel Aviv: Masada, 1985.
Gutman, "Jews in General Anders' Army"
Yisrael Gutman, "Jews in General Anders' Army in the Soviet Union." *Yad Vashem Studies*, 12 (1977): 231–296. Available at: https://www.yadvashem.org/odot_pdf/Microsoft%20Word%20-%206217.pdf
Gutman, "Shoyn?"
Gutman, Meyer Bar. "Shoyn? – Men hot zikh gezen!" *Vokhnblat* (newspaper of the Holocaust survivors in Germany DP camps), December 9, 1949.
Haaretz, "Dzigan metakhnen"
"Dzigan metakhnen hatsagot be'ivrit." *Haaretz*, October 3, 1960.
Haaretz, "Yiśra'el Shumacher – Limnuḥot"
"Yiśra'el Shumacher – Limnuḥot." *Haaretz*, May 23, 1961.
Haboker, "Dzigan ṿeShumacher"
"Dzigan ṿeShumacher betokhnit ḥadasha." *Haboker*, October 18, 1957.
Haboker, "Hofa'at habekhora"
"Hofa'at habekhora shel Dzigan–Shumacher." *Haboker*, March 17, 1950.

Haboker, "Shiḥrur mimas"
"Lo buṭal shiḥrur mimas lehatsagot 'Pargod' shel Dzigan veShumacher." *Haboker*, October 15, 1958.
Hador, "Dzigan veShumacher be'ivrit"
"Dzigan veShumacher be'ivrit." *Hador*, April 29, 1950.
Hador, "Ḥatul shaḥor"
"Ḥatul shaḥor bein Dzigan veShumacher." *Hador*, June 30, 1955
Ha'olam haze, "Haḥok hu tseḥok"
"Haḥok hu tseḥok." *Ha'olam haze*, November 23, 1950.
Har-Gil, "Gonvim mikol"
Har-Gil, Shraga. "Gonvim mikol haba' layad." *Maariv*, December 25, 1972.
Har-Gil, "Humor yehudi"
Har-Gil, Shraga. "Koḥo shel humor yehudi." *Maariv*, April 9, 1974.
Harshav, *Manifesṭim*
Harshav, Benjamin, editor. *Manifesṭim shel modernizm.* Expanded and updated edition. Jerusalem: Carmel, 2001.
Harshav, *The Meaning of Yiddish*
Harshav, Benjamin, *The Meaning of Yiddish.* Berkeley, CA: University of California Press, 1990.
Hasan-Rokem, "Carl Schmitt and Ahashver"
Hasan-Rokem, Galit. "Carl Schmitt and Ahashver: The Idea of the State and the Wandering Jew." *Behemoth: A Journal on Civilisation* 2 (2008): 4–25.
Hasan-Rokem, "Hatarbut ha'amamit"
Hasan-Rokem, Galit. "'Al ḥeker hatarbut ha'amamit." *Te'orya uvikoret* 10 (1997): 5–14.
Hatzofe, "Dzigan metakhnen hatsagot"
"Dzigan metakhnen hatsagot be'ivrit." *Hatzofe*, October 3, 1960.
Hoberman, *Bridge of Light*
Hoberman, J. *Bridge of Light: Yiddish Film between Two Worlds*. New York: Museum of Modern Art, 1991.
Hon, "Dzigan kimvaker"
Hon, Shaul. "Dzigan kimvaker hamedina." *Maariv*, April 22, 1970.
Hon, "Tsu Niusia Golds kumen"
Hon, Y. "Tsu Niusia Golds kumen keyn Poyln." *Dos naye lebn* (Łódź), November 15, 1948.
Horn, "Dzigan shaft"
Horn, Y. "Sh. Dzigan shaft a teater." *Di idishe tsaytung* (Tel Aviv), October 4, 1960.
Hutcheon, *Theory of Parody*
Hutcheon, Linda. *A Theory of Parody: The Teachings of Twentieth-Century Art Forms.* New York: Methuen, 1985.
Idishe tsaytung, "A bazukh"
"A bazukh fun Dzigan–Shumacher in 'Di idishe tsaytung.'" *Idishe tsaytung* (Buenos Aires), April 4, 1951.
Izban, "Di grine aktyorn"
Izban, Shmuel. "Di grine aktyorn vos vitslen zikh af dem khesbm fun der Yisroel-regirung." *Der morgn zhurnal* (New York), November 11, 1950.
Janasowicz, "A shmues"
Janasowicz, Isaac. "A shmues mit Shimen Dzigan." *Di prese* (Buenos Aires), December 27, 1967.

Janasowicz, “Der ershter program”
Janasowicz, Isaac. “Der ershter program fun ‘L.Y.T.’ – ‘Nu, vu vos vayter?’” *Dos naye lebn* (Łódź), December 30, 1947.
Janasowicz, “Vos far a kleynkunst”
Janasowicz, Isaac. “Vos far a kleynkunst darfn mir.” *Dos naye lebn* (Łódź), August 11, 1947.
Jerusalem Post, “Beersheba Councillors”
“Beersheba Councillors Go to Theatre Instead.” *Jerusalem Post*, December 2, 1958.
Kagedan, *Soviet Zion*
Kagedan, Allan Laine. *Soviet Zion: The Quest for a Russian Jewish Homeland.* New York: St. Martin’s Press, 1994.
Kants, “A simkhe”
Kants, Shimen, “A simkhe fun lakhn un epes mer.” *Letste nayes* (Tel Aviv), April 30, 1979.
Karo, “Dzigan ṿeShumacher”
Karo, Baruch. “Dzigan ṿeShumacher: ‘Tseḥoḳ ṿelo’ ya‘avor,’ hofa‘at ’orḥim.” *Haboker*, October 20, 1950.
Katsizne, “Milkhike gevisns”
Katsizne (Kacyzne), Alter. “Milkhike gevisns: Birobidzhan.” *Fraynd* (Warsaw), December 14, 1934.
Kaufman-Simhon, “Lemale’ ḥalal”
Kaufman-Simhon, Sarit. “Lemale’ ḥalal: Te’aṭron baśafa hamagrebit beYiśra’el.” *Te’aṭron 30* (2010): 94–106.
Kaynar, “National Theatre”
Kaynar, Gad. “National Theatre as Colonized Theater: The Paradox of Habima.” *Theatre Journal* 50, no.1 (1998): 1–20.
Kedourie, “Nationalism and Self-Determination”
Kedourie, Elie. “Nationalism and Self-Determination.” In *Nationalism*. Edited by John Hutchinson and Anthony D. Smith, 49–55. Oxford: Oxford University Press, 1994.
Keisari, “Dzigan beli ’ipur”
Keisari, Uri. “Dzigan beli ’ipur.” *Maariv*, May 10, 1965.
Keisari, “Hasaṭira”
Keisari, Uri. “Hasaṭira hayiśre’elit nikhtevet be’idish.” *Maariv*, April 23, 1971.
Keisari, “Kol Dzigan”
Keisari, Uri. “Kol Dzigan.” *Haaretz*, October 19, 1960.
Kelai, “Hatsaga shelo”
Kelai, Sh. “Hatsaga shelo hi’ bivḥinat hafta‘a ki tamid yesh ba mashehu, she’af eḥad lo’ ḥoshev ‘alav.” *Herut*, March 31, 1961.
Kelai, “Ṿiduyaṿ”
Kelai, Sh. “Ṿiduyaṿ shel śaḥḳan ‘ivri.” *Herut*, October 5, 1960.
Keneder odler, “Dzigan un Shumacher”
“Dzigan un Shumacher – Di veltmayster fun humor, kumen keyn Montreal.” *Keneder odler*, April 15, 1954.
Khantshin, “Di gastroln”
Khantshin, Ya. “Di gastroln fun byalistoker melukhishn yidishn teater.” *Der emes* (Moscow), February 15, 1941.
Khrabolovsky, “Palestine, Birobidzhan”
Khrabolovsky, Elkana. “Palestine, Birobidzhan un di prese.” *Nyu-Yorker vokhnblat* (New York), February 22, 1935.

Kidron, "Ethnography of Silence"
Kidron, Carol A. "Toward an Ethnography of Silence: The Lived Presence of the Past in the Everyday Life of Holocaust Trauma Survivors and Their Descendants in Israel." *Current Anthropology* 50 (2009): 2–27.
Kimmerling, "Miliṭarizm"
Kimmerling, Baruch. "Miliṭarizm baḥevra hayiśre'elit." *Te'orya uviḳoret* 4 (1993): 123–139.
Kipnis, "A shpatsir"
Kipnis, Menakhem. "A shpatsir iber di teatern un kontsert-zaln." *Haynt* (Warsaw), September 18, 1932.
Kipnis, "A velt"
Kipnis, Menakhem. "A velt mit nisim! Dos naye program fun Ararat in teater Novoshtshi." *Haynt* (Warsaw), October 28, 1935.
Kipnis, "Afn varshever yarid"
Kipnis, Menakhem. "Afn varshever yarid." *Haynt* (Warsaw), March 1, 1937.
Kipnis, "Moyshe-Kapoyer"
Kipnis, Menakhem. "Moyshe-Kapoyer." *Haynt* (Warsaw), December 26, 1935.
Kipnis, "Tate, du lakhst?"
Kipnis, Menakhem. "Tate, du lakhst?" *Haynt* (Warsaw), April 11, 1938.
Kirshenblatt-Gimblett and Taylor, "What's Wrong with These Terms?"
Kirshenblatt-Gimblett, Barbara, and Taylor, Diana. "What's Wrong with These Terms? A Conversation with Barbara Kirshenblatt-Gimblett and Diana Taylor." *PMLA* 120 (2005): 1497–1508.
Kishon, "Dzigan ṿeShumacher lashilṭon"
Kishon, Efraim. "Dzigan ṿeShumacher lashilṭon!" *Maariv*, July 25, 1955.
Klaus, "Canaanism"
Hofmann, Klaus. "Canaanism." *Middle Eastern Studies* 47, no. 2 (2011): 273–94.
Kliger, "'Ish matsḥiḳ"
Kliger, Noah. "'Ish matsḥiḳ haya." *Yedioth Ahronoth*, May 18, 1980.
Kohansky, *Hate'aṭron ha'ivri*
Kohansky, Mendel. *Hate'aṭron ha'ivri*. Translated by Aviv Meltser. Jerusalem: Veidenfeld ṿeNikolson, 1974.
Konigsberg, "Our Children"
Konigsberg, Ira. "'Our Children' and the Limits of Cinema: Early Jewish Responses to the Holocaust." *Film Quarterly* 52, no. 1 (1998): 7–19.
Kowzan, *El Signo*
Kowzan, Tadeusz. *El Signo y el teatro*. Madrid: Arco/Libros, 1997.
K-R, "Shoshanes"
K-R, "Shoshanes-yankev." *Nayer fraydenker* (Łódź), March-April 1928.
Kramer, "Dzigan Headlines"
Kramer, Mendel. "Shimon Dzigan Headlines Yiddish Revue." *The Gazette*, November 11, 1968.
Krimsky, "Nokh a mol"
Krimsky, M. "Nokh a mol Ararat." *Der moment* (Warsaw), May 29, 1931.
Kronfeld, *Margins of Modernism*
Kronfeld, Chana. *On the Margins of Modernism: Decentering Literary Dynamics*. Berkeley: University of California Press, 1996.

La'isha, "'Al timshekheni"
"'Al timshekheni balashon." *La'isha*, April 16, 1961.
Lamerḥav, "Dzigan mitkonen lehatsig"
"Dzigan mitkonen lehatsig be'ivrit." *Lamerḥav*, October 3, 1960.
Langer, "Undzere Kinder"
Langer, Lawrence L. "'Undzere Kinder': A Yiddish Film from Poland." In Lawrence L. Langer, *Preempting the Holocaust*. 157–165. New Haven: Yale University Press, 1998.
Lastik, "Undzere kinder"
Lastik, Shmuel. "Vegn yidishn film 'Undzere kinder' – A por bamerkungen." *Dos naye lebn* (Łódź), April 12, 1950.
Lederman, *Fun yener zayt*
Lederman, Dovid. *Fun yener zayt forhang*. Buenos Aires: Tsentral-farband fun poylishe yidn in Argentine, 1960.
Leneman, "Abi men zet zikh"
Leneman, Leon. "Abi men zet zikh." *Keneder odler* (Montreal), September 6, 1949.
Letste nayes, "Artist Shimen Dzigan"
"Artist Shimen Dzigan vegn zayn nay-gegrindetn satirishn teater in nomen fun Moyshe Broderzon." *Letste nayes* (Tel Aviv), October 3, 1960.
Letste nayes, "Dzigan–Shumacher in 'Beit-Lid.'"
"Dzigan–Shumacher in 'Beit-Lid.'" *Letste nayes* (Tel Aviv), December 22, 1950.
Letste nayes, "Mevatel"
"Dos mevatel makhn di shtayern-hanokhes far 'Pargod' vet firn tsum ufleyzn dos teater." *Letste nayes* (Tel Aviv), October 20, 1958.
Letste nayes, "Prezident af der forshtelung"
"Prezident af der forshtelung fun Dzigan un Shumacher." *Letste nayes* (Tel Aviv), February 1, 1953.
Letste nayes, "Sh. Dzigans satirish-teater"
"Sh. Dzigans satirish-teater in nomen fun Moyshe Broderzon – Ongehoybn zayne forshtelungen." *Letste nayes* (Tel Aviv), October 10, 1960.
Levavi, *Hahityashvut*
Levavi, Ya'akov. *Hahityashvut hayehudit beBirobidjan*. Jerusalem: The Historical Society of Israel, 1965.
Levin, "Teaters in Yisroel"
Levin, B. "Teaters in Yisroel." *Der tog-morgn zhurnal* (New York), December 23, 1960.
Levin, *Tekufa besograyim*
Levin, Dov. *Teḳufa besograyim: 1939–1941: Temurot beḥayei hayehudim ba'azorim shesupḥu liVrit haMo'atsot bitḥilat milḥemet ha'olam hasheniya*. Tel Aviv: Hakibbutz hameuchad, 1989.
Levin, "He lekha ṿe'al tivke"
Levin, Vera. "'He lekha ṿe'al tivke' – Dzigan ṿeShumacher." *Haaretz*, October 14, 1955.
Levy-Weinrib, "Pesaḳ hadin shel bagats"
Levy-Weinrib, Ella. "Hahashlakhot shel pesaḳ hadin shel bagats: Nitsaḥon hisṭori 'o nezeḳ lakalkala hayiśre'elit?" *Globes*, March 28, 2016. http://www.globes.co.il/news/article.aspx?did=1001113171.
Lewy, *Hayeḳim*
Lewy, Tom. *Hayeḳim ṿehate'aṭron ha'ivri: Bama'avaḳ bein ma'arav lemizraḥ 'Eiropa*. Tel Aviv: Resling, 2016.

L. F., "Perasei Yiśra'el"
L. F. "Perasei Yiśra'el le'sifrut ṿe'omanut: Hanna Rovina." *Lamerhav*, April 24, 1956.
Liberman, "Balebatish un demokratish"
Liberman, A. "Balebatish un demokratish." *Unzer vort* (Paris), July 12, 1949.
Liberman, "Men zet zikh?"
Liberman, A. "Men zet zikh? – Shoyn." *Unzer vort* (Paris), September 26, 1949.
Lifshitz, "Badkhonim un letsim"
Lifshitz, Yekhezkel. "Badkhonim un letsim ba yidn – Material tsu a verterbukh." In *Arkhiv far der geshikhte fun yidishn teater un drame*. Edited by Jacob Shatzky, 25–45. Vilna and New York: YIVO, 1930.
Lilienshteyn, "Dzigan un Shumacher"
Lilienshteyn, Y. "Dzigan un Shumacher in Pariz." *Arbeter-vort* (Paris), September 9, 1949.
Lipsker, "Young Yiddish Poetry"
Lipsker, Avidov. "The Albatrosses of Young Yiddish Poetry: An Idea and Its Visual Realization in Uri Zvi Greenberg's Albatros." *Prooftexts* 15/1 (1995): 89–108.
Literarishe bleter, "Lodzher kameral"
"Lodzher kameral- un kleynkunst-teater 'Ararat' – Kinstlerisher onfirer – Moyshe Broderzon: Dos 24ste program. " *Literarishe bleter* 9 (Warsaw), February 5, 1932, 95.
Literarishe bleter, "Revyu-teater 'Ararat'"
"Der lodzher revyu-teater 'Ararat.'" *Literarishe bleter* 5 (Warsaw), December 7, 1928, 969.
Litvak, *Peliṭim*
Litvak, Yosef. *Peliṭim yehudim miPolin biVrit haMo'atsot 1939–1946*. Tel Aviv: Hakibbutz Hameuchad, 1988.
L. P., "Dzigan matslif"
L. P. "Dzigan matslif." *Kol ha'am*, April 2, 1965.
M., "Hasivuv hasheni"
M. "Hasivuv hasheni shel Dzigan ṿeShumacher." *Maariv*, October 13, 1950.
McGrath, "The Cheviot"
McGrath, John. "The Year of the Cheviot." Introduction to *The Cheviot, the Stag, and the Black, Black Oil*. London: Methuen, 1981.
Maariv, "'Eshbot ra'av"
"Dzigan: 'Eshbot ra'av 'al pesilat tokhniti laṭeleṿizya." *Maariv*, April 22, 1976.
Maariv, "Hanof hapeḳiduti'"
"'Hanof hapeḳiduti' mukar lo – Haḳomiḳai Dzigan gila shegam be'Ameriḳa ḳayemet 'masoret hateh.'" *Maariv*, March 1, 1962.
Maariv, "Nim'as lehitlotsets"
"Nim'as lehitlotsets 'al Bi. Gi." *Maariv*, October 24, 1958.
Maariv, "'Ośim tseḥoḳ"
"Dzigan ṿeShumacher 'ośim tseḥoḳ." *Maariv*, March 2, 1955.
Maariv, "Yad lapeh"
"Yad lapeh." *Maariv*, May 17, 1955.
Maariv, "Yode'a gam lin'om"
"Dzigan yode'a gam lin'om." *Maariv*, December 1, 1958.
Malinowski, "Yung Yiddish"
Malinowski, Jerzy. "The Yung Yiddish (Young Yiddish) Group and Jewish Modern Art in Poland, 1918–1923." *Polin: Studies in Polish Jewry* 6 (1991): 223–230.

Mastboym, "In Ararat"
Mastboym, Yoel. "In Ararat." *Nayer folksblat* (Warsaw), December 23, 1928.
Mayzel, "Afn varshaver yarid"
Mayzel, Nakhmen. "Afn varshever yarid." *Literarishe bleter* 14 (Warsaw), February 19, 1937, 126.
Mayzel, "Ararat in Lodzh"
Mayzel, Nakhmen. "Tsu gast baym 'Ararat' in Lodzh," *Literarishe bleter* 9 (Warsaw), January 29, 1932, 78.
Mayzel, "Ararat in Varshe"
Mayzel, Nakhmen. "Ararat in Varshe." *Literarishe bleter* 8 (Warsaw), May 1, 1931, 343.
Mayzel, "Ferter"
Mayzel, Nakhmen. "Ferter 'Azazel'-program." *Literarishe bleter* 138 (Warsaw), December 24, 1926, 866–867.
Mayzel, "Mikoyekh"
Mayzel, Nakhmen. "Mikoyekh dem shund-roman." *Literarishe bleter* 10 (Warsaw), November 10, 1933, 709–710.
Mayzel, *Yidishe tematik*
Mayzel, Nakhmen. *Yidishe tematik un yidishe melodyes bay bavuste muziker: Notitsn un materialn*. New York: Ikuf, 1952.
M.D., "Tsenzorim"
M. D. "Sodot shel tsenzorim." *Maariv*, January 31, 1950.
Meir, *My Life*
Meir, Golda. *My Life*. New York: G. P. Putnam's Sons, 1975.
Melzer, *Ma'avaḳ medini bemalkodet*
Melzer, Emanuel. *Ma'avaḳ medini bemalkodet: Yehudei Polin, 1935–1939*. Tel Aviv: Tel Aviv University, Diaspora Research Institute, 1982.
Mestel, *Undzer teater*
Mestel, Yankev. *Undzer teater*. New York: Ikuf, 1943.
Miron, *Hatsad ha'afel*
Miron, Dan. *Hatsad ha'afel bitsḥoḳo shel Shalom Aleichem*: *Masot 'al ḥashivuta shel haretsinut beyaḥas leyidish ulesifruta*. Tel Aviv: Am Oved, 2004.
Modras, "The Catholic Church and Antisemitism"
Modras, Ronald E. "The Catholic Church and Antisemitism: Poland, 1933–1939." *Polin: Studies in Polish Jewry* 13 (2000): 401–405.
M-m., "Dzigan un Shumacher"
M-m, Shimen. "Dzigan un Shumacher (tsu zeyere uftritn in Tel-Aviv)." *Letste nayes*, January 2, 1953.
M. P., "Dzigan ṿeShumacher"
M. P. "Dzigan ṿeShumacher haleitsanim hayehudim (medabrim 'al 'atsmam)." *'Ashmoret*, March 16, 1950.
Mukdoni, *In Varshe un in Lodzh*
Mukdoni, A. *In Varshe un in Lodzh: Mayne bagegenishn*. vol. 2. Buenos Aires: Tsentral-farband fun poylishe yidn in Argentine, 1955.
N., "Dzigan ṿeShumacher."
N. "Dzigan ṿeShumacher." *Herut*, October 19, 1955.
Na'aman, "'Ayin 'aḥat bokha"
Na'aman, Idit. "'Ayin 'aḥat bokha, 'ayin aḥat tsoḥeḳet." *Yedioth Ahronoth*, April 4, 1975.

Na‘aman, “Dzigan ‘ole”
Na‘aman, Idit. “Dzigan ‘ole ‘al habariḳadot.” *Yedioth Ahronoth*, May 16, 1976.
Na‘aman, “Monolog hapereda”
Na‘aman, Idit. “Monolog hapereda shel Dzigan.” *Yedioth Ahronoth*, April 17, 1977.
Nadava, “Ṭov kele’ be’Yiśra’el”
Nadava, Yosef. “Ṭov kele’ be’Yiśra’el mishulḥan ‘arukh be’Amerika.” *Yedioth Ahronoth*, April 8, 1954.
Nahor, “Dzigan ṿeShumacher”
Nahor, Asher. “Dzigan ṿeShumacher.” *Yedioth Ahronoth*, May 15, 1959.
Nahor, “‘Erev ‘im”
Nahor, Asher. “‘Erev ‘im Dzigan ṿeShumacher.” *Herut*, January 9, 1953.
Nahor, “Holekh”
Nahor, Asher. “LeDzigan ṿeShumacher holekh.” *Yedioth Ahronoth*, October 9, 1958.
Nahor, “Humor”
Nahor, Asher. “Dzigan ṿeShumacher ṿe[ha]humor [ha]yiśre’eli.” *Herut*, October 14, 1955.
Nahor, “’Idilya”
Nahor, Asher. “’Idilya ugvura yehudit ba’ariza senṭimenṭalit.” *Yedioth Ahronoth*, September 29, 1960.
Nahor, “Ledarkam”
Nahor, Asher. “Ledarkam shel Dzigan ṿeShumacher.” *Herut*, April 19, 1957.
Nahor, “Pegisha mera‘anenet”
Nahor, Asher. “Pegisha mera‘anenet ‘im Dzigan.” *Yedioth Ahronoth*, November 11, 1960.
Nahor, “Sendvitsh”
Nahor, Asher. “Sendvitsh shel Dzigan ṿeShumacher.” *Yedioth Ahronoth*, March 2, 1955.
Nahshon, “Habima’s Production of ‘The Dybbuk’”
Nahshon, Edna. “Hebrew, Jewish, Russian: Habima’s Production of ‘The Dybbuk.’” *Jewish in Russia and Eastern Europe* 2 (1998): 56–68.
Nakdimon, “Ha‘eṭ shemetaḳen”
Nakdimon, Shlomo. “Ha‘eṭ shemetaḳen shegi’ot.” *Herut*, May 15, 1959.
Nay-velt, “Dzigan–Shumacher”
“A ufname far Dzigan–Shumacher.” *Nay-velt* (Tel Aviv), February 2, 1953.
Naye prese, “Shabes, zuntik un montik”
“Shabes, zuntik un montik gastovntn fun di barimte folks-artistn Dzigan un Shumacher.” *Naye prese* (Paris), September 14, 1949.
Nayman, “Ararat”
Nayman, Yekhezkl-Moyshe [A foygl]. “‘Ararat’ in Varshe.” *Haynt* (Warsaw), May 5, 1931.
Nayman, “Dzigan ṿeShumacher”
Nayman, Yekhezkl-Moyshe. “Dzigan ṿeShumacher: Lehofa‘atam ba’arets.” *Devar hashavu‘a*, June 1, 1950.
Nayman, “Planvirtshaft”
Nayman, Yekhezkl-Moyshe. “Planvirtshaft in der yidisher film-produktsye.” *Literarishe bleter* 15 (Warsaw), February 3, 1938, 91–92.
Neyr, “In gevirbl”
Neyr. “In gevirbl fun ideologyes: Palestine, Birobidzhan un teritorialism.” *Baginen* 6 (Vilna), October 6, 1934, 5–12.

N. M., "Dzigan–Shumacher"
N. M. "Dzigan–Shumacher: Men meg zey zen, men darf zey hern." *Di naye tsayt* (Buenos Aires), May 18, 1951.
Nora, "Between Memory and History"
Nora, Pierre. "Between Memory and History: Les Lieux de Mémoire." *Representations* 26, Special Issue: Memory and Counter-Memory (Spring, 1989): 7–24.
Novak, "Yesh leDzigan"
Novak, Ḥana. "Yesh leDzigan 'artsonet." *Davar*, April 7, 1968.
Novershtern, *Ḳesem hadimdumim*
Novershtern, Avraham. *Ḳesem hadimdumim: 'Apoḳalipsa umshiḥiut besifrut yidish*. Jerusalem: Magnes Press, 2003.
Noy, "Haḳayemet"
Noy, Dov. "Haḳayemet bediḥat 'am Yehudit?" *Maḥanayim* 67 (1962): 152–163.
Nudelman, "Kleynkunst"
Nudelman, Moyshe. "Kleynkunst- un marionetn-teaters tsvishn beyde velt-milkhomes." In *Yidisher teater in Eyrope tsvishn beyde velt-milkhomes (Materialn tsu der geshikhte fun yidishn teater)*. Edited by Itzik Manger, Jonas Turkow, and Moyshe Perenson, 152–163. New York: Alveltlekher yidisher kultur-kongres, 1968.
Nudelman, "Shumacher z"l"
Nudelman, Moyshe. "Yisroel Shumacher z"l (tsu di shloyshim)." *Letste nayes* (Tel Aviv), June 22, 1961.
N. Z., "Dzigan un Shumacher in Pariz"
N. Z. "Sh. Dzigan un Y. Shumacher in Pariz." *Unzer vort* (Paris), August 23, 1949.
Ohad, "Sheva' parotai"
Ohad, Mikhael. "'Eifo sheva' parotai hashmenot?" *Haaretz*, April 4, 1975.
Ohana, "Politics of Political Despair"
Ohana, David. "The Politics of Political Despair: The Case of Political Theology in Israel." In *By the People, For the People, Without the People? The Emergence of (Anti)Political Sentiment in Israel and in Western Democracies*. Edited by Tamar Hermann, 356–378. Jerusalem: The Israel Democracy Institute, 2011.
Olin, "Lanzmann's *Shoah*"
Olin, Margaret. "Lanzmann's *Shoah* and the Topography of the Holocaust Film." *Representations* 57 (Winter 1997): 1–23.
Olsvanger, *Rejte Pomeranzen*
Olsvanger, Immanuel. *Rejte Pomeranzen: Ostjüdische Schwänke und Erzählungen*. Berlin: Schocken, 1935.
Omer, "Te'aṭron saṭiri"
"Dzigan heḳim te'aṭron saṭiri be'idish." *Omer*, March 10, 1960.
Opalski, "Polemics on the Jewish Question"
Opalski, Magdalena. "*Wiadomości Literackie*: Polemics on the Jewish Question, 1924–1939." In *The Jews of Poland between Two World Wars*. Edited by Yiśra'el Gutman et al., 434–449. Hanover: University Press of New England, 1989.
Oppenheimer, "Hanoch Levin"
Oppenheimer, Yochai. "Yitsug hamilḥama 'etsel Hanoch Levin: Saṭira, ḳomedya, ṭragedya." In *Hanoch Levin – Ha'ish 'im hamitos ba'emtsa': 'Iyunim bitsirato haṭe'aṭronit shel Hanoch Levin*. Edited by Nurit Ya'ari and Shimon Levi, 173–186. Tel Aviv: Hakibbutz Hameuchad, 2004.

Oren, "'Ilu hayiti"
Oren, Dudu. "Dzigan: 'Ilu hayiti yoter tsa'ir hayiti mitnatser ṿeyored meha'arets." *La'isha*, May 15, 1978.
Orian, *Habe'aya ha'adatit*
Orian, Dan. *Habe'aya ha'adatit bate'aṭron hayiśre'eli*. Tel Aviv: Open University, 2005.
Oring, *Israeli Humor*
Oring, Elliott. *Israeli Humor: The Content and Structure of the Chizbat of the Palmah*. Albany: State University of New York Press, 1981.
Oyslender, *Yidisher teater*
Oyslender, Nokhem. *Yidisher teater 1887–1917*. Moscow: Der emes, 1940.
Perelmuter, "Dzigan un Shumacher"
Perelmuter, Sholem. "Dzigan un Shumacher (tsu zeyer ershtn uftrit in Nyu-York)." *Der teater-shpigl* 3 (1954), 21.
Perle, "Kleynkunst"
Perle, Yoshue. "Kleynkunst – Vegn lodzher Ararat." *Der moment* (Warsaw), August 19, 1932.
Picon-Vallin, *Le théâtre juif soviétique*
Picon-Vallin, Béatrice. *Le théâtre juif soviétique pendant les années vingt*. Lausanne: Cité – Age d'homme, 1973.
Pilowsky, *Tsvishn yo un neyn*
Pilowksy, Aryeh Leyb. *Tsvishn yo un neyn: Yidish un yidish-literatur in Erets-Yisroel: 1907–1948*. Tel Aviv: Veltrat far yidish un yidisher kultur, 1986.
Pinkus, *Yahadut brit hamo'atsot*
Pinkus, Benjamin. *Yahadut brit hamo'atsot: 1917–1973*. Jerusalem: Zalman Shazar Center, 1974.
Portnoy, "Puppet Theatre"
Portnoy, Edward. "Modicut Puppet Theatre: Modernism, Satire, and Yiddish Culture." *The Drama Review* 43 (1999): 115–134.
Postlewait, "Autobiography and Theatre History"
Postlewait, Thomas. "Autobiography and Theatre History." In *Interpreting the Theatrical Past: Essays in the Historiography of Performance*. Edited by T. Postlewait and B. A. McConachie, 248–272. Iowa City: University of Iowa Press, 1989.
Prylucki, "Yidishe bineshprakh"
Prylucki Noyekh. "Di yidishe bineshprakh." *Yidish teater* (Warsaw) 1, no. 2 (1927): 129–144.
Pulaver, *Ararat*
Pulaver, Moyshe. *Ararat un lodzher tipn*. Tel Aviv: Y. L. Peretz, 1972.
Pulaver, *Geven iz a geto*
Pulaver, Moyshe. *Geven iz a geto*. Tel Aviv: Y. L. Peretz, 1963.
Puś, "Jews in Lódz"
Puś, Wiesław. "Jews in Lódz 1820–1939." *Polin: Studies in Polish Jewry* 6 (1991): 3–19.
Rabon, *Balut*
Rabon, Yisroel. *Balut: Roman fun a forshtot*. Warsaw: Literatur fond baym fareyn fun yidishe literatn un zhurnalistn, 1934.
Radin, *The Trickster*
Radin, Paul. *The Trickster: A Study in Native American Mythology*. New York: Schocken Books, 1956.

Raḥeli, "Ḳela'im"
Raḥeli, H. "Ḳela'im umasakim." *Herut*, March 3, 1949.
Rancière, *Emancipated Spectator*
Rancière, Jacques. *The Emancipated Spectator*. Translated by Gregory Elliott. London: Verso, 2009.
Rapaport, "Dzigan ṿeShumacher"
Rapaport, Azaria. "Dzigan ṿeShumacher." *Yedioth Ahronoth*, March 11, 1955.
Rapaport, "'Omanei hatseḥoḳ"
Rapaport, Azaria. "'Omanei hatseḥoḳ – Dzigan–Shumacher be'am." *Maariv*, January 4, 1953.
Rapaport, "Yehudim tsoḥaḳim"
Rapaport, Azaria. "Tov lir'ot yehudim tsoḥaḳim. Dzigan ṿeShumacher ḥazru 'eleinu mimerḥaḳim." *Maariv*, December 26, 1952.
Rav-Nof, "Yahalom"
Rav-Nof, Ze'ev. "Yahalom meḥapeś misgeret." *Yedioth Ahronoth*, May 17, 1976.
Redlich, *Life in Transit*
Redlich, Shimon. *Life in Transit: Jews in Postwar Lodz, 1945–1950*. Brighton, MA: Academic Studies Press, 2010.
Reinelt and Roach, *Critical Theory*
Reinelt, Janelle G., and Joseph R. Roach. *Critical Theory and Performance.* Ann Arbor: University of Michigan Press, 1992.
Richard, *Cabarets*
Richard, Lionel. *Cabaret, Cabarets: Origines et Décadence*. Paris: Plon, 1991.
Rimon, "Dzigans uffirung"
Rimon, Yitskhok. "Dzigans uffirung 'Sholem-Aleichem-yidn' geyt shoyn khadoshim-lang in Yisroel mit a groysn derfolg." *Di prese* (Buenos Aires), February 14, 1967.
Rivkes, "Der lakh-spektakl"
Rivkes Y. [Yankev-Tsvi Lemel]. "Der lakh-spektakl 'Lakht gezunterheyt' fun Dzigan un Shumacher." *Unzer gedank* (Buenos Aires), October 15, 1953.
R-n, "Ararat"
R-n, "Ararat." *Fraynd* (Warsaw), October 10, 1934.
Roach, *Cities*
Roach, Joseph, *Cities of the Dead.* New York: Columbia University Press, 1996.
Robakowski, "Łodz Progressive Art Movement"
Robakowski, Josef. "Łodz Progressive Art Movement." In *Żywa Galeria. Łódzki progresywny ruch artystyczny.* Vol. 1. Edited by Jozef Robakowski, 14–21. Łodz: Łódzki Dom Kultury – Galeria FF, 1969–1981.
Rokem, "'Hadibuk' be'Erets Yiśrael"
Rokem, Freddie. "'Hadibuk' be'Erets Yiśra'el: Hate'aṭron, habiḳoret ṿehitgabshuta shel hatarbut ha'ivrit." *Ḳatedra* 20 (1981): 183–202.
Rokem, "Hebrew Theater"
Rokem, Freddie. "Hebrew Theater from 1889 to 1948." In *Theater in Israel.* Edited by Linda Ben-Zvi, 51–84. Ann Arbor: University of Michigan Press, 1996.
Rojanski, *Yiddish in Israel*
Rojanski, Rachel. *Yiddish in Israel: A History.* Indiana: Indiana University Press, 2020.
Ron, "Hofa'ato ha'aḥarona"
Ron, Moshe. "Hofa'ato ha'aḥarona 'al habama." *Davar*, May 18, 1980.

Ron, "Tsores fun der televizye"
Ron, Moshe. "Tsores fun der televizye in Yisroel." *Di yidishe nayes* (Tel Aviv), May 14, 1976.
Roshanski, "A mayster-program"
Roshanski, Shmuel. "A mayster-program fun Dzigan un Shumacher." *Di idishe tsaytung* (Buenos Aires), October 14, 1953.
Roshanski, "Yisroel Shumacher"
Roshanski, Shmuel. "Yisroel Shumacher." *Di idishe tsaytung* (Buenos Aires), May 24, 1961.
Roskies, *Against the Apocalypse*
Roskies, David. *Against the Apocalypse: Responses to Catastrophe in Modern Jewish Culture*. Syracuse: Syracuse University Press, 1999.
Rotman, *Habama*
Rotman, Diego. *Habama kebayit 'ara'i: Hate'aṭron shel Dzigan ṿeShumacher, 1927–1980*. Jerusalem: Magnes, 2017.
Rotman, "Hadibuḳ 'einenu Moshe Sneh"
Rotman, Diego. "Hadibuḳ 'einenu Moshe Sneh: 'Al haparodya hasaṭirit 'Hadibuḳ heḥadash' shel Dzigan ṿeShumacher (1957)." In *'Al na' tegarshuni: 'Iyunim ḥadashim be"Hadibuḳ."* Edited by Dorit Yerushalmi and Shimon Levi, 179–197. Tel Aviv: Safra, 2009.
Rotman, "Performens kebiḳoret tarbut"
Rotman, Diego. "Performens kebiḳoret tarbut: Mif'al hate'aṭron shel Dzigan ṿeShumacher 1927–1980." PhD dissertation, The Hebrew University of Jerusalem, 2012.
Rotman, "Performing Homeland"
Rotman, Diego. "Performing Homeland in Post-Vernacular Times: Dzigan and Shumacher's Yiddish Theater after the Holocaust." In *Spiritual Homelands: The Cultural Experience of Exile, Place and Displacement among Jews and Others*. Edited by Asher D. Biemann, Richard I. Cohen, and Sarah E. Wobick-Segev, 81–98. Berlin, Boston: De Gruyter, 2019.
Rotman, "Political Satire"
Rotman, Diego. "The 'Tsadik from Plonsk' and 'Goldenyu'" Political Satire in Dzigan and Shumacher's Israeli Comic Repertoire." In *A Club of Their Own: Jewish Humorists and the Contemporary World. Studies in Contemporary Jewry* 29. Edited by Eli Lederhendler and Gabriel N. Finder, 154–170. Oxford: Oxford University Press, 2016.
Rotman, "Language Politics"
Rotman, Diego. "Language Politics, Memory, and Discourse: Yiddish Theatre in Israel (1948–2003)." In *Skenè. Journal of Theatre and Drama Studies 6 (2)* (2020): 115–145.
Rotman, "Yidish teater in Medines-Yisroel"
Rotman, Diego. "Yidish teater in Medines-Yisroel: Tsu der retorisher konstruktsye funem yidish teater in an eynshprakhikn kultur-milye 1948–2003." MA thesis, The Hebrew University of Jerusalem, 2004.
Rouse, "Textuality"
Rouse, John. "Textuality and Authority in Theater and Drama: Some Contemporary Possibilities." In *Critical Theory and Performance*. Edited by Janelle G. Reinelt and Joseph R. Roach, 146–157. Ann Arbor: University of Michigan Press, 1992.
Rozenberg, "Ararat"
Rozenberg, Yisroel. "Ararat." *Nayer folksblat* (Warsaw), January 30, 1928.
Rozenberg, "Di premyere"
Rozenberg, Yisroel. "Di premyere fun Ararat." *Nayer folksblat* (Warsaw), October 28, 1927.

Rozenberg, "Dos 5te program"
Rozenberg, Yisroel. "Dos 5te program fun 'Ararat.'" *Nayer folksblat* (Warsaw), March 19, 1928.
Rozenberg, "Nisim"
Rozenberg, Yisroel. "Nisim min hashamoyim." *Nayer folksblat* (Warsaw), December 30, 1927.
Rozier, *Moyshe Broderzon*
Rozier, Gilles. *Moyshe Broderzon: Un écrivain yiddish d'avant-garde*. Saint-Denis: Presses Universitaires de Vincennes, 1999.
Rubel, "Lahaḳat ha'Yung-teater'"
Rubel, Elinor "Lahaḳat ha'Yung-teater.'" MA thesis, The Hebrew University of Jerusalem, 1990.
Sadan, *Masot ʿal sofrei yidish*
Sadan, Dov. *'Avnei miftan: Masot ʿal sofrei yidish*. Tel Aviv: Y. L. Peretz, 1962.
Sadan, "Peras Manger"
Sadan, Dov. "'Im peras Manger hashata." *Yedioth Ahronoth*, June 25, 1976.
Safran, "Language, Ideology, and State-Building"
Safran, William. "Language, Ideology, and State-Building: A Comparison of Policies in France, Israel, and the Soviet Union." *International Political Science Review* 13, no. 4 (1992): 397–414.
Said, "Reflections on Exile"
Said, Edward W. "Reflections on Exile." In *Altogether Elsewhere: Writers on Exile*. Edited by Marc Robinson, 137–149. Boston: Faber & Faber, 1994.
Salisbury, *Samuel Beckett*
Salisbury, Laura. *Samuel Beckett: Laughing Matters, Comic Timing*. Edinburgh: Edinburgh University Press, 2012.
Sandrow, *Vagabond Stars*
Sandrow, Nahma. *Vagabond Stars: A World History of Yiddish Theater*. New York: Syracuse University Press, 1996.
Sauber, "Le Théâtre Yiddish"
Sauber, Mariana. "Le Théâtre yiddish et sa langue." *Les Temps Modernes* 41 (1984): 557–567.
Schechner, *Performance Theory*
Schechner, Richard. *Performance Theory*. Revised and expanded edition, with a new preface by the author. New York: Routledge, 2003.
Schmitt, *Political Theology*
Schmitt, Carl. *Political Theology: Four Chapters on the Concept of Sovereignty*. Translated by George Schwab. Cambridge, MA: MIT Press, 1985.
Schnitzer, " 'Aḥaron habadḥanim"
Schnitzer, Shmuel. "'Aḥaron habadḥanim." *Maariv*, May 8, 1980.
Schrire, "Shivrei hagola"
Schrire, Dani. *Isuf shivrei hagola: Ḥeḳer hafolḳlor hatsioni lenokhaḥ haShoah*. Jerusalem: Magnes Press, 2018.
Scott, *Domination*
Scott, James C. *Domination and the Arts of Resistance: Hidden Transcripts*. New Haven: Yale University Press, 1990.
Segalovitsh, "Ararat"
Segalovitsh, Zusman. "Ararat." *Der moment* (Warsaw), April 24, 1931.

Segalovitsh, "Di 'samerodne' yatn"
Segalovitsh, Zusman. "Di 'samerodne' yatn... vegn 'Ararat.'" *Der moment* (Warsaw), October 14, 1934.
Segel, *Turn-of-the-Century Cabaret*
Segal, Harold B. *Turn-of-the-Century Cabaret: Paris, Barcelona, Berlin, Munich, Vienna, Cracow, Moscow, St. Petersburg, Zurich*. New York: Columbia University Press, 1987.
Segol, "Dzigan veShumacher"
Segol, "Dzigan veShumacher betokhnit ḥadasha." *Davar*, October 27, 1950.
Seidman, "Ghost of Queer Loves Past"
Seidman, Naomi. "The Ghost of Queer Loves Past: Ansky's 'Dybbuk' and the Sexual Transformation of Ashkenaz." In *Queer Theory and the Jewish Question*. Edited by Daniel Boyarin, Daniel Itzkovitz, and Ann Pellegrini, 228–245. New York: Columbia University Press, 2003.
Seidman, *Marriage Made in Heaven*
Seidman, Naomi. *A Marriage Made in Heaven: The Sexual Politics of Hebrew and Yiddish*. Berkeley: University of California Press, 1997.
Sfard, "Af dem rikhtikn veg"
Sfard, Dovid. "Af dem rikhtikn veg." *Dos naye lebn* (Łódź), February 15, 1948.
Sfard, "Tsum ershtn uftrit"
Sfard, Dovid. "Tsum ershtn uftrit fun Sh. Dzigan un Yisroel Shumacher in Lodzh." *Dos naye lebn* (Łódź), September 14, 1947.
Shaked, "'Or vatsel"
Shaked, Gershon. "'Or vatsel, 'aḥdut veribui: Hasiporet ha'ivrit behitmodedut di'aleḳṭit 'im metsi'ut mishtana." *'Alpayim* 4 (1991): 113–139.
Shaked, *Sipurim umaḥazot*
Shaked, Gershon. *'Al sipurim umaḥazot: Peraḳim bisodot hasipur vehamaḥaze*. Jerusalem: Keter, 1992.
Shamir, "'Inyan retsini"
Shamir, Ami. "'Humor hu' 'inyan retsini me'od,' 'omer Shimon Dzigan." *Lamerhav*, March 19, 1965.
Shandler, *Yiddish*
Shandler, Jeffrey. *Yiddish: Biography of a Language*. New York: Oxford University Press, 2020.
Shandler, *Yiddishland*
Shandler, Jeffrey. *Adventures in Yiddishland: Postvernacular Language & Culture*. Berkeley, CA: University of California Press, 2006.
Shapira "Ben-gurion vehaTanakh"
Shapira, Anita. "Ben-Gurion vehaTanakh: Yetsirato shel naraṭiv hisṭori?" *'Alpayim 14* (1996): 207–231.
Shapira, *Yehudim ḥadashim*
Shapira, Anita. *Yehudim ḥadashim, yehudim yeshanim*. Tel Aviv: Am Oved, 2003.
Shavit, *Me'ivri 'ad kena'ani.*
Shavit, Ya'akov. *Me'ivri 'ad kena'ani*. Jerusalem: Domino, 1984.
Shavit, "Lama 'ani 'atsuv"
Shavit, Yosef. "Lama 'ani 'atsuv befurim ze." *Yedioth Ahronoth*, March 24, 1967.
Shem-Or, "Be'idish ze matsḥik"
Shem-Or, Mirit. "Be'idish ze matsḥiḳ." *Maariv*, April 23, 1976.

Shiper, *Geshikhte fun yidisher teater-kunst*
Shiper, Yitskhok. *Geshikhte fun yidisher teater-kunst un drame: Fun di eltste tsaytn biz 1750*. Warsaw: Kultur Lige, 1923.
Shlomi, "Hit'argenut"
Shlomi, Hanna. "Hit'argenut shel śeridei hayehudim bePolin le'aḥar milḥemet ha'olam hasheniya." In *Ḳiyum ṿeshever – Yehudei Polin ledoroteihem*. Edited by Israel Bartal and Israel Gutman, 523–548. Jerusalem: Zalman Shazar Center, 1997.
Shmeruk, "Sifrut ha'shund'"
Shmeruk, Chone. "Letoldot sifrut ha'shund' beyidish." *Tarbiẓ* 52 (1983): 325–350.
Shner, "Varshever yidisher kunst-teater"
Shner, Mordkhe. "Varshever yidisher kunst-teater (VIKT)." In *Yidisher teater in Eyrope tsvishn beyde velt-milkhomes (Materialn tsu der geshikhte fun yidishn teater)*. Edited by Itzik Manger, Jonas Turkow, and Moyshe Perenson, 53–72. New York: Alveltlekher yidisher kultur-kongres, 1968.
Shepard, "Theater"
Shepard, Richard. "Theater: 'Joy' Opens Yiddish Season." *The New York Times*, October 25, 1979.
Shin, "Dzigan ṿeShumacher"
Shin, "Dzigan ṿeShumacher – Yeshalmu 'o lo' yeshalmu misim?" *Yedioth Ahronoth*, October 20, 1958.
Shmulevitsh, "Komiker Shimen Dzigan"
Shmulevitsh, Y. "Komiker Shimen Dzigan vet shpiln in Nyu-York." *Forverts* (New York), October 3, 1968.
Shofti, "Kol 'od neshama be'api"
Shofti, Shimshon. "Kol 'od neshama be'api – Śaḥeḳ 'aśaḥeḳ." *Al hamishmar*, June 23, 1978.
Sholem Aleichem, *Tevye*
Sholem Aleichem, *Tevye the Dairyman and Motl the Cantor's Son*. Translated from Yiddish by Aliza Shevrin. New York: Penguin, 2009.
Shtern, "'Oḳtsanut"
Shtern, Ḳ. "'Oḳtsanut ṭovat-lev." *Maariv*, October 15, 1957.
Shtif, *Yidishe literatur*
Shtif, Nokhem. *Di eltere yidishe literatur: Literarishe khrestomatye*. Kiev: Kultur-lige, 1929.
Sh. V., "Hatokhnit haḥadasha"
Sh. V. "Hatokhnit haḥadasha shel Dzigan ṿeShumacher." *Haboker*, October 7, 1955.
Shtshavinsky, "Ze vi du geyst?!"
Shtshavinsky, Y. "Ze vi du geyst?!" *Yidishe tsaytung* (Tel Aviv), October 10, 1958.
Shurer, "Dzigan ṿeShumacher"
Shurer, Haim. "Dzigan ṿeShumacher." *Davar*, December 1, 1959.
S. K., "A derfolg un a bavayz"
S. K. "A derfolg un a bavayz (tsu di gastshpiln fun Dzigan un Shumacher)." *Kultur-yediyes* (Paris), August 1949.
Silver, "Israeli Revue"
Silver, Lee. "Israeli Revue at the Casino." *Daily News*, December 11, 1961.
Shteyman, *Dramen*
Shteyman, Beinush. *Dramen*. Warsaw: Kultur-Lige, 1922.
Słonimski, "Kronika Tygodniowa"
Słonimski, Antoni. "Kronika Tygodniowa." *Wiadomości Literackie*, January 5, 1936.

Steinlauf, "Dybbuks"

Steinlauf, Michael. "Dybbuks on and off the Polish Jewish Stage." In *The Jews in Poland*. Vol. 2. Edited by Andrzej K. Paluch and Sławomir Kapralski, 273–284. Krakow: Jagiellonian University, Research Center on Jewish History and Culture in Poland, 1999.

Steinlauf, "Y. L. Peretz and the Canonization of Yiddish Theater"

Steinlauf, Michael. "Fear of Purim: Y. L. Peretz and the Canonization of Yiddish Theater." *Jewish Social Studies NS* 1, no. 3 (1995): 44–65.

Stern, "From Jester to Gesture"

Stern, Zehavit. "From Jester to Gesture: Eastern European Jewish Culture and the Re-imagination of Folk Performance." PhD dissertation, University of California, Berkeley, 2011.

Stow, *Jewish Dogs*

Stow, Kenneth. *Jewish Dogs: An Image and Its Interpreters*. Stanford, CA: Stanford University Press, 2006.

Strapontin-Tsushoyer, "Teater-notitsn"

Strapontin-Tsushoyer, A. "Teater-notitsn: Dzigan un Shumacher hobn ayngenumen...." *Afn tsimbl* (Paris), September 23, 1949.

Stutschinsky, "A shpatsir"

Stutschinsky, A. "A shpatsir ibern yidishn Pariz." *Yidishe nayes* (Sydney), October 3, 1949.

Sullivan, "Nikita Baliev's Le théâtre"

Sullivan, Lawrence. "Nikita Baliev's Le théâtre de la chauve-souris: An Avant-Garde Theater." *Dance Research Journal* 18, no. 2 (1986): 17–29.

Sverdlin, "Shimen Dzigen farlirt"

Sverdlin, G. "Shimen Dzigan farlirt 35000 tsushoyer." *Der tog-morgn zhurnal* (New York), April 6, 1967.

Szeintuch, "Mordkhe Strigler"

Szeintuch, Yechiel. "Vuhin? Mordkhe Strigler un David Ben-Gurion." *Forverts* (New York), May 9, 2008.

Sydow, *Folklore*

Sydow, Carl Wilhelm von. *Selected Papers on Folklore: Published on the Occasion of His 70th Birthday*. Edited by Laurits Bodker. Copenhagen: Rosenkilde and Bagger, 1948.

Szedlecki, *Album*

Szedlecki, Ann. *Album of My Life*. Toronto: The Azrieli Foundation and Others, 2009.

Tartakovsky, *Habima*

Tartakovsky, Elena. *Habima – Hamoreshet harusit*. Tel Aviv: Safra, 2013.

Taylor, *Archive*

Taylor, Diana. *The Archive and the Repertoire*. Durham and London: Duke University Press, 2003.

Topas, *Iron Furnace*

George Topas, *The Iron Furnace: A Holocaust Survivor's Story*. Lexington: University Press of Kentucky, 1990.

Ts. K. B., "Dzigan un Shumacher in Daytshland."

Ts. K. B. "Dzigan un Shumacher af a bazukh in Daytshland." *Di tsienistishe shtime* (Munich), October 26, 1949.

Tsanin, "Der 'heyliker' tsorn"

Tsanin, Mordkhe (Mordechai). "Der 'heyliker' tsorn." *Letste nayes* (Tel Aviv), December 11, 1950.

Tsanin, "Fun undzer televizye"
Tsanin, Dora. "Fun undzer televizye." *Letste nayes* (Tel Aviv), September 26, 1975.
Tsanin, "Hakokhav hanoded"
Tsanin, Mordkhe. "Hakokhav hanoded shekava – Shana lemoto shel Shumacher," *Lamerhav*, June 7, 1962.
Tsanin, "Nayn mos gelekhter"
Tsanin, Mordkhe (Mordechai). "Nayn mos gelekhter un nokh epes." *Letste nayes* (Tel Aviv), October 23, 1957.
Tsanin, "Shumacher z"l"
Tsanin, Mordkhe (Mordechai). "Yisroel Shumacher z"l." *Ilustrirte velt vokh* (Tel Aviv), May 31, 1961.
Tsanin, "Tsu der premyere"
Tsnanin, Mordkhe (Mordechai). "Tsu der premyere fun Dzigan un Shumacher 'Es blaybt baym altn.'" *Letste nayes* (Tel Aviv), November 27, 1959.
Tsharnes, "Tsu der premyere"
Tsharnes, Pinchas. "Tsu der premyere fun Dzigan un Shumacher 'Es blaybt baym altn.'" *Letste nayes* (Tel Aviv), May 27, 1954.
Tunkeler, "Al khet"
Tunkeler, Der (Yoysef Tunkel). "Al khet Shekhatose." *Der moment* (Warsaw), October 11, 1934.
Tunkeler, "*Di royte fon*"
Tunkeler, Der (Yoysef Tunkel), ed. *Di royte fon: A humoristish blat af sukes*. Mohilov, 1921.
Tunkeler, *Fort a yid*
Tunkeler, Der (Yoysef Tunkel). *Fort a yid keyn Erets-Yisroel*. Warsaw: M. Nomberg, 1932.
Tunkeler, "Hitler"
Tunkeler, Der (Yoysef Tunkel). "Hitler – Der oyev-Yisroel." *Der moment* (Warsaw), September 20, 1935.
Tunkeler, *Sefer hahumoresḳot*
Tunkeler, Der (Yoysef Tunkel). *Sefer hahumoresḳot ṿehaparodyot hasifrutiyot beyidish: Mivḥar ketavim humorisṭiyim ʿal yehudei mizraḥ Eiropa ṿetarbutam bePolin bein shetei milḥamot haʿolam*. Edited by Yechiel Szeintuch. Jerusalem: Magnes Press, 1990.
Tunkeler, "Tsvey yidishe filmen"
Tunkeler, Der (Yoysef Tunkel). "Tsvey yidishe filmen." *Der moment* (Warsaw), May 3, 1936.
Tunkeler, "Umshedlekher"
Tunkeler, Der (Yoysef Tunkel). "Umshedlekher gaz," *Der moment* (Warsaw), January 12, 1938.
Tunkeler, "Vagones"
Tunkeler, Der (Yoysef Tunkel). "Vagones far yidn." *Der moment* (Warsaw), November 1, 1936.
Tunkeler, "Vos volt Hitler geven"
Tunkeler, Der (Yoysef Tunkel). "Vos volt Hitler geven ven er zol nisht zayn keyn antisemit?" *Der moment* (Warsaw), September 2, 1932.
Turkow, "A mageyfe"
Turkow, Jonas. "A mageyfe vos ruft zikh shund." *Literarishe bleter* 15 (Warsaw), January 7, 1938, 27.
Turkow, *Farloshene shtern*
Turkow, Jonas. *Farloshene shtern*. Buenos Aires: Tsentral-farband fun poylishe yidn in Argentine, 1953.

Turkow-Grudberg, *Af mayn veg*
Turkow-Grudberg, Yitskhok. *Af mayn veg. Shraybers un kinstler: Dermonungen un opshatsungen*. Buenos Aires: Tsentral-farband fun poylishe yidn in Argentine, 1964.
Turkow-Grudberg, *Yidish teater*
Turkow-Grudberg, Yitskhok. *Yidish teater in Poyln.* Warsaw: Yidish-bukh, 1951.
Turkow-Grudberg, "Yidish teater in Varshe"
Turkow-Grudberg, Yitskhok. "Yidish teater in Varshe tsvishn beyde velt-milkhomes." In *Yidisher teater in Eyrope tsvishn beyde velt-milkhomes (Materialn tsu der geshikhte fun yidishn teater)*. Edited by Itzik Manger, Jonas Turkow, and Moyshe Perenson, 73–126. New York: Alveltlekher yidisher kultur-kongres, 1968.
Turner, *Forest of Symbols*
Turner, Victor. *The Forest of Symbols: Aspects of Ndembu Ritual.* Ithaca, NY: Cornell University Press, 1967.
Unzer shtime, "Di artistn"
"Di artistn Dzigan un Shumacher in Pariz." *Unzer shtime* (Paris), August 25, 1949.
Unzer vort, "A bagegenish"
"A bagegenish fun di parizer prese-forshteyer mit di bakante artistn Dzigan un Shumacher." *Unzer vort* (Paris), April 14, 1949.
Unzer vort, "Dzigan un Shumacher in Pariz"
"Dzigan un Shumacher in Pariz." *Unzer vort* (Paris), September 8, 1949.
Unzer vort, "Shturmisher"
"Shturmisher derfolg fun Dzigan un Shumacher." *Unzer vort* (Paris), September 21, 1947.
Vedenyapin, *Doctors Prescribe Laughter*
Vedenyapin, Yuri. *"Doctors Prescribe Laughter": The Yiddish Stand-up Comedy of Shimen Dzigan. Harvard Judaica Collection Student Research Papers 9.* Cambridge, MA: Harvard College Library, 2008.
Veidlinger, *Moscow State Yiddish Theater*
Veidlinger, Jeffrey. *The Moscow State Yiddish Theater: Jewish Culture on the Soviet Stage.* Bloomington: Indiana University Press, 2000.
V. Gr., "Broderzon un Dzigan"
V. Gr. "M. Broderzon un Sh. Dzigan." *Folksblat* (Tel Aviv), October 27, 1976.
Warnke, "Patriotn"
Warnke, Nina. "Patriotn and Their Stars: Male Youth Culture in the Galleries of the New York Yiddish Theatre." In *Inventing the Modern Yiddish Stage: Essays in Drama, Performance, and Show Business*. Edited by Joel Berkowitz and Barbara J. Henry, 161–183. Detroit, MI: Wayne State University Press, 2012.
Weichert, "Azazel"
Weichert, Michael. "Azazel." *Literarishe bleter* 3 (Warsaw), February 2, 1926, 109–110.
Weichert, *Zikhroynes*
Weichert, Michael. *Zikhroynes*. Tel Aviv: Menora, 1960.
Weinberg, *Stalin's Forgotten Zion*
Weinberg, Robert E. *Stalin's Forgotten Zion – Birobidzhan and the Making of a Soviet Jewish Homeland: An Illustrated History, 1928–1996.* Berkeley: University of California Press, 1998.
Weinreich, *Yidisher shprakh*
Weinreich, Max. *Geshikhte fun der yidisher shprakh: Bagrifn, faktn, metodn*. New York: Yidisher visnshaftlekher institut – YIVO, 1973.

Weitz, "Fanṭazya"
Weitz, Yechiam. "'El hafanṭazya uvaḥazara: Madu'a heḥliṭ Ben Gurion laredet liSde Boḳer." *'Iyunim bitḳumat yiśra'el* 8 (1998): 298–319.
Wiesel, "Der komiker Dzigan"
Wiesel, Eliezer. "Der komiker Dzigan iz geven troyerik purim." *Forverts* (New York), April 6, 1974.
Wolitz, "Between Folk and Freedom"
Wolitz, Seth L. "Between Folk and Freedom: The Failure of the Yiddish Modernist Movement in Poland." *Yiddish* 8, no. 1 (1991): 25–51.
Wolitz, "Di Khalyastre"
Wolitz, Seth L. "'Di Khalyastre,' The Yiddish Modernist Movement in Poland (After WWI): An Overview." *Yiddish* 4, no. 3 (1991): 5–19.
Yahav, "Drama bebagats"
Yahav, Telem. "Drama bebagats: Hashofṭim biṭlu 'et mitẏe hagaz." *Ynet*, March 27, 2016. http://www.ynet.co.il/articles/0,7340,L-4783716,00.html
Yasni, "Artist Shimen Dzigan redt zikh"
Yasni, Volf. "Artist Shimen Dzigan redt zikh arop fun hartsn," *Letste nayes* (Tel Aviv), October 7, 1966.
Yozma, "Hatslaḥatam"
"Hatslaḥatam shel Digan ẏeShumacher – 'Ein saṭira poliṭit beli ḥofesh ẏe'ein ḥofesh beli saṭira poliṭit." *Yozma*, January 25, 1951.
Yehuda, "Dzigan ẏehaṭeliẏizya"
Yehuda, G. "Dzigan ẏehaṭeliẏizya." *Davar*, November 5, 1976.
Yedioth Ahronoth, "Hanaśi' ẏehaḳomiḳanim"
"Hanaśi' ẏehaḳomiḳanim." *Yedioth Ahronoth*, February 6, 1953.
Yedioth Ahronoth, "Haśaḥḳan Shumacher – Limnuḥot."
"Haśaḥḳan shumacher – Limnuḥot." *Yedioth Ahronoth*, May 22, 1961.
Yedioth Ahronoth, "Humor yiśre'eli"
"Humor yiśre'eli." *Yedioth Ahronoth*, October 20, 1958.
Yedioth Ahronoth, "Lanashim nim'as"
"Lanashim nim'as." *Yedioth Ahronoth*, March 6, 1953.
Yedioth Ahronoth, "Minisṭer me'aḥorei haḳela'im"
"Minisṭer me'aḥorei haḳela'im." *Yedioth Ahronoth*, May 21, 1950.
Yedioth Ahronoth, "Shenei ba'alei miznon"
"Shenei ba'alei miznon." *Yedioth Ahronoth*, October 15, 1958.
Y. Ḥ. "'Emesh bate'aṭron"
Y. Ḥ. "'Emesh bate'aṭron: Tish'a ḳabin shel Dzigan ẏeShumacher." *Haaretz*, October 15, 1957.
Yerushalmi, "Betsila shel Hanna Rovina"
Yerushalmi, Dorit. "Betsila shel Hanna Rovina." *Zemanim* 99 (2007): 26–37.
Yerushalmi, "Hisṭoryot shel 'Hadibuk'"
Yerushalmi, Dorit. "Hisṭoryot shel 'Hadibuḳ.'" In *'Al na' tegarshuni: 'Iyunim ḥadashim be"Hadibuḳ."* Edited by Dorit Yerushalmi and Shimon Levi, 22–29. Tel Aviv: Safra, 2009.
Yerushalmi, "The Habimah 'Dybbuk'"
Yerushalmi, Dorit. "The Habimah 'Dybbuk': A Study of the Role of Exorcism." *Assaph Studies in the Theatre C*, 14 (1998): 193–214.

Yitskhoki, "Dzigan un Shumacher"
Yitskhoki. "Dzigan un Shumacher – Tsu zeyer veyln in Pariz." *Di tsienistishe shtime* (Paris), September 2, 1949.
Y. L., "Shumacher – 'Einenu"
Y. L. "Yiśra'el shumacher – 'Einenu." *Maariv*, May 22, 1961.
Y. V. "Mir lebn!"
Y. V., "Mir lebn! A groyse forshtelung fun di kinder-heymen in Poyln." *Dos naye lebn* (Łódź), May, 4, 1948.
Yuris, "Dzigan–Shumacher"
Yuris, Avrom-Shmuel. "Dzigan–Shumacher in 'Dzigan–Shumacher.'" *Letste nayes* (Tel Aviv), October 23, 1957.
Yuris, "Dzigan un Shumachers mizug-galuyot"
Yuris, Avrom-Shmuel. "Dzigan un Shumachers mizug-galuyot." *Letste nayes* (Tel Aviv), October 24, 1958.
Yuris, "Lakht gezunterheyt"
Yuris, Avrom-Shmuel. "'Lakht gezunterheyt' – Dzigan un Shumacher un di problematik fun humor un satire in Yisroel." *Nayvelt* (Tel Aviv), April 22, 1955.
Yuris, "Red tsu der zakh"
Yuris, Avrom-Shmuel. "Red tsu der zakh." *Der tog-morgn zhurnal*, May 18, 1963.
Z., "'Undzere kinder"
Z. "'Undzere kinder – Mit Dzigan un Shumacher." *Unzer vort* (Paris), October 10, 1952.
Zak, "Di krizis-shtimung"
Zak, Avrom. "Di krizis-shtimung in Lodzh." *Haynt* (Warsaw), November 1, 1926.
Zarrilli, "For Whom Is the King a King?"
Zarrilli, Phillip. "For Whom Is the King a King? Issues of Intercultural Production, Perception, and Reception in a Kathakali King Lear." In *Critical Theory and Performance*. Edited by Janelle G. Reinhelt and Joseph R. Roach, 16–40. Ann Arbor: University of Michigan Press, 1992.
Ze'ev, "Makirim 'otkha"
Ze'ev, Ron. "Makirim 'otkha, dod!" *Omer*, May 15, 1959.
Zeitlin, "Dzigans un Shumachers nign"
Zeitlin, Arn. "Dzigans un Shumachers yidish-poylisher nign." *Ilustrirte literarishe bleter* (Buenos Aires) 9 (1954): 5–6.
Zeitlin, "Dzigan un Shumacher"
Zeitlin, Hillel. "Dzigan un Shumacher af a bazukh in Daytshland." *Der moment* (Warsaw), May 26, 1922.
Zemanim, "'Eḥad miḳra"
"'Eḥad miḳra ṿe'eḥad targum." *Zemanim*, October 7, 1955.
Zer-Zion, "Beyond Habima"
Zer-Zion, Shelly. "Beyond Habima: Hebrew Theater Performances in Eastern Europe." *Jews in Russia and Eastern Europe* 57, no. 2 (2006): 85–110.
Zer-Zion, *'Habima' beBerlin*
Zer-Zion, Shelly. *'Habima' beBerlin: Misudo shel te'aṭron tsioni*. Jerusalem: Magnes Press, 2009.
Zer-Zion, "Ha'Vilner trupe'"
Zer-Zion, Shelly. "Ha'Vilner trupe' – Prolog lehisṭorya shel 'Habima.'" *Biḳoret ufarshanut* 41 (2009): 65–92.

Zerubavel, "Mythological Sabra"
Zerubavel, Yael. "The 'Mythological Sabra' and Jewish Past: Trauma, Memory, and Contested Identities." *Israel Studies* 7, no. 2 (2002): 115–144.
Zhitlowski, *Geklibene verk*
Zhitlowski, Haim. *Geklibene verk*. Edited by Yudl Mark. New York: Tsiko, 1955 [1913].
Zilberberg, "Vos Dzigan hot gezogt."
Zilberberg, Yoysef. "Vos Dzigan hot gezogt." *Forverts* (New York), May 1, 1967.
Žižek, *Plague*
Žižek, Slavoj. *The Plague of Fantasies*. London: Verso, 2008.
Zohar, "Dzigan, Shalom Aleichem"
Zohar, Avital. "Dzigan, Shalom Aleichem, ṿeYehoshua Rabinovits," *Yedioth Ahronoth*, April 8, 1977.
Zonder, "Tseḥok"
Zonder, Y. "Tseḥoḳ 'o ḥozeḳ?" *Hador*, December 3, 1950.
Zylbercweig, *Leksikon*
Zylberzweyg, Zalmen. *Leksikon fun yidishn teater*. New York – Mexico City: Elisheva, 1934–1969.

Index of Names

Abbot and Costello 50
Ackerly, Chris 107
Aderet, Ofer 149
Adler, Richard 229
Adler, Yankl (Jakob) 6, 7, 22, 58, 74
Adler, Yulius (Julius) 5
Agamben, Giorgio 77
Akshteyn, Al. 182
Alexander, David 219, 220
Almogi, Yosef 245, 246
Alperin, Yaakov 182
Alterman, Natan 230
Alter, Sh. 126
Altman, Nathan 7, 228
Amichai, Yehuda 168
Amid, Yehudit 153
Amihud, Dalia 153, 180
Anabela (Ya'akov-Kelner) XIX
Anderson, Mark 126
Anders, Władysław 95
An-sky, Sh. XVI, 2, 58, 96, 227–229, 234, 236, 238, 240, 241
Appenszlak, Jakub 50, 75, 76, 80
Appignanesi, Lisa 9, 10
Ararat XI–XV, XVI–XIX, 1, 3–6, 8–10, 14, 18, 19, 21–49, 54, 70, 79, 81, 90, 95, 101, 131, 140, 192, 206, 218, 258
Arciszewska, Tea 3
Arnshteyn, Mark 15
Aronson, Nahum 48
Atzmon-Wircer, Shmuel (Shmulik) XIX, 36, 102, 173, 175, 182
Austin, John 55
Aviani, Sara 180
Avidan, David 168
Avi-Miriam, M. 162
Avrahami, Yitsḥak 156, 165, 166, 170, 178
Avrekh, Mira 50, 53
Azazel 3, 4, 8, 10, 24, 28, 31

Bakhtin, Mikhail Mikhailovich 65
Baliev, Nikita 10
Barczyński, Henoch (Henryk) 8
Barkat, Reuven 222
Bar-Noy, Shimshon 196
Bar-On, Modi 173
Bar-On, Ya'akov 124, 138, 159, 170, 187, 190, 191
Bar-Yosef, Yehoshua 149, 158, 161, 175, 183, 192
Bashan, Rafael 29, 31, 35, 47, 54, 74, 81, 95, 157, 169, 264
Bauman, Richard XIV
Beckett, Samuel 64, 107
Beck, Józef 64
Begin, Menachem XV, 170, 208, 223, 224, 234
Belkin, Ahuva XIII
Belting, Hans 100
Ben-Ami, Naḥman 182, 192, 220, 249
Ben-Amotz, Dan 166
Ben-Gurion, Amos 222
Ben-Gurion, David XVI, 223–225, 227–235, 239, 242, 245–249, 251, 252, 255, 260
Ben-Meir (Abba Ahimeir/ Abba Shaul Geisinovich) 171, 172, 175
Bennet, Susan 34, 232
Ben-Porat, Yesha'yahu 220
Ben-Porat, Ziva 226
Ben-Shlomo, M. 246
Ben-Yishai, Aharon Ze'ev 194, 195
Ben-Ze'ev, Mordechai 166, 195–197
Ben-Zvi, Yitzhak 170
Berezovsky, Shaul 22, 29, 87, 154, 225, 226, 228, 229
Bergelson, Dovid (David) 2, 53
Bergman, Yoel (Joel) 48, 87, 218
Berg, Nicholas 204
Berg, Yehudit. (*See* Iza Harari)
Berkowitz, Joel V, XIII, XVII, XVIII
Berlewi, Henryk 3
Berlinksi, Ze'ev 166
Berman, Leyb 23
Bernard, Tristan 48
Bertal, Marcel 66
Bevin, Ernst 141
Beygelman, Dovid (David) 22, 23, 28, 29, 47

https://doi.org/10.1515/9783110717693-012

Bey, Hakim 110
Beylin, Gustav 219
Bialik, Haim Nahman 227
Bilu, Yoram 235, 241, 242
Birnboym, Dovid (David) 218
Blin, Roger 107
Blitental, Dan 154, 225
Blum, Shmuel 22, 29
Bodo, Yaakov 173
Bornshteyn, Yitskhok 101, 102, 131
Borvin 140
Boshes, Heda 154, 193
Botoshansky, Yankev 52, 57
Boyarin, Daniel 149
Brat, Yitskhok 14, 49, 164, 199, 202, 214, 216, 223
Breslauer, Hans Karl 73
Bresler, Zeev-Volf 6
Brezhnev, Leonid 215, 217
Brin Ingber, Judith 84, 91, 92
Brizon, Michael 220
Broder Zinger 6, 11–14
Broderzon, Moyshe (Moshe) XI, XVI, 1–4, 6–11, 13–15, 17–29, 31, 32, 35, 37–40, 42, 43, 47, 48, 57, 59, 61, 65, 70, 74, 86, 87, 89, 90, 117, 122, 153, 155, 182, 192, 199, 218, 261
Broderzon, Sheyne-Miriam 18, 22, 33, 44, 47, 54, 70
Brook, Peter 108
Broyde, Gershon 7
Broyner, Ida 8
Broyner, Yitskhok 7, 9, 22, 29
Buᵌat, Mirosᵌawa 3, 24
Buloff, Joseph (Yosef) 152, 181, 184
Bunim, Shmuel 166
Burshteyn (family) 186
Butler, Judith 255
Buzik, Maks 61

Carlebach, Azriel 148, 169, 189
Carlson, Marvin 14
Certeau, Michel de 241
Chagall, Marc 48
Chaplin, Charlie (Charles) 13, 14, 66
Chaver, Yael 109, 258
Chitron, Chagai 132
Cohen, Nathan 53, 55, 56, 67, 75, 77, 78
Cohen, Nurit 275
Cohen, Uri 275
Cohen, Ya'akov 196
Cohen, Yehuda Leyb 199
Cutler, Yosl 98

Daniderff, Leo 66
Dayan, Moshe 223, 224, 234, 245, 251, 255, 260
Deleuze, Gilles and Félix Guattari 41, 257
Der Blaue Vogel 10, 21, 29
Der byalistoker melukhisher yidisher minyatur-teater 86
Dobrushin, Yekhezkel 87, 91
Dolska, Maria (Miriam) 22
Dorf, Asher 139
Dror, A. 225
Dymov, Osip 35
Dzigan (Feygnblum), Eva 50
Dzigan, Moyshe 15
Dzigan, Nekhe 15

Eban, Abba 223, 245, 249
Edwards, Christine 20
Efrat, Moshe 168, 171, 242
Efron, John XVI, XVII
Efros, Yisroel 109, 116
Elam, Keir 28
Elboym, Moyshe 22, 48, 181
Elior, Rachel 232, 242
Ellenberg, Al 191
Epelberg, Heshel 16
Erik, Maks XIII, 11, 84
Ertel, Rachel 2
Eshkol, Levi 179, 183, 209, 223, 234
Estraikh, Gennadii 7, 84
Evron, Boaz 167
Eynsman, Haim 153

Falek, Wilhelm 22
Fater, Issachar 8, 28
Feinberg, Leonard 241
Fejgenbaum, Julius 57
Feldman, Karol 21, 182
Fertreter, A. 67, 76, 80
Feterman, Mashe 22, 218

Feuerstein, Emil 42, 156, 161, 165, 166, 167, 169, 181, 182, 193, 194, 226, 239
Feygnblum Dzigan, Eva 50
Fibich, Felix 84, 87, 91, 140
Filma'i (A Film Critic) 137
Finder, Gabriel 54, 122, 133, 135, 138
Finkin, Jordan 50, 51
Fishman, Joshua 145, 152
Flanagan and Allen 50
Florsheim, Ella 102
Fogg, Mieczysław 66
Folman, Lola 47, 87
Forbert, Adolf 61
Ford, Alexander 122, 133
Foucault, Michel 77, 111
Fredersdorf, Herbert 122
Freud, Sigmund 64
Fridvald, Zenon 48
Friedman-Cohen, Carrie 123
Friedman, Shraga 197
Frukhter, Rudi 153
Frumkin, Eshter 84
Fuchs, Esther 168
Fuks, Khayim-Leyb 32, 33, 42
Fuks, Sarit 187, 189

Gadron, Daniel 182
Galay, Asaf 173
Gallagher and Shean 50
Gamzu, Haim 156, 162, 167, 175, 179–181, 187, 190–193, 255
Gavrieli-Nuri, Dalia 248
Gebirtig, Mordkhe 28, 39, 48, 88, 133
Gelbert, Stefan 156, 165, 172, 175, 182, 190
Gennep, Arnold van 81
Gershenzon, Moyshe 152
Geyhoyz, Volf 37–39
Gilboa, Menucha 4
Gilboa, Yehoshua 158, 173, 174, 187
Gilula, Leah XIV
Giora, M. 176, 196
Glatstein, Israel 3
Glatstein, Jacob 111
Glickman, Dovale (Dov) 173
Glik, Hirsh 131, 132
Gluzman, Michael 72, 255
Godik, Vladek (Władysław) 3, 87
Goldenberg, Eliyahu 175, 176
Goldfaden, Avrom (Avraham) 5, 12, 19, 23, 100, 129, 152, 199
Gold (Goldberg), Niusia 124, 128
Goldgran, Henry 139, 140
Goldin, M. 101, 140
Goldin, Sidney 58
Goldman, Nachum 222, 223, 250
Goldshteyn, Shmulik (Shmuel) 15, 41, 44, 48, 61, 87, 218
Goldshteyn, Yoysef-Shimen 5, 27, 44, 48, 49, 51, 54, 56, 60, 67, 70, 72, 75, 83, 87, 89, 93, 139, 199, 219
Goldstein, Mark 122
Gontarski, Stanley 107
Gorby, Sara 140
Gordin, Jacob 5, 34, 58, 62, 100, 152
Göring, Hermann 64, 76, 79, 260
Gorlitska, Zise Girl 22, 218
Gornshteyn, Pavel 100, 146, 149, 150
GOSET 3, 21, 88, 94, 108
Goskind, Shaul XII, 60, 123, 138, 146, 226
Goskind, Yitskhok 146
Grafman, Avrom-Yitskhok 44, 49, 65, 70, 80, 114, 131, 219
Granovskii, Aleksandr 3, 21
Greenberg, Uri Zvi XX, 2, 78, 116
Green, Jooseph 60
Grin, Dovid. *See* David Ben-Gurion
Grinhoyz-Turkow, Shura 276
Grinshteyn, Mikhael 153, 182, 229
Grodner, Yisroel 12
Grosher, Eliezer 176
Gross, Natan XII, 58, 59, 62, 122–125, 127, 130, 138, 261
Guilat, Yael 180
Gutman, Meyer Bar 143, 144
Gutskov, Karl 34

Habima XIII, XIV, XVI, 3, 21, 29, 32, 153, 161, 181, 197, 219, 226–228, 232, 234, 242, 281
Halperin, Menashe 7
Halpern, Dina 276
Halpern, Moyshe-Leyb 4, 21
Harari (Vainberg), Iza. *See* Berg, Yehudit
Hart, Dovid (David) 152

Hart, Hersh 195
Hasan-Rokem, Galit V, 116, 200
Hefer, Haim 166, 225
Heftman, Yosef 148
Heiblum, Yosef 153, 182, 199, 203
Heller, Binem 124, 125, 131, 134
Herman, Dovid (David) 2, 3, 9, 20, 35, 39, 227, 264
Hermon, Shlomo 153
Herzl, Theodor 72
Heyman, Mayzel 34
Hirshbeyn, Perets 2, 20, 152
Hirshbeyn trupe 2
Hitler, Adolf 53–56, 64–66, 75, 76, 78, 79, 83, 128, 189, 217
Hoberman, James 59
Holland, Agnieszka 135
Hollender 48
Holzer, Rokhl 47, 59, 152
Hon, Shaul 183
Hon, Y. 124
Hussein, Saddam 217
Hutcheon, Linda 240

Ivlev, N. 87, 91
Izban, Shmuel 157

Janasowicz, Isaac 107, 109, 118, 139, 141, 153, 183, 258
Jaracz, Stefan 33
Jeannot, Leon 58, 61
Jung Wien 9
Jushny, Jascha 10

Kaczerginski, Shmerke 225
Kaganovits, Lazar 210, 211
Kaganovski, Froym (Efraim Kaganowski) 9
Kagedan, Allan 70
Kahn, Lazar 5, 20
Kamen (Kamien), Yoysef (Yosef) 75, 76
Kaminska, Ida 3, 62, 100, 184
Kaminsky (family theater) 9, 218
Kants, Shimen 190, 191
Karni, Avraham 153
Karo, Baruch 162, 171, 172, 175, 177, 178
Karpinovitz, Avraham 187, 205
Katsizne (Kacyzne), Alter 3, 49, 62, 70
Katzenelson, Yitsḥak 6, 8, 15, 28
Katz, Gregory 90
Katz, Pinchas 64
Katz, Zishe 47
Kaufman-Simhon, Sarit XIV
Kazanover (Moyshe Kosman) XIX, 21, 22, 33
Kedourie, Eli 145
Kein, Alexander 21
Keisari, Uri 55, 182, 192–194, 220
Kenig, Haim 276
Kenig, Leo 7
Kenig, Y. 22, 29
Kerman, Peysakh 47
Kerr, Alfred 33
Kesel, Dovid 34
Khad-gadye 8–9, 28
Khantshin, Ya 88
Khlebnikov, Viktor 6
Khrabolovsky, Elkana 70
Khrushchev, Nikita 211
Kidron, Carol 104, 133, 134
Kimmerling, Baruch 255
Kinarti, Arye 172
Kipnis, Menakhem 29, 44, 49, 55, 65, 80, 219
Kirshenbaum, Moti 220
Kirshenblatt-Gimblett, Barbara V, XV
Kishon, Efraim 154, 166, 170, 182, 199, 210, 211, 225
Kisielewski, Jan August 9
Kisilov, Ya'akov 147, 148
Kletzkin, Boris 49
Kletzkin, Rafael 154, 182
Kohansky, Mendel 166, 167, 187
Kolev, Karl 122
Kon, Henekh 3, 4, 8, 9, 22, 23, 28, 29, 58, 59, 61, 154
Konigsberg, Ira 122, 128, 133
Kon, Motl 21, 22, 218
Kosygin, Alexei 215, 217
Kowzan, Tadeusz 28
Kraus, Karl 9
Krimsky, M. 25
Kronfeld, Chana 1
Kulbak, Moyshe 21–23, 27, 84
Kvanisberg 87

Lahat, Shlomo 183
Landau, H. 178
Langer, Lawrence 122, 128
Lastik, Shlomo 130
Laurel and Hardy 50, 70
Lavon, Pinchas 222
Le Chat Noir 9
Lederman, Dovid 47, 83, 84, 86, 87, 89
Lender, Pinchas 177
Leneman, Leon 102, 103, 139
Le Picador 10
Lerski, Tomasz 57
Letuchaya Mysh 10
Levanon, Chaim 223
Levavi, Ya'akov 70
Lev, Eitan 153
Levi, Izidor 21
Levin, B. 158, 165
Levin, David 220
Levin, Dov 36, 40, 63, 84–86
Levin, Hanoch 220, 241
Levin, Lena 61
Levin, Vera 158
Levi-Strauss, Claude 63
Levkovitz, Y. 15
Lewy, Tom XIV, 145
Leyvik, H. 23, 48, 218
Liberman, A. 48, 140, 141
Lichtenstein, Yitskhok 7
Liliana, Lili (Zielińska) 47
Lilienshteyn Y. 140
Lilienthal, Peter 135
Lilit, Ola (Lolya Tsederboym) 3
Lindenfeld, Pola 8
Lipman, Moyshe 21
Lipsker, Avidov 2
Lissitzky, El 6, 7
Liton, Eni 261
Litvakov, Moyshe 84
Litvak, Yosef 83, 85, 87, 95–98
Livni, Avida 173
Lubitz, Zina 61

Malinowsky, Jerzy 7, 8
Malkin, Dov-Ber 52
Mandelblit, Yankev 39
Mané-Katz, Emmanuel 178
Manger, Itsik 28, 186, 190
Man, Lena 22
Margolis, Berl Broder 11
Marinis, Marcus de 28
Mark, Berl 49, 86
Markish, Perets 2
Markovits, M. 91
Markovits, Ze'ev 139, 146, 147
Marmari, Hanoch 220
Marten, Aleksander (Marek Tenenbaum) 58, 59, 62
Mastboym, Yoel 28, 33, 39
Matus, Dina 8, 22, 29, 48
Mauban, Louis 66
Mayakovsky, Vladimir 6
Mayzel, Nakhmen 2, 4, 43, 44, 48, 49, 53, 65, 199
McGrath, John 80
Medem, Vladimir 110, 130
Meir, Golda 223–225, 247–251, 252, 254, 255
Melzer, Emanuel 69
Mendele Moykher Sforim 5
Mestel, Yankev XIII
Meyerhold, Vsevolod 6, 10
Michael, B. 173, 220
Mikhoels, Shlomo 40
Miron, Dan 41, 42, 153, 248
Modras, Roland 65
Molodowsky, Kadia 49
Molotov, Vyacheslav 141
Moravsky, Mark 277
Morel, Adam 153
Morevski, Avrom (Abraham Morewski) 59, 86, 152
Moses, Erich 228
Moskovits, Yoysef 21, 23
Motil, Adam 153
Mukdoni, A. 5

Na'aman, Idit 183, 185, 193
Nadava, Yosef 161
Nadir, Moyshe 22, 27, 48
Nahor, Asher 156, 165, 166, 171, 172, 175, 181, 182, 195
Nahshon, Edna XIII, 227

Nakdimon, Shmuel 157
Namir, Mordechai 222
Natan, Simkhe 61
Navon, Yitzhak 189
Nayman, Yekhezkl-Moyshe 4, 5, 8, 9, 13, 43, 44, 45, 50, 53, 56, 58–61, 74, 80, 156, 165
Nelken, Moyshe 22, 23, 27, 33
Neses, Dr. 21, 22
Netanyahu, Benjamin 259
Neyr 70
Niborski, Yitskhok 129
Ninio, Avraham 182
Niv, Kobi 220
Nixon, Richard 247, 248, 250
Nora, Pierre 99, 120
Noy, Dov 168
Nudelman, Moyshe XVII, XVIII, 3, 4, 9, 22, 28, 47, 49, 51, 54, 56, 65, 67, 69, 72, 75, 76, 83, 87, 89, 93, 139, 154, 181, 182, 199, 203, 208, 212, 225

Oberzhanek, Yankev 4, 9, 22, 23, 27, 49, 199
Ogieiv, Dovid 21
Ohad, Mikhael 183, 184
Oksenberg, Yosef 153, 180
Okulicki, Leopold 94, 95
Olin, Margaret 135, 136
Olsvanger, Immanuel 200
Opalski, Magdalena 74
Openheim, Menashe 61
Oppenheimer, Yochai 241
Oren, Dudu 184, 187, 189
Orian, Dan XIV
Orit, Miriam 153
Osterwa, Juliusz 33
Oyerbakh, Rokhl 123, 128, 133–135
Oyslender, Nokhem XIII

Perron, Alfred 107
Picon-Vallin, Béatrice 3
Pilowksy, Arie Leyb 145
Pinskier, J. 111, 141
Plotner, Izik 48
Pope Paul VI 249
Postlewait, Thomas XIV, XVII, XVIII
Potashinski, Moyshe 39
Preter, Maurice 138
Prusicka, Irena 21, 22
Pryłucki, Noyekh 40
Pulaver, Moyshe XVIII, 15, 19–23, 27, 29, 31–33, 35, 38, 40, 45, 47, 49, 65, 66, 75, 218
Puś, Wiesław 5

Quatre Gats 9
Quid Pro Quo 10

Rabinovitz, Yehoshua 209
Rabin, Yitzhak 159, 190, 220, 224, 234, 245
Rabon, Yisroel 5, 6
Racheli, H. 139
Rakitin, Yitskhok 86
Rakov, Nekhemiya 34
Rancière, Jacques 31
Rapaport, Azaria 156–158, 162, 169, 174, 179
Rapaport, Nathan 120
Rapel, Zina 124
Rappel, Malvina 39, 47
Ravitch, Melech 111
Ravni, Gavriel 153
Rav-Nof, Ze'ev 190, 193
Rayske, Roza 141
Redlich, Shimon 99–101, 138
Reinelt, Janelle XVI
Reinhardt, Max 2
Reynglas, Yankev 21, 22, 27, 33, 182, 218
Reyzen, Avrom 21
Richard, Lionel 9
Rikhnberg, Natan 39
Ringelblum, Emanuel 123, 134
Ritterman-Abir, Ḥaim (Henryk) 153, 154, 182, 199, 222
Rivkes, Y. 140
Rivkin, Avrom 62
R-K 31
Roach, Joseph XVI
Robakowski, Jozef 8
Roden, Raḥel 153
Rojanski, Rachel XIV, XVI, XVII, 146, 242
Ron, Moshe 184, 188, 261
Roshanski, Shmuel 156, 181
Roskies, David 103, 118, 134, 138

Ross, Jerry 229
Rotbaum, Jacob 124
Rotenberg, Yekusiel 87
Rotman, Ayzik 47
Rotman, Diego XIV, XVII, 102, 122, 138, 146, 152, 153, 167, 173, 182, 184
Rotsheyn, Meytek 87
Rouse, John 28, 253
Rovina, Hanna XIV, XVI, 226, 232, 234, 235, 242, 255
Rozenberg, Liyuva 278
Rozenberg, Yisroel 29, 32–34
Rozen, Pinchas 223
Rozental, Roman 21, 22, 38
Rozental, Yankev 23
Rozier, Gilles XVI, 6, 7, 9, 15, 20, 23, 25
Rozner, Edi 97
Rubel, Elinor 2
Rubin 278
Rubin, Herts 22, 29, 48
Rubinstein, Eliakim 259
Rumkowski, Khayim Mordkhe (Chaim Mordechai) 126
Ruszkowski, Wojciech 66
Ryba, Henry 47
Rybak, Yisakhar 6
Rydz-Śmigły, Edward 95

Słonimski, Antoni 74
Sadan, Dov 12, 190
Safran, William 145
Safrin, Hortzy (Hirsh) 141
Sagi, Eli 182
Salem family 15
Samoilov, I. 87, 90
Sandler, Chaim 3
Sandrow, Nahma XVI, 12
Sauber, Mariana 40
Schechner, Richard XV, 63, 64
Schiller, Friedrich 34
Schmitt, Carl 77, 233
Schnitzer, Shmuel 14, 194, 261
Schwartz, Maurice 152, 218
Scott, James 79, 260
Segal, Harold 9, 10, 11
Segalovitsh, Clara 278
Segalovitsh, Zusman 5, 28, 41, 42, 44, 48, 49
Segal, Shmulik 175
Segal, Yiśra'el (Yisroel) 152
Seidel, Hillel 170
Seidman, Naomi 238, 254, 255
Seltzer, Anat 173
Sempoliński, Ludwik 66
Serlin, Yosef 170
Sfard, Dovid 101, 140
Shaked, Gershon 219
Shalmoni, Haim 225
Shandler, Jeffry V, XI, 12, 110
Shapira, Anita 232, 233, 246
Sharett, Moshe 170
Sharon, Ariel 223, 224
Shavit, Edna 220
Shavit, Ya'akov 191
Shavit, Yosef 164, 167, 183, 187
Shazar, Zalman 170
Shem-Or, Mirit 50, 159, 189
Shepard, Richard 191
Sheyn, Yosef 181
Shifer 87
Shifer, Chayele 218, 225, 229
Shifman, Marian 153
Shimel, Moyshe 28
Shiper, Yitskhok XIII
Shlomi, Hanna 98, 99, 124, 126, 139
Shmargad, Ludvig (Ludvig Zonsheyn) 48
Shmeruk, Chone 2
Shmulevitsh, Y. 183
Shner, Mordechai 2
Sholem Aleichem XVII, XX, 2, 5, 15, 18, 21, 33, 41, 42, 49, 61, 72, 86, 103, 107, 130–134, 152, 153, 182, 192, 202, 204, 222, 248
Sholem Asch 2, 5, 9, 180, 218
Shteyman, Beynish 21, 22
Shtif, Nokhem 12
Shtshavinsky, Y. 170
Shulman, Avrom 120, 182, 215, 216, 223
Shumacher-Ophir, Lydia V, XIX, 19, 53, 60, 69, 92, 115, 121, 136, 142, 143, 147, 154, 155, 160, 164, 182, 205, 207, 210, 216, 221, 237
Shumacher, Peyke 18, 19
Shumacher, Yankev 18, 19
Shurer, Haim 174
Shvartshteyn, Ber 48

Sidon, Ephraim 173, 220
Sidon, Sidonia and Mark 249
Silver, Lee 191
Singer, Israel Joshua 5, 218
Sneh, Moshe XVII, 102, 155, 182, 223, 235
Sokolow, Nahum 4
Somberg, Ayzik 34
Sommerstein, Emil 99
Spektor, Mordkhe (Mordecai) 5
Sprinzak, Yosef 170
Stalin, Joseph 70, 71, 84, 189, 211
Stal (Shumacher), Celina 19, 20, 50, 136, 141
Stanislavski, Konstantin 2, 6
Steinlauf, Michael XIII, 227
Sten, Efraim 185
Stern, Zehavit V, XIII, 11, 12
Stow, Kenneth 66
Strugatsh, Yoysef 3, 39
Stutschinsky, A. 139
Sullivan, Lawrence 10
Svislotsky, Shmuel 156, 179, 208
Szedlecki, Ann 118
Szeintuch, Yechiel V, 3, 246
Szlanger, Lea XIX, 153, 182, 225, 229
Szwarc, Marek 7, 8
Szymaniak, Karolina 95

Tabet 21
Tartakovsky, Elena XIV
Tauber, Garda 153
Taylor, Diana XV, 118, 120
Topas, George 57
Tovi, Esther 153
Tran and Helle 50
Troupes XIII, 2, 3, 38, 40, 54, 86, 87, 166, 167, 191, 192, 220
Trunk, Yekhiel Yeshaye 5
Trzeciak, Stanisław 65, 79, 260
Tsanin, Dora 184
Tsanin, Mordkhe (Mordechai) 13, 14, 42, 52, 165, 166, 172, 177, 178, 181, 225
Tsharni, Daniel 7
Tshaykov, Yoysef (Iosif Chaikov) 6, 7
Tunkeler, Der (Yoysef Tunkel) 3, 9, 22, 23, 27, 48, 56, 59, 69, 199, 202, 254
Turkow-Grudberg, Yitskhok XIII, 9, 84, 86, 96
Turkow, Jonas 2, 3, 37, 83
Turkow, Roza 152
Turkow, Rut 61
Turkow, Zygmunt 3, 58, 61, 152
Turner, Bernard 137
Turner, Victor 81
Tuwim, Julian 10

Uger, Yeshaye 5
Umansky, Adam 87, 94, 95
Urbakh (Ben-Zvi), Shmuel 34

Vakhtangov, Evgeniĭ 227, 228
Valinska, Miriam 153
Vayter, A. 2
Vedenyapin, Yuri XVI, XVII, 70–73, 188, 208
Veidlinger, Jeffrey XIII, 3, 40, 88, 94, 108
Veytsman, Yoysef 48
VIKT (Varshever yidisher kunst-teater) 2
Vilner trupe (Vilna Troupe) 2, 39, 40, 75, 227
Vinder, Meyer 47, 83
Vinitsky, Yosef 182, 243
Volkonsky, Sergey 48

Wajda, Andrzej 135
Warnke, Nina 34
Waszyński, Michał 28, 227
Weichert, Michael 2, 4, 20
Weinberg, Robert 70
Weinreich, Max 12
Weintraub, Władysław 3
Weitz, Yechiam 231, 234
Wiesel, Eliezer 126, 187
Wolitz, Seth 1, 2
Wulfowitz, Nathan (Nosen) 152, 153
Wycieczka, J. 48

Yafe, Shlomo 154
Yagil, Gadi 173
Yakobovsky, Wanda 122
Yavlon, Henrik 22
Yehuda, G. V, XIX, 86, 161, 185, 226
Yelin, Y. 21
Yerozolimski, Y. 22
Yerushalmi, Dorit XIV, 235, 242
Yeshurun, Avot 168
Yitskhoki 140

Yung-teater 2, 22, 28
Yuris, Avrom-Shmuel 165, 166, 176, 199, 225, 226, 239, 240

Zak, Avrom 6
Zakov, Amnon 169, 188, 189, 195
Zaltsman, Bronke 153, 180, 182
Zandberg, Yitskhok 5
Zarrilli, Philip XIV
Ze'ev, Ron 165, 174, 175
Zeitlin, Arn 111, 159
Zeitlin, Hillel 9, 159
Zelkind, Eliezer 132
Zelkovits, Yoysef 21
Zemach, Nahum 3
Zerubavel, Ya'akov 122, 145, 177, 178
Zerubavel, Yael 113, 191, 255
Zer-Zion, Shelly XIV, 3, 40
Zhitlowski, Haim 109, 110
Zhivov, M. 91
Zielony Balonik 9
Zilberberg, Yoysef 186, 217
Zilberg, Yokheved 47
Zilberman, Leah (Lola) 21, 22, 33
Zilber, Yoel 182
Zonder, Y. 156
Zustanvits, Yankev 39
Zylbercweig, Zalman XX, 3, 9, 12, 227

www.ingramcontent.com/pod-product-compliance
Lightning Source LLC
Chambersburg PA
CBHW020829160426
43192CB00007B/579
9783111114590